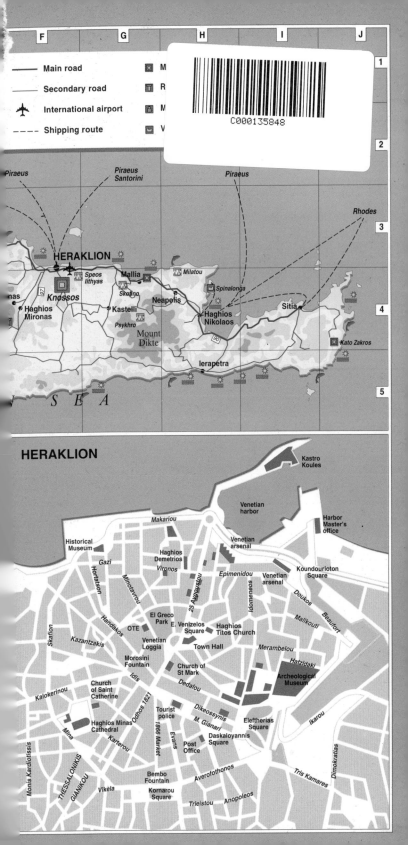

Legend

—	Main road	▣ M	
—	Secondary road	⛨ R	
✈	International airport	▣ M	
---	Shipping route	▣ V	

C000135848

Piraeus

Piraeus
Santorini

Piraeus

Rhodes

HERAKLION

Speos
lithyas

Mallia

Milatou

Spinalonga

nas

Knossos

Skotino

Neapolis

Haghios
Mironas

Kastelli

Haghios
Nikolaos

Sitia

Psykhro

Mount
Dikte

Kato Zakros

Ierapetra

S E A

HERAKLION

Kastro
Koules

Venetian
harbor

Makariou

Venetian
arsenal

Harbor
Master's
office

Historical
Museum

Haghios
Demetrios

Epimenidou

Venetian
arsenal

Koundourioton
Square

Gazi

Vironos

Doukos

Hortatsiou

Minotavrou

Mallkouti

Beaufort

El Greco
Park

25 Avgoustou

Idomeneos

Skafion

Handakos

OTE

E. Venizelos
Square

Haghios
Titos Church

Merambelou

Kazantzakis

Venetian
Loggia

Town Hall

Hatzidaki

Morosini
Fountain

Church of
St Mark

Archeological
Museum

Idis

Church
of Saint
Catherine

Dedalou

Dikeossynis

Kalokerinou

Odhos 1821

Tourist
police

M. Gianari

Eleftherias
Square

Ikarou

Mira

Haghios Minas
Cathedral

1866 Market

Evans

Post
Office

Daskaloyannis
Square

Monis Kardiotissis

Karterou

Averofothonos

Tris Kamares

THESSALONIKIS
GIANIKOU

Bembo
Fountain

Dimokratias

Vikela

Kornarou
Square

Trieistou

Anopoleos

Heraklion, the capital of Crete, was Nikos Kazantzaki's favourite city. In his novel *Freedom or Death*, he describes the city and, in particular, the harbor with its Venetian fort: "the great, thick-walled tower, decorated with Venetian winged lions, which loomed to the right of the harbor entrance."

"Although this island suffered slavery through the centuries, the spark of freedom was never extinguished in the heart of her children. Crete has stirred up emotions and sacrifices which have never troubled other lands. Here, it is not only the land itself which yields itself to our gaze, which begets such an aching in our breast."

Pandelis Prevelakis

The Morosini fountain at Heraklion.

EVERYMAN GUIDES
PUBLISHED BY DAVID CAMPBELL PUBLISHERS LTD, LONDON

CRETE ISBN 1-85715-832-6

© 1995 David Campbell Publishers Ltd
© 1995 Editions Nouveaux-Loisirs, a subsidiary of Gallimard, Paris

MANY SPECIALISTS AND ACADEMICS HAVE
CONTRIBUTED TO THIS GUIDE. SPECIAL THANKS
TO MONIQUE KAMARI IN CRETE:

EDITORS: Françoise Botkine, Catherine Bray,
Emmanuelle Laudon, Anne Nesteroff,
Sophie Nick
TRANSLATION: Marc Budin, Monique Kamari
LAYOUT: Philippe Marchand
TYPESETTING: Jean Jottrand

NATURE: M. Alibertis, Gérard G. Aymonin,
M. Bretagnon (astronomer, Paris
Observatory), Eric Fouache, Alexis Fossi and
Apostolos Trichas (Cretan Institute of Marine
Biology at Heraklion)
HISTORY: Yolande Triantafyllidou-Balladié,
Louisa Karapidakis (Historical Museum at
Heraklion)
LANGUAGE: Maria Couroucli, Monique Kamari
ARTS & TRADITIONS: Michele Manganas
(Cretan costume), Jacques Brûlé (dance and
music), Philippe Garcin (weaving, embroidery
and lace), Mme Guest-Papamanoli (St
George's Day, Orthodox Easter, pottery),
Sophie Nick (island of olives), Monique
Kamari (cafes and tavernas)
ARCHITECTURE: Alexandre Farnoux, François
Brosse
CRETE AS SEEN BY PAINTERS: Marina Canacakis,
Monique Kamari, Michèle Manganas
CRETE AS SEEN BY WRITERS: M. Lassithiotakis
(Neo-Hellenic Center of Heraklion) and
M. Jacques Lacarrière

ITINERARIES: John Freely, Monique Kamari,
Louisa Karapidakis (Historical Museum of
Heraklion), Alexandra Karetsou
(Archeological Museum of Heraklion),
Jean-François Laguenière (Association of the
Friends of N. Kazantzaki), Christoforos
Vallianos (Museum of Ethnology at Vori),
Mme Vlazaki (Archeological Museum of
Khania)

PRACTICAL INFORMATION: Sandrine Duvillier,
Monique Kamari (Crete), Michèle Manganas
(Crete), Sophie Nick

ILLUSTRATIONS
NATURE: Sophie Lavaux, Jean-François Péneau
ARCHITECTURE: François Brosse, Jean-François
Péneau, Iusse Perret
MAPS: Jean-François Binet, Pierre-Xavier
Grézaud
COMPUTER GRAPHICS: Jean-Francois Binet,
Pierre-Xavier Grézaud

PHOTOGRAPHY: François Brosse, Jean-Marc
Cholet, Dominique Cros, Christian Ferrare,
Bernard Hermann, Monique Kamari, Bernard
de Larminat, Michèle Manganas, Sophie Nick,
Nikos Psilakis, Guido Alberto Rossi

PRODUCTION
Éditions Didier Millet
77, rue du Cherche-Midi
75006 Paris

WE WOULD LIKE TO THANK: Metaxia
Tsipopoulou (Archeological Museum
of Haghios Nikolaos), Kostas Mamalakis
(collector), George Anemoyannis
(Kazantzaki Museum, Myrtia), Mssrs
A. Legakis and K. Paragamian (Cretan
Institute of Marine Biology), Nikos
Yannadakis (Vikelaia Library, Heraklion),
Irini Skhizaki (Heraklion), M. Aymonin
(Museum of Natural History, Paris), M.
Pirazzoli, Alexandre Rivier.

TRANSLATED BY SUSAN MACKERVOY AND LAURA WARD.
EDITED AND TYPESET BY BOOK CREATION SERVICES, LONDON.
PRINTED IN ITALY BY EDITORIALE LIBRARIA.

EVERYMAN GUIDES
79 Berwick Street
London W1V 3PF

CRETE

EVERYMAN GUIDES

CONTENTS

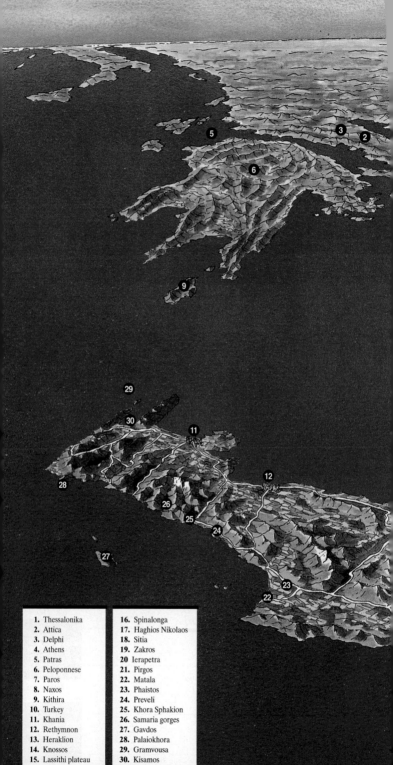

CRETE

1. Thessalonika
2. Attica
3. Delphi
4. Athens
5. Patras
6. Peloponnese
7. Paros
8. Naxos
9. Kithira
10. Turkey
11. Khania
12. Rethymnon
13. Heraklion
14. Knossos
15. Lassithi plateau
16. Spinalonga
17. Haghios Nikolaos
18. Sitia
19. Zakros
20 Ierapetra
21. Pirgos
22. Matala
23. Phaistos
24. Preveli
25. Khora Sphakion
26. Samaria gorges
27. Gavdos
28. Palaiokhora
29. Gramvousa
30. Kisamos

How to Use this Guide

(Sample page shown from the guide to Venice)

The symbols at the top of each page refer to the different parts of the guide.

■ NATURAL ENVIRONMENT

● KEYS TO UNDERSTANDING

▲ ITINERARIES

◆ PRACTICAL INFORMATION

The itinerary map shows the main points of interest along the way and is intended to help you find your bearings.

The mini-map locates the particular itinerary within the wider area covered by the guide.

★ The star symbol signifies that a particular site has been singled out by the publishers for its special beauty, atmosphere or cultural interest.

At the beginning of each itinerary, the suggested means of transport to be used and the time it will take to cover the area are indicated:

🚤 By boat
🚶 On foot
🚲 By bicycle
🕐 Duration

● ▲ ■ ◆
The symbols alongside a title or within the text itself provide cross-references to a theme or place dealt with elsewhere in the guide.

THE GATEWAY TO VENICE ★

PONTE DELLA LIBERTA. Built by the Austrians 50 years after the Treaty of Campo Formio in 1797 ● *34*, to link Venice with Milan. The bridge ended the thousand-year separation from the mainland and shook the city's economy to its roots as Venice, already in the throes of the industrial revolution, saw

🚶 Half a day

BRIDGES TO VENICE

NATURE

Crete's present geological structure was produced by the movements of the earth's tectonic plates. The earth's plates can move apart (opening up oceans) or together (forming mountain chains, faults and volcanos). The history of the island's formation can be summarized in two stages. During the Mesozoic era a vast area of ocean opened up between the Eurasian plate to the north and the African plate to the south. Towards the end of the Mesozoic, and then more rapidly at the beginning of the Tertiary period, these two plates moved toward each other again, reducing the ocean area and producing a folded mountain chain, the Alpine chain, which extends into the Hellenic chain in continental Greece and the South Aegean arc; Crete is the largest island on this arc between the Peloponnese and Anatolia.

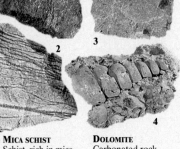

GNEISS
Metamorphic rock consisting of feldspar, quartz, mica and various other elements (**5**).

CALCITE
Section of a stalactite formed from calcite, in varying degrees of purity (**6**).

LIMESTONE
Limestone gorges of Pantocrator (Trias).

MICA SCHIST
Schist, rich in mica flakes, is the product of metamorphic clay (**1**).

OPHIOLITE
Red and green rock, threaded here with veins of calcite (**2**).

DOLOMITE
Carbonated rock formed from deposits of sediments (**3**).

SHELLY LIMESTONE
Sedimentary rock formed from the remains of fossilized organisms (**4**).

HEMATITE
The most common form of iron ore (**7**).

LIMESTONE TUFF
Formed by a chemical reaction in evaporating spring water (**8**).

SEDIMENTARY ROCKS
Undifferentiated molasse
Undifferentiated flysch
Undifferentiated limestone
Undifferentiated marine conglomerates
METAMORPHIC ROCKS
Schist
Gneiss
SURFACE FORMATIONS
Holocene and Quaternary alluvial embankments
Lakeside conglomerates and Pleistocene
OTHER FORMATIONS
Ophites

GEOLOGICAL MAP OF CRETE

CHANGING LAND LEVEL
The shoreline of two thousand years ago now lies some 13 feet below sea level to the east of the island, and over 28 feet above it at the western end (above).

CRETE TILTING
Notches in the rocky cliffs made by marine erosion over 16 feet above sea level on the Gramvousa peninsula in western Crete (right). Traces of former shorelines can be seen on both the northern and southern coasts, at progressively higher levels toward the southwest. Modern carbon dating methods have revealed that the land level rose after a tectonic upthrust around the beginning of the 5th century, which was itself probably caused by the earthquake of AD 438.

7

8

SUBDUCTION
When the African tectonic plate sank it created the Hellenic gulf, below the convex arc of the Aegean plate, stretching from the Ionian islands to the Peloponnese and southern Crete. Friction caused by this movement under the Aegean plate produced higher levels of volcanic activity. Materials and sediments from the African plate gradually shifted downward along the sloping plane, becoming hotter and then melting, producing a magma which periodically forced its way through to the surface. This is how the Aegean volcanic arc was formed. It is largely inactive today, but still remains a real threat, as was demonstrated by the violent eruption of Thera (Santorini). The process of subduction continues steadily: Africa and continental Europe are still creeping closer together, by 2 inches each year on average.

THERA (SANTORINI) HARBOUR
At the beginning of the 7th century BC, this volcanic island exploded: as the ground sank the sea rushed into the circular bay thus formed. This cataclysm may well have been responsible for destroying the first Minoan palaces at Knossos ▲ *161* and Mallia ▲ *192*. There have been many earthquakes during subsequent centuries, the most recent in 1925–6, 1928 and 1956.

The Cretan sky is very clear as humidity levels are minimal in the summer. This offers superb conditions for studying stars, especially over Heraklion and Haghios Nikolaos. Around 130 BC the Greek astronomer Hipparchus introduced the system of magnitudes, placing the stars in six categories according to their brightness, ranging from the first magnitude (the brightest) to the sixth (those least visible to the naked eye).

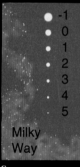

SCALE OF APPARENT STELLAR MAGNITUDE IN USE TODAY

THE MILKY WAY
Looking toward the south in summer you can see a broad, luminous white trail stretching from the constellation of Sagittarius to beyond Cassiopeia. This is our galaxy, seen in cross-section. The sun is just one of the billions of stars – 100 billion at least – of which it is made.

APPROXIMATE POSITION OF THE SUN IN OUR GALAXY

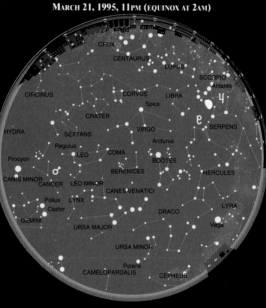

MARCH 21, 1995, 11PM (EQUINOX AT 2AM)

JUNE 21 1995, 11PM (SOLSTICE AT 8AM)

THE GALAXY OF ANDROMEDA
M31 (the galaxy of Andromeda) is the neighbor and twin of our own galaxy, and the furthest object which can be seen by the naked eye – it is visible as an elongated mark in the autumn sky. It is located in the constellation of Andromeda, 2.2 million light-years away. A light-year is the distance traveled by light in one year, or in other words over 6000 billion miles.

☿ Mercury
♀ Venus
♁ Earth
♂ Mars
♃ Jupiter
♄ Saturn
♅ Uranus
♆ Neptune
♇ Pluto

VENUS
Visible to the naked eye after the sun has set, or just before the sun rises, Venus is the brightest planet in the sky. It is known as the Shepherd's Star as its course echoes the rhythms of the shepherd's life, which follows the sun.

SEPTEMBER 21, 1995, 10PM (EQUINOX ON 23 AT NOON)

GRUS
PHOENIX
SCULPTEUR
Fomalhaut
PISCES AUSTRINUS
FORNAX
ERIDANUS
CAPRICORN
AQUARIUS
CETUS
Mira
♄
PISCES
AQUILA
PEGASUS
TAURUS
Altair
ANDROMEDA
ARIES
Pleiades
Aldebaran
CYGNUS
M 31
PERSEUS
LYRA
Deneb
Capella
CASSIOPEIA
AURIGA
CEPHEUS
Vega
CAMELOPARDALIS
Polaris
DRACO
URSA MINOR

DECEMBER 21, 1995, 11PM (SOLSTICE ON 22 AT 8AM)

PUPPIS
VELA
COLUMBA
LEPUS
CANIS MAJOR
CIRCINUS
HYDRA
ERIDANUS
Rigel
Sirius
MONOCERUS
Procyon
CRATER
CETUS
ORION
SEXTANS
Betelgeuse
CANIS MINOR
Regulus
Aldebaran
CANCER
LEO
TAURUS
GEMINI
Pollux
Pleiades
Castor
LEO MINOR
ARIES
LYNX
Algol
AURIGA
Capella
URSA MAJOR
CANES
PERSEUS
VENATICI
CAMELOPARDALIS
CASSIOPEIA
Polaris
DRACO
URSA MINOR

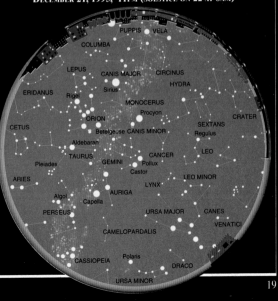

19

THE BAY OF ELOUNDA

The Bay of Elounda is protected by the Spinalonga peninsula; its depth, currents and sediments combine to make it an excellent habitat for plant life. The commonest plants in the bay are flowering plants like the sea grasses Cymodocea and posidonia. Over decades the posidonia has formed what the fishermen call a "mat", fastening its roots into the sand as it grows: this plant-reef provides a good environment for a wide range of animal life. Sometimes the posidonia dies off here and there, as part of its natural life cycle; however, human actions are more generally responsible for destroying the bay's vegetation.

AUDOUIN'S GULL

HERRING GULL

GRAY HERON

POSIDONIA
A marine plant named after the god Poseidon, with a thick, brown, scaly stem and green flowers. The stem is sheathed in two rows of translucent leaves. The fruits are olive-sized.

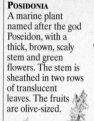

SEA CUCUMBER
This creature has suckers on its underside and retractable papillae on its back.

JELLYFISH

POSIDONIA

SEA SLUG

PEACOCK WORM
Marine worm with a crown of tentacles as much as 6 inches across.

SPONGE "VERENGIA AEROPHOBA"
A sea creature of varying shape; its porous skeleton provides the substance we use in the bathroom.

CUTTLEFISH
This mollusc has an internal shell. It can squirt black ink when attacked and change color to match its surroundings.

ROSULARIA
Rocks provide shelter for this plant, one of the stonecrops, with its clustered, fleshy leaves and yellow or pink flowers.

POSIDONIA BALLS
Pieces of leaf which have broken from the "mat" and have been rolled by the tide into gray, fibrous balls.

BELLFLOWER
Magnificent, short-lived, single-flowered campanulas cling to the rocks.

MAIDENHAIR FERN
Humid limestone rocks are the typical habitat of this delicate fern.

SPIKE MOSS
Its flowers, which look like moss, form a dense carpet over the rocks.

SEA ANEMONE

"CAULERPA PROLIFERA"
The most common form of seaweed in the bay.

GOBY

SEA SQUIRT

THORNBACK RAY

BANDED SEA-PERCH

COMMON SOLE

STARFISH
Often lives buried in the sand, coming out at night to feed.

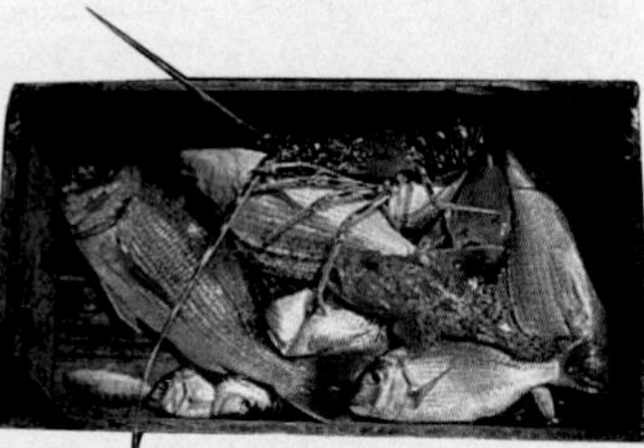

Fishing has gained importance in Crete over the last twenty years: the demand for fish has grown with the rise of tourism. Fishing takes place mainly off the north shores of the island, particularly at Khania and Heraklion. Crete has some 1,100 working fishing boats of less than 20 feet in length, and around 100 boats of more than 40 feet. Various fishing techniques are used, ranging from the net to the line; often nets and lines are used alternately on the same boat. The typical Cretan boat is the *trehadiri* – a local variant of the small fishing boats used throughout the Aegean.

DEEP-SEA LINE FOR RED BREAM

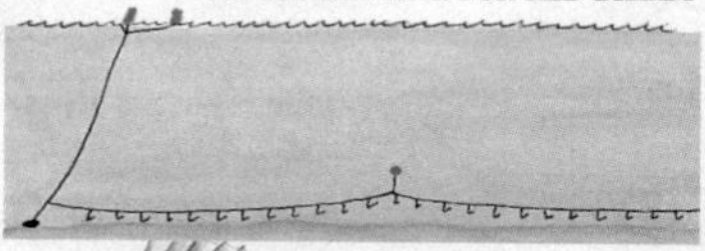

SEA BREAM
Lives at a depth of 65 to 160 feet.

COMMON DENTEX
One of the largest predators of the Mediterranean: its mouth is equipped with four to six teeth.

A *trehadiri* arrives at the fishing ground.

Preparing the *paragadia* nets.

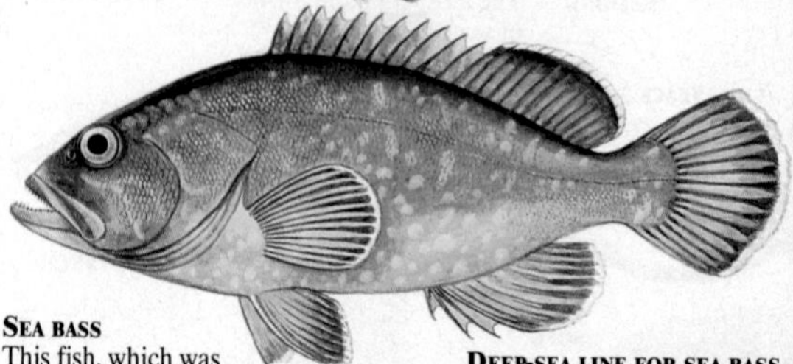

SEA BASS
This fish, which was until recently classified as a member of the *Serranides* family, is caught at depths of up to 700 feet.

DEEP-SEA LINE FOR SEA BASS

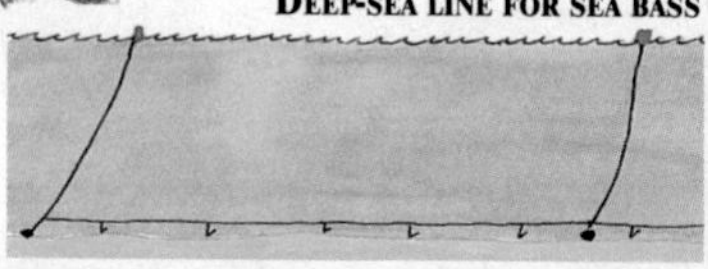

Fixing the baited hooks.

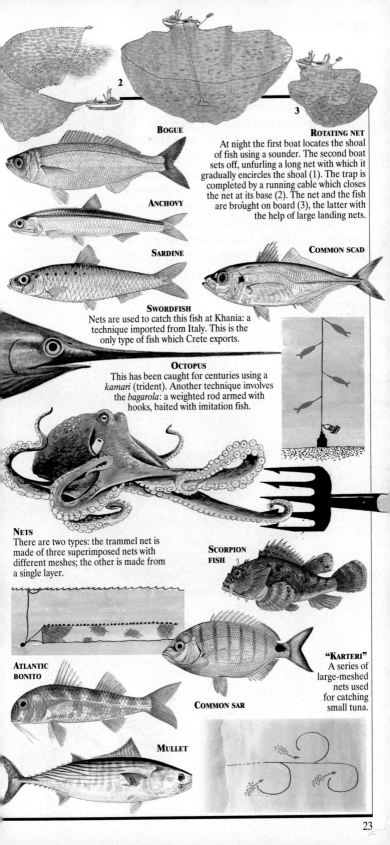

BOGUE

ANCHOVY

SARDINE

ROTATING NET
At night the first boat locates the shoal of fish using a sounder. The second boat sets off, unfurling a long net with which it gradually encircles the shoal (1). The trap is completed by a running cable which closes the net at its base (2). The net and the fish are brought on board (3), the latter with the help of large landing nets.

COMMON SCAD

SWORDFISH
Nets are used to catch this fish at Khania: a technique imported from Italy. This is the only type of fish which Crete exports.

OCTOPUS
This has been caught for centuries using a *kamari* (trident). Another technique involves the *bagarola*: a weighted rod armed with hooks, baited with imitation fish.

NETS
There are two types: the trammel net is made of three superimposed nets with different meshes; the other is made from a single layer.

SCORPION FISH

ATLANTIC BONITO

COMMON SAR

"KARTERI"
A series of large-meshed nets used for catching small tuna.

MULLET

Olives were first cultivated in the Mediterranean three thousand years ago, imported by the Minoans from Asia Minor or Africa. Since then the olive tree has spread throughout the Mediterranean basin, so successfully that it has come to be almost a symbol of the region. Its ideal altitude is below 1,000 feet, but it can grow from sea level to heights of 2,000 feet. Olives for eating are harvested from September to October (green olives) and November to January (black olives). Olives for extracting oil are gathered between December and February.

AN ANCIENT TRADITION
The Greeks of today, like their ancestors, harvest olives by shaking them down, using poles of different lengths. The flavor of olive oil has probably not changed since ancient times.

Olive groves are generally quite small, and need to be regularly tended. An olive tree starts producing fruit after three or four years, reaching its maximum yield when it is fifteen to thirty years old. Trees are often cut short to make harvesting easier. The spaces between trees are also put to use: olive groves can be used for growing vines or as pasture in the spring when the last black olives have been harvested. The ripe olives fall on canvases spread beneath the trees.

BLACKCAP
A warbler; the male can be identified by his black crown.

WEEVILS
There are many species of weevil on Crete; they have a long proboscis.

ROBIN
Solitary songbird which lives in the wooded mountains.

HOUSE SPARROW
A familiar inhabitant of the olive grove.

One flower in twenty produces an olive.

24

PLAIN AND OLIVE GROVES
This magnificent plain of olive trees is 30 miles long. As well as the young trees, arranged geometrically, there are much older trees, with enormous roots and wrinkled bark, dating from the 18th century and still producing 700 lb of olives. The olive tree is famous for its long life, bearing fruit up to its 150th year.

OIL BEETLE
This beetle has glossy black elytra (wing cases).

BROWN HARE
Can be seen throughout Greece.

HEDGEHOG

The olive tree belongs to the family Oleacea. The species grown in Crete is *Olea europaea*.

The ladder is still used widely in Crete for picking olives.

Olives were harvested by women in earlier times.

Electric harvesting poles were introduced in the late 1980's.

The name "phrygana" comes from a word coined by the Greek botanist Theophrastus in the 4th century AD to describe a type of low-lying terrain common throughout the Mediterranean – like the *tomillares* in Spain or the garrigue in France. Phrygana can be found throughout Crete, from the coastal regions up to the high plateaux. It consists of woody, often thorny vegetation forming an uneven carpet on dry, hot terrain, generally limestone rocks. The floral life of the phrygana is extremely rich and varied, with plants, both annual and hardy, which burst spectacularly into flower in spring and autumn, when there is rain. The animal life of the phrygana includes many interesting birds, reptiles and insects.

CRETAN SPINY MOUSE
This rodent is common in Egypt and Israel but unknown in Europe, except for an isolated population in Crete. It has long bristles on its back and flanks.

CHUKAR
This species of partridge, which lives in the thorny shrubs, is sadly a favourite target for hunters.

CAT SNAKE
Many reptiles live in the phrygana, but none is dangerous to humans.

EASTERN STRAWBERRY TREE

KERMES OAK

BROOM

ASPHODEL

THORNY BURNET

SHRUBBY SAINFOIN

BALKAN GREEN LIZARD
Its scientific name, *trilinea*, refers to the three lines visible on the back of the juveniles.

A typical view of the phrygana, with its rolling surface of thorny gorse cushions. The gorse flowers in spring, but many aromatic plants give off strong perfumes in summer when the vegetation appears to be dry. As well as rosemary there are various types of sage, oregano and thyme, in different varieties from the herbs found in the garrigue of France.

SARDINIAN WARBLER
This little bird, which nests in thickets, has a red eye ring and a white throat. Its dark head is jet-black in the male; shown here is the female.

ORTOLAN BUNTING
This small bird has an olive-green head and breast, orange-buff underparts and a gray-brown rump. It nests at ground level.

HIVES AND HONEY
Honey was very highly prized in classical times. The bees feed on the nectar of the abundant aromatic plants. The hives, painted in different colours, are kept in enclosures sheltered from the wind.

ASPHODEL
Thanks to their deep tubers, asphodels are very hardy; they are abundant in some parts of the phrygana.

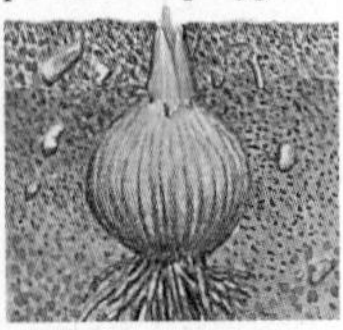

The herbaceous plants of the phrygana are either annuals with a short life cycle or hardy perennials which live off underground reserves. The seeds of the annuals, like the bulbs, are dormant during the dry season.

MALE "UROMENAS ELEGANS"
This large insect lives on the garrigues of the largest Mediterranean islands (Corsica, Sicily, Crete, Cyprus and Sardinia).

CHAMELEON
This reptile with its prehensile tail can change the colour of its skin to match its surroundings.

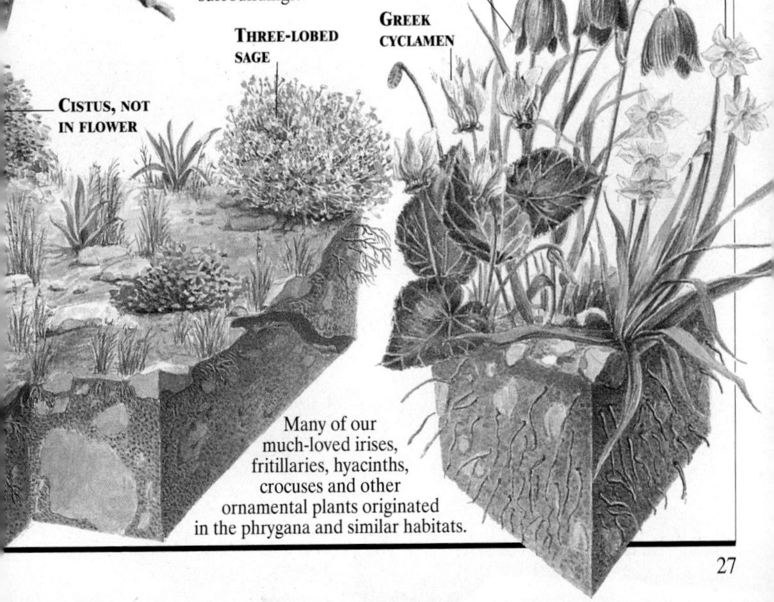

BLUE ROCK THRUSH
The male's plumage is blue all over, while the female is dark brown with pale spots.

NARCISSUS SEROTINUS

FRITILLARY

GREEK CYCLAMEN

THREE-LOBED SAGE

CISTUS, NOT IN FLOWER

Many of our much-loved irises, fritillaries, hyacinths, crocuses and other ornamental plants originated in the phrygana and similar habitats.

■ THE LASSITHI PLATEAU

The Lassithi plateau, at an altitude of 2,800 feet, is surrounded by mountains (including Mount Dikte, 7,050 feet high); it is some four miles long and three miles wide. Two passes give access to the plateau, one of them studded with windmills. Under the Venetian occupation, irrigation work transformed Lassithi into a fertile plain, and its produce is renowned throughout Crete. The windpumps which were used to bring up the water have gradually been replaced by motorized pumps. In summer the inhabitants of the twenty villages on the plateau enjoy relatively cool conditions.

PEACOCK ANEMONE
One of the most beautiful wild plants in the Mediterranean: its delightful, brightly colored flowers appear in spring. Many cultivated anemones derive from this species.

MYRTLE
Grows on the slopes above the plateau. Its white flowers and evergreen foliage give off a sweet, heady perfume.

CRETAN CYCLAMEN
Found only on Crete and Karpathos, its flowers are pure white, rarely very pale pink.

LARGE QUAKING GRASS
An annual grass; its flower spikelets are a silver-green in color, often tending toward brown. Its elegant appearance makes it a favourite for dried flower arrangements.

CRETAN ARUM
Its tiny flowers, borne on a yellow "spadix", are partially enclosed by a fleshy pale sheath or "spathe".

SPANISH BROOM
This large bush – 3 to 10 feet high – has narrow stems bearing large yellow flowers and often grows by the wayside.

WHEAT

FOOD CROPS

WILD RABBIT

CRETAN STONE MARTEN

Plantation of fruit trees near the village of Mohos, on the road from Stalida, east of Heraklion; one of the stone windmills, where the local people came to grind their wheat and rye up to the beginning of the century.

BLACK-EARED WHEATEAR
The two dark patches on either side of its head give this bird its name. It visits the island in summer.

SHORT-TOED TREECREEPER ▶
A non-migrant which likes to nest under loose bark.

TAWNY PIPIT
Lives in the arid parts of the mountains around the plateau.

BEE-EATER
This vivid summer visitor snaps up wasps and bees in mid-air in the fruit orchards.

SKYLARK
This resident, with its little crest, feeds mainly on seeds and cereals.

GREEN TOAD
Enjoys the humidity of the farmland; its sweet, crystal-clear song can be heard at night.

SUBALPINE WARBLER
Likes to live in the mountains flanking the plateau.

TREE FROG
This small frog can cling to leaves using the suckers on its feet.

WINDPUMP

FRUIT TREES (APPLES, PEARS, PLUMS, PEACHES ETC.)

UNDERGROUND WATER SOURCE

Crete has many wild orchids – some eighty species have been recorded, several of them endemic – and they attract both specialist and amateur botanists to the island. They are all land-flowering plants, sometimes with tubers or rhizomes. Their flowers are generally bisexual, often with male and female parts which are compatible. In these cases pollination is achieved in ingenious ways. The bee orchid is a good example here: the flowers mimic insects, with a "mirror" on the lower petal and a perfume like that of bees' hormones. Male bees are attracted and carry off pollen which comes into contact with the stigma (female organ) on another flower, resulting in fertilization.

BLUE BEE ORCHID

BEE ORCHID
Its flower is a good illustration of the orchid's structure: a pink external corolla made of three sepals; a large single petal (the lip) with an attractive pattern and hairy lobes, crowned by a beak-like anther, which is split into two masses of pollen, and the female stigma, flanked by two small furry petals.

THE "ORCHIS" FAMILY
The six species shown right (from left to right) illustrate the diversity of the *Orchis* family in Crete: the Anatolian orchid, its stem 4 to 16 inches high with a thick, sparsely clustered spike; the Italian man orchid, with a sturdy stem and a heavily clustered, conical head; the toothed orchid, with fragrant flowers, which grows in the phrygana. The Provence orchid is stocky, with yellow flowers, and prefers shady slopes; *Orchis prisca* is endemic and *Orchis boryi* is native to Crete and southern Greece.

As well as endemic varieties of various species, like the rare and protected orchids of the Samarian gorges, common European orchids can also be seen on Crete, such as the late-flowering autumn lady's tresses (left), as can orchids which are common only in the Mediterranean like Robert's orchid (centre). The violet bird's nest orchid, which lacks chlorophyllous leaves but has a very long, deep root and a purple stem, lives as a parasite in wooded areas. Its large flowers have a long spur (right).

LONG-LIPPED SERAPIAS
Serapias orientalis (below, left) is found in damp meadows, marshes and by streams.

TUBER
Orchids derive their name from the Greek word *orchis* (testicle) – owing to the shape of some of the tubers.

DIVERSITY OF THE ORCHID FAMILY
Cross-fertilizations can produce irregular, intermediate varieties of orchid, confounding even the botanists and producing a family of great diversity. However their survival is threatened by theft, and by pesticides which kill both the pollinating insects and the plants themselves. The bright yellow Wasp orchid contrasts with the more somber Cretan orchid. *Ophrys candica* has a pattern around a brown-red area, while the Brown orchid is related to *Ophrys iricolor*.

BEE ORCHID
There are several different varieties of this striking orchid in southern Greece and the Aegean islands, although its presence in Crete is doubtful. There are, however, similar varieties with a less hairy lip.

MAN ORCHID
Has a long spike of flowers, each shaped like a hanged man.

31

JUNIPER   **CYPRESS**

PINE

Cutting into the limestone mountains of Crete are a number of gorges – very narrow, dark and cool. The gorges of Samaria and of the Levka Ori (White Mountains) in the west are famous for their impressive sheer drops. This botanic corridor, 11 miles long, provides a habitat for numerous species of flora and fauna, some of them endemic, such as the Cretan wild goat known locally as the *kri-kri* or *agrimi*. Calabrian pines and extraordinary cypresses with flat crowns stand above the sheer cliff faces of the gorges, while clumps of creeping shrubs cling to the dry areas of the rock face.

TORRENTS HAVE CUT A GROOVE WHICH RUNS TO THE SEA

HOLM OAKS, PINES AND OLEANDERS

THE GORGES SERVED AS A REFUGE FOR CRETANS DURING THE TURKISH OCCUPATION

GOLDEN EAGLE
This magnificent bird of prey has slotted wings spanning 7 feet and a golden crown; it builds its huge cliff nest on an inaccessible ledge.

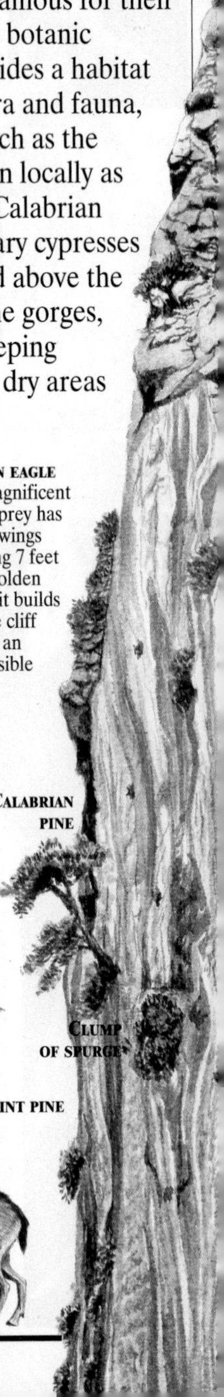

CALABRIAN PINE

CLUMP OF SPURGE

CRETAN WILD GOAT

JOINT PINE

The alpine flora include species peculiar to each of the three massifs with altitudes of over 6,500 feet. These plants descend from very ancient families which suffered little from the effects of the last ice age. All are unique to Crete, showing marked differences from their relatives on the neighboring land masses.

SPRING FLOWERS
Clusius' peony, with its white flowers, is found only in Crete and Karpathos **(1)**; rock tulip with large pink sepals marked with yellow **(2)**; Cretan iris, a species with narrow leaves and single violet flowers **(3)**; a bush of Clusius' peonies **(4)**.

CRETAN MAPLE
This evergreen shrub is often destroyed by flocks of grazing sheep but survives here and there on the mountains.

SAMARIAN ORCHID
This species flowers from mid-May to June.

PRICKLY JUNIPER
A shrub or small tree, silver-grey in color, and from 3 to 26 feet high. Its green fruits ripen to a red-brown color.

CRETAN ZELKOVA
Related to the "Siberian elm" (which is in fact Caucasian), this plant dates from the Tertiary period and exists nowhere else in Europe.

STAEHELINA
This member of the daisy family has narrow leaves with silver-haired undersides. It loves rocky ground and steep slopes (below).

PETROMARULA
This member of the bellflower family (Campanulaceae) grows in the Samarian gorges and is endemic to Crete. It has a very attractive spike of mauve flowers.

SMALL COMMON DRAGON ARUM
The enormous purple flower has a fetid fragrance. The stems are marked with striking black blotches and reach a height of 3 feet.

DITTANY OR BURNING BUSH
This plant is now very rare in Crete, having been over-picked for its many medicinal properties.

■ THE HAGHIA PARASKEVI CAVE

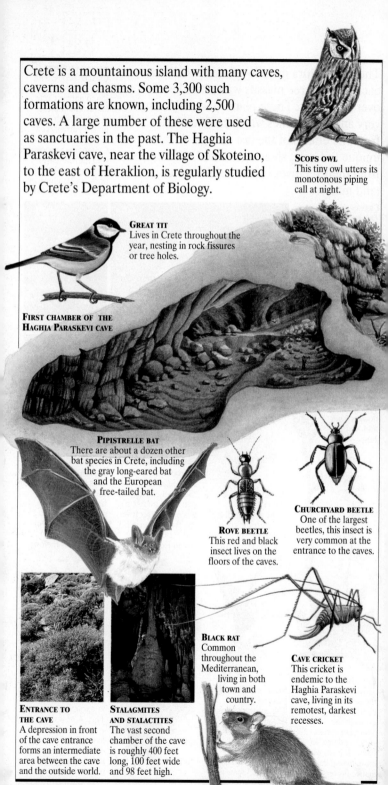

Crete is a mountainous island with many caves, caverns and chasms. Some 3,300 such formations are known, including 2,500 caves. A large number of these were used as sanctuaries in the past. The Haghia Paraskevi cave, near the village of Skoteino, to the east of Heraklion, is regularly studied by Crete's Department of Biology.

SCOPS OWL
This tiny owl utters its monotonous piping call at night.

GREAT TIT
Lives in Crete throughout the year, nesting in rock fissures or tree holes.

FIRST CHAMBER OF THE HAGHIA PARASKEVI CAVE

PIPISTRELLE BAT
There are about a dozen other bat species in Crete, including the gray long-eared bat and the European free-tailed bat.

ROVE BEETLE
This red and black insect lives on the floors of the caves.

CHURCHYARD BEETLE
One of the largest beetles, this insect is very common at the entrance to the caves.

BLACK RAT
Common throughout the Mediterranean, living in both town and country.

CAVE CRICKET
This cricket is endemic to the Haghia Paraskevi cave, living in its remotest, darkest recesses.

ENTRANCE TO THE CAVE
A depression in front of the cave entrance forms an intermediate area between the cave and the outside world.

STALAGMITES AND STALACTITES
The vast second chamber of the cave is roughly 400 feet long, 100 feet wide and 98 feet high.

34

History

The Greek myths are impressive stories dramatizing fictional or real events; they are popular, legendary tales based on what the Greeks knew of their ancient history. The writings of Hesiod and Homer are the main sources for our knowledge of Greek mythology. In his *Theogeny*, Hesiod tells the story of the creation of the world; the birth of Gaia (Earth) and Uranos (Sky). Crete has a very special place in this mythological drama.

FAMILY TREE
Zeus had a number of brothers and sisters, including Poseidon, Hera and Metis. He also had large numbers of children (among them Athena, Apollo, Dionysos, Minos), by both goddesses and mortal women. Below is a simplified family tree, and Gaia, mother of Cronos, the youngest of the Titans.

RHEA'S TRICK

Cronos knew that he would be supplanted by one of his children and adopted the extreme solution of eating them as soon as they were born. Rhea, tired of supplying her husband's infanticidal appetites, went to Crete, to the Cave of Dikte to give birth. She returned to Olympus and gave her husband a stone in place of her newborn son, Zeus; he swallowed the stone in one gulp.

THE CURETES

Zeus was a lively child, even when young given to thunderous outbursts. Rhea ordered the Curetes, a semi-divine people, to dance and clash their shields and lances in noisy rituals, so that Zeus' father did not hear him crying. The young god and the satyr Pan, his foster brother, were brought up on Crete by the goat (or nymph) Amalthea.

ZEUS, KING OF THE GODS

Aided by the Cyclops, Zeus fought the Titans and the Giants, casting them down beyond the underworld into the depths of the abyss. After this he did indeed supplant his father: he put a herb into the wine cup of Cronos, which forced him to regurgitate the offspring he had devoured. Zeus divided the world up by drawing lots. The underworld became the province of Hades, while Poseidon was given the seas. Zeus kept the heavens for himself, becoming god of the universe, "father of the gods" and "father of men", presiding over all fates, human and divine.

ZEUS' MARRIAGE

Zeus' first wife was the magical Titan goddess Metis (Prudence and Shrewdness). Zeus was informed by an oracle that her child could endanger his supremacy; so when she became pregnant he tricked her into turning into a fly, and instantly swallowed her (thus uniting within himself Power and Reason). Some time later he suffered a violent headache. Hephaistos pierced his temple to relieve the pain, and Athena emerged from Zeus' head, fully armed.

THE RAPE OF EUROPA

Europa, daughter of the king of Phoenicia, was playing on the beach at Tyre with her companions, when Zeus – who was certainly not averse to liaisons with mere mortals – became captivated by her youthful beauty. He transformed himself into a pure white bull; Europa caressed the beast's soft skin and then, becoming bolder, sat upon its back. Zeus headed straight for the sea and swam away, with Europa holding on to one of his horns. They arrived on Crete, where the plane trees of Cortyne have evergreen leaves in memory of their union. They had three children: Minos, Rhadamanthys and Sarpedon. The bull whose shape Zeus had taken became a constellation and a sign of the zodiac. Although it is refuted by Herodotus (Histories, IV. XLV), it is said that the continent of Europe was named after the young girl who left the shores of Asia to settle in the West.

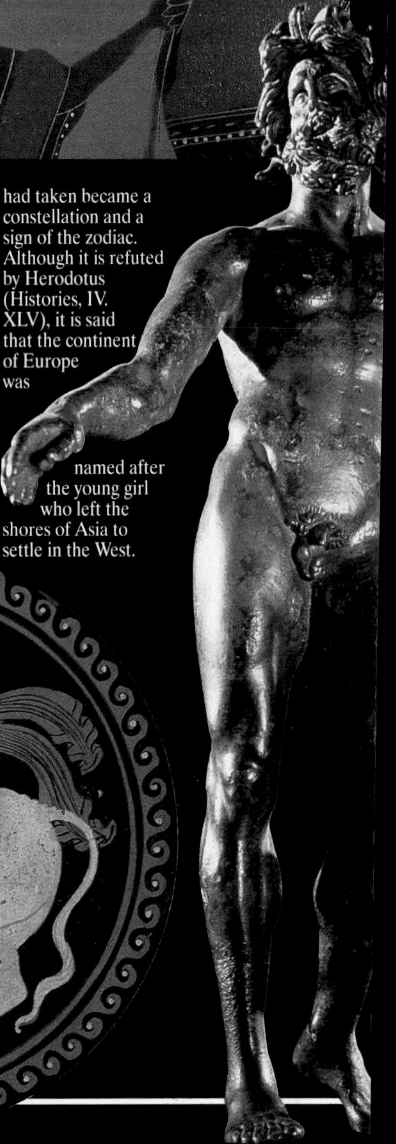

A BROKEN PROMISE

In order to convince his brothers that he was meant to reign alone over Crete and that the gods were on his side, Minos asked Poseidon to send a bull from the sea, which he promised to sacrifice. Minos became king: the animal was so superb, however, that he decided not to kill it but to breed from it with his herds. Minos married Pasiphaë, daughter of Helios (the Sun), by whom he had many children including Ariadne and Phaedra.

MONSTROUS LIAISON

Poseidon, angry at this breach of faith, avenged himself on Minos by inspiring the king's wife Pasiphaë with a guilty passion for the magnificent bull. She did not know how to satisfy her passion, and asked Daedalus, an Athenian architect exiled in Crete, to help her. He designed a wooden cow; the queen hid herself in this perfect decoy, the bull was deceived, and the unnatural coupling took place.

THE MINOTAUR

After this ill-fated liaison, Pasiphaë bore a creature with the body of a man and the head of a bull, which fed on human flesh. Minos ordered Daedalus to build the Labyrinth to hide the monster. After his victory over Athens, Minos demanded fourteen young Athenians as a tribute every three years, to be sacrificed to the Minotaur. The Athenian Theseus offered himself as a victim, but Ariadne fell in love with him at first sight.

THE LABYRINTH, THE MINOTAUR'S PRISON
Ariadne gave Theseus a ball of string so that he would not get lost in the labyrinth, and he unraveled it on his way to the Minotaur's lair. After a violent struggle, Theseus emerged victorious. He then had only to follow Ariadne's thread to retrace his steps to daylight. Ariadne, fearing Minos' anger, fled by boat with Theseus and the other Athenians.

ARIADNE AND DIONYSOS
At the port of Naxos, Theseus left Ariadne sleeping on the sand. She woke later to see the Athenians' ship just a dot on the horizon. But her sadness soon lifted: Dionysos, dazzled by her beauty, carried her up to Olympus, married her and made her immortal.

THE FLIGHT AND FALL OF ICARUS

The Minotaur's death and Ariadne's flight with Theseus enraged Minos: he shut Daedalus and his son Icarus in the labyrinth. But Daedalus, whose name means "skillful craftsman" in Greek, came up with an idea. He made two pairs of wings from feathers for himself and his son. He fixed them to their shoulders with wax, and they both flew off. Unfortunately, Icarus did not pay heed to his father's advice: intoxicated with the sense of freedom, he flew too near the sun. The wax on his wings melted and he fell to his death; the sea he fell into was later called the Icarian sea after him. It is said that Daedalus recovered his son's body and buried it on the island now called Icaria. But still Minos did not relent. He pursued the Greek architect to the court of the king of Sicily, where he died, scalded to death in a bathtub invented by Daedalus.

PHAEDRA AND THESEUS

Phaedra married Theseus. She bore him two children, but fell for her stepson Hippolytus, who was banished and killed in spite of his innocence. Phaedra later hanged herself. Above, Phaedra and her servant.

The symbolism of the Cretan myths has been as constant source of inspiration for many artists. They have returned again and again to the image of the naïve young girl abducted by the brute force of the bull, disguised under the dazzling whiteness of its beautiful coat. The image of the Minotaur reappears in all its power around the turn of the century in Vienna and then during the Surrealists' political phase before the war. The Surrealists were drawn to this myth by its "superhuman", unnatural, "surreal" qualities.

THE "MINOTAUR"
Covers designed by Picasso (right) and Dali (left) for the journal founded by Albert Skira, the first issue of which appeared in February 1933.

ICARUS IMMORTALIZED
This drawing after Picasso for Serge Lifar's ballet expresses man's joy at the conquest of the skies.

THE MINOTAUR SYMBOL IN VIENNA
Around 1897 Gustav Klimt, together with a small group of other artists, founded a movement known as the Vienna Secession, which aimed to present an alternative to official art, especially academic art. In this poster designed for the Secession's first exhibition, Klimt depicts figures drawn from the mythology of Crete (Theseus and the Minotaur) and of Greece (Athena and the Gorgon). The empty square in the middle represents the space of the temple or the labyrinth, and the narrow dark strip at the top shows the monster's lair, where the individual faces a perpetual and terrible struggle with his own instincts. It is perhaps worth noting that Sigmund Freud was formulating the basic concepts of psychoanalysis at precisely this time, with the hypothesis that the psyche is divided into three elements: the unconscious, the subconscious and the conscious. Klimt was to make Athena an emblem for the Secessionist movement: she represents primitive power and sensitivity, controlled by the guiding force of moral conscience.

BULLFIGHTING
The Minotaur is a major theme in Pablo Picasso's unique pictorial world. He used this ancient symbol of the struggle between light and dark, good and evil, love and death, with its affinities to the world of bullfighting, and produced a very human version of the "monster", at once both executioner and victim.

> "WHEN A SYMBOL IS TRANSPOSED INTO A NEW LANGUAGE, IT SETS OFF UNEXPECTED RESONANCES WHILE REMAINING FAITHFUL TO THE ORIGINAL INSPIRATION, AND THERE IS A COHERENCE AMONG SUCCESSIVE INTERPRETATIONS." J. CHEVALIER

The Rape of Europa by Titian.

ORIGINS

Opposite, geometric decorative motifs from neolithic pottery.

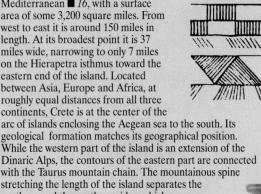

6500 BC
Neolithic Europe: Beginnings of cereal farming and rearing of sheep and goats.

Neolithic figurines. Archeological Museum of Heraklion

3800 BC
Villages surrounded with defensive walls.

3500 BC
Use of rudimentary horse-drawn ploughs.

3000–2100 BC
Maritime trade between Crete and the Greek archipelago.

2000–1600 BC
Connections established between the Minoans, Byblos and Egypt.

Pitcher in the Kamares style from the palace of Phaistos, 1900–1700 BC.

GEOLOGICAL FORMATION. Crete is one of the largest islands in the Mediterranean ■ *16*, with a surface area of some 3,200 square miles. From west to east it is around 150 miles in length. At its broadest point it is 37 miles wide, narrowing to only 7 miles on the Hierapetra isthmus toward the eastern end of the island. Located between Asia, Europe and Africa, at roughly equal distances from all three continents, Crete is at the center of the arc of islands enclosing the Aegean sea to the south. Its geological formation matches its geographical position. While the western part of the island is an extension of the Dinaric Alps, the contours of the eastern part are connected with the Taurus mountain chain. The mountainous spine stretching the length of the island separates the northern and the southern sides, which are very different from each other in terms of climate and vegetation. Three principal massifs divide the island into three regions: in the west the White Mountains (Lefka Ori), which dominate the Khania region; in the center Mount Ida (Oros Idi), sloping steeply to the plain of Messara; and in the east Mount Dikte (Oros Dikti), surrounded by a more complex region made up of high plateaux and hills leading towards the Sitia Mountains (Sitiaka Ori), which reach a maximum altitude of about 4,800 feet. Crete's geographical position, its temperate climate and the fertility of its soil made it attractive to outsiders at a very early stage, and it has been under foreign rule a number of times.

FIRST NEOLITHIC PERIOD (6100–3800 BC).
The earliest traces of human habitation on Cretan soil go back to around the end of the 7th millenium (6100 BC). Many of the myths and beliefs of antiquity suggest that the island had a native population. However, even if a primitive population did exist in earlier times, it is probable that Crete was first settled properly by peoples from elsewhere. The Phoenicians, a seafaring people, definitely established settlements on the island; gradually a number of them settled permanently, introducing important features of their civilization. Cave dwellings, such as Dikteon Antron on Mount Dikte where bones and stone tools have been found, are typical of the first Neolithic period, as are settlements of simple houses.

SECOND NEOLITHIC PERIOD (3800–2800 BC). Pottery appeared during this period, made of terracotta and fired in an open fire. Neolithic pottery is generally dark or black in color, consisting of cooking utensils, ladles, pitchers and vases, as well as idols. Objects of bone and crystal have also been found. Traces of advanced cultivation have been discovered: cereals, barley, lentils, as well as animal bones (goats, sheep, pigs, and more rarely cattle). At the end of the Neolithic age, metals were introduced to Crete: an early bronze axe provides evidence of this.

Sir Arthur Evans divided the Minoan era into three periods: Early Minoan, Middle Minoan and Late Minoan, each broken into periods I, II and III. Nicolas Platon

MINOAN CIVILIZATION (2700–1200 BC)

Following its relatively slow development during the Neolithic period, Crete began a new era around 2800 BC, a golden age of prosperity which lasted some fifteen hundred years, with an exceptionally high level of civilization in all spheres. The Minoan age is named after King Minos, who is supposed to have reigned over the island ● 39. Alongside developments in agriculture, stock-breeding and craftsmanship, this period brought denser habitation and the growth of trade with Egypt, Syria and Asia Minor.

later created a dating system referring to the Cretan "palatial system".

Votive figurine, from the period of the first palaces.

1900 BC
Hieroglyphic writing in Crete.

THE FIRST PALACES
(PROTO-PALATIAL PERIOD). The first palace at Knossos was built around 1900 BC. Knossos was clearly the main administrative center on the island, although further palaces were built at Phaistos, Mallia and Haghia Triada at around the same time, following the same architectural design. These buildings indicate a comfortable and highly developed lifestyle, including bathrooms and a channeling system which supplied drinking water, sometimes from considerable distances: the pipes supplying the palace of Knossos ● 88 came from the area of Mount Jouchtas, some six miles away. The artistic life of the period – painting, theater, bullfighting – also reveals a high level of civilization, as does the appearance of an early form of writing, hieroglyphics like those inscribed on the disk of Phaistos ● 66. As trade developed with nearby or distant countries, the Minoans expanded their seafaring fleet: Crete became an important maritime power during this period and in later centuries.

Opposite, a superb rhyton in rock crystal from the palace of Zakros, 1450 BC

1550 BC
Myceneans in Greece.

1450 BC
Mycenean civilization supplants that of the Minoans.

Dolphin fresco from the palace of Knossos, around 1600 BC.

THE SECOND PALACES
(NEO-PALATIAL PERIOD). The first palaces were destroyed around 1750 to 1700 BC, very probably by a natural catastrophe, perhaps a series of violent earthquakes such as often occurred on the island. However, the palaces were rebuilt after this disaster; furthermore, new ones were erected, including those at Tylissos, Pressos and Zakros. The next three centuries, between 1700 and 1450 BC, saw another phase of unprecedented economic and cultural growth; this was the golden age of Minoan civilization.

Chief's goblet, from Haghia Triada, 16th century BC.

A matchless piece of Minoan jewelry: a gold bee pendant found on the site of Mallia ▲ *192* (around 1500 BC).

The population grew and new towns sprang up across the island. The script known as "Linear A" appeared at this time. Minoan civilization was very influential, especially on the islands of the Aegean Sea. Excavations undertaken on the island of Thera (Santorini) some thirty years ago supplied proof of this. Minoan influence also reached as far as the Peloponnese. This great civilization, however, whose remains still astonish us today, fell victim to a mysterious catastrophe during the course of the 15th century BC. Historians, archeologists and other specialists disagree as to the cause. The most plausible explanation seems to be the eruption of the volcanic island of Thera, which took place at around this time. The explosion produced a gigantic tidal wave and deposits of volcanic ash ■ *17*, inflicting serious damage from which the Minoan civilization could not recover.

THE MYCENEANS AND THE DORIANS (1450–700 BC)

Helmet of boar's teeth, 1450–1300 BC. Opposite, a

Mycenean gold plaque depicting a shrine decorated with a double set of horns.

END OF 13TH TO BEGINNING OF 12TH CENTURY BC
Trojan War.

POST-PALATIAL PERIOD (1450–1100 BC).
Other historical theories ascribe the disappearance of the Minoans to the waves of invaders who attacked the island during the same period. The invaders, from the Peloponnese mainland, were Acheans, more commonly known as Myceneans. During this period, referred to as the Creto-Mycenean civilization, the two cultures merged: Minoan civilization had a particularly clear influence on the Myceneans' way of life. The effect of Mycenean culture on the Cretans can be seen in the introduction of religious elements, the Greek language and the script known to us as "Linear B". Many tablets bearing this type of writing were discovered throughout Crete, notably in the palace of Knossos, and on the Peloponnese ● *66*; they were eventually deciphered by the English scholars Ventris and Chadwick.

CRETE AND ANCIENT GREECE (700–67 BC)

1150 BC
End of Mycenean civilization: cities and palaces abandoned.

Mycenean gold goblet, 15th century BC.

DORIAN PERIOD (1100–700 BC). The period which followed represented a complete break with earlier times. The invasion of the Dorians, a race which came originally from the northeast, began in Greece and proceeded in waves from the end of the 13th to the beginning of the 12th centuries BC. The new arrivals were completely different from other Greek peoples in terms of their economic, social, cultural and political systems. The Dorians arrived in Crete around 1100 BC, settling at first around the center of the island, at Knossos, Driros and at Gortys (the last of which grew into an important town under

their rule). The Dorian period saw significant changes in the political system (an aristocratic regime) and morals. Some decline in terms of lifestyle and the arts is apparent; a number of old towns like Knossos, on the other hand, were given a new lease of life, while new cities were created (including Lato to the north of Mount Dikte). In addition the population grew and trade expanded, especially with Asia Minor. After the Dorian invasion, Crete tended to become indistinguishable from the rest of Greece in terms of customs, religion, language and writing. This period also corresponds with what is known as the Iron Age.

ARCHAIC AND CLASSICAL PERIODS (700–330 BC).

During the Archaic and Classical periods, after the Dorians had settled, Crete seems to have remained on the margins of the Hellenic world. When Athens was at the height of its artistic and commercial powers, the rest of Greece was involved in the wars with the Medes – although the Cretans seem to have played no part in these. By contrast, closer links developed with Libya and Cyrenaica (the town of Cyrene was founded in 630 BC), and a number of Cretans emigrated to these areas. Nonetheless the Cretans, highly trained in the military arts since the Dorian invasion, probably supplied seven thousand mercenary archers to Alexander the Great for his Asian expedition.

HELLENISTIC PERIOD (330 BC–67 BC).

Alexander the Great, who had succeeded his father Philip II of Macedon in 336 BC, gained control of most of Asia Minor by the year 333 BC, when he defeated Darius III of the Medes. When he died in Babylon ten years later his generals, the Diadochi, divided up his empire among themselves. A part of Crete, Cyrenaica and some islands in the Aegean fell to the Ptolemies of Egypt. However, rivalries in dividing up the island produced political confusion and piracy flourished as a result: the Romans were to come and suppress this disorder.

GRECO-ROMAN ERA (67 BC–AD 330)

After several abortive attempts, Quintus Caecilius Metellus finally managed to conquer Crete around 67 BC. The island became a Roman eparchy attached to the province of Cyrenaica. It remained under Roman rule until the 4th century AD. The Roman governor was based at Gortyna, where ruins from this era can still be seen today, not far from the plain of Messara ▲ 176. The constant communication and trade with Cyrenaica meant that Crete, and particularly the southern part of the island, enjoyed a time of prosperity. For their part the Romans undertook major construction works: irrigation works to improve farming, road building, and so on. They also allowed some towns to mint coins. Christianity made its appearance in Crete at the same time: Saint Paul

Decorative motifs taken from pottery from LMI and LMII (1500–1400 BC).

900 BC
Beginning of the Geometric period.

9TH CENTURY BC
Homeric poems.

7TH CENTURY BC
Archaic period.

The lady of Auxerre, a Cretan figurine in the Egyptian style, 650–600 BC.

5TH CENTURY BC
Classical period: dominance of Athens; century of Pericles and Socrates.

4TH CENTURY BC
Hellenistic period.

3RD CENTURY BC
Rome controls Italy.

31 BC
Greece becomes a Roman province.

3RD CENTURY AD
Decline of the Roman Empire. Rise of Christianity.

Roman bust from the first Flavian dynasty (AD 69–96) and mosaic, 3rd century AD.

made many conversions when he traveled through Crete in AD 59, accompanied by the bishop Titus. After Saint Paul left the island, Titus settled at Gortyna and continued to spread the Christian faith, as did his successor Philip. The remains of the great basilica which was later built at Gortyna and dedicated to Saint Titus ● *100* bear witness to the early years of Christianity on the island. In the mid-third

century AD, under the emperor Decius, Christians on Crete suffered great persecution, as they did in the rest of the Roman Empire: there were many victims in Gortyna and the surrounding area.

BYZANTINE CRETE (330–1204)

Opposite, Byzantine cross, 6th–7th century.

5TH CENTURY
Barbarian invasions

6TH CENTURY
Reign of Justinian (527–565): construction of the St Sophia basilica at Constantinople (Byzantium).

7TH CENTURY
Reign of Heraclius (610–641). The Arabs conquer Egypt and settle in northern Africa.

Arab coin, 9th century. Historical Museum, Heraklion.

FIRST BYZANTINE PERIOD (330–824). In 330, the Roman Empire was divided into the eastern and western empires. Crete joined the former in 395, becoming a province of the Byzantine Empire. It was to remain unaffected by major political upheavals until the beginning of the 9th century when it came under threat from the Arabs.

ARAB OCCUPATION (824–961).
At the beginning of the 9th century the Arabs (or Saracens) of Andalusia were expelled from Spain following disputes with the Emirate of Cordoba. They settled in Northern Africa, using this as a base for pirate raids throughout the Mediterranean, including the eastern territories. Their repeated attacks on the islands of the Aegean Sea and the Mediterranean coasts were a threat to the Byzantine Empire. They were attracted by Crete's geographical position and by its wealth, and attacked it several times before capturing it in 828; they ruled the island for around 130 years. For the Byzantines its loss was a disaster; for the Arabs, Crete was a convenient base for their piratical activities. They founded the town of al-Khandaq, now Heraklion, and built fortifications around it. The Byzantines tried to reconquer the island several times, but in vain: their campaigns, especially that of 949, proved very costly in terms of both money and human life. In July 960, Nikephoros Phokas laid siege to Khandaq at the head of a large armada and a strong army of infantry and cavalry. After several months' resistance the Byzantine strategist captured Khandaq on March 7, 961; he then took the other Arab-occupied cities, destroying their fortifications.

8TH CENTURY
Reign of Leon III (717–41). Conflict with the Arabs. Constantinople under threat. Charlemagne (747–814) becomes Holy Roman Emperor in 800.

SECOND BYZANTINE PERIOD (961–1204). Once they had reconquered Crete the Byzantines founded the town of Temenos, to the south of Khandaq. They put considerable

"THE MINDS OF THE UNCULTIVATED INVADERS WERE ENNOBLED BY THEIR CONTACT WITH GREECE."

HORACE

Arab army, 9th–10th century.

9TH CENTURY
Photius, ruler of Constantinople.

11TH CENTURY
1054, schism of the Greek church. 1071, Battle of Mantzikert: Byzantines are beaten by Seljuk Turks.

12TH CENTURY
Restoration of the Byzantine Empire under the Comnene dynasty (1057-1185).

effort into re-establishing Christianity, which had been jeopardized under Arab rule, notably by sending missionaries to the island, including Saint Nikon and Athanase the Athonite. Many noble Byzantine families settled on the island where they were granted estates and privileges. As peace returned so did Crete's prosperity, and trade developed not only with Constantinople, the capital of the Byzantine Empire, but also with Russia. Crete was to remain under Byzantine rule for just over two centuries, up to the fourth crusade in which the Franks and the Venetians took part. The crusaders captured and sacked Constantinople in 1204, causing the break-up of the Eastern Empire.

Saint Theodore, 11th century. Historical Museum, Heraklion.

VENETIAN OCCUPATION (1204–1669)

United under Boniface of Montferrato, king of Thessalonika, the conquerors of Constantinople divided up the spoils of the Byzantine Empire. They encountered difficulties with the various parties involved, especially between the Genoans and the Venetians who laid claim to the same territories. The Venetian Republic emerged victorious, acquiring a part of the ancient Byzantine capital where it established a Latin and Venetian patriarch, Tomaso Morosini. In this way Venice became the spiritual protector of all the Europeans in the east. In the meantime Venice had taken command of several provinces in the western part of the former Byzantine empire, the western coast of Greece from Durazzo to Navpaktos, the Ionian

1204
Fourth crusade, in which the Venetians took part. Sacking of Constantinople and break-up of the Byzantine Empire.

1261
Recapture of Constantinople by the Byzantines.

1261–1453
Renaissance of Byzantine arts and literature under the Paleologues.

1275
The Venetian Marco Polo travels to China.

14TH CENTURY
Venice at the height of her economic powers, enriched by trade with the Orient.

Opposite, the fortress of Rethymnon.

49

The Doge Dandolo sends Rainieri to conquer Crete in 1207.

1438
Councils of Ferrara and Florence: attempt to unite the eastern and western churches.

1445
First printed book produced by Gutenberg.

Candia, 1488.

islands, the coasts of the Peloponnese, some islands in the Aegean and the large island of Euboea: this made the conquest of Crete almost as important as that of Constantinople, in strategic and economic terms. The island was an excellent naval base, located at the junction of various sea routes: it could guarantee Venice commercial dominance of the Mediterranean. Crete was also rich in agricultural produce – cereals, wines, olive oil, fruits and vegetables – which would bring in substantial revenues. In August 1204 the Venetians bought Crete from Montferrato: they finally gained full control in 1212, despite attempts by the Genoese to prevent it.

GOVERNMENT OF THE ISLAND. The Venetians set up a political, legal and social system modeled, by and large, on their own. A governor, the Duke of Crete, was appointed by the Great Council of Venice to take charge of the island's administration. In order to consolidate the conquest, Crete was divided into nearly two hundred fiefs which were allocated to members of the Venetian nobility; they were charged with defending the island and obliged to surrender a

1453
Constantinople conquered by Mehmet II: the Turks dominate the eastern Mediterranean.

1492–1498
Discovery of America and the Atlantic sea routes by Christopher Columbus and Vasco da Gama.

Lion of Saint Mark from the fortress of Candia.

portion of their agricultural output to "La Serenissima". A few Venetian commoners were granted official positions; others settled as traders in the capital, which was renamed Candia. The orthodox church was placed under the jurisdiction of the Latin church. The great Byzantine families – the Paleologues, the Skordhiles, the Kallergis, the Vlastos and many others – were kept out of public affairs, retaining only their financial privileges. The Cretan population, the peasantry in particular, was submitted to a highly centralized and oppressive system of regulations and burdened with statutory labor, enforced service in the galleys and high taxes.

REVOLTS. The Venetian rulers encountered lively resistance, especially in the 13th and 14th centuries. There were no less than ten revolts in the 13th century alone, many involving considerable loss of life; the rebellion of 1282, led by the Byzantine governor Alexis Kallergis, was particularly ferocious. Venice was forced to make numerous concessions: authorizing mixed marriages, reinstating the high clergy of the orthodox church, freeing slaves, and so on. Despite these measures the rebellions did not stop. During the 14th and

"COMMEMORATING THE DUKE OF BEAUFORT, ADMIRAL OF FRANCE, AND THE FRENCH OFFICERS, SOLDIERS AND SAILORS, ONE THOUSAND IN NUMBER, WHO FELL BENEATH THE WALLS OF CANDIA."

INSCRIPTION

15th centuries, civilian unrest repeatedly threw the country into turmoil. The last rebellions, in 1527, were extremely serious and were bloodily put down by the authorities. However, after this the tide of events began to turn, and relations improved between the Cretan leaders and the Venetian authorities. The 16th century heralded a welcome return to peace, which allowed Crete to experience an unprecedented phase of growth.

ECONOMIC GROWTH. The disturbances and rebellions did not stop the Venetians from making the most of Crete's agricultural resources. The island became an important center for trade at the end of the 15th century, when new trading routes were opening up. It was a valuable port of call for many types of produce sent from the Red Sea to the Mediterranean, destined for western Europe: these included, for example, spices from the Far East, which were bought in the market-place. On Crete itself, the Venetians at first favored cereal crops. However, towards the end of the 15th century they gave priority to vines, transforming almost the whole of Crete into an immense, highly productive vineyard. The island's economy grew rapidly, bringing higher living standards and population growth: despite frequent plagues and earthquakes, which devastated the island from time to time, Crete sustained around 200,000 inhabitants towards the end of the 16th century.

CANDIA, KHANIA, RETHYMNON. The 16th century also brought even closer ties between Crete and Venice. The Cretan middle classes sent their children to study medicine, law or philosophy at Italian universities, in Bologna, Padua, and Venice itself, where a large Cretan community developed. Crete's three main towns, Candia, Khania and Rethymnon, became cultural as well as commercial centers, as the artistic production of the period reveals. The Venetians undertook restoration work in these towns and erected a variety of buildings: a ducal palace with loggia, an armory, the cathedral of San Marco, the Church of St Titus, the Morosini fountain, and a large number of splendid private residences were built at Candia ▲ *144*. The port was renovated and arsenals were built. The Venetians also carried out general improvements: roads were re-laid, for example, and irrigation systems were set up to increase the productivity of the land.

Venetian coin, 15th century. Historical Museum, Heraklion.

FIRST HALF OF THE 16TH CENTURY
The Spanish and Portuguese controlled the new spice routes. Decline of the Arabs, of Venice and of Genoa.

The Ottoman Empire reached its height under the reign of Sultan Suleyman the Magnificent (1520–66).

In Europe: Humanism, the Renaissance and the rise of the middle classes.

Town gateway at Rethymnon.

SECOND HALF OF 16TH CENTURY
Rise of the English navy.

1570
The Turks take full control of the former Byzantine Empire.

17TH CENTURY
France dominant in Western Europe, under Louis XIV.

1669
Turkish conquest of Crete.

The Venetian arsenals at Khania.

Two official documents prove that the famous painter Domenikos Theotokopoulos, known as El Greco ("The Greek"), was born at Heraklion in 1541, while Crete was under Venetian rule. The artist underwent his apprenticeship as a painter in the Cretan capital, but left there in 1566 at the age of twenty-five, heading initially for Venice where he was most probably a pupil of Titian. He arrived in Rome in 1570, and there met Luis Castilla, whose brother Diego, dean of the chapter at Toledo cathedral, was to be his patron in Spain. It is here that he reached the height of his powers as an artist, developing the very personal style for which he is known. El Greco died at Toledo in 1614.

This self-portrait dates from 1563. Opposite, Saint Anne, the Virgin and Child, which reveals a number of Byzantine features.

"VIEW OF MOUNT SINAI"
Dating from around 1570, this is the only work by El Greco exhibited in Crete, at the Historical Museum in Heraklion ▲ 152. The painting, in oils on tempera-primed wood, shows an imaginary view of Mount Sinai with the famous monastery of Saint Catherine and a group of pilgrims in the foreground. The misshapen, stylized mountains give a foretaste of the painter's later style.

In his biographical note of 1619 on the painter, Giulio Cesare Mancini reports an incident which may help to explain why El Greco stayed only briefly in Italy. Pope Pius V, who held office between 1566 and 1572, planned to have some details of Michelangelo's *Last Judgment* in the Sistine Chapel (of 1536) painted over, considering them to be indecent. The young Cretan painter is supposed to have declared that if he were entrusted with the task he could do just as well as the great Roman master, while also observing the proprieties. "Having aroused the indignation of all painters and lovers of painting", Mancini concludes, "he was forced to leave for Spain."

BYZANTINE INFLUENCE

El Greco's artistic and historical connections with his native Crete are still a matter of investigation and dispute today among art historians. How important is the Byzantine influence on his work? Some see traces of this tradition in the fact that his pictures are theological rather than religious in character: they make a clear distinction between the divine world and the material world, which are shown as separate but mutually accessible areas.

THE CRETAN SCHOOL

Left, a detail from the *Adoration of the Myrrh-bearers*, an icon by Damaskinos ▲ *148*, one of the main representatives of the 16th-century Cretan School, to which El Greco's early works also belong.

Ceramic dish, 16th century. Historical Museum, Heraklion.

1674
Signing of the "New Capitulations", trade agreements between France and the Ottoman empire.

1687
The Venetians recapture Morea.

Lion of Saint Mark, emblem of Venice, engraving of 1651.

1699
Decline of the Ottoman Empire: treaty of Karlowitz, the Turks lose Hungary.

1702
Foundation of St Petersburg, capital of the Russian Empire.

1718
The Turks defeated by the Austrians.

1768–1774
War between the Ottoman Empire and Russia: the Turks lose the Crimea and the Russians win the right to cross the Dardanelles.

Woman of Sfakia, C. Vecelio, 1590.

THE TURKISH THREAT.

Crete's prosperity was in imminent danger, however. To east and west, to north and south, whole regions had been falling under Turkish control since the capture of Constantinople. The Turkish or Ottoman Empire reached its height in the 16th century under the reign of Suleyman I the Magnificent (1520–66). During the second half of the century, the Western nations tried to stop the Turkish advance: Selim II (1566–74) seized Cyprus in 1570; in retaliation the West, under Spanish leadership, destroyed the sultan's fleet at the Battle of Lepanto in October 1571. Crete, the last bastion of Christianity to the east, was attacked a number of times.

PAX TIBI MAR CE EVAN GELIS TA MEVS

RAMPARTS AND FORTIFICATIONS.

After 1550, in the face of this growing threat, the Venetians reinforced their defenses. The remains of extensive fortifications from the 16th and 17th centuries can still be seen at Heraklion (Candia): the ramparts with their seven bastions, monumental gateways studded with escutcheons, and extensive underground passages show how much importance the Venetians attached to the defence of Crete. Fortifications were also constructed at Khania and the bay of Souda, following roughly the same design. After a Turkish attack in 1571, the Venetians built a fortress at Rethymnon on the rocky platform of the ancient acropolis. Forts and fortifications sprang up throughout the rest of the island, including the fortresses at Gramvoussa in the west and at Spinalonga in the east (the latter is still well preserved). Completing this defensive effort, the Venetians built walls around market towns and many towers on the island's shores.

THE TURKISH CONQUEST.

These measures held the Turks at bay for a time, but their advance through the eastern Mediterranean was inexorable. On June 23, 1645, Crete, the last Venetian colony, was attacked by the army of Sultan Ibrahim (1640–8). The Turks came ashore in the bay of Khania. Within a few months the town and all of western Crete except the fortress of Gramvoussa had been conquered. The following year saw the fall of Rethymnon. In 1647 the Turks gained control of the rest of the island, except for the fortress of Spinalonga and the town of Candia, which continued to resist. The siege of Candia is famous for its length and for the emotions it aroused throughout Christian Europe; many were killed, both within the besieged town and among the Europeans who came to its aid. In 1669 the Turks finally broke into the fortress. After the surrender of Candia, Crete was conquered, except for the fortresses of Gramvoussa and Spinalonga, which were the last to hold out.

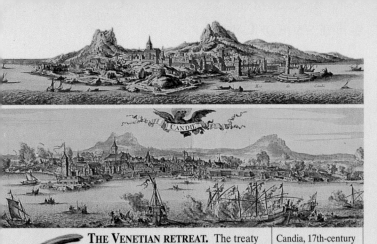

THE VENETIAN RETREAT. The treaty imposed by the conquerors was lenient toward the Venetians, who were able to withdraw with their weapons, archives and possessions. The Cretans were also permitted to leave the island with their possessions. Thousands of them, nearly half the population, opted for exile: some sought refuge in the Ionian islands which were still under Venetian control, others settled in Venice. As for the Turks, now the rulers of the island, they tried at first by various means to appease the hostility of the local population, in particular by re-establishing the freedom of the orthodox church. The Turkish occupation was to last a little over two centuries.

THE CONSEQUENCES. Taking a broader view, it could be argued that the Venetians' loss of Crete had important consequences for the rest of Western Europe. The withdrawal of Venice marked the end of the medieval era and the beginning of modern times. As will be seen later, it enabled France to extend its economic and religious influence into this region.

Candia, 17th-century engravings.

1789
French Revolution.

1797
End of the Venetian Republic.

1798
Battle of Aboukir.

Turkish inscription, Rethymnon.

The Turkish fleet off Candia, mural painting.

● THE SIEGE OF CANDIA

After the fall of Constantinople in 1453, the Ottoman Empire extended in the eastern Mediterranean, with the conquests of Euboea, Rhodes, the Peloponnese, Nauplia, Monemvasia, Chios, and finally Cyprus in 1571. Venetian Crete, the last bastion of Christianity in this part of the world, was to be the next stage of this advance: quite apart from its agricultural resources and the wealth of its warehouses, the island held a strategic military and economic position. At Candia, where the Duke of Crete and the *capetan general* (in charge of the Venetian army) were based, the Rocca al Mare fortress was reinforced in the mid-16th century.

CANDIA'S FORTIFICATIONS

Between 1550 and 1560, imposing walls designed by the architect Sanmicheli (1484–1559) were built around the city. The walls, some 2 miles long, formed a star shape, and included seven polygonal bastions. The ramparts consisted of an external parapet and a platform protected by a second wall. The bastions had a central recess at a higher level, protected by a third wall; they were linked by a system of tunnels.

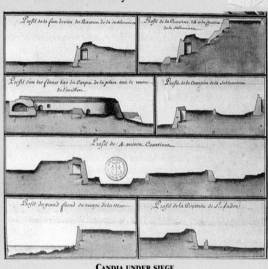

CANDIA UNDER SIEGE

The Turks conquered Khania and western Crete in 1645, and Rethymnon the following year. In 1647 the fortresses of eastern Crete fell one by one, followed in 1648 by the fortress of Souda. Only Candia remained. The Turkish land army headed for the capital, destroying the fortresses of Haghios Dimitrios and Nova Candia as it went. The siege of the great citadel, the "Megalo Kastro", began on May 1, 1648.

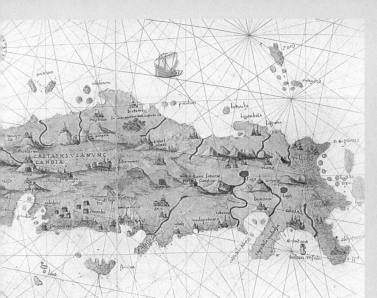

CANDIA IN ISOLATION

During the first two years of the siege, the Turks surrounded Candia on all sides, destroyed the aqueducts which supplied the town with water, and attacked almost daily. Despite the difficult living conditions the inhabitants of the beleaguered town held firm and the siege dragged on without any major developments between 1650 and 1666. Candia remained in Venetian hands despite the Turks' repeated raids.

CHRISTIAN CRUSADE

Nearing the end of their resources, the Venetians eventually called on the Western powers for assistance, thereby turning the conflict into an international issue. The defence of Candia became in itself a crusade for Christian Europe: from 1666 onwards, considerable military forces were sent to reinforce the town, as well as weapons, ammunition and other equipment; a formidable artillery was deployed and major defenses were constructed.

1666–7

In November 1666, Sultan Mehmet IV (1648–77) sent his leading strategist, the Grand Vizir Ahmet Köprülü, to lead the siege. The Venetians, for their part, appointed Francesco Morosini (right) to the head of their army. Despite serious damage caused by the constant bombardment, and despite the difficulties in obtaining supplies, the town did not despair: the Western powers regularly sent reinforcements and the citadel seemed impregnable. But then Colonel Andrea Barrozi gave himself up to the Turks and revealed to them the weak points in Candia's fortifications.

DESPONDENCY

When this treachery became known, it unleashed a wave of panic; Venetian soldiers began to desert in increasing numbers. The situation became ever more critical and tension rose. The European mercenaries suffered from the weather, epidemics, and from the disagreements which prevented their leaders from coordinating their actions effectively.

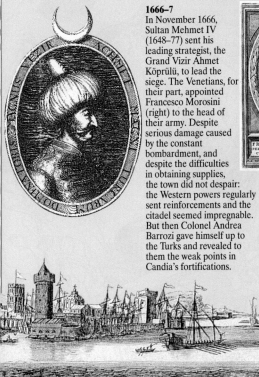

In 1668 the Marquis de Saint-André Montbrun came to Candia at the head of a force of sixty-eight officers. A few months later the Duc de Feuillade landed, with an armed unit of six hundred men. However, their attack on the Turks ended in defeat. The French finally withdrew in January 1669. In June, the dukes of Beaufort and Navailles led a new expedition to the besieged town, which also failed. Morosini gave up hope and surrendered.

Marquis de Montbrun.

EUROPEAN INTERVENTION
More aid was sent to Candia in the form of money, provisions, weapons and men. The Order of Teutonic Knights sent 200 men, the Republic of Venice 900, the Duke of Hanover 4,000 and Leopold I of Germany 2,000, in addition to 2,500 soldiers enlisted by the German count Waldeck. Further reinforcements arrived from France: 6,000 soldiers commanded by the Duke of Navailles (right, above) and Admiral François de Vendôme (right, below). A squad of gunners and soldiers arrived from Bavaria and Strasbourg.

Nonetheless, a fatal lack of coordination between the different commanders meant that these forces could not be fully effective, and each of the many attacks they launched only increased the numbers of soldiers lost.

THE FALL OF CANDIA

The Duke of Beaufort was killed in a general attack on the Turks. The Duke of Navailles withdrew in August 1669, after losing nearly 2,000 men. His departure prompted many defections among the allied ranks. Soon Francesco Morosini had no more than 3,000 Venetians under his command, worn out by illness and hardship, and he decided to negotiate the surrender of the citadel. The treaty of surrender was signed on September 16. The Venetians evacuated the town, along with a number of Cretans who took refuge initially on the island of Dia, before seeking exile in Venice or the Ionian islands. When Grand Vizir Köprülü finally entered the citadel on September 27, 1669, he found Candia deserted and in ruins. Although Venice had spent over 120 million ducats, and although her navy and army had fought with great bravery to defend Candia, "La Serenissima" was ultimately unable to hold on to the capital of Crete, where she had held sway for almost half a millenium.

OUTCOME

After this the whole of Crete was under Turkish control. The fall of Candia, after more than twenty years of siege, 69 attacks by the Turks, 849 attacks by the Venetians and their allies, 110,000 Turkish and 30,000 Christian dead, finally marked the end of the Venetian Republic's powers. It was to have significant repercussions on the balance of power in the Mediterranean and on subsequent events in the region.

TURKISH OCCUPATION (1669–1898)

1821–27
Greek War of Independence.

1827
Victory of the Greek allies in the Battle of Navarin.

1830
Greek independence confirmed by the Protocol of London.

1832–1862
Otho I proclaimed King of Greece.

Cretan costumes of the 17th century. Historical Museum, Heraklion.

THE NEW ORDER. After the Turks took power they divided the island into three districts, each governed by a pasha. The pasha of Khania was the most powerful of the three, and governor of the island as a whole. The lands which had belonged to the Venetian nobility or to leading Byzantine families were confiscated, and re-allocated to military leaders and officials who had taken part in the conquest. However, the new incumbents were only given the right to work the land: under Turkish law, all lands belonged to the sultan. A strong military presence was maintained throughout the island. The Ottoman authorities, their officials, and traders from Asia Minor settled in the cities; the Cretan population withdrew to the countryside, as most of them were forbidden to live in the towns. Only a few Jewish traders continued to live in Khania, only a few Armenians in Candia. In order to take full control of the island's economy, the Turks established new forms of taxation and changed the legal system (setting up religious tribunals under the jurisdiction of the *qadis*, or Muslim judges).

1834
Athens is designated capital of Greece.

1854–1856
Crimean War.

Scene of a massacre.

Turkish map of Crete.

TRADE WITH FRANCE. Around the time that Crete fell under Turkish rule, France signed the "New Capitulations" (1674) with the Ottoman Empire, allowing its ships free right of passage in the eastern Mediterranean and enabling its merchants to settle in Turkish ports, the "Ports of the Levant". Although Crete was financially ruined following the conquest, it was soon to benefit from these agreements. It offered a product for which there was a great demand in France: olive oil, which was used by the soap manufacturers of Marseilles. Barely five years after the conquest, a French consulate was established at Khania and French merchants settled there. These merchants bought most of the olive oil produced in Crete but also other products including wax and silk. Responding to this increased demand, the Cretans established new olive plantations. In his account of his travels, the botanist Pitton de Tournefort noted in 1700: "the area around La Canea is admirable, from the town up to the nearby mountains. It is covered by olive trees, as high as those in Toulon or Seville. At Candia [here Candia refers to

Portrait of Melitakas, commander during the Cretan revolution of 1821–30.

the whole of the island] they never die because there is never a frost. The forests of olive trees are interspersed with fields, vines, gardens, streams: and the streams are bordered with myrtle and oleander."

LIFE IN CRETE UP TO THE EARLY 19TH CENTURY.

The relative peace allowed Crete to enjoy a degree of economic stability during the 18th century. In other spheres the results were not so positive: culturally, the island was very inward-looking at this time, producing no significant intellectual or artistic developments. In the late 18th century war broke out between the Turks and the Russian Empire; Russian agents incited the Cretan population to revolt. In 1770 a rebellion broke out in the mountainous region of Sfakia ▲ *263*, and was brutally suppressed by the Turks. The Russo-Turkish war was settled in 1774 with the treaty of Küçük Kaïnardji, which heralded the decline of the Ottoman Empire. Soon after this the Cretans, like the rest of the Greeks, were granted a number of rights, mainly concerning freedom of navigation in the Mediterranean.

1862
King Otho I deposed.

1863–1913
George I, King of Greece. Ionian islands and Thessaly become part of Greece.

1869
Opening of the Suez Canal.

THE 19TH CENTURY

POPULAR UPRISINGS IN THE 19TH CENTURY. The Greek War of Independence began in 1821, and in June of the same year the Cretans revolted. The uprising failed and was brutally suppressed, but the next ten years saw a series of revolts in Crete. When Greece was proclaimed independent in 1827, the British intervened to ensure that Crete remained under Turkish rule, placing it under the jurisdiction of the Egyptian pasha. In 1840 Crete again became a Turkish province and saw a period of relative calm, especially between the reforms of 1839 and 1856, following the treaty of Paris under which the sultan promised to improve conditions for Christians within his empire. As a result Crete's economy improved; the island was represented at the International Exhibition in Paris in 1855. After 1864 the troubles started again. The year 1866 saw several bloody massacres, the most notorious at the monastery of Arkadi, which provoked a wave of sympathy throughout Europe ▲ *222*. The great powers negotiated with the Ottoman Empire, which accepted some of Crete's demands, including the recognition of two official languages. However these reforms were poorly implemented and did not prevent more disruption. After the revolt of 1896, the great powers forced through Crete's independence in 1898, placing the island under the rule of Prince George of Greece, who received the title of High Commissioner.

Cretan revolutionary.

Eleftherios Venizelos (1864–1936) left his mark on the history of Greece as a whole for nearly half a century. He was elected President of the Chamber in 1909 and Premier in 1910; in 1911 he won the national elections and founded the liberal party. After this Venizelos began his great political work, instigating important changes in economic and social policy. His clarity of vision helped realize the dream of a Hellenic nation and the creation of an enlarged Greek state with a strong presence on the international scene. His activities, his successes and his political audacity aroused violent antipathies: he was the target of eleven assassination attempts.

THE HELLENIC MISSION

Venizelos was born at Mournies in 1864. He was a barrister in Khania from 1887 onward. His clear vision and his brilliant mind had by this stage already impressed politicians such as Georges Clemenceau and Joseph Chamberlain. In 1897 he called for Crete to be united with Greece, as the only possible solution to the "Cretan question". In 1901 his disagreement with Prince George's policies led to his dismissal. After this he became a focus for the political opposition, which demanded a revision of the Cretan constitution in 1905. After the Therissos revolution Venizelos created a "provisional Cretan government", amidst general jubilation. Three years later the Greek government declared Crete united with Greece.

ATTACK. On July 20, 1920, the Sèvres agreements were signed between the allies and the Turkish Empire. Venizelos was attacked by Greek officers at the railway station in Lyon, as he prepared to return to Athens.

WORLD WAR ONE

A supporter of the Western Allies, Venizelos set up a provisional government at Thessalonika. In 1915 he traveled to Egypt with Markandonakis.

THE FATE OF HELLENISM

In 1919, when the peace treaties were signed, Venizelos represented the interests of Greece: the dream of an enlarged Greek nation seemed to be taking shape. But the Turks retaliated and Greece was defeated in Asia Minor. Venizelos lost the 1920 elections and went into exile. After this, with a characteristic display of obstinacy and diplomacy, he fought to retain Greek territories and tried to contain the losses; on July 24, 1923 he signed the treaty of Lausanne, which set limits to the frontiers of the Turkish state. Greece went through a time of recession and political instability between the two wars. In 1928 Venizelos was called back from exile to take an active part again in the political life of his nation. At the same time he worked to improve Greece's relations with neighboring countries.

BURIED IN STATE
After a series of setbacks, Venizelos finally retired from politics in 1932 and left Greece. He died in Paris in 1936 and was buried at Khania, on the Akrotiri peninsula.

1913
Assassination of George I; accession of Constantine I.

George I.

1917–20
Constantine I deposed and exiled. Venizelos is Prime Minister.

Constantine I.

1916–18
Greece enters World War One on the side of the Allies.

1920–22
Mustapha Kemal becomes the first president of the Turkish Republic.

War between Greece and Turkey. The Greek army is routed.

Cretan deputies, safe from the winds of European war in 1911.

1924
Proclamation of the Greek Republic.

1935
Monarchy restored under George II.

CRETAN INDEPENDENCE (1898–1913). During the time of peace which followed, many exiles returned to Crete: the population grew; the economy, trade and agriculture all developed, and the island experienced a renaissance in its cultural life. Despite this progress the Cretans were not happy: they wanted full union with Greece, and it was then that Eleftherios Venizelos appeared on the political scene.

THE 20TH CENTURY

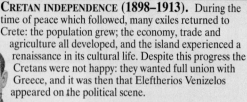

UNION WITH GREECE (1913). In 1908, the Young Turks of the nationalist Union and Progress committee took power in what was left of the Ottoman Empire. In 1910, when called by the king of Greece to form the Greek government, Venizelos declared that *Enosis* (union with Greece) was a military question. And indeed annexation was to be the result of war. In 1911 war broke out between Italy and Turkey, followed in 1912 by Greece's involvement in the Balkan wars. The Allies asked Constantinople to introduce reforms in the empire. When this was refused, the Greeks invited Cretan deputies to join their government. The Turks, defeated by the Greeks, had to abandon the island once again. On May 17, 1913, the Treaty of London officially united Crete with Greece. After this the island was governed by a Governor General and reorganized in four *nome* (departments): Heraklion, Rethymnon, Khania and Lassithi.

THE "ASIA MINOR DISASTER".
In 1916, Crete supported Venizelos' policy of entering the war against Germany. Crete also supported the Greco-Turkish conflict, which had been rumbling on since 1912: in 1919 Greece won western Thrace, but had to concede eastern Thrace in 1923, after defeats inflicted by Turkey under Mustapha Kemal. The "Asia Minor Disaster" was to result in a significant exchange of population: the Turks who left the island were replaced by Greeks from Asia Minor.

> "CRETE IS A CRADLE, AN INSTRUMENT, A TEST TUBE IN WHICH A VOLCANIC EXPERIMENT IS UNDER WAY."
>
> HENRY MILLER

1936–41
Dictatorship of General Metaxas.

APRIL 1941
German offensive launched on Crete.

MAY 21–31, 1941
Battle of Crete. German occupation of the island.

Bombing of Heraklion.

1944
The Germans withdraw from Crete.

1947
Return of George II. He is later succeeded by Paul I and Constantine II.

Hitler and his commanders discuss their plans for Crete.

1955–63
C. Karamanlis, Prime Minister.

1964–7
George Papandreou, Prime Minister

1967–74
Dictatorship of the Colonels in Greece.

1974
Restoration of the Greek Republic.

1980
Karamanlis elected president of the Greek Republic.

1981
Greece joins the EC. Election of Andreas Papandreou.

1986
Greece becomes a full member of the Common Market.

WORLD WAR TWO. On October 28, 1940, Greece joined the Allied coalition. Three days later, in agreement with the Greek government, British troops moved into the Cretan military base on the bay of Souda, and set up air bases at Rethymnon and Heraklion. In April 1941, the Germans launched their offensive on Greece. The Greek forces had to withdraw to Crete, under protection of the British navy. The German high command decided to attack Crete from the air: a series of punishing aerial bombardments got the better of Crete's towns; the British evacuated them one after another, suffering heavy losses. The Cretan resistance was formed, and harassed the German occupying forces until liberation. In his *Memoirs*, Sir Winston Churchill declared: "Goering's victory in Crete was a Pyrrhic one: the forces he expended here could easily have obtained him Cyprus, or Iraq ...".

CRETE, PROVINCE OF GREECE. After the war, Crete set about modernizing its agriculture, its industry (then more or less non-existent), and its trade. Today it has over 500,000 inhabitants. It is a fertile island with an equable climate, and exports its agricultural produce through much of Europe. Yet tourism is today the main source of income. Several internationally renowned writers have made its cultural life famous. Crete is currently one of the most prosperous provinces of Greece and one of the major tourist destinations in the Mediterranean.

Hieroglyphic writing consists of ninety different signs, in addition to a number of ideograms, only the most common of which have as yet been identified. The various shapes inscribed on the disk of Phaistos (details above) represent men and women, animals, plants, tools and boats, among other things.

LINEAR A
This script consists of 70 signs and over 164 ideograms. Most of the tablets which have been found are religious texts or financial records: only the numbers have been identified. Although this syllabic script has not yet been deciphered, it has been established that it was read from left to right and from top to bottom.

THE FIRST FORMS OF WRITING

HIEROGLYPHIC WRITING. The earliest examples of writing discovered in Crete are stone seals from the Pre-palatial period (2600–1900 BC), with ideograms which were doubtless influenced by Egyptian writing. During the Paleo-palatial period (1900–1700 BC), while the Minoans were building the first large palaces, the ideograms evolved towards a more stylized form of hieroglyphs: several examples of this type of writing have been discovered on the major Minoan sites like Knossos and Mallia. The famous disk of Phaistos (details above), dating from around 1700–1600 BC, is a mysterious and fascinating object; many theories have been devised to explain its provenance and purpose ▲ 180.

LINEAR A. Hieroglyphic writing co-existed for a time with the Linear A script, which appeared during the Neo-palatial period (1700–1450 BC), corresponding with the second phase of Minoan civilization when the large palaces were rebuilt. It is called "linear" because it consists of signs which intersect without seeking to depict real objects. It includes syllabic signs and a few logograms: some of the characters are stylized forms of earlier hieroglyphs. Words are separated by dots or bars. Texts written in Linear A have been found outside Crete, in continental Greece and on some islands of the Aegean Sea, within the area covered by Minoan trade. The largest collection of tablets in Linear A was discovered at Haghia Triada ▲ 264, near Phaistos; however the number of extant texts is not enough for the writing to be deciphered.

LINEAR B. During the 1890's, Sir Arthur Evans ▲ 168 discovered engraved stones in antique shops in Athens which he thought could be fragments of prehistoric writing. He traced their source to Crete, where there were stones, worn by women as amulets. This clue led him to undertake excavations at the site of Knossos, which had already been discovered. The excavations were, of course, a success. Evans discovered tablets bearing writing which he thought was also Minoan, and which he christened Linear B. In fact this turned out to be an adaptation of Linear A to the Greek language, devised by the Myceneans who dominated Greece during the Post-palatial period (1450–1100 BC). The large number of texts discovered at Knossos enabled the architect and polyglot Michael Ventris to decipher the writing in 1952. Documents in Linear B were written on clay tablets,

> "THE LANGUAGE OF NEO-HELLENIC LITERATURE DOES NOT CONTAIN A MESSAGE. THE LANGUAGE IS THE MESSAGE. A WRITER'S FORM OF EXPRESSION IS THE ARGUMENT OF THE BOOK."
>
> VASSILIS VASSILIKOS

shaped in either "palm-leaf" or "page" shape. The tablets survived thanks to being hardened in fires.

THE KOINE. The system of writing continued to evolve during the course of what are known as the "dark ages": the Proto-geometric, Geometric and Archaic periods. With the dawning of the classical era (500–330 BC) the Greeks adopted a consonantal alphabet, following that of the Phoenicians. This highly rational system of phonetic transcription promoted the unification of the Greek languages – in the common tongue known as the *koine* – and the emergence of a written literature: the orally transmitted tales by the bard Homer were transcribed in the 8th century BC.

LINEAR B
This syllabic script uses eighty-seven "syllabograms" combined with around one hundred ideograms, figures and phonetic signs. Mycenean officials recorded all their information about the kingdom on these tablets: they are one of our primary sources of information on the administrative organization of the palaces.

THE ORIGINS OF MODERN GREEK

Today's spoken Greek is the product, first, of the historic evolution of the spoken language and secondly, of a series of reforms undertaken since the creation of the Greek state. On the eve of the War of Independence, a new language had to be chosen for the new nation. An intellectual movement headed by Koraïs, a Greek writer living in Paris, proposed a compromise between the "classical" language of the church and the language of the middle classes. As the Greeks were

descended directly from the Hellenic race, Koraïs considered that the new Greece should be reborn from the mulch of classical culture. For this reason the popular language was to be replaced by one with its roots in the past, purged of all foreign words.

GREECE'S TWO LANGUAGES. Greece therefore has two languages: the 'pure' language, *katharevoussa* (from *katharos*, pure), mainly written, and the official language; and the popular language, *dhimotiki* (from *dhimos*, people), which evolved with spoken Greek. Literary figures fought for the recognition of the popular language, though it was not until 1975 that the Neo-Hellenic language, as it was thence to be known, became Greece's official language.

CRETAN DIALECT. The Cretan dialect is a southern form of Greek, distinguished by its own form of pronunciation and by numerous archaisms in its morphology, syntax and vocabulary. Up to the first half of this century, words from ancient Greek or Byzantine, or even from Italian or Turkish, were used in Crete as viable alternatives to the Athenian terms. However, most of these are now scarcely used, except by the oldest inhabitants of Crete, village-dwellers or shepherds. Urbanization has imposed the language of the capital in recent years.

HOMER'S "ILIAD"
The founding masterpiece of Greek literature, set in the time of the Trojan War, was printed in the Greek language for the first time in Florence, in 1488.

CRETAN LITERATURE

The earliest written examples – whether literary texts or legal documents – in the neo-Cretan dialect (a mixture of dialect elements and scholarly Greek) do not appear until the 14th and 15th centuries. Cretan literature was influenced by the Italian Renaissance, while perpetuating the Greek and Byzantine traditions; it includes great works written in dialect, especially from the 16th century onward: *Erotocritos* and *Abraham's Sacrifice* by Vincent Cornaros, or Hortatzis' *Erophile*. After the Turkish occupation, a whole new generation of writers appeared, at a time when the language question was dividing the Greek world. Between the wars, some of these writers helped establish a literary language which drew mainly on the spoken word.

NIKOS KAZANTZAKI (1883–1957) ▲ *146.* The humanist issues which underlie his work culminate in a "heroic aesthetic of life", tinged with idealism. His most prominent literary themes include a devotion to action, an aesthetic renunciation, and also his deep-rooted, passionate attachment to his native island.

MANUSCRIPTS
Crete's many monasteries carefully preserve the work of their copyist monks. Above, a manuscript from the monastery of Gonia.

An ardent socialist and patriot, Kazantzaki was a great defender of the popular Cretan language, introducing to it a number of new words, both popular and ancient; he began work on a major dictionary.

PANDELIS PREVELAKIS (1909–86). He studied philosophy and law at Athens. From 1937 he taught history of art at the Academy of Arts there, where he was appointed director.

THE "EROTOCRITOS"
This immensely long poem – with 10,502 lines – was probably composed around 1645. It combines the metrical form of the Byzantine novel and the epic/lyrical style of the Italian Renaissance with the lively wit of Cretan literature and the simplicity of its dialect.

In his trilogy *The Cretans* (1948–50), *Chronicle of a City* (1958), and *The Paths of Creation* (1959–66), his accounts of historical events and portraits of everyday life have an almost poetic quality. His style is infused with the lyricism of landscape and people, the magic of legends and destinies.

ODYSSEUS ELYTIS. He discovered Surrealism in 1935, through his friend the poet Andreas Embirikos, and this influenced his poetry. He published his first poems in the 1940's (*Sun, the first*, 1943), then moved to France. His collections *Axion Esti* (1951), *Six and a remorse for the sky* (1960), *Maria Nefeli* (1978) draw their inspiration from Crete's sad history and the island's magnificent colors. He received the Nobel Prize for Literature in 1979.

ARTS AND TRADITIONS

● TRADITIONAL CRETAN COSTUME

Traditional Cretan dress is best known for its men's costume, the *vraka*, named after the trousers that the men wear. The *vraka* is one of the most complicated and elegant trouser styles in Greece. On other islands the male costume was the first to give way to modern styles of dress: in Crete, however, it is still worn, an indication of the island's continuing attachment to tradition.

Cretan costumes of the 18th century – particularly the headdresses – were clearly influenced by Turkish fashions.

On the left, the woman wears a luxuriant Turkish-style hat and a dress with very wide sleeves, a typical feature of the period.

WOMEN'S COSTUME
The female costume, and especially the woven motifs on it, vary from village to village. The women wear long white cotton trousers, covered at the front with an apron, and at the back with a half-skirt or *sartza*. The waistcoat is often very short, in dark blue or black wool, sometimes embroidered with gold. A scarf is worn over the head. Today women's traditional costume is worn only on special occasions.

MINOAN FRESCOS
These reveal the ceremonial costume worn by priestesses in 1500 BC. They were regarded as goddesses of fertility and wore a tightly waisted corset revealing bare breasts, above a flared skirt with flounces or covered with aprons.

MEN'S COSTUME
In memory of Crete's past loss of freedom, several elements of the traditional male costume are black: the hat, the boots, and sometimes even the shirt. A black net scarf is tied around the head, often with the fringes hanging over the forehead. This is supposed to have been introduced to Crete by pirates from Algeria.

THE "KIOUSTEKI"
The watch hangs on a silver chain, the *kiousteki*, attached to a double-breasted waistcoat, which is usually embroidered.

CRETAN TROUSERS
The *vraka* is held in place by a belt 9 yards in length. Wound several times around the waist, this holds the traditional silver knife or *bassalis*. The back panel of the trousers used to be longer than it is today.

● DANCE AND MUSIC

The tunes and instruments of popular Cretan music are different from those of the rest of Greece. The *mantinades*, which stem from a long oral tradition, are improvised serenades on the subject of love. They are composed of rhymed thirteen-syllable lines. *Rizitikas* have developed from laments sung during periods of occupation, with words expressing the desire for freedom in allegorical form. In Yannis Markopoulos's definition, Cretan music is "free and human, with no unnecessary flourishes, rough and unpolished but as beautiful and sensitive as a bird's plumage".

THE "SYRTO"
Originating from the Dodecanese islands, the *syrto* is supposed to derive from classical Pyrrhic dances. This dance, of which there are several variants in Crete, is full of grace and lightness. Men and women form a circle around the person leading the dance and perform wave-like movements: the handkerchiefs they hold call to mind the foaming crests of waves.

THE "PENDOZALIS"
This dance has five steps. Manly and war-like, it requires strength and suppleness. According to legend it was inspired by the classical *pyrichios* danced by the Curetes

● *37*, Crete's protecting spirits. The Curetes hit their shields with their lances to drown the cries of the newly born Zeus, whose mother's cunning had saved him from the evil appetite of his father Cronos.

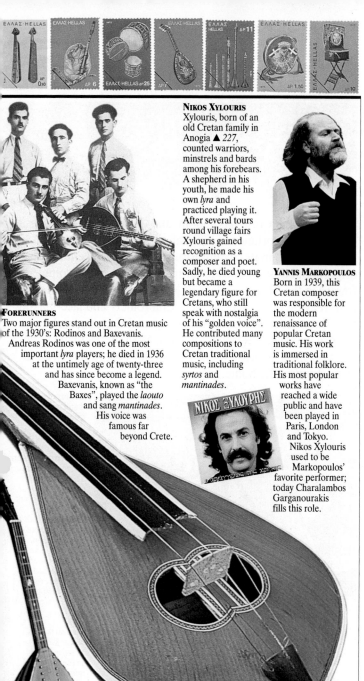

NIKOS XYLOURIS

Xylouris, born of an old Cretan family in Anogia ▲ *227*, counted warriors, minstrels and bards among his forebears. A shepherd in his youth, he made his own *lyra* and practiced playing it. After several tours round village fairs Xylouris gained recognition as a composer and poet. Sadly, he died young but became a legendary figure for Cretans, who still speak with nostalgia of his "golden voice". He contributed many compositions to Cretan traditional music, including *syrtos* and *mantinades*.

FORERUNNERS

Two major figures stand out in Cretan music of the 1930's: Rodinos and Baxevanis.

Andreas Rodinos was one of the most important *lyra* players; he died in 1936 at the untimely age of twenty-three and has since become a legend.

Baxevanis, known as "the Baxes", played the *laouto* and sang *mantinades*. His voice was famous far beyond Crete.

YANNIS MARKOPOULOS

Born in 1939, this Cretan composer was responsible for the modern renaissance of popular Cretan music. His work is immersed in traditional folklore. His most popular works have reached a wide public and have been played in Paris, London and Tokyo.

Nikos Xylouris used to be Markopoulos' favorite performer; today Charalambos Garganourakis fills this role.

THE "LYRA"

A specifically Cretan instrument constructed from old wood – mulberry, walnut or maple.

It has three strings tuned in perfect fifths and is played with a small bow (sometimes with bells attached), which is held in the right hand. The musician's left hand skims the strings, without depressing them. The *lyra* is often accompanied by the *laouto*, the Cretan version of which is the largest and most curved in Greece.

73

Every house in Crete has a loom, and this is evidence of the continuing importance of the craft of weaving, which seems to have existed in its current form since the 11th century. Its origins doubtless go back to far more remote times: some frescos in the Minoan palace of Knossos provide evidence that weaving was practiced then. Embroidery and lace-making are also practiced today: there is a special Cretan geometric pattern known as "Rethymnot" lace. Most pieces made to be worn on special occasions, or for interior decoration, are still crafted within the home.

The art of weaving is still passed down from mother to daughter. Up to around 1870, designs were traditionally geometrical, featuring diamond shapes. There are local variants: for example, the pairs of interlocking diamonds which are typical of Crete's central region. After this time motifs inspired by nature and historical events began to appear.

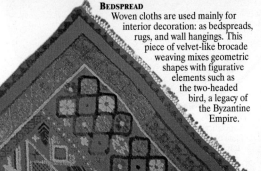

BEDSPREAD
Woven cloths are used mainly for interior decoration: as bedspreads, rugs, and wall hangings. This piece of velvet-like brocade weaving mixes geometric shapes with figurative elements such as the two-headed bird, a legacy of the Byzantine Empire.

LACE
Lace-making is still actively practiced, both in the home and commercially. The oldest surviving Cretan lace – trimmings for women's garments – dates from the 17th century.

> ## "WHILE SHE EMBROIDERED, THE YOUNG BRIDE TOLD THE STORY OF THE EARTH AND THE SKY."
>
> CRETAN POEM

LACE-MAKING CUSHION
The cushion allows the lace to be stretched, using pins, while it is made following a pattern. The lace-maker unwinds the thread from a collection of bobbins.

CRETAN APRON
The traditional Cretan women's costume includes a white cotton apron embroidered in red, matching a maroon half-skirt which is draped at the back.

EMBROIDERED HANDKERCHIEF
On the women's ceremonial dress, embroidery is used mainly to decorate the waistcoat (gold thread on black felt) and the apron. Other less obvious accessories – handkerchiefs and scarves – may also be embroidered.

● POTTERY

The art of pottery in Crete goes all the way back to the 7th millennium BC. The Cretan tradition of making *pithoi*, or large jars, is historically related to the technique and lifestyle of Crete's itinerant potters. These teams of craftsmen would camp for around six months at a time on the outskirts of oil-producing villages, near a source of water. They threw ten *pithoi* at a time, on a row of ten wheels, methodically adding a stage to each jar in succession. The firing day, once a week, was a day of great celebration. Master potters such as these made the famous *pithoi* of Knossos, Phaistos and Mallia. Some potters' workshops still exist today, notably at Trapsano, a town famous for its pottery.

On May 21, St Constantine's Day, the potters would leave Trapsano ▲ *197* in groups of five or six: the *mastoras* (master potter), the *soto-mastoras* (assistant), the *trocharis* (turner), the *xylas* (in charge of the wood), the *chomatas* (in charge of the clay) and the *kouvalitis* (porter-apprentice). Each member of the group had his own tools and donkey. After several days on the road, they arrived at their work site and immediately built a kiln with rough bricks.

In the lower part of the furnace, a stout, round pillar propped up the arches supporting a grill. At the center was the fire, with a thick circular wall of bricks and stones around and over it.

"I HAD WISHED DEEP IN MY HEART TO MARRY THE TOWN, AND I MARRIED AT THRAPSANO TO SIEVE THE EARTH."

POPULAR SONG

2. After being beaten thoroughly, the clay soil is sieved.

3. The finely sieved clay is slowly and carefully mixed with water.

1. The *chomatas*, in charge of the clay, beats the soil with a club.

4. The clay paste is kneaded with the feet, in a regular rhythm.

5. The *mastoras* places the base of the future jar on the wheel.

6. After spreading the base, the *mastoras* places the first lump of clay on top of it.

7. The *mastoras* and the *trocharis* raise the walls of the jar.

8. The *trocharis* turns the wheel at the speed indicated by the *mastoras*.

9. The first section of the jar must be able to bear the weight of its contents.

10. Every one of the jars bears the personal mark of the *mastoras* who made it.

11. After being left to dry for several days, the jars are put in the kiln.

12. Once it is full of jars and pots, the kiln is covered with metal sheets and clay.

13. Firing lasts from dawn until late in the night.

14. In the morning the top of the furnace is broken off, and the new pots are brought out.

77

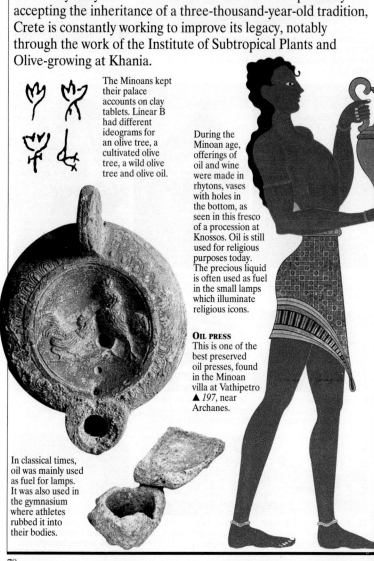

A number of products are derived from olives. Nearly all the olives produced in Crete are made into olive oil, which is known throughout the Mediterranean for its high quality. Olive oil has been one of the island's most valuable resources since the Minoan age. Olive groves are passed on down the generations, and can be given as the dowry of an olive farmer's daughter. Olive-growing is a long-term investment, which can be destroyed by fire in a few minutes. Far from complacently accepting the inheritance of a three-thousand-year-old tradition, Crete is constantly working to improve its legacy, notably through the work of the Institute of Subtropical Plants and Olive-growing at Khania.

The Minoans kept their palace accounts on clay tablets. Linear B had different ideograms for an olive tree, a cultivated olive tree, a wild olive tree and olive oil.

During the Minoan age, offerings of oil and wine were made in rhytons, vases with holes in the bottom, as seen in this fresco of a procession at Knossos. Oil is still used for religious purposes today. The precious liquid is often used as fuel in the small lamps which illuminate religious icons.

OIL PRESS
This is one of the best preserved oil presses, found in the Minoan villa at Vathipetro ▲ 197, near Archanes.

In classical times, oil was mainly used as fuel for lamps. It was also used in the gymnasium where athletes rubbed it into their bodies.

> "BLESSED TREE, UNKNOWN IN ASIA, INVINCIBLE AND IMMORTAL
> TREE, THE FOOD OF OUR LIFE, PALE-COLOURED OLIVE TREE
> PROTECTED BY ATHENA, GODDESS WITH THE BRIGHT EYES."
>
> SOPHOCLES, "HYMN TO THE OLIVE TREE"

In Crete, 100,000 families (in other words nearly all
the population) produce some 100,000 tons of oil each
year. A mature olive tree – around fifteen to thirty years
old – yields on average 26 pounds of olives every two
years, which can produce up to 2 litres of oil.

TRADITIONAL OIL PRESSES
The olives are crushed by
rotating grindstones.

The olive paste is spread
on circular mats which are
stacked and then pressed.

The oil from the first pressing
is the best, containing less
than one percent oleic acid.

Green olives are harvested in autumn; black olives,
which are riper, in winter. To reduce their bitterness
the olives are soaked in brine. In Crete, black olives
are often simply mixed with salt.

The use of olive oil
in the manufacture
of soap has declined
considerably in recent
years. Today there is
only one factory in
Crete which makes
such soap.

Union oil, which
was awarded an
international prize.

79

Greek churches are dedicated to the Virgin Mary, to Christ, the Holy Trinity or a patron saint. On the saint's feast day, the villagers organize a *panigiri*, an event both secular and religious, including masses, processions, music, dance and feasting. One of the most venerated saints in Crete is Saint George, alongside Saint Nicholas, the patron saint of sailors. Saint George is seen as the patron of car-drivers, peasants and shepherds. Innumerable chapels are dedicated to him, and he has become virtually a mythological hero. St George's Day, on April 23, is an occasion for special celebrations, notably in Asi Gonia, Haghii Deka, Plakias and Kasteli. On this day everyone brings out their best bottles of old wine.

THE LEGEND
Saint George, a general under the Roman emperor Diocletian, was martyred in AD 305. His cult began in Palestine in the 5th century, subsequently spreading through both the East and the West. Today he is the patron saint of Genoa, Venice, Barcelona and England.

IMAGES
On icons and on many other objects, such as this carved wooden distaff (left), the most common image of the saint depicts an episode from his youth, supposedly in Beirut: Saint George, riding a white horse, is shown defeating a dragon which is threatening a princess.

As a Roman general, Saint George is a link between the military and religious worlds. He is the patron saint of the Greek army and is pictured on its flags and emblems.

"WE PRAYED TO THE SAINTS TO GIVE A HELPING HAND, TO PRODUCE A MIRACLE, EVEN IF THIS DID PLAY HAVOC WITH THE DIVINE ORDER ...!"

PANDELIS PREVELAKIS

SHEPHERDS' DAY

St George's Day is a holiday in many Cretan villages – notably in those, like Asi Gonia, where there are still a large number of shepherds. Here the liturgy is longer than elsewhere in Greece, and all the shepherds take part along with their flocks. According to popular belief, the absence of a shepherd can make the saint angry. Indeed, one legend relates how the saint struck a shepherd and woke his children in the middle of the night to make them take their sheep to the church. He is also supposed to have taken one flock there himself. This festival coincides with the shepherds' departure for the pastures on the White Mountains.

THE FEAST DAY

Hundreds of sheep, washed and decorated with bells on the previous evening, flock through the roads of the village. When they are called by the priest, each flock, skillfully separated from the others, enters the place of assembly – the *courta* – with its shepherd or shepherds.

The shepherds receive the blessing. They kiss the priest's hand and cross and receive a small round loaf or *artos*.

THE BLESSING

While the shepherds milk the sheep, the priests recite the liturgy of Saint George in the village church. Once the milking of a flock has finished, the priests break off to bless the animals and, chanting, touch them with an olive branch.

The milk is collected together, boiled, blessed, and offered to all the villagers, who exchange good wishes.

Easter, in late April or early May, is the most important feast in the Orthodox calendar. It took over the tradition of the Jewish Passover and also of ancient spring rituals. The Orthodox Easter celebrates Christ's Resurrection and the renewal of life in spring. For families and communities it is a landmark, shaped by the Byzantine tradition, highly colored and charged with emotion. The Greek Orthodox church, traditionalist in all aspects of its rituals, uses the Gospels in their original version, which the people can understand, as well as psalms which are fifteen centuries old. The rites take place in the midst of much glittering gold and the heady perfumes of incense and flowers.

BYZANTINE CROSS
This cross decorating the Gospels bears witness to the survival of Byzantine Orthodoxy, which combined Christianity and Hellenic culture.

BISHOP OF RETHYMNON
From the first centuries of the Byzantine Empire up to the present, the Orthodox Greek clergy has played a major role in transmitting the Greek language, culture and imagery through religious festivals; these festivals have become a key element of the national consciousness.

HOLY WEEKS
On the Thursday, the Passion is enacted symbolically: the Christ figure on the cross, covered with crowns and flowers, is at the heart of long religious services. During the night, the women decorate the *Epitaphios*, representing Christ's tomb, with brocades and flowers. The *Epitaphios* is carried in procession on the Friday evening, followed by worshipers holding candles and chanting ancient lamentations. On the Saturday at midnight the light of the Resurrection, symbolized by candles, is passed around while fireworks and firecrackers are let off all around. Late in the night people gather for the first Easter meal. On the Sunday the perfumes of flowers mingle with the smell of roast lamb, which is eaten around a large table covered with Easter dishes, before the dancing starts.

ANASTASIS

The risen Christ ascends toward the light, symbolized here by the dome. He carries Adam, Eve and all of humanity out of Hell, the doors of which lie shattered under his feet. The Hebrew kings Solomon and David worship him, dressed in the costume of Byzantine emperors of the Macedonian dynasty.

THE LAMB

The lamb, a symbol of Christ's innocence and sacrifice, is embroidered on this priest's vestment; it is also roasted on a spit for the Easter meal. It is called *ovelias*, like the ancient offerings.

RED EGGS

On Wednesday of Holy Week, women dye eggs red – the color of Christ's blood and of joy. At Easter the eggs are exchanged, symbolizing the message of the Resurrection: *Christos Anesti*.

EASTER CANDLES

White, the symbol of purity, is everywhere: in the whitewashed houses and walls, and in the candles which transmit the purifying flame announcing the Resurrection. Easter candles, especially those made for children with ribbons and decorations, are everywhere in the shops.

The recipe for *xaratigana* uses the main traditional ingredients of Cretan cuisine: honey, oranges, and olive oil. This type of sweet pastry, oriental in origin, can be eaten as a dessert or passed around when friends come to visit, as is the custom in Crete.

2. In a bowl, mix together the flour, salt, orange juice, two spoons of oil, and water, to make a thick dough. Cover and leave to rest for an hour.

3. On a floured surface, roll the pastry until it is paper-thin and cut into pieces about 4 by 6 inches.

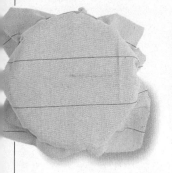

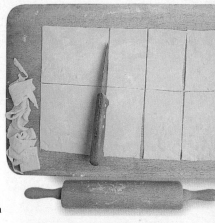

4. Heat the rest of the oil, and when it is boiling put in the pastries one by one. They will puff up in the hot oil. Take them out when they are a light golden color.

5. Place the pastries on a dish covered with absorbent paper to absorb the excess oil, and pour the syrup over them.

1. Ingredients: 2 cups of flour, 1 teaspoon of salt, 1½ cups of olive oil, ½ cup of orange juice, 3 tablespoons of water, ½ cup of honey.

1 cup of sugar, chopped mixed nuts, cinnamon powder and sticks, sesame seeds, 2 cloves.

6. Making the syrup: Making the syrup: in a saucepan mix the honey, sugar, ½ cup of water, a piece of cinnamon stick and 2 cloves.

Remove the scum which forms when the mixture boils. Pour the syrup over the *xaratigana* and sprinkle with nuts, sesame seeds and powdered cinnamon.

● SPECIALTIES

Embroidery.

Olive oil, retsina (dry white wine), castillo (red wine).

Cretans are very fond of weapons, especially knives.

"LYRA"
These typically Cretan instruments are still made by hand on the island.

"KOULOURA"
Bread and pastry.

JEWELRY
Reproductions of Minoan jewelry and original pieces
◆ *304*.

CHEESE. Made from sheep's or goat's milk; there are several regional varieties: *mitzithra*, *kaskavali* and *kritiko*.
NEWSPAPERS. Each town has its own daily newspaper.

ARCHITECTURE

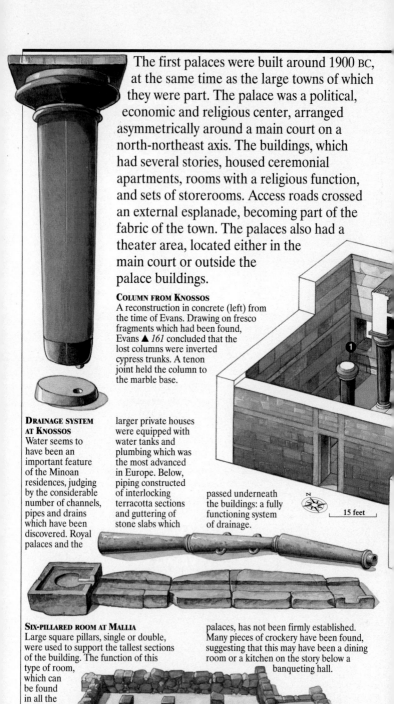

The first palaces were built around 1900 BC, at the same time as the large towns of which they were part. The palace was a political, economic and religious center, arranged asymmetrically around a main court on a north-northeast axis. The buildings, which had several stories, housed ceremonial apartments, rooms with a religious function, and sets of storerooms. Access roads crossed an external esplanade, becoming part of the fabric of the town. The palaces also had a theater area, located either in the main court or outside the palace buildings.

COLUMN FROM KNOSSOS
A reconstruction in concrete (left) from the time of Evans. Drawing on fresco fragments which had been found, Evans ▲ 161 concluded that the lost columns were inverted cypress trunks. A tenon joint held the column to the marble base.

DRAINAGE SYSTEM AT KNOSSOS
Water seems to have been an important feature of the Minoan residences, judging by the considerable number of channels, pipes and drains which have been discovered. Royal palaces and the larger private houses were equipped with water tanks and plumbing which was the most advanced in Europe. Below, piping constructed of interlocking terracotta sections and guttering of stone slabs which passed underneath the buildings: a fully functioning system of drainage.

15 feet

SIX-PILLARED ROOM AT MALLIA
Large square pillars, single or double, were used to support the tallest sections of the building. The function of this type of room, which can be found in all the larger palaces, has not been firmly established. Many pieces of crockery have been found, suggesting that this may have been a dining room or a kitchen on the story below a banqueting hall.

6 feet

SECTION OF A STOREROOM, KNOSSOS. Storerooms were long, windowless chambers, arranged in rows and served by a corridor with a single entrance to the shrines. Jars of oil and wine were kept here. Pits in the floor, covered by stone slabs, were used to store perishable produce (oil) and precious objects. Fragments of crystal, crockery and gold have been discovered in them.

RECONSTRUCTION OF THE PALACE AT MALLIA. The main features of Minoan architecture are asymmetry (with façades jutting from the main buildings), agglutination and stacked constructional blocks. The flat roofs and wooden uprights give the buildings a "cubist" appearance. The external façades, which often adjoined those of surrounding buildings, are plain; those overlooking the esplanade are more ornate, their rooftops decorated with the double-horn symbol.

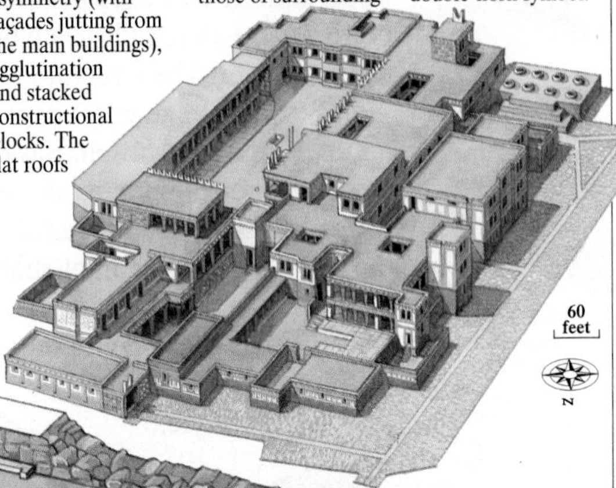

60 feet

N

KING'S MEGARON, KNOSSOS Minoan palaces and villas had a Cretan-style megaron or *polythyron*, a ceremonial room which was paved, with openings on several sides. A nearby light-shaft ensured that the room was well lit and aired (**1**). The room had a portico with columns on the outside (**2**). The megaron was adapted in Crete to suit the island's climate: the walls were not solid but had openings and doors (**3**). Openings between the pillars could be closed by wooden pivoting doors which fitted into the embrasure of the pillars.

LUSTRAL BATH AT MALLIA This half-sunken room was entered by a winding staircase: it was probably used for purification rites, and privacy was guaranteed by its transverse wall. At Mallia this room is quite small; elsewhere it can be much larger. It is one of the most striking features of Minoan architecture.

3 feet

N

89

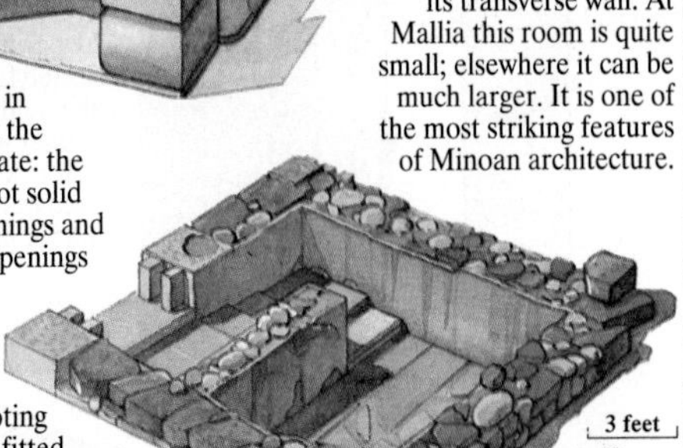

The Minoans used materials drawn from the natural resources of the island, where schists, limestone, easily worked *anmouda* (sandstone), wood and the clay used by bricklayers and potters were all readily available. Marble is rare, however. The structure of the buildings seems to have been very adaptable to the nature of the site chosen. Basic structural elements are common to all the buildings, fitting into an overall rectangle or square shape: the central court, the light-shaft, the *polythyron*, the lustral bath and the storerooms. There are no curves, vaults or domes to break up the straight lines of this architectural style.

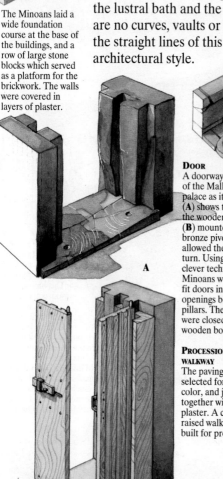

The Minoans laid a wide foundation course at the base of the buildings, and a row of large stone blocks which served as a platform for the brickwork. The walls were covered in layers of plaster.

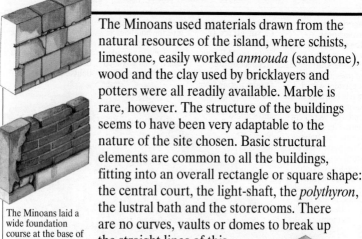

DOOR
A doorway of the Mallia palace as it is today (**A**) shows traces of the wooden uprights (**B**) mounted on bronze pivots which allowed the door to turn. Using this very clever technique, the Minoans were able to fit doors into the openings between pillars. The doors were closed by a wooden bolt.

PROCESSIONAL WALKWAY
The paving slabs were selected for their color, and joined together with red plaster. A central raised walkway was built for processions.

THE VATHIPETRO PRESS
Archeologists have found many presses, for oil or wine (above). The room is designed specially for this purpose. The grape must was collected in a trench cut into the floor. The pots in the kitchen (above) were set into a bench made of brickwork and covered in plaster. They were used to heat food, over hot ashes.

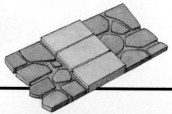

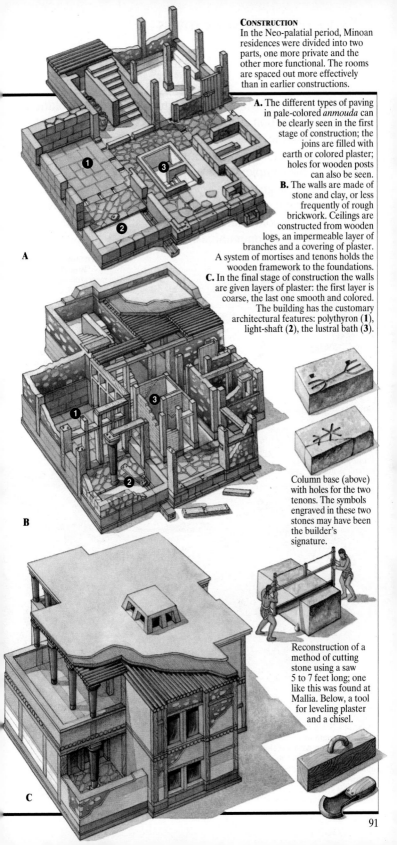

CONSTRUCTION

In the Neo-palatial period, Minoan residences were divided into two parts, one more private and the other more functional. The rooms are spaced out more effectively than in earlier constructions.

A. The different types of paving in pale-colored *anmouda* can be clearly seen in the first stage of construction; the joins are filled with earth or colored plaster; holes for wooden posts can also be seen.

B. The walls are made of stone and clay, or less frequently of rough brickwork. Ceilings are constructed from wooden logs, an impermeable layer of branches and a covering of plaster. A system of mortises and tenons holds the wooden framework to the foundations.

C. In the final stage of construction the walls are given layers of plaster: the first layer is coarse, the last one smooth and colored. The building has the customary architectural features: polythyron (**1**), light-shaft (**2**), the lustral bath (**3**).

Column base (above) with holes for the two tenons. The symbols engraved in these two stones may have been the builder's signature.

Reconstruction of a method of cutting stone using a saw 5 to 7 feet long; one like this was found at Mallia. Below, a tool for leveling plaster and a chisel.

A

B

C

91

The development of Minoan architecture reflects the evolution of Minoan civilization, over a period of nearly 1500 years, stretching from the earliest known house – the "oval house" of Chamezi, a building with several rooms enclosed by a curved wall – up to the complete destruction of the sites around 1450 BC. Archeologists have analyzed the different types of architectural remains: the plans of these sites have given rise to many theories concerning the social organization and lifestyle of Minoan communities.

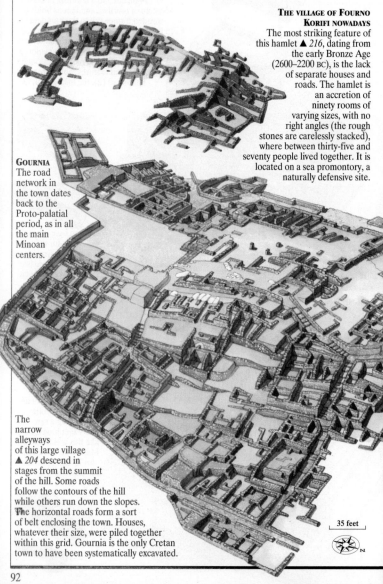

THE VILLAGE OF FOURNO KORIFI NOWADAYS
The most striking feature of this hamlet ▲ *216*, dating from the early Bronze Age (2600–2200 BC), is the lack of separate houses and roads. The hamlet is an accretion of ninety rooms of varying sizes, with no right angles (the rough stones are carelessly stacked), where between thirty-five and seventy people lived together. It is located on a sea promontory, a naturally defensive site.

GOURNIA
The road network in the town dates back to the Proto-palatial period, as in all the main Minoan centers.

The narrow alleyways of this large village ▲ *204* descend in stages from the summit of the hill. Some roads follow the contours of the hill while others run down the slopes. The horizontal roads form a sort of belt enclosing the town. Houses, whatever their size, were piled together within this grid. Gournia is the only Cretan town to have been systematically excavated.

35 feet

N

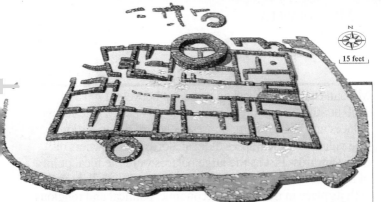

HAGHIA FOTHIA (AROUND 2000 BC)

Here for the first time we can see right angles and a rectangular, highly organized ground plan. The beginnings of a main courtyard can be seen. Several families lived here together, in separate dwellings. The presence of a town wall suggests a need for protection: this would seem to contradict the myth of the Minoans as a peace-loving civilization. A round cistern or silo for grain storage can be seen at the bottom; at the top is a circular tomb, from a later date. At the foot of the walls is a course of bare stones joined by rough mortar. The walls of the houses were made of clay, cobs or rough bricks held together by wooden grids.

15 feet

PILLAR CRYPT AT MALLIA

The appearance of towns and the first palaces, toward 1900 BC, indicates significant population growth and a more sophisticated urban structure. Different social classes emerged: at Mallia there is clearly a special quarter for craftsmen (potters, stonemasons, etc.) ▲ 192. The pillar crypt is another new architectural feature, to which a number of functions have been ascribed: a political center outside the palace, a council chamber for the elders – all of which suggest a Minoan community life. This type of room has two halls with benches: the rooms are of different sizes, opposite each other, and have access to a series of storerooms. The lay-out maximizes visibility and mobility. The pillars supporting the ceiling are out of line with the axis of the rooms. The use of cut blocks of stone shows how far building techniques had been developed by this stage.

VILLAGE OF GOURNIA

The village dates from the age of the second palaces (1700–1450 BC), the peak of the Minoan civilization. The houses, with several stories, are grouped in blocks of ten or fifteen surrounded by alleys (shown in blue) with guttering to drain off dirty water. The doorways of the houses are made of stone, and the roofs are flat. This type of dwelling is similar to the houses in traditional Cretan villages.

RECONSTRUCTION OF GOURNIA

The houses of the poor had only one room, which was also used as a workshop. A long square and a small palace overlook the village from the summit of the hill.

● MINOAN VILLAS

Minoan civilization reached its height between 1700 and 1450 BC: this was a time of peace and prosperity. The second palaces and villas feature impressively ornate decoration. The villas were the houses of local "lords", landowners or their stewards. Just as the large palaces were the focal point of Minoan cities, so villages grew up around the villas, each with its place in the chain of economic, political and religious structures. Seals and documents found on tablets written in Linear A prove the existence of an administrative hierarchy. A road network connected the villas with larger towns.

VILLA OF AMNISSOS, 1600 BC
All the walls of this villa ▲ *190* were covered with whitewash and decorated with frescos; the most famous of these, the Lilies fresco, can be seen in the Archeological Museum at Heraklion ▲ *158*. The floors were paved with slate or colored marble, joined with colored plaster. The customary architectural features are here: living rooms (**1**), *polythyron* (**2**) opening onto a terrace (**3**) with a view over the sea, and a light-shaft (**4**).

Pieces of earthenware depicting façades were discovered at Knossos: they show what the front of a Minoan villa looked like.

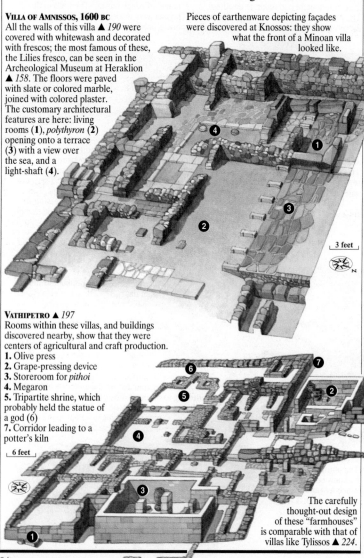

3 feet

N

VATHIPETRO ▲ *197*
Rooms within these villas, and buildings discovered nearby, show that they were centers of agricultural and craft production.
1. Olive press
2. Grape-pressing device
3. Storeroom for *pithoi*
4. Megaron
5. Tripartite shrine, which probably held the statue of a god (**6**)
7. Corridor leading to a potter's kiln

6 feet

The carefully thought-out design of these "farmhouses" is comparable with that of villas like Tylissos ▲ *224*.

The rooms dedicated to religious purposes suggest that palaces were ruled by "priest-kings" holding both earthly and religious powers. Shrines, where ceremonies were held and sacrifices were made to unknown gods, were found in cities and private houses, on mountain tops and in caves. Tombs with possessions of the dead person show that the Minoans believed in an afterlife. Minoan religious symbols and accessories included the rhyton, the double horn, and the double ax. Tombs were built in a variety of ways and were either private or communal.

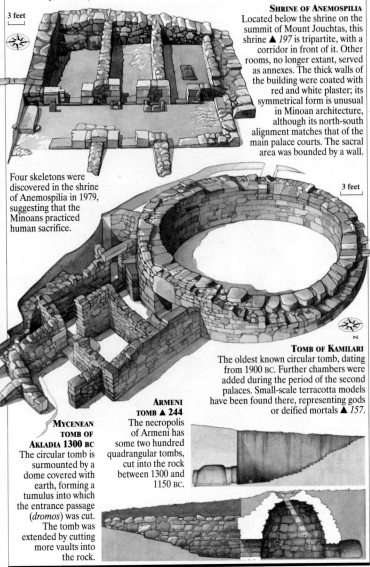

3 feet

SHRINE OF ANEMOSPILIA
Located below the shrine on the summit of Mount Jouchtas, this shrine ▲ 197 is tripartite, with a corridor in front of it. Other rooms, no longer extant, served as annexes. The thick walls of the building were coated with red and white plaster; its symmetrical form is unusual in Minoan architecture, although its north-south alignment matches that of the main palace courts. The sacral area was bounded by a wall.

Four skeletons were discovered in the shrine of Anemospilia in 1979, suggesting that the Minoans practiced human sacrifice.

3 feet

TOMB OF KAMILARI
The oldest known circular tomb, dating from 1900 BC. Further chambers were added during the period of the second palaces. Small-scale terracotta models have been found there, representing gods or deified mortals ▲ 157.

MYCENEAN TOMB OF AKLADIA 1300 BC
The circular tomb is surmounted by a dome covered with earth, forming a tumulus into which the entrance passage (*dromos*) was cut. The tomb was extended by cutting more vaults into the rock.

ARMENI TOMB ▲ 244
The necropolis of Armeni has some two hundred quadrangular tombs, cut into the rock between 1300 and 1150 BC.

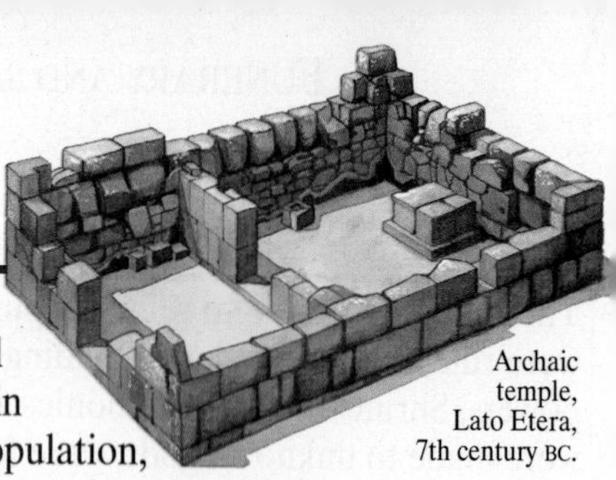

Archaic temple, Lato Etera, 7th century BC.

After the destruction of the palaces and the Post-palatial period, new settlers arrived in Crete. The island's native population, descendants of the Minoans, sought refuge in the mountains where they built new cities, notably on Mount Karfi. Between 1100 and 900 BC the Dorians imported the architecture of mainland Greece. During the geometric and archaic periods (900–500 BC), around a hundred city-states were established and the first temples were built. In the classical and Hellenistic periods (500–67 BC), Crete was a Greek province; after 67 BC it was a Roman province, together with Cyrenaica.

THE ODEON OF GORTYN

Gortyn ▲ 176 was a prosperous town, widely famed in antiquity; the Romans developed it into a brilliant city with many public buildings, making it the capital of the island. The Odeon was built in the 1st century AD on the site of older buildings (archaic and Hellenistic); it was rebuilt in the 3rd century. It was designed for musical performances, with two entrances to the north. The Romans incorporated the famous inscription of the Laws of Gortyn (5th century BC); these were originally carved on a circular building so that all citizens could peruse them. Today the inscription is protected by a brick portico (1). The stage was decorated with statues placed in niches, and the orchestra was paved with black and white tiles.

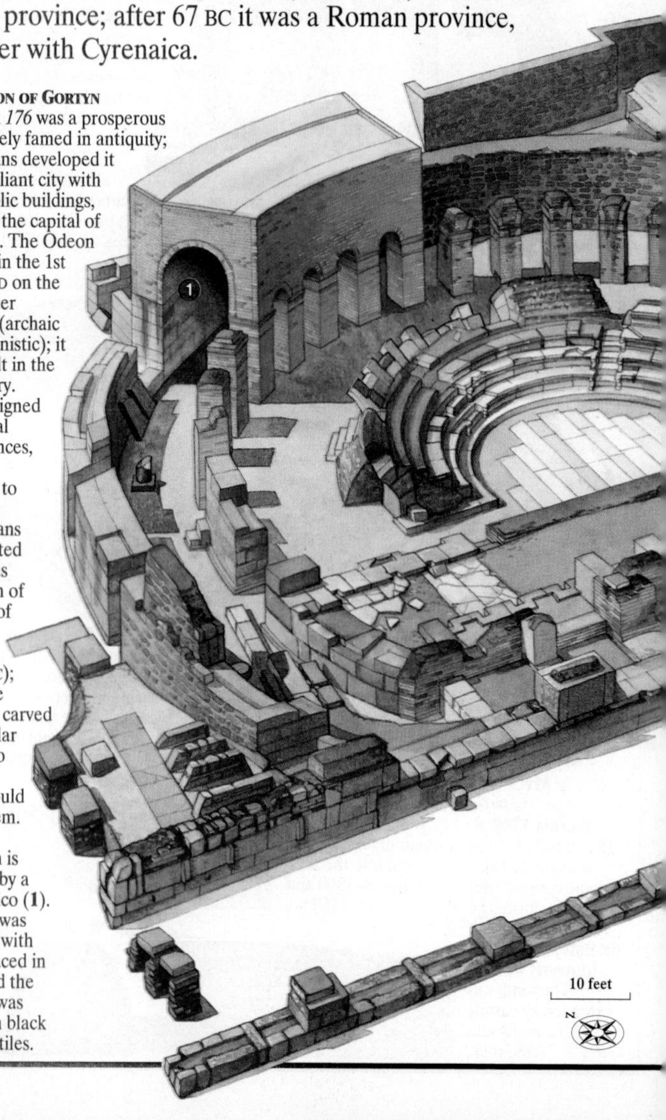

10 feet

ROMAN CISTERN, APTERA
Reserves of water were collected in case of drought: these cisterns were either carved into the rock or built of brick, as here at Aptera ▲ *252*.

15 ft

TEMPLE OF APOLLO, GORTYN
The shrine (above) was dedicated to Pythian Apollo; it was built around 650 BC, during the archaic period, on the site of a Minoan building (**1**), and modified around 200 BC, in the Hellenistic period (**2**). During the Roman period an apse (**3**) and an external altar (**4**) were added to the building, as well as eight Corinthian columns in the center, the remains of which can still be seen.

PLAN OF DELPHINIAN TEMPLE, DRIROS
This is the earliest Cretan version of the well-known Greek temple ▲ *196*. It is in the geometric style, and dates from 750 BC. It consists of an entrance porch with portico, a wooden framework supported by pillars, a central hollow (altar or fireplace) and a bench for offerings and religious statues (the statues of Apollo, in hammered bronze, can be seen at the Archeological Museum in Heraklion ▲ *154*).

MAGISTRATES' HOUSE AT LATO, 350 BC
Magistrates sat in the building shown below, located to the north of the agora (marketplace) at Lato ▲ *204*. It consists of two council chambers lined with benches and two small rooms for archives. The massive stairway was flanked by two towers, the bases of which can still be seen.

6 feet

10 feet

97

The church of Haghios Dimitrios, in the Rethymnon district, is typical of the Greek Byzantine style of the 11th to 12th centuries, when it was built. The ground-plan is in the shape of a Greek cross set within a square. Here stone has been chosen rather than brick, although bricks are used for the tambour and for the ornamental external arches which follow the lines of the internal vaulting. The building rises from the square ground-plan up to a circular cupola, progressing through a system of pendentives supported by four columns. The conical roof on the cupola is typical. The main interior ornaments are frescos and the iconostatis, a type of screen with icons separating the shrine from the nave.

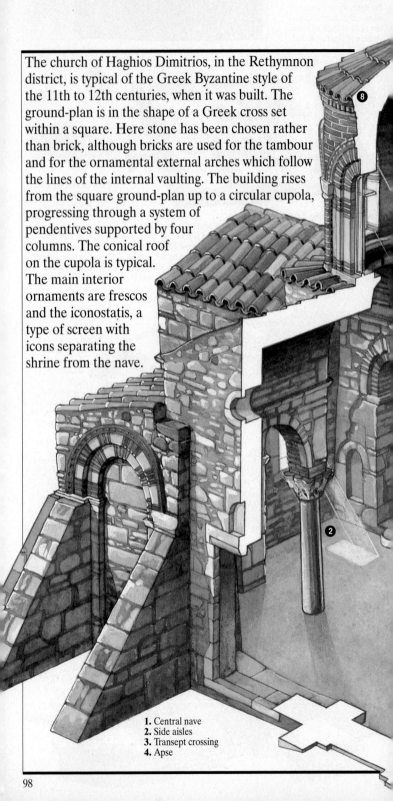

1. Central nave
2. Side aisles
3. Transept crossing
4. Apse

Iconostasis of the church of Moni Kremaston. The arrangement is fixed: Christ to the right of the doorway, the Virgin and Child to the left, and then the Saints. Above are icons of the *dodecaorton*.

FRESCOS AND ICONS
The Byzantines introduced their own style of religious imagery, which can be seen in all their churches in the form of frescos or icons. The Cretans assimilated this new iconography and expressed it in a distinctive style from the 15th century onward.

5. Fresco fragments of the 14th century
6. Pendentives
7. Tambour
8. Cupola

The first Byzantine period in Crete (330–824) is the time when the Christian faith was being established. During the second Byzantine period (961–1204), following a century of Arab occupation, the re-affirmation of Byzantine power accompanied a renewal of religious fervor. The architectural legacy of these periods was a number of churches and monasteries decorated with frescos and icons. The Byzantine style persisted under the Venetian occupation (1204–1669).

HAGHIOS TITOS, 6TH CENTURY, GORTYN ▲ *177*
Built during the first Byzantine period, its style is strongly influenced by the architecture of Constantinople. The church is crowned by a cupola and consists of a central nave flanked by two side aisles. All that can be seen today are the square chapels and the vaulted apse at the east end.

EVOLUTION OF BYZANTINE CHURCH ARCHITECTURE
From the 4th to the 6th centuries churches were built in the basilica style, mostly with three naves separated by colonnades or pillars, and ending in a semicircular apse; in the 6th century the Byzantines incorporated a cupola. From the classical period (8th to 12th centuries), the ground-plan of a Greek cross crowned with a cupola became most common; raised tambours were introduced and the cupolas were covered with conical roofs.

CHURCH OF THE PANAGHIA, FODELE ▲ *219*
This church (left) was built in the 13th century, on the site of an early 8th-century basilica. It is built on a square, cruciform ground plan, with a cupola.

CHURCH OF PANAGHIA KERA, 13TH TO 14TH CENTURY, KRITSA
Panaghia Kera in the village of Kritsa ▲ *203* originally consisted of a single nave with cupola. Two barrel-vaulted side aisles were later added to north and south. These 14th-century additions were reinforced by buttresses, giving the church its very distinctive outline. The east façade ends in three apsidioles; right, the entrance façade, to the west.

Apse windows from the Katholikon at Moni Arvis, the church of Haghios Antonios at Moni Arvis, and the church of the Panaghia, Archanes.

APSE WINDOWS

The main ornaments on church exteriors are the carvings around doors and the apse windows. The window designs show varying degrees of sophistication, with plant-based or geometric patterns, and sometimes figures in silhouette.

SOUTH FAÇADE OF THE CHURCH OF HAGHIOS FANOURIOS, MONI VALSAMONERO ▲ *188*
This church has two naves, bordered on the west by a third which functions as a narthex and exonarthex. The north nave, dedicated to the Panaghia, dates from 1326; the south nave, dedicated to Saint John the Baptist, dates from 1400–7; the narthex, dedicated to Saint Fanourios, was added in 1426–31, and the exonarthex in the late 15th or early 16th century. The south façade is especially elegant, with inlaid disks at the top of the exonarthex.

CHURCH OF MICHAEL THE ARCHANGEL, EPISKOPI-KISSAMOS
Episkopi ▲ *274* was, as its name suggests, a bishop's seat during the Venetian period. Its church is one of the oldest in Greece, and is unusual in being constructed around a rotonda dating from the 7th to 8th or from the second half of the 10th century.

Apse window from the church of Moni Kera Kardiotissa ▲ *183*.

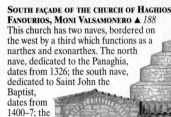

101

During the Venetian occupation, the work of the Italian architects Serlio (1475–1554) and Palladio (1518–80) had a significant influence in Crete, serving as an inspiration to local craftsmen. The influence of the Italian Renaissance is clear in numerous churches and monasteries built in the 16th century: these include the churches of Santa Maria at Rethymnon, of Moni Arkadi and Moni Haghia Triada on the Akrotiri peninsula. The basic church designs remained the same: the Greek cross with cupola or the triple-naved basilica.

Corinthian chapter (above) decorated with acanthus leaves, former church of San Francesco, Khania ▲ *258*.

COLUMN BASE, MONI GOUVERNETO
This sculpture of a mythical creature is typical of 16th-century Venetian style ▲ *265*.

WEST FAÇADE OF THE CHURCH OF MONI ARKADI
Moni Arkadi (1538) ▲ *221* is the most famous of the monasteries from the Venetian occupation. The west façade of its double-naved church is typical of what has been called "Cretan Renaissance" style: a mixture of Romanesque and Baroque elements. At the lower level it has double Corinthian columns and Romanesque arches; higher up, pilasters and Gothic arches. Arabesques and Baroque garlands complete the attractive ornamentation.

SAN MARCO BASILICA, HERAKLION
The basilica was built in 1239 and
partially destroyed by two earthquakes;
it was restored in 1508 ▲ *145*. It is a
classical basilica, with a central nave
flanked by two side aisles. At the
front is a porch supported
by an arcade with six
columns of green marble,
the latter doubtless from
a Roman temple.
The pointed arches
inside the church
still belong to the
Gothic style, while
the round arches
on the outside are
Renaissance.

The second period of Venetian occupation was very productive in artistic terms.
What became known as the "Cretan Renaissance", in the 15th century, was the product of two artistic movements: the Italian Renaissance, imported by the Venetians, and the Byzantine style which had already become established on the island. New arrivals in Crete included leading artists from Constantinople and Greece who had fled the invading Turks. In the sphere of religious art, a very large number of churches and monastic centers were built, often serving as refuges; the Cretan school revived the art of the fresco and icons, incorporating Italian elements and creating new Byzantine forms.

HAGHIOS GEORGIOS GALATAS CHAPEL, ON THE SITE OF HAGHIA TRIADA
This modest Byzantine chapel with its single barrel-vaulted nave probably dates from the beginning of the 14th century. It has an apse at the east end, and ossuaries on the north and south sides, which were added in the Venetian period ▲ 183.

HAGHIA EKATERINI CHURCH, HERAKLION
This church was built in 1555 ▲ 151, and was attached to the famous monastery of Saint Catherine on Mount Sinai. The building, in the Greek cross shape, was altered by the Turks in the 17th century and reveals a mixture of Venetian and Turkish architecture: its ribbed cupola is built on a tambour supported by squinches rather than pendentives, a type of construction often used in mosques.

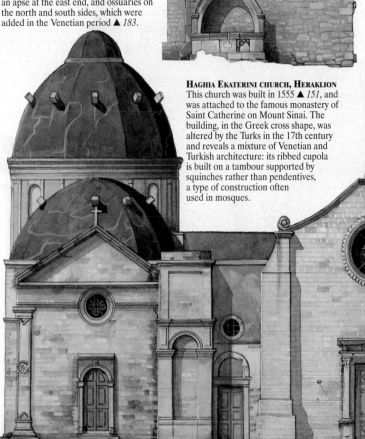

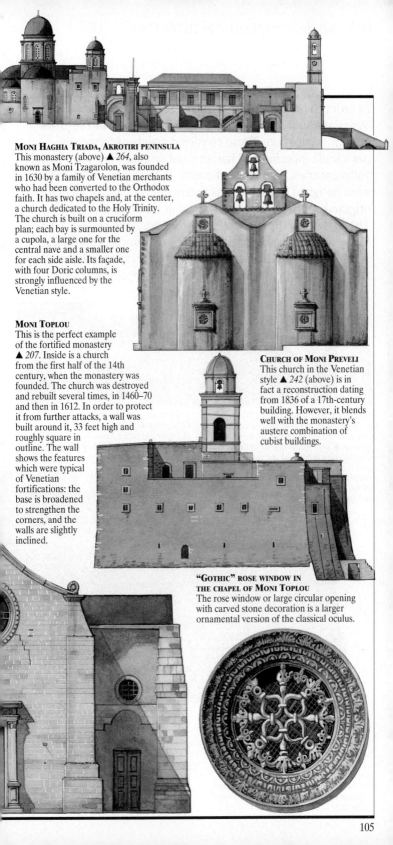

MONI HAGHIA TRIADA, AKROTIRI PENINSULA
This monastery (above) ▲ *264*, also
known as Moni Tzagarolon, was founded
in 1630 by a family of Venetian merchants
who had been converted to the Orthodox
faith. It has two chapels and, at the center,
a church dedicated to the Holy Trinity.
The church is built on a cruciform
plan; each bay is surmounted by
a cupola, a large one for the
central nave and a smaller one
for each side aisle. Its façade,
with four Doric columns, is
strongly influenced by the
Venetian style.

MONI TOPLOU
This is the perfect example
of the fortified monastery
▲ *207*. Inside is a church
from the first half of the 14th
century, when the monastery was
founded. The church was destroyed
and rebuilt several times, in 1460–70
and then in 1612. In order to protect
it from further attacks, a wall was
built around it, 33 feet high and
roughly square in
outline. The wall
shows the features
which were typical
of Venetian
fortifications: the
base is broadened
to strengthen the
corners, and the
walls are slightly
inclined.

CHURCH OF MONI PREVELI
This church in the Venetian
style ▲ *242* (above) is in
fact a reconstruction dating
from 1836 of a 17th-century
building. However, it blends
well with the monastery's
austere combination of
cubist buildings.

**"GOTHIC" ROSE WINDOW IN
THE CHAPEL OF MONI TOPLOU**
The rose window or large circular opening
with carved stone decoration is a larger
ornamental version of the classical oculus.

In order to protect their much-coveted territory, the Venetians built many fortifications during the four centuries of their occupation. These consisted mainly of fortresses, town walls, storehouses, harbors and arsenals. In the 15th and 16th centuries, defences at Khania, Rethymnon and Heraklion were designed by the famous architect Michele Sanmicheli, originally from Verona and trained in Rome and Venice. The harbors in these towns date from the same period. These Venetian buildings were damaged by earthquakes and, more seriously, by Turkish attacks: nonetheless they still show what a strong impression Venice made on the island.

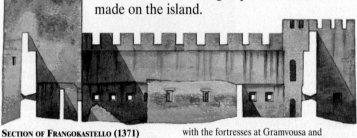

SECTION OF FRANGOKASTELLO (1371)
Only the external walls and four massive towers remain of this powerful Venetian fortress ▲ 247, today without its cannons. On the south side above the entrance portal is a coat of arms in relief showing the lion of Saint Mark. This is one of the surviving Venetian masterpieces on Crete, along with the fortresses at Gramvousa and Spinalonga ▲ 203 and the Fortetza of Rethymnon (right). These fortresses proved their effectiveness in holding out against the Turks for many years.

KASTRO KOULES, HERAKLION
The capital's harbor is protected by Kastro Koules (above) ▲ 160, which was rebuilt by the Venetians in 1523–40, on the site of Arab and, later, Genoese constructions. This formidable building complemented the defensive system surrounding the city: a triangular city wall some two miles long, reinforced with seven bastions.

VENETIAN ARSENALS AT KHANIA
The arsenals at Khania ▲ *257*, like those at
Heraklion, were built in two phases, in the
15th and 17th centuries. Today only nine of
the twenty-three storehouses have retained
their vaulted ceilings and remain in use.

FORTETZA OF RETHYMNON
This Venetian building was designed by
Michele Sanmicheli and built by Sforza
Pallavicini, then Ioannis P. Therari
▲ *236*, between 1573 and 1583. The
entrances are surmounted by massive
vaults. The surrounding wall, nearly
one mile in circumference, has four
impressive bastions. Inside are the
remains of administrative buildings,
quarters, barracks and storehouses for
weapons and supplies. In the
center was a church, no longer
standing. All that remains is a
small mosque built by the Turks.

**BELOW, VENETIAN ARSENALS AT
HERAKLION, 16TH CENTURY**

Following their native style, the Venetians built monuments, fountains and sumptuous houses in the Cretan towns. The Loggia at Heraklion was built in 1626–8 by the architect Francesco Basilicata, following the precepts established by Andrea Palladio (1508–1580) and developed in Crete by Michele Sanmicheli (1484–1559). Here the harmony of the whole is created through simplicity of form: the upper balustrade emphasizes the structure of the façade with its seven arcades, interspersed with Doric columns on the first story and Ionic columns above. This Loggia was the model for the Venetian pavilion in the Rome exhibition of 1911.

MOROSINI FOUNTAIN, HERAKLION
The fountain was completed in 1628 ▲ 145. The basin with its eight lobes (plan, far right) is decorated with magnificent carvings of nymphs and tritons. The upper bowl supported by lions was part of an earlier Venetian fountain, probably dating from the 14th century.

ABOVE, SPILI FOUNTAIN (DETAIL)
The verdant market town
of Spili ▲ *242* grew up around
a famous spring. Here the
Venetians built an elegant and
unusual fountain with twenty-five
spouts, nineteen of them in the
shape of lions' heads spouting
the water into the basin.

RIMONDI FOUNTAIN, RETHYMNON
This monumental fountain
(right) dates from 1629 ▲ *237*.
It shows a mixture of different
styles: the four Corinthian
columns are reminiscent of
ancient Greece; the three lions'
heads spouting water are typically
Venetian; the wall behind the
fountain was restored by the Turks.

BEMBO FOUNTAIN, HERAKLION
This dates from 1588 and bears the coats
of arms of the Bembo family ▲ *151*, flanking
a headless
Roman statue
discovered at
Ierapetra by
the architect
Z. Bembo.

**LOGGIA OF
HERAKLION**
(below)

109

The houses in Cretan villages are generally tightly packed; the streets are narrow and the houses are arranged in semicircular rows. The villages, which fit perfectly with their natural environment, are often divided into different groups of dwellings: there is the *kato chorio*, the lower village, the *meso chorio* or middle village, and the *pano chorio* or upper village. The villages bear the mark of successive occupations, and are often located in naturally defensive sites: on hilltops, in gorges, or on mountainsides.

The earliest houses are very narrow, comprising a single room with a fire in the corner for cooking. The chimney is covered with a pierced pot, which is stopped up with a stone when it rains.

"MITADO" OR "KOUMOS"
This type of small house is round and low, made of rough stones: it is the most basic form of traditional Cretan architecture. It is used seasonally by shepherds and can be found on mountain slopes.

The simplest Cretan houses are rectangular, with a single story, a flat roof, few openings in the walls and a long, low façade. Inside there is just one large all-purpose room, for cooking, sleeping, storage of provisions and harvest, even shelter for the animals. The old villages, built in stone, sometimes merge completely with the rocks of the surrounding landscape. Below, the single room of a simple Cretan house.

WINDMILL HOUSE ON THE PLAIN OF LASSITHI
These windmills ▲ 198 were built of stone and were still used to grind corn at the beginning of this century.

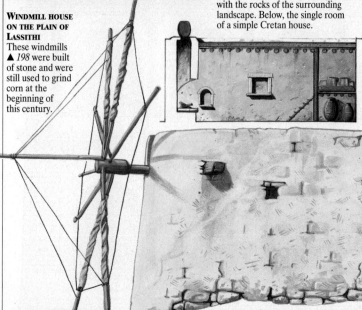

Stones are used in their natural state, and walls are built using rubble to hold them together. The small internal niche holds a water jug.

"KAMAROSPITO" RAISED BY ONE STORY (ABOVE)
The best examples of this type of house can be found at Khora Sphakion, in the southwest of Crete ▲ 272. The walls are plastered and whitewashed; doors and windows are painted a cheerful blue or brown. Below, the narrow façade of a harborside house.

MYRIODOMANOLIS HOUSE AT DOULIANA
This is a typical example of the composite house with two stories, built in an L-shape. Roofs are often tiled rather than flat in western Crete. The tiles, in the Byzantine style, are fixed with mortar. The living room, kitchen with fireplace, and courtyard are on the first story; the bedrooms are on the second.

"KAMAROSPITO" (ABOVE)
In this type of house the flat roof above the internal court is supported by a stone arch (*kamara*). It is generally found in those regions of Crete where there is not enough wood to make large beams for the roof.

111

During the two centuries of their occupation, the Turks mainly added the buildings they needed for practicing the Muslim religion: mosques, minarets and fountains for ritual ablutions. These monuments, reminders of a dark time in Crete's history, were neglected or even systematically destroyed afterward. Many of those which survive are now being carefully restored.

HOUSE IN RETHYMNON

Many houses in the Turkish style still exist in the old quarters of Rethymnon. They can be spotted by the wooden kiosks jutting out on the second story ▲ 232. This architectural feature derived originally from the Balkans, and was doubtless related to the Byzantine *iliakos*.

SARDIVAN, HERAKLION

This fountain for ritual washing was built close to the Church of the Holy Savior, which had been converted into a mosque. Several of its facets had *sebil* or "paths of God" on them, used by worshipers as they washed before going to prayers.

MOSQUE IN THE HARBOR AT KHANIA

The Janissaries' mosque ▲ 236, built in 1645, is square in shape and modest in scale. Its dome is more spherical than usual: this doubtless made it necessary to add the support of four flying buttresses, which, like the rest of the building, are made of beautifully cut stone.

MINARET OF THE NERANTZES MOSQUE, RETHYMNON

The Turks converted a number of churches into mosques: generally this involved little more than adding a minaret ▲ 237.

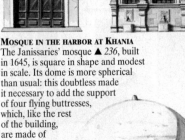

CRETE AS SEEN
BY PAINTERS

> "EVEN WHEN THE WIND BLOWS IT DOES NOT REFRESH US, AND
> THE SHADOWS ARE THIN UNDER THE CYPRESSES."
>
> GEORGES SEFERIS

The paintings of
EVANGHELOS
MARKOYANNAKIS
(1874–1956) can be
seen in Heraklion,
in the Vikelas
library and at the
Chronakis house;
they constitute a
unique record of
the last years of
Turkish occupation.
Here the work
called *Turks at
the Fountain* (1)
shows Heraklion
at the beginning
of the century, with
the old Pantocrator
Square, now Khania
Gate ▲ 144.

Y. GHIORGHIADIS,
born in 1935,
studied art in
Lyons. He is a
painter but also
a pianist and a
lover of the theater,
a cosmopolitan
and elegant man
who was initially
influenced by
Impressionism
and Cubism. After
this he returned
to his Cretan roots.
Shades of orange
and ocher dominate
his landscapes and
his portraits. In
*Haghios Trios
Church at Gortyn*
(2) he conveys the
impressive, austere
theatricality of the
ruins of Gortyn,
bathed in the
majestic light of
a southern evening
▲ 176. The serene,
harmonious
landscape of *The
Hills of Haghia Irini*
(3), a village near
Knossos, displays
a sensitivity more
clearly inspired by
the French
Impressionists.

1	2
	3

"NIGHT AS BIG AS THE METAL SHEET ON THE TINSMITH'S WALL. SONG
AS PRECIOUS AS A COB LEAF. ON THE SPONGE FISHERMAN'S TABLE.
AND HERE IS THE CRETAN MOON, HURTLING OVER THE SHINGLE."

YANNIS RITSOS

Draftsman, humorist, author of the celebrated "nonsense" poems and an inveterate traveler, EDWARD LEAR (1812–88) ▲ *126* visited Crete in the spring of 1864. His lively account of his adventures in Crete is far more personal than those of his compatriots and predecessors Pashley and Spratt. The text is accompanied by drawings and watercolors, mostly executed in the classical manner, generally in light tones. Left, *Mount Ida before Sunrise*, a subject which inspired Lear to make a series of drawings, widely considered to be the finest work he produced in Crete.

In the 1850's, CAPTAIN THOMAS A. B. SPRATT made several journeys to Crete on behalf of the British Admiralty. His *General Description of the Island of Crete* appeared in London in 1865. During his visits, Captain Spratt spent much time discovering the island's rich archeological sites, but his interests tended more toward cartography and meteorology. He was fascinated by the sea and explored all the Cretan coasts. *The Sponge Fishers* (left) depicts the strenuous labors of the men of Kalimnos and Kalkis, in a dark, stormy atmosphere. Sponge fishing was practiced mainly off the east coasts of Crete, up to the beginning of the 20th century.

The work of
LEFTERIS
KANAKAKIS (1934–85)
uses imagery closely
connected with his
homeland, Crete.
His artistic world is
an intense, silent
one, marked by his
political conscience
(*The Decorations* **(1)**,
painted in 1973), his
love for simple or
symbolic objects and
his ideal of humanity.
His introverted
temperament finds
expression in dark
colors and austere
compositions. A
translucent light
confers a striking
unity on his oeuvre as
a whole. Rethymnon
dedicated its museum
of modern art to
Kanakakis, hailing
him one of the most
outstanding modern
painters ▲ *198*.

ARISTIDE VLASSIS
(born in 1947) was
inspired more by the
lost world of Greece
and the shores of
Anatolia than by
Cretan landscapes; he
developed a very
personal style –
combining dream and
reality, as in *Moni
Gonias* **(2)** ▲ *275* –
whose resonances
often call to mind the
Surrealist poetry of
Andreas Embiricos.

E. MARKOYANNAKIS,
in his *Church of the
Savior at Heraklion*
(3), offers a charming
image of this
Venetian church in
an Impressionist
style; the church was
converted into a
mosque under the
Turks, and torn
down in 1973.

	2
1	
	3

"A SEA OF DARK BLUE, IMMENSE, STRETCHING TO
THE AFRICAN SHORES. IN THE MORNING IT WAS AS
FRAGRANT AS WATERMELON."

NIKOS KAZANTZAKI

CRETE AS SEEN BY PAINTERS

The characteristic style of ARISTIDE VLASSIS is displayed in this strongly structured work, entitled *On the Walls* **(1)** : a distant landscape, precise and yet dreamlike (here Kastro Koules at Heraklion ▲ *160*), with figures in the foreground who have a magical, timeless quality.

In *Parea* **(2)**, P. TETSIS (born in 1925) depicts a familiar and timeless scene in the Mediterranean world: seated villagers conversing quietly at nightfall.

The work of TAKIS PERAKIS (born in 1952) is decidedly hyper-realistic. *South* **(3)** has a strong architectural quality, and is dominated by the flat, intense blues of the south.

CRETE AS SEEN
BY WRITERS

● CRETE AS SEEN BY WRITERS

OF MYTH AND MAN

Crete plays an important part in Greek myth and legend. Home of the birthplace of Zeus, the island has also given rise to a rich fund of tales concerning the powerful King Minos. These fables have inspired many writers, including the English poet, novelist and dramatist Robert Graves (1895–1985), whose own creative muse was kindled by highly unorthodox mythological interpretation.

66The parentage of Daedalus is disputed. His mother is named Alcippe by some; by others, Merope; by still others, Iphinoë; and all give him a different father, though it is generally agreed that he belonged to the royal house of Athens, which claimed descent from Erechtheus. He was a wonderful smith, having been instructed in his art by Athene herself.

One of his apprentices, Talos the son of his sister Polycaste, or Perdix, had already surpassed him in craftsmanship while only twelve years old. Talos happened one day to pick up the jawbone of a serpent or, some say, a fish's spine; and, finding that he could use it to cut a stick in half, copied it in iron and thereby invented the saw. This, and other inventions of his – such as the potter's wheel, and the compass for marking out circles – secured him a great reputation at Athens, and Daedalus, who himself claimed to have forged the first saw, soon grew unbearably jealous. Leading Talos up to the roof of Athene's temple on the Acropolis, he pointed out certain distant sights, and suddenly toppled him over the edge. Yet, for all his jealousy, he would have done Talos no harm had he not suspected him of incestuous relations with his mother Polycaste. Daedalus then hurried down to the foot of the Acropolis, and thrust Talos's corpse into a bag, proposing to bury it secretly. When challenged by passers-by, he explained that he had piously taken up a dead serpent, as the law required – which was not altogether untrue, Talos being an Erechtheid – but there were bloodstains on the bag, and his crime did not escape detection, whereupon the Areiopagus banished him for murder. According to another account he fled before the trial could take place.

Daedalus took refuge in one of the Attic demes, whose people are named Daedalids after him; and then in Cretan Cnossus, where King Minos delighted to welcome so skilled a craftsman. He lived there for some time, at peace and in high favour, until Minos, learning that he had helped Pasiphaë to couple with Poseidon's white bull, locked him up for a while in the Labyrinth, together with his son Icarus, whose mother, Naucrate, was one of Minos's slaves; but Pasiphaë freed them both.

It was not easy, however, to escape from Crete, since Minos kept all his ships under military guard, and now offered a large reward for his apprehension. But Daedalus made a pair of wings for himself, and another for Icarus, the quill feathers of which were threaded together, but the smaller ones held in place by wax. Having tied on Icarus's pair for him, he said with tears in his eyes: 'My son, be warned! Neither soar too high, lest the sun melt the wax; nor swoop too low, lest the feathers be wetted by the sea.' Then he slipped his arms into his own pair of wings and they flew off. 'Follow me closely,' he cried, 'do not set your own course!'

. . . They had left Naxos, Delos, and Paros behind them on the left hand, and were leaving Lebynthos and Calymne behind on the right, when Icarus disobeyed his father's instructions and began soaring towards the sun, rejoiced by the lift of his great sweeping wings. Presently, when Daedalus looked over his shoulder, he could no longer see Icarus; but scattered feathers floated on the waves below. The heat of the sun had melted the wax, and Icarus had fallen into the sea and drowned. Daedalus circled around, until the corpse rose to the surface, and then carried it to the near-by island now called Icaria, where he buried it. A partridge sat perched on a holm-oak and watched him, chattering for delight – the soul of his sister Polycaste, at last avenged. This island has now given its name to the surrounding sea.**99**

ROBERT GRAVES, *THE GREEK MYTHS*,
PUB. CASSELL & COMPANY LTD, LONDON, 1968

THE BIRTH OF A LEGEND

Dame Emilie Rose Macaulay (1881–1958), novelist, essayist and travel writer, was educated at Somerville College, Oxford. Her travel writings include "They Went To Portugal", and "The Pleasure of Ruins" (1953) from which the following extract is taken.

❝Most dramatically in Crete, where, after the speculations and partial explorings of travellers had groped for two thousand years after the ruins of a mighty civilization whose ghost has always haunted the mountains and shores of that mysterious island, and of the the Greek mainland, the legend at last took shape, rising from the earth in the shape of cities, palaces, and the rich decorations of a culture that was a thousand years before Homer, seventeen centuries before the age of Pericles, over two thousand [years] before the Christian era. The legends became real: Minos in his great palace, the minotaur in the labyrinth that Daedalus had made for him, Theseus, Ariadne, the birth of Zeus, even 'Europa, a young lady, swimming into Crete upon a prestigious bull'; they all sprang to life, among palaces and pleasures, corridors of huge Aladdin jars, vivid frescos of flowers, sea creatures, bull fights, youths and maidens, huge-pillared courts, labyrinthine mazes of rooms, subterranean dungeons, and the most admirable plumbing *a l'anglaise*. In 1898 Sir Arthur Evans bought a plot of land from the Turks; within two years there had been uncovered the prehistoric palace of Knossos, its great Throne Room, its frescos, its vast warren of chambers, corridors and courts. Sir Arthur, their discoverer and presiding genius, threw up a skeleton tower from which to survey the ruins, and settled near them in the Villa Ariadne, lunching his friends under the olives, while wine flowed and mandolins played and Cretans danced; a brilliant showman, having conjured a civilization out of the earth he enjoyed it so much, and made everyone else enjoy it so much, that there was never a dull moment. From excavation he proceeded to reconstruction, building sham ruins on to ancient ones, causing to be painted gaudy frescos of bulls, erecting columns with a downward taper that greatly vexes many archaeologists, throwing up bulls' horns over porticos, making the palace so nearly habitable that it has been one of the pleasures of tourists staying at the Villa Ariadne (lately the Cretan headquarters of the British archaeological school in Athens, now handed over to the Greek

government) to roam about the ruins assigning the various rooms to themselves and their relations for dwellings. The Minoan civilization has been brought across the threshold of the western modern imagination, to become part of the familiar landscape of our minds, like the Hellenic and the Roman, only still with that mysterious and monstrous strangeness which lends to pre-Hellenic ages something of the dissolving, uneven quality of dreams. It is almost too much for us to take.

For now all Crete has sprung into ancient life, its soil everywhere yielding up traditions and legends of antique myth, carved in stone palaces, cities and streets. No sooner had Sir Arthur Evans uncovered Crete than Miss Boyd of the American Exploration Society saw a ridge at Gournia, near the bay of Mirabello, got thirty diggers to work, and in three days got down to a Bronze Age city – houses, paved streets, vases, a palace – and had found the most complete pre-Hellenic town yet discovered. Middle Minoan, it was built before the great palace period of the Cretan golden age; its small palace, less pretentious than Knossos or Phaestos, was more like a country manor house later enlarged and adorned into a palace. In the centre of the town was a shrine with its goddess idol, twined with snakes and doves. Italians meanwhile discovered Agia Triada, and the most impressive palace in Crete, Phaestos, standing on the spur of a hill range. A contemporary and rival of Knossos, with Gortyna, one of the three chief Cretan cities, Phaestos must have been almost as magnificent; its general effect today is more so, and its different periods less confused. It has the same intricate jumble of corridors, courts, stairways, chambers, cellars, terraces, walls, bathrooms and lavatories, brilliant frescos and precious inlay. No reconstruction has been done on Phaestos, which stands bare and stark on its hill, a ruin for three thousand years, stripped now of the Greek and Roman and later habitations which once hid it.**

ROSE MACAULAY, *PLEASURE OF RUINS*,
PUB. WEIDENFELD AND NICOLSON, LONDON, 1953

CRETAN PAINTING

This piece by Patrick Leigh-Fermor (b. 1915) is taken from his book "Mani: Travels in the Southern Peloponnese".

**Cretan painting is more a step aside than a regression. Those bonds of tradition which Mistra had shaken loose are there, but they have changed; where they induced a droop in the Macedonian school, they are worn in the Cretan with a swagger. The muscular and etiolated faces assume an unearthly frown of defiance, sometimes a scowl; and in their robes the flow of multiple folds and pleats in contrasting colours, as though of shot material – one of the great features of all Eastern painting – take on something more violent; they become taut radiations of

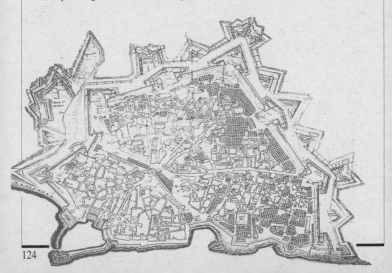

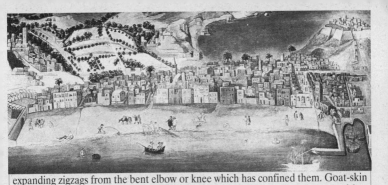

expanding zigzags from the bent elbow or knee which has confined them. Goat-skin becomes shaggier, caves in the mountain-side look as though torn open with a blade and the jutting Sinais and the stepped and toppling crags, sundered by ravines with all the fierceness of the actual Cretan ranges, are in a state of faction: they are an insurrection of colossal geometric ghosts. As in the island itself, dramatic tension is stretched between those soaring commotions of rock – golden or peach-coloured, or vitreous or ice blue or hard as steel or ashen and aghast – on taut invisible threads. The figures, like the Cretans themselves, are illuminated and intensely masculine, a manic-depressive compound of brooding melancholy and exaltation; and the inner light, which the Macedonians lost in a measure, shoots from the sinister shadows undimmed. But in spite of their energy, there is nothing uncouth or brutal in these painted saints as there was among the Cappadocians; and, for all their vigour, they are instinct with Byzantine introversion. They are far removed from materialism, and the tension, the violence and the tragedy are all in the world of the spirits. The detail is subtle and delicate: the cartographic wrinkles and circling contour-lines on the saints' faces, the line of nose and nostril, the sweep of those hoary eyebrows over each of which beetles an outlined irascible and though-indicating bulge; the dark and, by contrast, etiolating triangles that project point downwards from the lower lids, the bristling curl of the white locks round foreheads that catch the light like polished teak, the prescribed complexity of their beards cataracting in effulgent arcs or erupting like silver quills from swarthy physiognomics – all of this, on close inspection, proves to be built up of complementary planes of brick red and apple green applied with delicate impressionism to the black phantom of the saint or paladin beneath. The emergence of this dark background under a luminous and fragmentary carapace of skilfully superimposed light and colour (a technique explained in precise detail by Dionysios of Phourna for those wishing to paint *Krétika*) is the earmark of the Cretan mode. I am tempted to relate this very strange technique, especially in ikons of Our Lord, with reasons that are not purely plastic. It calls irresistibly to mind a charactistic passage of St. Dionysios the Areopagite: 'The Divine Dark', writes this other Dionysios, 'is the inaccessible Light in which God is said to dwell, and in this Dark, invisible because of its surpassing radiance and unapproachable because of the excess of the streams of supernatural light, everyone must enter who is deemed worthy to see or know God.'**

PATRICK LEIGH-FERMOR, *MANI – TRAVELS IN THE SOUTHERN PELOPONNESE*,
PUB. JOHN MURRAY, LONDON, 1958

THE CRETAN LANDSCAPE

For all its beauty, Crete has inspired mixed reactions in travelers over the centuries. The Scotsman William Lithgow (1582–1645) was one of Crete's more eccentric visitors. He took with him a portable coffin, and if his lurid accounts are to be believed he was probably wise to do so. His Cretan journeys took him by way of Souda, which at that time was much sought after by Spain as a harbor for refueling their ships.

**South-west from this famous harbour, lieth a pleasant plaine surnamed the Valley of Suda: It is twenty Italian Miles long, and two of breadth: And I remember, or I discended to crosse the Valley, and passe the haven, me thought the whole planure resembled to me a greene sea; and that was onely by reason of infinite Olive trees grew there, whose boughes and leaves over-toppe all other fructiferous trees in that plaine: The Villages for losse of ground are all built on the skirts of Rockes, upon the South side of the Valley; ye, and so difficile to climbe them, and so dangerous to dwell in them, that me thought their lives were in like perill, as he who was adjoyned to sit under the poynt of a two handed sword, and it hanging by the haire of a horse tayle.

Trust me, I told along these Rockes at one time, and within my sight, some 67. Villages; but when I entred the valley, I could not find a foote of ground unmanured, save a narrow passing way wherein I was: The Olives, Pomgranets, Dates, Figges, Orenges, Lemmons, and Pomi del Adamo growing all through other: And at the rootes of which trees grew Wheate, Malvasie, Muscadine, Leaticke Wines, Grenadiers, Carnobiers, Mellones, and all other sorts of fruites and hearbes, the earth can yeeld to man; that for beauty, pleasure, and profit it may easily be surnamed, the garden of the whole Universe: being the goodliest plot, the Diamond sparke, and the Honny spot of all Candy: There is no land more temperate for ayre, for it hath a double spring-tyde; no soyle more fertile, and therefore it is called the Combat of Bachus and Ceres; nor region or valley more hospitable, in regard of the sea, having such a noble haven cut through its bosome, being as it were the very resting place of Neptune. **99**

WILLIAM LITHGOW, *RARE ADVENTURES AND PAINEFULL PEREGRINATIONS*,
PUB. JAMES MACLEHOSE & SONS, GLASGOW 1906

THROUGH AN ARTIST'S EYES

Edward Lear (1812–88) visited Crete in 1864. He is probably best known for his poems and stories for children but produced many notable paintings, using his travel writings to record keen visual detail. A rather pessimistic tone in these accounts betrays his tendency toward ill health and depression, but never manages to engulf his sense of delight in experiencing the Cretan landscape at first hand.

66We went on, always above the plain, skirting the mountain bases: what ruined houses – walls – churches! Yet, very tiny churches are still abundant. We tried many short cuts, but unforeseen ravines made us haste back. Asphodels and squills covered the ground, with thousands of flowers, and about 10.30 we came to a spot where vast lots of that brutal-filthy yet picturesque plant grew: the black arum, which first I recollect to have seen at Marathon, in 1848. All the plain of Hania is grand, as far as food goes, but unavailable for drawing: the long flat tubular line of Akrotíri alone – and hardly – relieves it. Walking on, about Mourniés, the olives grow finer, and there is a richer vegetation of gardenism. Birds are plentiful: ravens, hooded crows, orioles, bee-eaters and hoopoes. At twelve we reach a high olive tree, and sit in its shade to lunch: eggs, wine, lamb and bread and oranges. No dogs – no nothing – no annoyances. For a while I think the same hills, flowers, sounds, tastes, etc... are here as about the Tivoli hills in 1837; so strange and dreamlike is life, it seems to me. In vain I try to draw hence; the few dry olives forbid. We walk on. Ever small ruined churches, and here and there one not ruined. But there is no intoxication of beauty here, as at Damascus, Palermo, etc. (Cistus and *fern* abound.) At two I draw above a ruined monastery, over gulfs of fern and underwood, looking, beyond great olives and lemon groves, to the plain and city. Thence we still went west, till it was time to strike back, and so we crossed deep dells *full* of 'lemon groves', most remarkable in extent and richness. The olives here too were older and larger than heretofore, and one or two drawings ought to be made here – Perivólia. In the villages we passed the very few villagers we saw never moved, but said 'καλως ωρισατε' ['welcome'] as if they saw strangers daily. Greater olives make lovelier scenes, and we pass Katsistrohóri and get into great cornfields, with the snow hills beyond the dark olives. (A Turkish farm, the inmates unlike the Greeks: woolly-headed children playing.) Passing two or three villages, and fearing to draw lest time should fail, we walked on, and got to Halépa by six. A charming day, and calm. . . . Rose at five. Very lovely, and George and I off at six; I in great pain from some unknown cause in left foot – left wrist also very painful. Out of spirits. Hobbled to the streets by the gate and drew a little, so that now I can

make a drawing of it. Then by the paved Turkish road, drawing a picturesque tomb, towards the Perivólia villages. Drew below a large olive – at this part of the plain there are really fine trees . . . foreground a great waving pale green corn meadow, then large olives deep gray beneath the green down-like hills, topped by a snow range. Beyond this, at nine, we threaded through ruined villages – what a state they are in! – hardly seeing a soul, to the west of the plain; but then, missing our way, had to work back till we reached the huge olive boles, whence all the plain is seen, a blaze of colour: the yellow-green of the plain and the frittery bright lemon groves, the darker orange, gray olive, red cliffs, lilac hills and blue sea! Nightingales delighted by singing, orioles and hoopoes by showing themselves. Nor were we molested, once only being spoken to by a suspicous Turk: 'Are you drawing lemons? And why lemons?' Certainly this corner of the plain of Haniá is wonderfully lovely, and the lemon groves are positively amazing. We began about eleven to wind below the hills toward Mourniés, meeting three leprous men on horseback. The hedges hereabouts are full of most *enormous* aloes, and the ground one sheet of rosy cistus bloom. At twelve we lunched . . . not very far from the monastery of Harodhiá. But everything, except nature, is in ruin here.**99**

EDWARD LEAR, *THE CRETAN JOURNAL*,
PUB. DENISE HARVEY & COMPANY, ATHENS 1984

THE VIVID ELEMENTS

A visit to Phaistos is described by the American novelist and essayist Henry Miller (1891–1980). Typically violent and laden with bizarre imagery, Miller's surreal prose nevertheless echoes the sentiments of other writers who have visited this ancient site.

66We swung through the dilapidated gate in a cloud of dust, scattering chickens, cats, dogs, turkeys, naked children and hoary vendors of sweets to right and left; we burst at full speed into the drab and dun terrain of gutta percha which closes in on the city like mortar filling a huge crack. There were no wolves, buzzards or poisonous reptiles in sight. There was a sun flooded with lemon and orange which hung ominously over the sultry land in that splashing, dripping radiance which intoxicated Van Gogh. We passed imperceptibly from the quick bad lands to a fertile rolling region studded with fields of bright-colored crops; it reminded me of that serene steady smile which our own South gives as you roll through the State of Virginia. It set me dreaming, dreaming of the gentleness and docility of the earth when man caresses it with loving hands. I began to dream more and more in the American idiom. I was crossing the continent again. There were patches of Oklahoma, of the Carolinas, of Tennessee, of Texas and New Mexico. Never a great river, never a railroad, however. But the illusion of vast distances, the reality of great vistas, the sublimity of silence, the revelation of light. On the top of a dizzying crag a tiny shrine in blue and white; in the ravine a cemetery of terrifying boulders. We begin to climb, curving around the edges of precipitous drops; across the gulch the earth bulges up like the knees of a giant covered with corduroy. Here and there *a* man, *a* woman, the sower, the reaper, silhouetted against billowy clouds of suds.

We climb up beyond the cultivated lands, twisting back and forth like a snake, rising to the heights of contemplation, to the abode of the sage, the eagle, the storm cloud. Huge, frenzied pillars of stone, scarred by wind and lightning, grayed to the color of fright, trembling, top-heavy, balanced like macrocosmic fiends, abut the road. The earth grows wan and weird, defertilized, dehumanized, neither brown nor gray nor beige nor taupe nor ecru, the no color of death reflecting light, sponging up light with its hard, parched shag and shooting it back at us in blinding, rock-flaked splinters that bore into the tenderest tissues of the brain and set it whimpering like a maniac.

This is where I begin to exult. This is something to put beside the devastation of man, something to overmatch his bloodiest depredations. This is nature in a state of dementia, nature having lost its grip, having become the hopeless prey of its own elements. This is the earth beaten, brutalized and humiliated by its own violent treachery. This is one of the spots wherein God abdicated, where He surrendered to the cosmic law of inertia. This is a piece of the Absolute, bald as an eagle's knob, hideous as the leer of a hyena, impotent as a granite hybrid.

. . . We roll down a crisp, crackling mountain side into an immense plain. The uplands are covered with a sheath of stiff shrub like blue and lavender porcupine quills. Here and there bald patches of red clay, streaks of shale, sand dunes, a field of pea green, a lake of waving champagne. We roll through a village which belongs to no time and no place, and accident, a sudden sprout of human activity because some one some time or other had returned to the scene of the massacre to look for an old photograph amidst the tumbled ruins and had stayed there from force of inertia and staying there had attracted flies and other forms of animate and inanimate life. **"**

HENRY MILLER, *THE COLOSSUS OF MAROUSSI*,
PUB. SECKER & WARBURG, LONDON 1942

THE CRETAN PEOPLE

William Lithgow suffers at the hands of Cretan bandits.

❝I was beset on the skirt of a Rocky Mountaine; with three Greeke murdering Renegadoes, and an Italian Bandido: who laying hands on me, beate me most cruelly, robbed me of all my clothes, and stripped me naked, threatning me with many grievous speeches.

At last the respective Italian, perceiving I was a stranger, and could not speake the Cretan tongue, began to aske me in his owne language, where was my money? to whom I soberly answered, I had no more then he saw, which was fourscore Bagantines: which scarcely amounted to two groats English: But he not giving credit to these words, searched all my linnen, and Letters of recommendations I had from divers Princes of Christendome, especially the Duke of Venice, whose subjects they were, if they had beene lawfull subjects: Which when he saw, did move him to compassion, and earnestly entreated the other three theeves to grant me mercy, and to save my life: A long deliberation being ended, they restored backe againe my

Pilgrimes clothes, and Letters, but my blew gowne and Bagantines they kept: Such also was their theevish courtesie toward me, that for my better safegard in the way, they gave me a stamped piece of clay, as a token to shew any of their companions, if I encountred with any of them; for they were about twenty Rascalles of a confederate band, that lay in this desart passage.

. . . I never could see a Greeke come forth of his house unarmed: and after such a martiall manner, that on his head he weareth a bare steele cap, a bow in his hand, a long sword by his side, a broad Ponard overthwart his belly, and a round Target hanging at his girdle. They are not costly in apparell, for they weare but linnen cloathes, and use no shooes but bootes of white leather, to keepe their legges in the fields from the prickes of a kind of Thistle, wherewith the Countrey is overcharged like unto little bushes or short shrubs which are marvelous sharpe, and offensive unto the inhabitants, whereof, often a day to my great harme, I found their bloody smart: The women generally weare linnen breaches as men do, and bootes after the same manner, and their linnen coates no longer then the middle of their thighes, and are insatiably inclined to Venery, such is the nature of the soyle and climate. They auncient Cretans were such notable lears, that the heathen Poet Epimenides, yea, and the Apostle Paul in his Epistle to Titus, did tearme them to have beene ever liers, evill beasts, and slow bellies: whence sprung these proverbs, as *Cretense mendacium, & cretisandum est cum cretensibus.* 99

WILLIAM LITHGOW, *RARE ADVENTURES AND PAINEFULL PEREGRINATIONS*, PUB. JAMES MACLEHOSE & SONS, GLASGOW 1906

AN INSUPERABLE FEAR

A sensitive exploration of the Greek-Turkish divide by Nikos Kazantzaki (1883–1957).

66The sole fear I had not succeeded in conquering up to that point was the fear of earthquakes. Megalo Kastro often shook to its very foundations. A rumble sounded below in the world's cellars, the earth's crust creaked, and the poor people above went out of their minds. Whenever the wind subsided abruptly, not a leaf moved, and a hair-raising hush settled over everything, the inhabitants of Kastro rushed out of their homes or shops and glanced first at the sky, then at the ground. They did not say a word lest the evil hear and come, but to themselves they thought fearfully, There's going to be an earthquake, and they made the sign of the cross.

One day our teacher, old Paterópoulos, tried to set our minds at ease. 'There is nothing to an earthquake, really,' he explained. 'Don't be afraid of it. It's just a bull beneath the ground. He bellows, butts the earth with his horns, and the ground shakes. The ancient Cretans called him the Minotaur. There's really nothing to it at all.'

But after being consoled in this way by our teacher, we found that our terror had increased all the more. The earthquake was a living thing in other words, a beast with horns; it bellowed and shook beneath our feet, and it ate people up.

'Why doesn't Saint Minas kill him?' asked chubby little Stratís, the sexton's son.

But the teacher became angry. 'Don't talk non-sense!' he shouted, whereupon he left his desk and twisted Stratís's ear to make him keep quiet.

One day, however, as I was racing through the Turkish quarter at top speed because the smell the Turks exuded disgusted me, the earth began to shake again, the windows and doors rattled, and I heard a great clatter, as though from collapsing houses. I stood petrified with fear in the middle of the narrow lane, my eyes riveted to the ground. I was waiting for it to crack and the bull to emerge and eat me, when suddenly a vaulted door swung open, revealing a garden, and out darted three young Turkish girls, bare-footed and unkempt, their faces uncovered. Quaking with fear, they scattered in all directions, uttering shrill cries like swallows. The entire lane smelled of musk. Ever since that moment earthquakes began to display a different face for me, one which endured my entire life. It was no longer the fierce face of the bull. They stopped bellowing and began to chirp like birds. Earthquakes and the little Turks became one. This was the first time I saw a dark force merge with the light and become luminous. **99**

NIKOS KAZANTZAKI, *REPORT TO GRECO*,
TRANS. P.A. BIEN, PUB. BRUNO CASSIRER, OXFORD 1965

ON THE ROAD TO KNOSSOS
Kazantzaki meets with compatriots on his way to Knossos.

66Crete's mystery is extremely deep. Whoever sets foot on this island senses a mysterious force branching warmly and beneficently through his veins, senses his soul begin to grow. But this mystery has become even deeper and richer since the discovery of this immensely versatile and varicolored civilization until then buried beneath the soil, this civilization filled with such great nobility and youthful joy.

I left the city and took the charming road which leads to the new cemetery. . . . I was surrounded by olive groves and vineyards. The vintage still had not begun; the grapes drooped heavily and touched the soil. The air smelled of fig

leaves. A little old lady came along. She halted. Lifting the two or three fig leaves which covered the basket she carried on her arm, she picked out two figs and presented them to me.

'Do you know me, old lady?' I asked.

She glanced at me in amazement. 'No, my boy. Do I have to know you to give you something? You're a human being, aren't you? So am I. Isn't that enough?'

Laughing a fresh girlish laugh, she began to hobble along once more toward Kastro.

The two figs were dripping with honey; I believe they were the most delicious I ever tasted. The old lady's words refreshed me as I ate. You are a human being. So am I. That's enough!

A shadow fell next to my own. Turning, I saw a Catholic priest. He looked at me and smiled.

'Abbé Mugnier,' he said, holding out his hand. 'Would you care to keep me company? I don't know modern Greek, only ancient: Μηνιν αειδε, θεα, Πηλιαδεο Ἀχιληοσ . . .'

'. . . ουλομενην, ν μυρι Ἀχαιοισ αλγε εθηξε . . .' I continued.

Laughing, we continued to declaim the immortal verses as we proceeded. . . .

The custodian hurried forward to greet us and explain the site. He was a simple, jovial Cretan who wore *vrakes* and carried a large crook. His name was David. In his many years as custodian and guide at Knossos he had learned much. He spoke of the palace as though it were his home, received us in the capacity of master of the house.

Taking the lead, he extended his crook to indicate the sites.

'Before you is the great royal court, sixty meters long, twenty-nine meters wide. Here are the storerooms with their huge decorated jars. In here the king stocked his produce in order to feed his people. We found sediment from wine and olive oil in the jars, also olive pits, beans, chick-peas, wheat, barley, and lentils. Everything was carbonized by great fires.'

We climbed to the upper story. On all sides: short, thick columns colored black and purple. In the passageways we saw wall paintings of flowers, shields, and bulls. We reached the high terrace. The happy domesticated landscape stretched all around us; at the center of the horizon lay Yioúchtas, Zeus's supine head. The half-crumbling, half-restored palace gleamed with brilliance after thousands of years, once more enjoying Crete's masculine sunlight. In this palace one does not see the balanced geometric architecture of Greece. Reigning here are imagination, grace, and the free play of man's creative power. This palace grew and proliferated in the course of time, slowly, like a living organism, a tree. It was not built once and for all with a fixed, premeditated plan; it grew by additions, playing and harmonizing with the ever-renewed necessities of the times. Man was not guided here by inflexible, untrickable logic. The intellect was useful, but as a servant, not a master. The master was something or someone else. What name could we give it?

Turning to the abbé, I revealed my thoughts and asked his opinion.

'You want to know who the master was?' he answered with a smile. 'What do you expect a priest to tell you except God? The Cretans' god was the master; He guided their hands and minds, and they created. God was the master builder. And this Cretan god was as nimble and playful as the sea which embraces the island. This is why landscape, palace, paintings, and sea have such a faultless harmony and unity.'

Descending the stone stairway, we gazed in silence at the paintings on the walls: bulls, lilies, fish in the blue sea, the flying fish that spread their fins to leap above the waves, as though water, their maternal instinct, stifled them and they wished to inhale a more rarified atmosphere❞

NIKOS KAZANTZAKI, *REPORT TO EL GRECO*,
TRANS. P.A. BIEN, PUB. BRUNO CASSIRER, OXFORD 1965

A SILENT STRANGER
Wartime service in Crete for Evelyn Waugh (1903–66) provided inspiration for his "Sword of Honour" trilogy, novels originally published under the titles "Men at Arms", "Officers and Gentlemen" and "Unconditional Surrender".

❝Sage and thyme, marjoram and dittany and myrtle grew all about Fido's mossy bed and, as the sun mounted over the tufted precipice, quite overcame the sour sweat of his fear.

The spring had been embellished, consecrated and christianized; the water glittered and bubbled through two man-made basins and above it an arch had been cut in the natural rock. Above the arch, in a flat panel, the head of a saint, faded and flaked, was still discernible.

Fido woke in this Arcadian vale to find standing near him and gazing fiercely down a figure culled straight from some ferocious folk-tale. His bearing was patriarchal, his costume, to Fido's eyes, phantasmagoric – a goat-skin jacket, a crimson sash stuck full of antique weapons, trousers in the style of Abdul the Damned, leather puttees, bare feet. He carried a crooked staff.

'Good morning,' said Fido. 'I am English, an ally. I fight the Germans. I am hungry.'

The Cretan made no answer. Instead he reached forward with his crosier, deftly hooked Fido's pack from beside him and drew it away.

'Here, I say. What d'you think you're doing?'

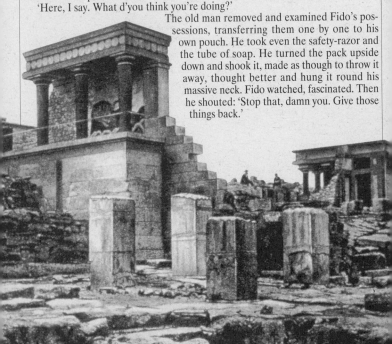

The old man removed and examined Fido's possessions, transferring them one by one to his own pouch. He took even the safety-razor and the tube of soap. He turned the pack upside down and shook it, made as though to throw it away, thought better and hung it round his massive neck. Fido watched, fascinated. Then he shouted: 'Stop that, damn you. Give those things back.'

The old man regarded him as though he were a fractious great-grandson. Fido drew his pistol.

'Give those back or I'll shoot,' he cried wildly.

The Cretan studied the weapon with renewed interest, nodded gravely and stepped forward.

'Stop,' cried Fido. 'I'll shoot.'

But his finger lay damp and limp on the trigger. The old man leant forward. Fido made no movement. The horny hand touched his and gently loosened his grip on the butt. The old man studied the pistol for a moment, nodding, then tucked it beside his daggers in the red sash. He turned and silently, surely, climbed away up the hillside.

Fido wept.**

EVELYN WAUGH,
OFFICERS AND GENTLEMEN,
PUB. EYRE METHUEN,
LONDON 1955

THE BUTCHER'S BULL

*Pandelis Prevelakis (1909–86) drew
from a seemingly inexhaustible supply of
anecdotes to furnish his novels with the richness,
the gaiety and – as related below – the occasional brutality of Cretan village life.*

**Going back to the village we came upon a group of children following Kanakis, the butcher, and the calf he was going to kill. He'd furled coloured paper in its horns and hung tassels of ribbon round its throat. He drove it into the village and sold it while still alive, piece by piece.

'When was there ever such a young bull? People of Pigi, come and buy, before it's all gone!' he cried as he drove it along.

Men came to the doors of their workshops. Some bought, others said nothing and went back to their benches. In front of Manousso's café two or three villagers got up together from their table, went across to the butcher and mumbled something to him.

'Hi!' the butcher shouted. 'The kidneys and the intestines are sold! . . . Hi! The head and feet are sold.'

The animal seemed to grow proud, and swung its ribbons. It was a fine sight, with its dark shiny coat, its white patch on the forehead, its intelligent eyes. The poor thing was unaware of its fate, and those that knew had forgotten, praising and complimenting it as if seeing it off to its wedding.

At lame Gregory's café lower down, the bloodless sacrifice continued. Some chose a cut from the ribs, others a cut from the shoulder, and another took the skin. The butcher's purpose was to involve the whole village in his crime before he actually killed the beast. If three kilos of meat remained unsold, the slaughter would be put off till the following Saturday.

The procession crossed over the square and disappeared into the alleys. At a bend of the road we heard a murmur of voices. There was quite a crowd at Matthew's café: workmen, labourers, each wanting a share of the meat. The bull-calf put a hoof on the doorstep, lowered its head into the café and stared at the men. It was as if it wanted to be sure of knowing them individually before it went to its Maker.

'Hey, Kanakis,' said Matthew, a bandy-legged fellow beside whom the bull seemed like a god. 'Will you keep the tail for me, to make a duster?'

A shudder passed over the bull, as if it understood what was said. It didn't object to giving its strength to people, but to become a fly-swat in the hands of that creature was too much for it.

Matthew took a copper coin from the pocket of his waistcoat and gave it to the slaughterer. Nothing of the bull must be given away: that coin was its first fare for

133

the lower world. Not even its hoofprints remained unsold!

Kanakis dragged the beast rudely by the horn into the lane that led to the slaughter-house, giving it a sharp smack on the rump with the small stick he carried. The decorated bull that had gone through the village like a prince was now hustled gracelessly away by its butcher. **99**

PANDELIS PREVELAKIS, *THE SUN OF DEATH*,
TRANS. PHILIP SHERRARD, PUB. JOHN MURRAY, LONDON 1965

HARD-HEADED PEOPLE

The English novelist, poet and travel writer Lawrence Durrell (1912–90) spent the latter years of his life in the Mediterranean region, basing many novels and non-fictional accounts upon his experiences in the Greek islands, Cyprus and Alexandria.

66Traditionally, Chanea is the home of the quince, and its quince *compote* has always been a famous local comestible. I also remember Chanea as greener and less dusty than other towns. There are small and pleasant prospects, where one can sit over an ouzo and think about nothing – just feeling the sunlight on your fingers, and tasting it in your glass. Traditionally, too, its inhabitants are thought more cosmopolitan and outward-looking than most Cretans. Certainly, they are sufficiently evolved (to use a word in its French sense) to make jokes about the duller aspects of the island character.

One of these, which illustrates Cretan hard-headedness, can be told with decency since it comes from a Cretan himself. During a parachute course in the Middle East the instructor, jump-training a group of commandos from various islands, saw one of them fumble with his harness and hesitate to advance into the bay for the jump. Incautiously, he made a pleasantry – asking if the novice was scared? The response was unexpected. 'Scared?', cried the young man, 'You dare to tell a Cretan that he is scared? I'll show you who is scared.' He unhooked his safety harness altogether and jumped to his certain death. So be careful what jokes you make when you are in Crete.

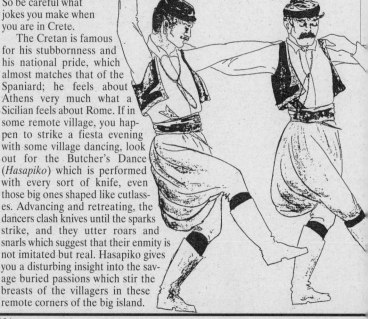

The Cretan is famous for his stubbornness and his national pride, which almost matches that of the Spaniard; he feels about Athens very much what a Sicilian feels about Rome. If in some remote village, you happen to strike a fiesta evening with some village dancing, look out for the Butcher's Dance (*Hasapiko*) which is performed with every sort of knife, even those big ones shaped like cutlasses. Advancing and retreating, the dancers clash knives until the sparks strike, and they utter roars and snarls which suggest that their enmity is not imitated but real. Hasapiko gives you a disturbing insight into the savage buried passions which stir the breasts of the villagers in these remote corners of the big island.

Hundreds of years of sieges and battles and famines have gone to make up this unyielding and obdurate character, with all its limitations as well. I once asked a friend who had spent two whole winters as a commando in Crete what had made the job he had done hardest. I expected some stock answer – the cold and chilblains, or fear of the enemy. But no; the hardest thing to cope with, he said, was the lack of conversation. There were only two permissable topics for men – the performance of pistols or small arms, and the cut of boots. This was worse than the Cavalry Club, he added; and went on to say that if one dared to open a book, there would be alarmed looks all round – you must be sickening for something; a friend would ask, 'Feeling off colour, old man?' But I doubt if remote village communities would be any different from those of the Cretan shepherds living on Mount Ida. **99**

LAWRENCE DURRELL, *THE GREEK ISLANDS*,
PUB. FABER AND FABER, LONDON 1978

CIVILIZATION

When Henry Miller decided, at the beginning of World War Two, to visit Greece at the invitation of his friend Lawrence Durrell, he had no idea what experiences were awaiting him. Having had no classical education, he lacked any academic or preconceived notion of this of this age-old civilization, and it is probably this innocence of perception – so rare in travel writers – that gives "The Colossus of Maroussi" such impact and authenticity. Crete was a very different place in 1939; tourists were thin on the ground, the rumblings of war were drawing ever closer.

66Greece is what everybody knows, even *in absentia*, even as a child or as an idiot or as a not-yet-born. It is what you expect the earth to look like given a fair chance. It is the subliminal threshold of innocence. It stands, as it stood from birth, naked and fully revealed. It is not mysterious or impenetrable, not awesome, not defiant, not pretentious. It is made of earth, air, fire and water. It changes seasonally with harmonious undulating rhythms. It breathes, it beckons, it answers.

Crete is something else. Crete is a cradle, an instrument, a vibrating test tube in which a volcanic experiment has been performed. Crete can hush the mind, still the bubble of thought. I wanted so long and so ardently to see Crete, to touch the soil of Knossus, to look at a faded fresco, to walk where "they" had walked. I had let my mind dwell on Knossus without taking in the rest of the land. Beyond Knossus my mind pictured nothing but a great Australian waste. That Homer had sung of the hundred cities of Crete I didn't know because I could never bring myself to read Homer; that relics of the Minoan period had been found in the tomb of Akhenaton I was ignorant of also. I knew, or believed rather, only that here at Knossus on an island which nowadays scarcely anybody ever thinks to visit there had been initiated some twenty-five or thirty centuries before the dawn of that blight called Christianity a way of life which makes everything that has happened since in this Western World seem pallid, sickly, ghost-ridden and doomed. The Western world, we say, never once thinking to include those other great social experiments which were made in South America and Central America, passing them over always in our rapid historical surveys as if they were accidents, jumping from the Middle Ages to the discovery of America, as if this bastard bloom on the North American continent marked the continuation of the line of true development of man's evolution. Seated on King Minos' throne I felt closer to Montezuma than to Homer or Praxiteles or Caesar or Dante. Looking at the Minoan scripts I thought of the Mayan legends which I had once glimpsed in the British Museum and which stand out in my memory as the most wonderful, the most natural, the most artistic specimens of calligraphy in

135

the long history of letters. Knossus, or what happened there almost fifty centuries ago, is like the hub of a wheel on which many spokes have been fitted only to rot away. The *wheel* was the great discovery; men have since lost themselves in a maze of petty inventions which are merely accessory to the great pristine fact of revolution itself.

. . . I went back to my room determined to plunge into that great unknown tract which we call Crete, anciently the kingdom of Minos, son of Zeus, whose birthplace it was.

> HENRY MILLER, *THE COLOSSUS OF MAROUSSI*,
> PUB. SECKER & WARBURG, LONDON 1942

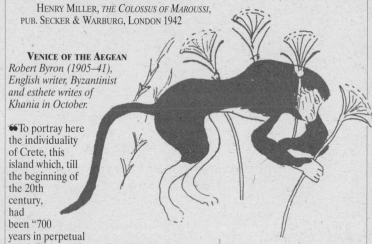

VENICE OF THE AEGEAN
Robert Byron (1905–41),
English writer, Byzantinist
and esthete writes of
Khania in October.

❝To portray here the individuality of Crete, this island which, till the beginning of the 20th century, had been "700 years in perpetual revolt," is scarcely possible. Our visit was a reconnoitre, a prelude perhaps, to further exploration. At first we remained in the capital, Canea. The buildings of this town epitomise the whole history of the Levant. Across the mouth of the harbour, as the rowing-boat enters, runs a mole ending in a Turkish lighthouse, a truncated minaret delicately embroidered with stone ornament. Nearer in, on the east, stands the earliest mosque on the island, a tiny building with a dome that resembles three-quarters of a doughnut and is supported by flying buttresses that might have been borrowed from St. George's Windsor. Look now across to the west. It is Venice. High, multi-coloured houses, each black window reflected in the sunlit water, jumble along the quay; and reveal, on closer view, that it was Venice, and that the lions of St. Mark still cry a weatherbeaten echo from the bellying walls. Behind, up the slope from the sea, it is the same. Twisting narrow streets, the houses so tall as to exclude all sun, display Renaissance porticoes, escutcheons of the Venetian nobility, and even bas-relievo portraits of the general of the Republic in plumed helmets. On one such there appeared also the stone fez of a later tenant. And above, as if to complete the tale, the cornice had been furnished with a row of Greek *acroteria*. Adjacent lies the old Turkish quarter, to-day the centre of commerce, where lanes of windowless shops are piled with the importations of the West, side by side with the traditional clothing and commodities of the island.

It was October. The weather was clearing. And the sun shone with golden warmth in the squares, upon the tall swinging men in their dress of top-boots, black Turkish trousers falling in a huge bag behind, and black cross-stitched shirts, to which were sometimes added blue cloaks embroidered and hooded. At all the street corners chestnuts were cooking on braziers. Fruit and game were piled high in the market. We lunched as a rule in a disused mosque, where we were always invited to choose our own partridge in the kitchen. ❞

> ROBERT BYRON, *THE STATION*,
> PUB. DUCKWORTH, LONDON 1928

ITINERARIES

▲ The harbor at Khania.   ▼ Rethymnon's inner harbor.

▼ Ierapetra, sited at the narrowest point of the island.

▼ Haghios Nikolaos with its picturesque harbor.

▼ Painted fishing boats to the east of the island.

▲ An attractive display of Cretan *koulourias*.

▲▼ Bustling and colorful market street, Heraklion.

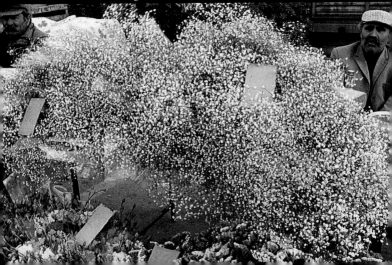

▲ Cretan Orthodox priest. ▼ Hairdresser in the village of Kastelli.

▼ Taverna in Heraklion, with the Bembo fountain in the background.

▲ The Falassarna site, to the southwest of the Gramvousa peninsula.

▲ Peaceful countryside, Rodopos peninsula   ▼ Gorge of Aradena

HERAKLION

1. ST ANDREW'S BASTION
2. PANTOKRATOS BASTION
3. KHANIA GATE
4. BETHLEHEM BASTION
5. MARTINENGO BASTION
6. JESUS BASTION
7. VITURI BASTION
8. SABIONERA BASTION
9. VRISI PRIULI FOUNTAIN
10. IDOMENEUS FOUNTAIN
11. HISTORICAL MUSEUM

Two days

THE SIEGE OF CANDIA
● *56.* The Turkish Sultan Ibrahim the Mad (reigned 1640–8) launched the first attack against Candia in spring 1648; so began a siege that was to last for twenty-one years. In 1666 Mehmet IV's troops laid siege to Candia, defended by Francesco Morosini the Younger, the *proveditore generale*. On September 5, 1669, Morosini capitulated, leaving the Turks in control of the town.

HISTORY

The classical geographer Strabo refers to the harbor of Knossos as "Heraclium". It was called this until Crete fell to the Saracens in AD 828, ● *48.* They rebuilt the Byzantine ramparts and erected a citadel, naming it *El-Khandak* after the ditch dug around it. European travelers softened the pronunciation, calling it Candia, or Candy. In the West the name was used to describe the whole of Crete until the 20th century. Little is left today of Heraklion from these ancient, Saracen or Byzantine times, other than Roman fragments reused in buildings of a later date, and museum artefacts. Under Venetian rule Candia underwent a dazzling cultural renaissance: most of the major figures in 16th- and 17th-century Greece attended its school, Haghia Ekaterini, the most famous being El Greco ● *52.* Following the Turkish victory in 1669 Candia was renamed *Megalo Kastro*, the "Great Fortress", after its Venetian fortifications. The town kept this name until 1923, when it was renamed Heraklion in a government move to hellenize city names. In 1971 Heraklion became the capital of Crete. Today it is the largest town on the island; its population of over 100,000 makes it the fifth largest in Greece.

Morosini, "defender of Candia", came from an old Venetian patrician family. He later acquired the sobriquet *il Peloponnesico* after recapturing the Morea and Athens.

144

12. St Minas' Cathedral and Church
13. St Catherine's Church
14. Kioska and Bembo Fountain
15. Market
16. Venizelos Square
17. Morosini Fountain
18. El Greco Park
19. St Mark's Church
20. Loggia
21. St Titus' Church
22. Eleftherias Square
23. Archeological Museum
24. Venetian Arsenals
25. Kastro Koules

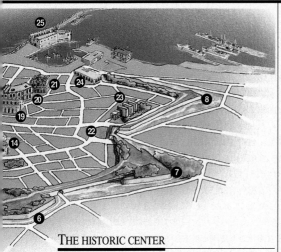

THE HISTORIC CENTER

VENIZELOS SQUARE (PLATEIA VENIZELOU). This is a lively meeting place with cafés, restaurants, bookstalls and antique shops. Its main feature is the Venetian Morosini fountain, commissioned in 1628 by Francesco Morosini, governor of Candia and uncle of the famous defender of the town in 1669. Vaulted ceilings in the shops are all that remain of the Duke of Crete's palace, the *Palazzo Ducale*, once the seat of Venetian government.

THE CHURCH OF HAGHIOS MARKOS ● *103*. The church of St Mark, at the northeastern corner of the square, is a fine basilica with an entrance portal of five bays. The original church, built in 1239, was destroyed by an earthquake in 1303 and was rebuilt only to suffer the same fate in 1508. The present church was built shortly after this. It became a mosque under the Turkish occupation and during further misfortunes even saw use as a cinema. Between 1956 and 1961 work undertaken by the Cretan Historical Society restored it to a style in keeping with its Venetian origins. Since then it has become a cultural and exhibition center, notably showing icons and copies of Byzantine frescos.

THE CHURCH OF HAGHIOS TITOS. The church is of Byzantine origin and is dedicated to Saint Titus, patron saint and first Bishop of Crete; a gold reliquary chalice here contains his head. Under the Venetians it was the church of the Latin archbishop's see; the Turks used it as a mosque. Turkish features added during restoration in 1872 have given it a rather unusual appearance.

THE CHURCH OF HAGHIOS TITOS
The church is situated behind the Loggia, with a vast paved courtyard in front of it. The actual date of its construction is unclear. The church suffered serious damage in a fire in 1544 and in the earthquake of 1856, and was rebuilt several times. It became the mosque of Vezir Tzami under Turkish occupation, when a minaret was added; this has since been replaced by a bell tower.

THE MOROSINI FOUNTAIN ● *108*
The raised sides of the basin form eight segments, with bas-relief scenes representing the sea gods of Greek mythology; nymphs and tritons are shown riding upon the backs of dolphins and sea monsters. In the center stands a squat plinth surmounted by four lions, from whose gaping mouths water flows. The lions in turn support a smaller basin, in which formerly stood an impressive statue of Poseidon; the Turks had this replaced by a peristyle, also subsequently lost.

145

▲ NIKOS KAZANTZAKI

The writer, poet and Cretan intellectual Nikos Kazantzaki ▲ *129* (he preferred the "s" at the end of his name to be omitted) was born in Heraklion on February 18, 1883. After studying law in Athens and philosophy in Paris under Bergson, Kazantzaki traveled widely: in Europe, Russia, the Middle East, China and Japan. His travel journals were instantly hailed as masterpieces on their publication in Greek. In 1919 he entered Cretan politics, appointed Secretary General of the Ministry of Public Welfare by Venizelos; as minister in the Sofoulis government in 1945 he founded the Socialist Workers' Union. He was made literary advisor to Unesco in 1947, but resigned in 1948 to concentrate on writing in Antibes, where he settled. He died in Germany on October 26, 1957. The funeral ceremony in Heraklion prompted displays of popular emotion throughout Greece, as the whole country honored the memory of a great patriot.

Nikos Kazantzaki is one of the outstanding figures in contemporary world literature. His various works cover a wide range of genres (the philosophical essay, poetry, the novel) and have been published in many languages; most frequently translated and best known are *Zorba the Greek*, *Christ Recrucified* and *The Last Temptation*, which was banned by the Catholic Church. Kazantzaki was also the Modern Greek translator of Dante's *Divine Comedy*, Goethe's *Faust* and Nietzsche's *Thus Spake Zarathustra*.

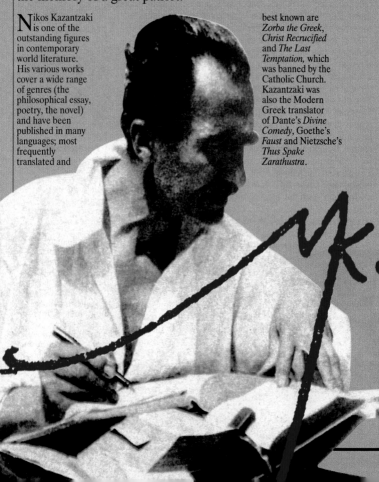

The painter Takis Kalmouchos, Kazantzaki's friend, sketched this portrait of the writer, with whom he visited the Sinai desert in 1927.

In 1931 Kazantzaki was on Aegina where he experienced one of his most intense periods of creativity. In a letter to Pandelis Prevelakis, he wrote, "The days are divine now that I am alone, I am working relentlessly hard . . . and I feel perfectly happy." He prepared entries for the Eleftheroudakis French-Greek dictionary ● 68, wrote The Poor Man of God, Zorba the Greek and his version of the 33,333 verses of The Odyssey, an immense work and the finest example of the living Homeric epic tradition.

A CALLIGRAPHIC SIGNATURE
Nikos Kazantzaki's magnificent signature is rooted in his native Cretan soil: the sweep of the first initial echoes the Minoan symbol of the double-headed axe.

The Church of St Catherine (Haghia Ekaterini), now the Museum of Religious Art, houses a superb collection of icons. Six icons from Moni Vrondisi, a monastery some 29 miles south of Heraklion, are among the finest works. These were executed by Mikhail Damaskinos (c. 1530–91), thought to have been the teacher of El Greco. Like other masters of the Cretan Renaissance, Georgios Klontzas or Theophanis Bathas, Damaskinos mastered both the "Greek manner", deriving from Paleologi tradition, and the "Italian manner". This embraced the technical and iconographic innovations of 15th- and 16th-century Tuscan and Venetian painters such as Veneziano, Pisanello, Gentile da Fabriano or Titian, whose works were widely copied.

THE "LAST SUPPER"
The Italian manner suffuses this piece, although it is mingled with echoes of Byzantine style whose anti-naturalistic principles were never abandoned by the painter. Here, the care taken in representing objects is worthy of a still-life; depth of perspective underpins the composition with the two servants in the foreground, the dogs under the table and the framing function of the architecture.

"THE WOMEN AT THE TOMB"
The principal scene shows Christ appearing to Mary Magdalene in the garden of Gethsemane. Byzantine sources are evident in the style of the mountains, the narrative sequence of the scenes of different sizes and the red-lettered inscription on Christ's gold halo; also, in the foreground, in Christ's detached pose (right). On the other hand, the kneeling Mary Magdalene corresponds to the ideals of beauty of Italian mannerist art in the 16th century.

THE "COUNCIL OF NICEA". This last known icon by Damaskinos dates from 1591 and marks a return to traditional techniques and esthetic notions. Yet the realistic faces (detail, above) and rendering of the bishops' veined hands show that the lessons from Italy have been absorbed.

THE "DIVINE LITURGY". This is represented by traditional iconographic interpretation. God the Father and the Son are surrounded by seraphim; the altar is draped with a gilded cloth; above, the Holy Spirit appears as a dove. Encircling angels celebrate the body of Christ. The icon dates from 1579 to 1584.

THE "ADORATION OF THE MAGI". This icon marks the high point of Western influence, calling on Italian iconography of the Nativity rather than Byzantine images of the Magi; hence the foreshortening and movement of the horses. The only Byzantine characteristics are in the depiction of the mountain and Joseph's detached attitude.

THE "VIRGIN WITH THE BURNING BUSH" Although the theme derives from Italian sources, Byzantine elements abound in the stylized mountains, the presence of Moses in each episode and, in the foreground, the two figures of Moses; the first, erect, listening to the voices of the angels, the second kneeling to fasten his sandal.

149

FAÇADE AND METOPE OF THE LOGGIA

This elegant two-story edifice was seriously damaged by bombing raids during World War Two. A careful replica of the original was constructed on the exact same spot. Today the Loggia hosts shows and exhibitions.

TURKISH KIOSK

On Kornarou Square once stood the Church of Tou Sotiros, converted by the Turks into the Valide mosque. Today a sculpture stands in honour of the *Erotokritos*. Next to the Bembo fountain the Turks built a fountain kiosk ● *112*, which today houses a café.

AUGUST 25 STREET. The street of August 25 Martyrs (Odos Martyron 25 Avgoustou) is the finest avenue and busiest commercial quarter in Heraklion and links Venizelos Square with the seafront boulevard of Sophokles Venizelou. It is dedicated to the memory of Cretans killed by the occupying Turks on August 25, 1898, three months before they were expelled ● *64*. During the clashes fire razed a large part of the quarter: most of the neoclassical buildings consequently date from recent times.

KALERGON SQUARE (PLATEIA KALERGON). North of Venizelos Square is Kalergon Square, bordered by El Greco Park to the northwest. In Venetian times it was called the *Piazza dei Signori* and was surrounded by residential palaces for the governor and council nobles.

THE MARKET. Venizelos Square extends from Nikephoros Phokas Square, the main focal point of Heraklion. To the south 1866 Street (Odos 1866) leads to the permanent market, the busiest and most colorful part of the town, with fresh Cretan produce displayed on open-air stalls and under cover. An eastern bazaar-like atmosphere reigns.

THE LOGGIA ● *109*. On the way down toward the harbor stands a superb Venetian building, the Loggia, constructed in 1727 for Francesco Morosini the elder. The architect, quite probably Basilicata, built it in the Palladian style with a lower-story Doric and an upper-story Ionic colonnade. The Doric order is surmounted by a sculpted frieze of Venetian emblems. The palace was the center of public life and provided a meeting place for the Venetian nobles.

THE TOWN HALL. Behind the Loggia is the *Dhimarhio*, within an old Venetian armory dating from the early 17th century. This was destroyed by a bomb in 1941 but was rebuilt to house the *Dimarkheion*, the town hall of Heraklion. Set into the north wall are fragments from the Sagredo fountain, named after the Venetian governor who commissioned it in 1602.

THE BEMBO FOUNTAIN ● *109.* 1866 Street leads to Kornarou Square, where a Turkish fountain kiosk has been converted into a café. Next to it stands the Venetian Bembo fountain whose façade consists of a colonnade of two pillars and two columns framing a toga-clad headless statue of Roman origin. The statue rests on a support decorated with bas-relief floral motifs; from a basin, water pours into what was probably the lower part of a sarcophagus. Here and there are sculpted the Bembo family's heraldic emblems.

ST CATHERINE'S (HAGHIA EKATERINI) SQUARE. St Catherine's Square has three churches, dominated by Haghio Minas, Heraklion's cathedral and the Metropolitan see of Crete. The imposing cathedral, based on a Greek cross plan, was built between 1862 and 1895 in a pseudo-Renaissance style. Its dome rises from a drum above the nave and is flanked by two campaniles. The cathedral can hold eight thousand worshipers, making it the largest in Greece. The small church of Haghio Minas next door contains an extremely fine iconostasis.

THE CHURCH OF HAGHIA EKATERINI ● *104.* The Church of St Catherine dates from the first period of Venetian rule (16th century). It was originally the *metocheion*, the see of the Monastery of St Catherine of Sinai. After the fall of Constantinople its school was one of the most renowned in the Greek world: famous pupils included the writers Vincent Kornaros and G. Hortatzis and the painter El Greco ● *52.* Today it houses the Museum of Religious Art and exhibits fresco fragments and icons from churches and monasteries throughout the island: of particular interest are the six icons by the famous Cretan painter Damaskinos ▲ *148.* A walk alongside the pleasant El Greco Park takes the visitor to the Historical Museum ▲ *152.*

THE BEMBO FOUNTAIN
It takes its name from the governor Ioannis Bembo, who erected it in 1588 using antique fragments, sarcophagi and a headless statue brought from the Roman ruins at Ierapetra, on Crete's south coast ▲ 215.

HAGHIA EKATERINI
The church was built in 1555 and stands at the northeast corner of St Catherine's Square. Like so many other churches it was converted into a mosque under Turkish occupation. Exhibitions of religious art are now held here.

VRISI PRIULI FOUNTAIN
An inscription indicates that this fountain was erected in 1666 by the *proveditore generale*, Antonio Priuli. Its façade is constructed in the manner of a classical Greek temple. Like all other towns or villages in Crete, Heraklion is embellished with magnificent Venetian or Turkish fountains. Also worth seeing: the beautiful Venetian fountain of Idomeneus, opposite the Historical Museum, referred to by Kazantzaki in his novel *Freedom or Death*.

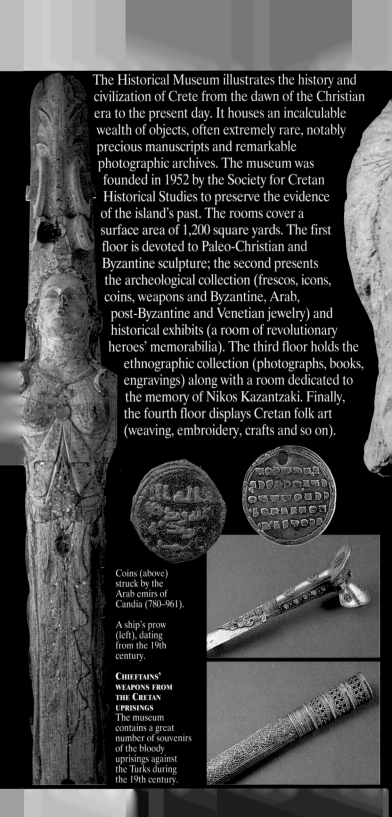

The Historical Museum illustrates the history and civilization of Crete from the dawn of the Christian era to the present day. It houses an incalculable wealth of objects, often extremely rare, notably precious manuscripts and remarkable photographic archives. The museum was founded in 1952 by the Society for Cretan Historical Studies to preserve the evidence of the island's past. The rooms cover a surface area of 1,200 square yards. The first floor is devoted to Paleo-Christian and Byzantine sculpture; the second presents the archeological collection (frescos, icons, coins, weapons and Byzantine, Arab, post-Byzantine and Venetian jewelry) and historical exhibits (a room of revolutionary heroes' memorabilia). The third floor holds the ethnographic collection (photographs, books, engravings) along with a room dedicated to the memory of Nikos Kazantzaki. Finally, the fourth floor displays Cretan folk art (weaving, embroidery, crafts and so on).

Coins (above) struck by the Arab emirs of Candia (780–961).

A ship's prow (left), dating from the 19th century.

CHIEFTAINS' WEAPONS FROM THE CRETAN UPRISINGS
The museum contains a great number of souvenirs of the bloody uprisings against the Turks during the 19th century.

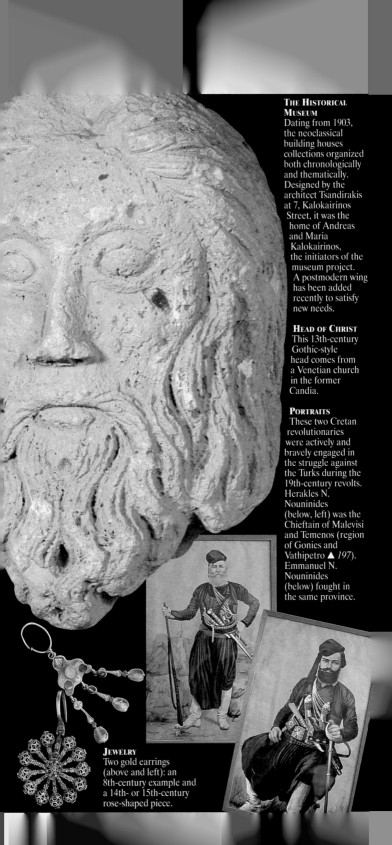

THE HISTORICAL MUSEUM

Dating from 1903, the neoclassical building houses collections organized both chronologically and thematically. Designed by the architect Tsandirakis at 7, Kalokairinos Street, it was the home of Andreas and Maria Kalokairinos, the initiators of the museum project. A postmodern wing has been added recently to satisfy new needs.

HEAD OF CHRIST

This 13th-century Gothic-style head comes from a Venetian church in the former Candia.

PORTRAITS

These two Cretan revolutionaries were actively and bravely engaged in the struggle against the Turks during the 19th-century revolts. Herakles N. Nouninides (below, left) was the Chieftain of Malevisi and Temenos (region of Gonies and Vathipetro ▲ 197). Emmanuel N. Nouninides (below) fought in the same province.

JEWELRY

Two gold earrings (above and left): an 8th-century example and a 14th- or 15th-century rose-shaped piece.

The Archeological Museum of Heraklion presents excavated finds from all over Crete, thus illustrating the ancient history of the island from Neolithic times (5700 BC) to the Greco-Roman period (5th century BC to 4th century AD). Yet the museum's chief uniqueness lies in its collection of exceptional specimens from the Minoan civilization (2000–1400 BC). Up until 1937 these treasures were housed within one room. The construction of a new building was rapidly considered indispensable: the architect P. Karandinos took on the task. Work began in 1951 when Nicolas Platon was Ephor of Antiquities and was completed in 1964 under the management of S. Alexiou. The museum contains twenty rooms with exhibits arranged according to chronology and provenance.

CRETAN POTTERY FROM THE PRE-PALATIAL TO THE ARCHAIC PERIOD

VASILIKI WARE
This style dates from the Pre-palatial era (2600–2000 BC) and derives its name from a site in eastern Crete. Vase surfaces are typically mottled with brown, red or black flecks. This effect is obtained by irregular firing. The fabrication process is unknown but indicates highly advanced technical skills. The shapes are extravagant, as this "teapot" with its exaggerated spout demonstrates.

This libation ewer (right) was discovered in a tomb near Heraklion

NEO-PALATIAL PERIOD
After the earthquake of 1700 BC Crete reached a new peak. A new style of pottery emerged. Vase shapes were more elongated and decorated naturalistically. Surface designs were either pale-colored patterns on dark grounds, or vice versa. Two styles predominated: the vegetal and the marine.

The celebrated "White Lily Vase" (above) from Knossos ▲ 161, dating from 1600 BC.

VEGETAL STYLE
This superb ewer from the Palace of Phaistos ▲ 178 typifies the style; its entire surface is covered with a dense pattern of reeds (1530 BC).

and dates from the end of the Palace period (1400 BC). The spine-like protuberances imitate examples of metalwork. The stylized argonauts and papyrus flowers are remarkable.

HARVESTER VASE
This famous rhyton
(1500 BC) was discovered
in the Villa of Haghia
Triada ▲ *182* and
reconstructs in bas-relief
a procession of peasants
returning from the fields,
followed by musicians.
One of the harvesters
trips; another turns
to him.

MARINE STYLE
Some of the finest
examples of this
style are from the
Palace of Zakros
▲ *212*, such as
this superb conical
rhyton, decorated
with starfish, shells,
tritons and rocks
and dating from
1500 BC. The small
amphora (above)
possesses several
vertically aligned
handles in the form
of large octopi
surrounded by
shells (1450 BC).

THE ARCHAIC PERIOD. This large jar constitutes a
rare and significant example of the pottery of this
era (650–500 BC). Its body is covered with bands
of raised reliefs, linear designs and pictographs,
decorated with a series of lion-headed spirals and
four sphinxes in relief.

155

Minoan art displays a sure grasp of the human form. Yet it is the miniature figurine that seems to characterize its statuary, making it quite unlike that of the Greek or Egyptian world. Only a few rare exceptions to this exist, one such being the two life-sized clay feet discovered in the Anemospilia Sanctuary. From the early Neolithic period figures that appear to be awkward actually reveal a sense of proportion and highly fluid lines. These figurines, frequently votive, become progressively more elongated. One of the most extraordinary and most discussed features is the incredible delicacy of their tiny size.

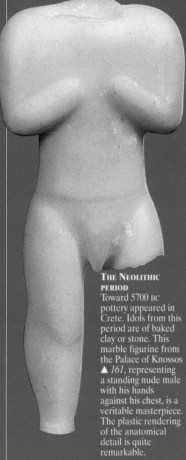

THE NEOLITHIC PERIOD

Toward 5700 BC pottery appeared in Crete. Idols from this period are of baked clay or stone. This marble figurine from the Palace of Knossos ▲ *161*, representing a standing nude male with his hands against his chest, is a veritable masterpiece. The plastic rendering of the anatomical detail is quite remarkable.

THE PROTO-PALATIAL PERIOD

During this period (2000–1700 BC) small-scale statuary flourished. A series of figurines was discovered during excavations of hilltop sanctuaries (Minoan Peak Sanctuaries). Pilgrims brought terracotta objects as offerings to the deity: (below, left) an idol from the Petsophas Sanctuary ▲ *211*. The seated female idol (below, right) with elaborate headgear was found at the Kophinas Sanctuary.

This highly stylized statuette of Neolithic origin comes from the cave at Eileithyia ▲ *190*. Incised decoration takes the place of anatomical detail.

This elegantly coiffed female head, from the sanctuary at Piskokephalo, dates from the end of the Proto-palatial period. The facial features are finely modeled.

Terracotta
statuette of the
Geometric period
representing a
lyre player.

**THE NEO-PALATIAL
PERIOD**
This terracotta
"model" from a
tomb at Kamilari,
near Phaistos ▲ *178*,
proves the existence
of funerary customs
in honor of the
dead. The façade
of the house
or temple,
with its two
columns, is
open; inside,
four figures
are seated
before
offertory
tables.

**THE
GEOMETRIC
PERIOD
1100–900 BC**
New influences entered
Crete, from Greek and Dorian
sources. The old and new styles
fused together. Iron appeared
and metallurgical skills evolved
to breathe new life into the human
form; contours were angular.
This tiny bronze idol, a seated
lyre player, is a perfect example.

Fresco painting constitutes one of the most impressive forms of Minoan art. Most of the frescos date from the Neo-palatial period (1700–1450 BC). Of the Proto-palatial period (2000–1700 BC), only minute fragments of decorative motifs have survived. The paint was applied *al fresco* then finished with the *fresco secco* technique. The varied colors were mineral or plant-based. The various themes are inspired by daily life, ceremonies, processions and above all, nature. The frescos were made to please the eyes and the soul, expressing fleeting joys and daily events, and thus being transformed into remarkable works of art.

BLUE BIRD
This delicate, richly coloured fragment (c. 1500 BC) comes from the House of the Frescos at Knossos ▲ *174*. Nature rules in splendor, creating an image of a peaceful world. It may even be that the scene represents the royal gardens at the palace, with an exotic bird set among the rocks, wild roses and irises.

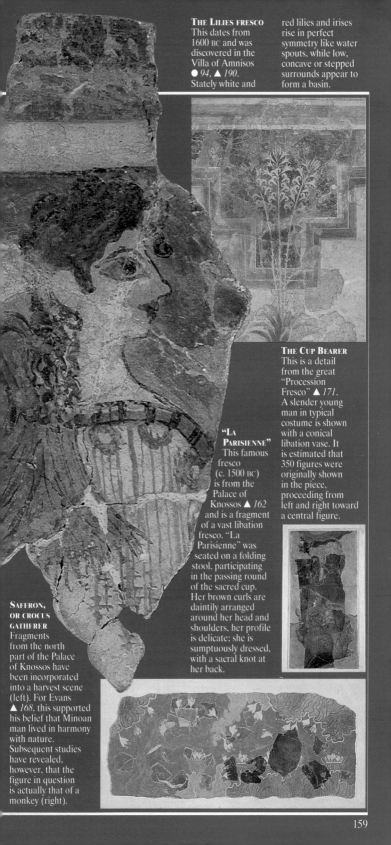

THE LILIES FRESCO

This dates from 1600 BC and was discovered in the Villa of Amnisos ● *94*, ▲ *190*. Stately white and red lilies and irises rise in perfect symmetry like water spouts, while low, concave or stepped surrounds appear to form a basin.

"LA PARISIENNE"

This famous fresco (c. 1500 BC) is from the Palace of Knossos ▲ *162* and is a fragment of a vast libation fresco. "La Parisienne" was seated on a folding stool, participating in the passing round of the sacred cup. Her brown curls are daintily arranged around her head and shoulders, her profile is delicate; she is sumptuously dressed, with a sacral knot at her back.

THE CUP BEARER

This is a detail from the great "Procession Fresco" ▲ *171*. A slender young man in typical costume is shown with a conical libation vase. It is estimated that 350 figures were originally shown in the piece, proceeding from left and right toward a central figure.

SAFFRON, OR CROCUS GATHERER

Fragments from the north part of the Palace of Knossos have been incorporated into a harvest scene (left). For Evans ▲ *168*, this supported his belief that Minoan man lived in harmony with nature. Subsequent studies have revealed, however, that the figure in question is actually that of a monkey (right).

THE HARBOR AND KASTRO KOULES

Sophokles Venizelou Boulevard leads to the Venetian harbor; this is sheltered by a huge harbor wall stretching out to Kastro Koules ● *106*. The fortress was built between 1523 and 1540 to face the threat posed by the Ottoman Empire, then at its peak under the reign of Suleyman the Magnificent. It has been fully restored over the last few years and is used as a theater for plays or musicals in summer. To the east, along the quayside of the old harbor, are the Venetian arsenals ● *107*, still used as warehouses, although one has retained its original arcade.

THE RAMPARTS

These are some three miles long and boast seven large bastions, built between 1550 and 1560 from the plans of Michele Sanmicheli, the Venetian architect, engineer and designer of some of the most important fortresses in the eastern Mediterranean ● *56*. Originally five gates were set in the walls, of which two are still visible today. The first bastion is St Andrew's and overlooks the sea. The second is dedicated to the Pantocrator, Christ the Almighty Ruler. Adjacent to it is Khania Gate, on whose inside wall is a magnificent vaulted portal bearing the date 1565; its fine freestone façade extends to the south. Next is the bastion of Bethlehem, followed by that of Martinengo: a path from the interior boulevard leads to the top of this bastion to reach the final resting place of the writer Nikos Kazantzaki ▲ *146*. The following bastion is dedicated to Jesus, next to the 1587 gate of the same name; its great vaulted portal still bears some original bas-reliefs. Vituri Bastion, the last but one, is bordered by a public garden with statues of Eleftherios Venizelos ▲ *62* and Emperor Nikephoros Phokas, along with a monument to the dead of the Battle of Crete. The ramparts terminate at the new port, ending with the Sabionera Bastion.

ELEFTHERIAS SQUARE (PLATEIA ELEFTHERIAS). Halfway between the final two bastions is Eleftherias, or Liberty Square, the largest and most pleasant square in the town. A moment to linger in one of its many cafés provides a refreshing pause before a tour of the nearby Archeological Museum ▲ *154*.

KASTRO KOULES
The original Venetian fortress was completed in 1303, probably on the site of an earlier Byzantine fort on the same rocky islet. It was destroyed by an earthquake at the beginning of the 16th century, but was rebuilt soon after. Under Turkish occupation it fell into disuse. It was damaged during World War Two but has since been restored.

THE PORT OF CANDIA
Photographed by Joubin during his 1891 trip.

KNOSSOS

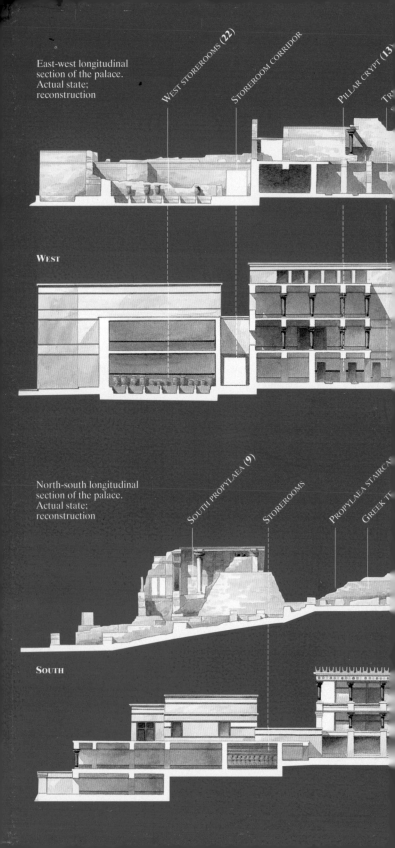

East-west longitudinal
section of the palace.
Actual state;
reconstruction

WEST STOREROOMS (22)

STOREROOM CORRIDOR

PILLAR CRYPT (13)

TR

WEST

North-south longitudinal
section of the palace.
Actual state;
reconstruction

SOUTH PROPYLAEA (9)

STOREROOMS

PROPYLAEA STAIRCAS

GREEK TE

SOUTH

36. Drains
37. Bathroom with clay tub
38. Shrine of the double axes
39. Lustral basin
40. House of the sanctuary
41. Southeast house
42. House of the Fallen Blocks
43. Monolithic pillar basement
44. East bastions
45. Central colonnade chamber
46. Stonecutters' workshop
47. Potters' workshop
48. Courtyard of the Stone Spout
49. Store of the giant *pithoi*
50. Corridor of the Draft Board

POTTERY
Cretan pottery displays very different characteristics from that of the mainland. From this Evans deduced the existence of a civilization quite distinct from that of the Myceneans. This

In 1900 Sir Arthur Evans began to excavate the Knossos site, having acquired a portion of the land. By 1906 a substantial part of the site had been uncovered. With his collaborators Duncan Mackenzie and later John Pendlebury, Evans devoted his life and his fortune to Knossos, up to his death in 1941. He published his findings in a work entitled *The Palace of Minos*. His imagination and his inventive turn of mind in its reconstruction incited much controversy, but he was the first to recreate and interpret the Minoan world. Evans wrote about the palace, "It was my idea, my work . . ."

he christened "Minoan" after Minos, the legendary king of Crete, establishing three periods: Early, Middle and Late Minoan
● *46*.

GAMES. Royal draft board of gold-plated ivory inlaid with rock crystal (early Neo-palatial). The game played an important part in the life of the Minoans who frequently depicted it in frescos, seals and other such objects.

THE EXCAVATIONS. Evans unearthed the theater area **(26)** in 1903. In November 1905 he reconstructed the grand staircase **(31)**, which was close to collapse, with a team of masons, carpenters and ironsmiths. He had no hesitation in using concrete, a new material of which he praised the strength. These undertakings led to heated controversy.

Evans was born in 1851 of a well-to-do family. During his wide travels (Lapland, Yugoslavia) he amassed archeological notes. Having closely followed the activities of Schliemann in Mycenae, he decided to research the undeciphered script of this civilization. Engraved stones discovered in Athens in 1889 led him to Crete.

169

The land of legends, Crete evoked the image of a treasure island with hoards of sacred riches. The town of Knossos, the capital of the island according to Homer, was the thriving center of Minoan power, and in its palace ruled King Minos. The wealth of material unearthed during excavations confirmed this image and enabled the tale of Minoan civilization to be told, or guessed at; its daily life, social rituals, religion and court splendor.

THE ACROBAT
This ivory figurine represents an athlete leaping over a bull; the animal has not been preserved. The magnificent sculpture, which John Pendlebury thought to be the "most exquisite" miniature of the ancient world, including Egypt, dates from around 1500 BC.

PRINCE OF THE LILIES
Evans readily reconstructed missing images to suit his theories. Thus the Lilies fresco (1500 BC), with the prince leading a griffin, is in fact composed of separate fragments from various frescos. Other interpretations have been put forward but Evans' remains on display in the Museum at Heraklion ▲ *158*, with a copy at the south entrance of the palace.

SOUTH PROPYLAEA (9)
In the restored part of this
impressive building a copy of
the Procession fresco has
been placed. Great sacred
horns once decorated one
of the windows.

THE FRESCOS
Minoan frescos are the
earliest examples of
painting in Greece. The
originals of those at
Knossos are displayed
in the Archeological
Museum at Heraklion

▲ 158. The palace is
decorated with
copies. The light-shaft
of the Throne Room
(19) is decorated with
copies of frescos from
various parts of the
palace (above, right).
The Ladies in Blue
fresco displays
elegantly beautiful
Minoan women,
whose immaculate
appearance (makeup,
hair adornments and
open bodices)
perhaps indicates
attendance at some
special event. The
Minoans seem to
have had a passion
for sporting exploits;
notably, it would
seem, perilous
acrobatic feats such
as is shown in this
Bull-fighting fresco.

THE PROCESSION
This frescoed homage
to Minos adorns the
walls of the corridor
of the same name **(4)**.
Only the Cup Bearer,
displayed in the
Museum ▲ *158*, is
still intact today.

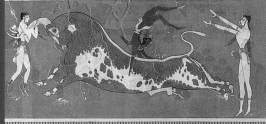

SNAKE GODDESSES
These faience idols (c. 1600 BC) were found in the rooms of the Treasury **(16)** in 1903. Both of them are bare-breasted, although their stance differs and the first is larger than the second (13 ½ inches).

THE THRONE ROOM
In 1900 Evans found the chamber **(19)** decorated with griffins (mythical monsters with the body of a lion and the head of an eagle) and gypsum benches by the walls. The room's religious function is indicated by the lustral basin, for ablutions, and at the far end a shrine with a double horn, double axe and statuette.

THE QUEEN'S MEGARON (34). Evans' fertile imagination was fired by these rooms, distinguished by their light-shaft, bathroom and toilet. Indeed, his interpretation of the sanitation system may be a little over-zealous. The Dolphins fresco ● *40*, among others, decorates this room. Wooden reproduction (left) of the throne.

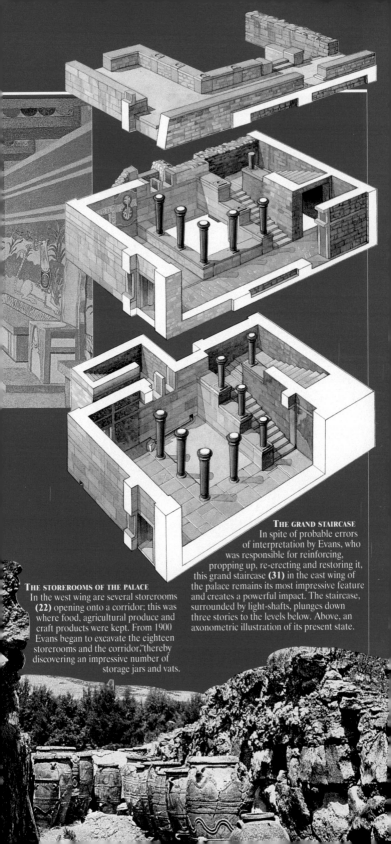

THE STOREROOMS OF THE PALACE
In the west wing are several storerooms
(22) opening onto a corridor; this was
where food, agricultural produce and
craft products were kept. From 1900
Evans began to excavate the eighteen
storerooms and the corridor, thereby
discovering an impressive number of
storage jars and vats.

THE GRAND STAIRCASE
In spite of probable errors
of interpretation by Evans, who
was responsible for reinforcing,
propping up, re-erecting and restoring it,
this grand staircase **(31)** in the east wing of
the palace remains its most impressive feature
and creates a powerful impact. The staircase,
surrounded by light-shafts, plunges down
three stories to the levels below. Above, an
axonometric illustration of its present state.

In the area around the palace there some interesting remains that were excavated and reconstructed by Evans: the Royal Road, leading from the theater area; the Little Palace, an impressive residence; the Minoan villas; the "Caravanserai", so called by Evans who imagined that the basins of fresh water were for passing travelers; the structure known as the "House of the High Priest", where a stone altar set between supports for double axes has been discovered; and the Royal Villa, thought to have been three stories high and set within gardens.

THE BULL'S HEAD RHYTON
Sacred vases were used as cult accessories, later becoming symbols. This fine example from the Little Palace is made from inlaid serpentine and dates from LM I (1500–50 BC)
▲ 152.

THE DOUBLE AXE
The ubiquitous emblem of the Minoan religion appears in every medium; drawn, engraved, painted or modeled, it is placed on the end of a shaft or between the double horns. Some are made of bronze, silver or gold. In Greek the axe is called a *labys*, thus linking it with the myth of the labyrinth ● 40.

THE ROYAL ROAD
This paved way has been dubbed the "oldest road in Europe". Private houses line it, such as the House of the Frescos that was decorated by the Blue Bird fresco ▲ 158.

THE PARTRIDGE FRESCO
Minoan man seems to have lived in harmony with nature. His depictions of its fauna give an impression of naturalness and freedom, as displayed by these partridges which animate the "Caravanserai" walls. The colors are flat, but create strong tonal contasts.

SOUTH OF HERAKLION

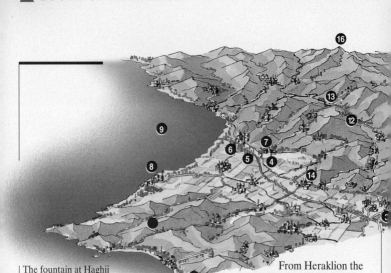

The fountain at Haghii Deka.

From Heraklion the main road leads to Venerato, twelve miles to the south; near here is the Paliani convent where the nuns support themselves by selling their needlecrafts to visitors. Beyond the Vourvoulitis pass the fertile Messara plain appears; descending towards it the road divides and the main route heads west to the village of Haghii Deka (the "Holy Ten").

GORTYS ★

THE CODE OF GORTYN
This was probably inscribed at the end of the 7th century or early 6th century BC and is a valuable source of information regarding ancient Crete. It would originally have been displayed in the *prytaneion*, a building used for public debates. It is divided into 12 columns of 52 lines, a total of 17,000 characters in ancient Doric, a Greek dialect. It is drawn up in the *boustrophedon* or "ox-plough" system, in which the sequence reads alternately from left to right, then right to left, in the way a peasant would plough his field.

The ruins of ancient Gortyn, called Gortys by the Cretans, are scattered about beneath the wild, untamed vegetation of the countryside around Haghii Deka.

HISTORY. Some ancient writers claim that Gortyn was established by the inhabitants of the Peloponnese at the end of the 3rd or beginning of the 2nd millennium BC. In the 5th century BC the laws of the city were laid down in the "Code of Gortyn", which constitutes the first known legislative system and is the most comprehensive example to survive from ancient Greece. From 67 BC Gortyn was the elected capital of the Roman province of Crete and Cyrenaica and as such possessed some fine buildings. After the arrival of Saint Paul in AD 59 and the nomination of Titus as Bishop, it became the center for the dissemination of the Christian faith. Gortyn remained the most important town in Crete during the first centuries of the Byzantine era, but pillaging raids by the Saracens in 824 destroyed the town, and it lost its former power for ever. The village of Haghii Deka gradually grew up over its ruins. Excavations began in 1884 under the archeologists Halbherr and Fabricius, and still continue today.

THE ROMAN CITY. The path starting at the chapel at Haghii Deka leads via the ruins of an amphitheater (with those of a stadium beyond it) to the *Megali Porta*, thought to be an arch from a 2nd-century AD thermal complex. Not far to the north are the remains of a nymphaeum, a monumental fountain

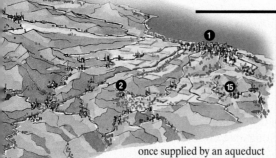

1. HERAKLION 2. VENERATO 3. GORTYS 4. MONASTERY OF KALIVIANI 5. PHAISTOS 6. HAGHIA TRIADA 7. VORI 8. MATALA 9. THE BAY OF MESSARA 10. MONASTERY OF ODIGITRIA 11. LENDAS 12. MONASTERY OF VALSAMONERO 13. KAMARES 14. MIRES 15. ARCHANES 16. MOUNT IDA

Four days

once supplied by an aqueduct whose pillars and arches are still visible against the slope of the hill. To the left, on the path running parallel to the main road, lie the ruins of another nymphaeum and those of a Praetorium, where the Roman governor lived. Beyond this are the remains of an archaic temple, dedicated to the Pythian Apollo; this was rebuilt during Hellenistic and Roman times. Shortly after is a theater and a sanctuary dedicated to Isis and Serapis, whose cult was introduced by Egyptian merchants during the Roman period.

HAGHIOS TITOS. The basilica of Saint Titus stands across the road, close to the bridge. It is thought that a church was first built on the site of Saint Titus' martyrdom. The present cruciform-plan basilica was erected during the reign of Justinian (527–65) and has been restored many times. The east end with its apse flanked by two square chapels is the finest section. Three naves can be deciphered from the still visible bases of what were their dividing columns. A narthex through which the congregation entered would have been at the west end ● *100*.

THE AGORA AND THE ODEON. Behind the basilica lies the as yet unexcavated agora, the ancient marketplace. On this site stood a temple dedicated to Asclepios, god of healing. The Odeon ● *96* stands beyond this.

THE ACROPOLIS. A few scant remains of the Hellenistic theater are sited on the other side of the river. On the hilltop is the acropolis of ancient Gortyn (the site of which is more easily reached from the village of Ambelouzos); here the foundations of a 7th- or 8th-century BC temple were discovered. Little remains of the acropolis itself, other than parts of the ruined bastion wall.

MONI KALIVIANI. Ten miles west of Gortys stands the monastery of Kaliviani whose one remaining ancient building, a 16th-century chapel, is decorated with original frescos. At the next intersection, take the minor road to Phaistos.

ODEON OF GORTYN This semicircular structure dates from the 1st or 2nd century AD. It was originally erected on the site of an older building and was used for musical performances. The stage was decorated with niches containing statues, and the orchestra paved with white and black flagstones. The marble seats are reasonably well preserved. Purely for decorative purposes, the Romans included the "queen of inscriptions" that was carved on a wall of the Hellenistic structure. The "Code of Gortyn" is today preserved in the vaulted outer corridor.

Icon, Monastery of Kaliviani.

177

The site of Phaistos was inhabited in the 3rd millennium BC. A palace was first built between 2000 and 1900 BC and destroyed around 1700 BC. A new, grander palace was erected that incorporated some of the earlier parts. An earth tremor destroyed it in c. 1450 BC. The site was reoccupied toward the end of the Bronze Age, and the Dorians subsequently founded a city-state, probably during the 8th century BC. This was destroyed in a war against Gortyn in the 2nd century BC.

THE UPPER COURT
Entrance to the site is through an upper court (1) to the northwest. The foundations of houses dating from the Hellenistic period are still visible. Along the west wall tombs dating from the early Christian era can be seen, along with seventeen holes for the wooden columns that supported the arcaded corridor. Straight terraces (2) along the wall of the court formed tiered rows from which the spectators watched ceremonies or processions. Two processional ways meet in the center of the west court (3). The circular structures visible to the south are cisterns and grain silos (4). The monumental entrance, or *propylaea*,

consists of a flight of steps (5), a propylon (6), a porch (7), a portico (8) and a light-shaft (9). To the left a staircase (10) led to the upper story; a corridor (11) led to a peristyle hall (12), the heart of the ancient palace. On a lower level to the right is a lustral bath (14) and its vestibule (13). Further along, an antechamber (15) opens onto a corridor with a central pillar (16) flanked by eleven storerooms (17) dating from the building of the new palace. Inside are two *pithoi* dating

from the Middle Minoan II period (1850–1750 BC). A staircase (18) leads to a gypsum-paved antechamber (19) that opens into the peristyle hall, an open court surrounded by a portico and a gallery facing toward Mount Ida. In the center are the foundations of a Pre-palatial Minoan house.

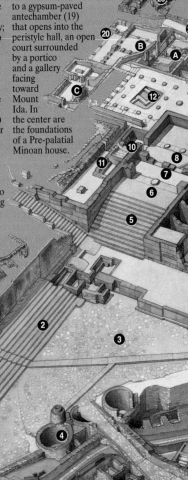

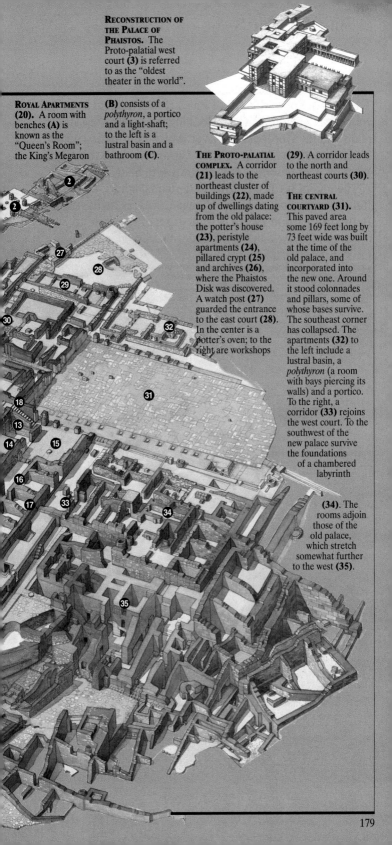

RECONSTRUCTION OF THE PALACE OF PHAISTOS. The Proto-palatial west court **(3)** is referred to as the "oldest theater in the world".

ROYAL APARTMENTS (20). A room with benches **(A)** is known as the "Queen's Room"; the King's Megaron **(B)** consists of a *polythyron*, a portico and a light-shaft; to the left is a lustral basin and a bathroom **(C)**.

THE PROTO-PALATIAL COMPLEX. A corridor **(21)** leads to the northeast cluster of buildings **(22)**, made up of dwellings dating from the old palace: the potter's house **(23)**, peristyle apartments **(24)**, pillared crypt **(25)** and archives **(26)**, where the Phaistos Disk was discovered. A watch post **(27)** guarded the entrance to the east court **(28)**. In the center is a potter's oven; to the right are workshops **(29)**. A corridor leads to the north and northeast courts **(30)**.

THE CENTRAL COURTYARD (31). This paved area some 169 feet long by 73 feet wide was built at the time of the old palace, and incorporated into the new one. Around it stood colonnades and pillars, some of whose bases survive. The southeast corner has collapsed. The apartments **(32)** to the left include a lustral basin, a *polythyron* (a room with bays piercing its walls) and a portico. To the right, a corridor **(33)** rejoins the west court. To the southwest of the new palace survive the foundations of a chambered labyrinth **(34)**. The rooms adjoin those of the old palace, which stretch somewhat further to the west **(35)**.

179

The rich and powerful city of Phaistos was built on a commanding hilltop site overlooking the fertile Messara plain and the Geropotamos river. Much information about Phaistos dates back to antiquity. Citing its role in the Trojan Wars, Homer describes it as a "town with many inhabitants". At the end of the last century Federico Halbherr, of the Italian Archeological Mission, began to excavate the region. Between 1950 and 1966 a new program of research, still ongoing today, was launched under the direction of Doro Levi of the Italian School.

POLYCHROMED KRATER WITH RELIEF FLOWERS
This superb example of Kamares ware, discovered at Phaistos, must have been part of a royal dinner service from the first palace. It is today exhibited in the Archeological Museum at Heraklion ▲ *154*, as are the jar (above, right) and the inscribed disk.

JAR IN MARINE STYLE
Also from the Palace of Phaistos, this *pithos* with its fish and net pattern is unique among the entire production of ware from the Kamares workshops.

Paved corridor leading to the central courtyard. Every corridor in the palace led to this court.

Legend relates that Phaistos was ruled by one of the three sons of Zeus and Europa, Rhadamanthys, whose rule was renowned for its wisdom and justice. He is credited with establishing the code of law observed in Crete that was to become a model for mainland Greece.

THE TWO SIDES OF THE PHAISTOS DISK

The baked clay disk is inscribed with a hieroglyphic script ● 66. It features new ideographs, such as the head of an Asiatic warrior with a pointed helmet. It is read in a spiral from center to rim. Each sign represents a syllable and each group of signs, broken by a vertical line, a word. Some of the signs have been deciphered (tools, animals), but the text remains an enigma.

The Italian Mission's excavations at the turn of this century.

**STAIRCASE OF
THE VILLA OF
HAGHIA TRIADA**
The first excavations
were carried out by
the Italian Mission at
the beginning of the
20th century, just
after the discovery of
Phaistos. A paved
road linked the two

sites. Objects from
the Haghia Triada site
include the celebrated
sarcophagus
(opposite), the
Chieftain's Cup
● 46, the Boxer Vase
made of steatite,
dating from 1700 to
1600 BC (below), and
the Harvester Vase;
all are on display in
the Museum at
Heraklion ▲ 154.

HAGHIA TRIADA ★

The site of Haghia Triada, named after the
ancient village of the same name, is situated
on the left bank of the Geropotamos some
2 miles west of Phaistos. The Villa of Haghia
Triada is a small Minoan palace thought to
have been used as a summer residence,
together with the surrounding buildings, by
the King of Phaistos
and his entourage.
HISTORY. The site was
occupied from the
Neolithic era, but only
remains of very basic
structures survive from
this and the Early and
Middle Minoan periods.
The structure whose ruins
can still be seen was erected after 1600 BC,
contemporary with the new palace of Phaistos.
From its position on the hill the villa looks over
the most magnificent and luxuriant part of the Messara
plain. Its scale is modest and the plan includes neither
central courtyard nor satellite buildings. The Villa of
Haghia Triada was destroyed in 1450 BC, at around the
same time as the new palaces of Knossos and Phaistos,
and no doubt for the same reason. At the end of the Late
Minoan III period (1200–1100 BC) a plain rectangular
building was constructed on the ruins of
the storerooms: this is the oldest known
example of a megaron, a feature of
mainland Mycenean Greece; its imposing
walls are still visible. The Mycenean colony
of Haghia Triada seems to
have died out during the Greek
Middle Ages. Around the 8th
century BC the site is thought
to have served as a sanctuary
dedicated to Zeus Velkhanos, god
of the willow and the principal
divinity of Phaistos.
THE VILLA OF HAGHIA TRIADA.
The villa occupies the southern part
of the archeological site, where the
various rooms are disposed in a rough reversed L-shape.
The north wing, forming the long side of the "L", was
greatly altered during Mycenean reconstruction. An
area with a central pillar can nonetheless be recognized,
with, some way further on, a royal apartment with its
light-shaft and *polythyron*. At the end of this wing a
staircase leads down to the ancient Phaistos road. At the
foot of this staircase a small wing must have contained
servants' quarters along with sanctuaries; the
southernmost construction has been identified as a
temple dating from the Late Minoan III. A ramp,
known as the "Sea Ramp" with the redans typical
of Minoan architecture, runs along the west wing
and serves the royal apartments.

Ανάκτορο Κνωσού. Η αίθουσα του θρόνου. 1450–1400 π.Χ.
Palace of Knossos. Throne Room. 1450-1400 BC.

ΚΝΩΣΟΣ
KNOSSOS

KN

3537386

ΕΙΣΙΤΗΡΙΟ ΕΙΣΟΔΟΥ
ΕΥΡΩ **6** EURO
ENTRANCE TICKET

It led to a staircase that ascended to the upper terrace. The six doors of the ramp opened into the large vestibule of the royal apartments which was decorated with frescos, some of which are today in the Archeological Museum in Heraklion ▲ *154*. The remains of a light-shaft can be seen at the end of the vestibule, and a room with benches round its walls; the room to the north probably housed the royal archives, as is implied by the clay seals and registers discovered there dating from the time of the town's destruction. Most of the surviving rooms to the south of the royal apartments were shops. The central space between the east and west wings has been called the "altar court" by Italian archeologists after the number of votive objects discovered there: male and female figurines; horses and bulls; the model of a boat. All these Late Minoan objects are on display in the Archeological Museum in Heraklion. From the court can be seen the 14th-century Church of St George ● *104* to the south; inside are original frescos.

THE TOMBS. The ruins of two circular vaulted tombs are situated approximately three hundred yards to the northeast of the site. These resemble the *tholos* (circular) tombs at Mycenae. The first one, to the east, dates from the Pre-palatial, and the second from the Post-palatial period. The Italian archeologists exhumed some five hundred skeletons, together with a variety of valuable funerary offerings now on display in the Museum in Heraklion.

VORI. The site of Vori, just over 3 miles from Haghia Triada, was occupied continuously from the 3rd millennium BC. Previously the main town of the Pirgiotisa district, the present village retains several houses from the 16th to the 19th centuries, along with three churches of 12th-, 16th- and 19th-century origin. Nearby, the 15th-century monastery church of Moni Kardiotisa is remarkable for its architecture and frescos. Vori possesses several artisans' workshops (pottery, weaving and carving) as well as a Museum of Cretan Ethnology, situated in the heart of the old district.

THE SARCOPHAGUS FROM HAGHIA TRIADA
This was found in one of the chambers unearthed to the south of the tombs. Its richly painted decoration dates from the 15th century BC when the Myceneans dominated Minoan Crete.

THE AGORA AT HAGHIA TRIADA
The north side of the site consists of the remains of a village dating from the end of the Minoan period. To the right is an area that corresponds to an agora, the marketplace during the Late Minoan III period, flanked by a portico-fronted row of shops.

18th-century house in Vori.

The Ethnological Museum is a recent foundation created by the Cultural Association of the Messara. It is affiliated to a research center responsible for ethnological study and the systematic acquisition of objects and publications. The exhibition follows the display principles of G.H. Rivière and presents objects from popular culture, mainly from the 18th and 19th centuries. In 1992 the museum received a special nomination from the Council of Europe's awards for the Best European Museum.

A twin-fluted Cretan horn (above). Flutes with mouthpieces (below). These musical instruments are primarily used by mountain folk. The geometric designs are influenced by the Byzantine High Middle Ages.

A gourd for carrying *tsikoudia*, Cretan *eau-de-vie*. It is basically a flask made from raw vegetable matter left to dry in the sun then finely chiseled by the shepherds who will use it.

Cypress planks used on the threshing floor to split ears of corn. Jagged pieces of silex have been thrust into deep grooves. Similar to the Latin *tribulum*, this simple but highly practical tool is found throughout the Mediterranean basin and dates back to Neolithic times.

Shepherds' wooden mugs; highly practical during long periods in the mountains.

EEL POT
Used to trap
the eels that thrive in
Cretan streams. This
one is woven from reeds
and alder twigs.

**LINEN STALK
GRINDER**
An instrument
which enables
fine vegetable
fibers to be
produced for
spinning and
weaving.

Traditional Cretan objects speak of a civilization dating back several millennia, and still very much alive today. Thus many forms of pottery have remained unchanged since the beginning of the 2nd millennium BC. In other traditional crafts such as weaving, ironwork or furniture-making, 11th- and 12th-century Byzantine influences are strongly felt. If the Venetians, and their successors the Turks, left a profound impression on architecture, the popular arts on the other hand reveal a stubborn resistance to foreign influence, and so preserve a truly Cretan heritage. The same may be said for songs, music, dance and social customs.

This pottery hive is used in central Crete. The shape of it has remained unaltered for over 4,000 years. From that distant era until recent times, honey was one of the island's main exports.

DRAGON HEADS
Such motifs decorate a variety of objects. Here they adorn the tips of saber sheaths, but are just as likely to be found decorating the arm of a chair. The motifs are stylized and date back to antiquity.

Oil lamps are still used today in Crete. The flame takes on a sacred significance when lit near an icon.

The locksmith has added a heart to the back of this lock, fixing it to the main pin of the spring; it would have been visible from inside the house.

This pear-shaped handle is influenced by Venetian forms; it is one of the rare examples of Western origin.

CRETAN HOE
An agricultural tool used since the 10th century that remains technologically irreplaceable.

AXE
This piece of iron is an all-purpose axe, just as massive and brutal as its Neolithic or Bronze Age ancestors.

The design of this door handle (above) owes much to Byzantine tradition, and perhaps to even more ancient influences. The intricate pattern is composed of motifs which probably once had a symbolic meaning.

187

▲ South of Heraklion

LEBENA
Black and white mosaic pebble floor from the crypt at the Sanctuary of Asklepios.

MONI VALSAMONERO
This church with three naves is all that remains of the great monastery. The north nave was completed in 1328 and the south nave

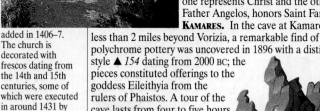

added in 1406–7. The church is decorated with frescos dating from the 14th and 15th centuries, some of which were executed in around 1431 by the Cretan painter Konstantinos Rikos.

ICON FROM MONI VRONDISI
The painter Mikhail Damaskinos ▲ 148 apparently lived in the monastery for a time: it once held six icons by the artist, all dating from between 1579 and 1584. Today they can be seen in St Catherine's Museum in Heraklion. Detail (right) of the "Virgin of the Burning Bush" icon ▲ 149.

THE SOUTH COAST AND THE ROAD TO KAMARES

MATALA. Matala is just over 6 miles southwest of Phaistos. Its magnificent beach is overlooked by sandstone cliffs riddled with caves hollowed out from the rock. The submerged ruins of ancient Matala, Minoan port of Phaistos, then of Gortyn, can still be seen to the northeast of the bay.

THE MONASTERY OF ODIGHITRIA. A road from a ridge on the peninsula leads to the partially walled monastery of Odighitria; its main entrance bears the date 1568. It once possessed five superb icons, two of which are now in St Catherine's Museum, Heraklion ▲ 145. The three *in situ* are by Father Angelos, a Cretan painter of the 15th century.

LENDAS. A road skirts the bay of Kali Limenes to Lendas. The village is situated close to the Lebena site, where the Sanctuary of Asklepios was built in the 3rd century BC. The ruins lie in a half-moon shape: to the east, two columns flank an altar; to the north, a marble flight of steps leads to a crypt, with an arch and a nymphaeum nearby. On the way back to Heraklion, a detour west toward Kamares is recommended.

THE MONASTERY OF VRONDISI. The mural paintings attest to its 14th-century origins. At the end of the Venetian period the monastery was famous for its school of painting and the erudition of its monks. Outside, note the splendid Venetian fountain decorated with sculpted figures of Adam and Eve. The *katholikon* is decorated with frescos dating from the first half of the 15th century.

THE MONASTERY OF VALSAMONERO ★. A road some 3 miles further along leads to Moni Valsamonero. Other than its frescos, the church has two fine icons: one represents Christ and the other, by Father Angelos, honors Saint Fanourios.

KAMARES. In the cave at Kamares, less than 2 miles beyond Vorizia, a remarkable find of polychrome pottery was uncovered in 1896 with a distinctive style ▲ 154 dating from 2000 BC; the pieces constituted offerings to the goddess Eileithyia from the rulers of Phaistos. A tour of the cave lasts from four to five hours and requires the accompaniment of a guide.

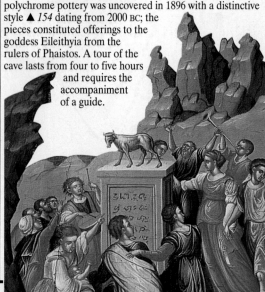

From Heraklion to Haghios Nikolaos

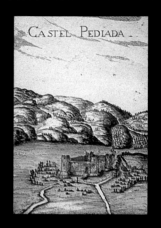

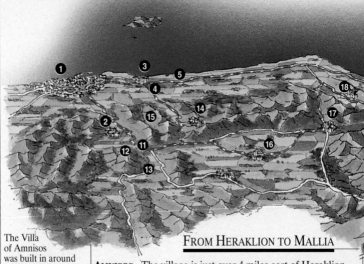

1. HERAKLION
2. KNOSSOS
3. AMNISOS
4. EILEITHYIA
5. NIROU KHANI
6. MALLIA
7. LATSIDA
8. VOULISMENI

The Villa of Amnisos was built in around 1600 BC and was destroyed by a fire in 1450 BC. It is known as the House of the Lilies from the frescos ▲ *158* that once decorated its walls; today these are displayed in the Museum at Heraklion, along with the two life-sized stone eagles that stood each side of the altar in the Sanctuary of Zeus.

This Neolithic figurine represents Eileithyia, daughter of Zeus and Hera and mother of Eros. The first objects were discovered in the cave in 1884 during excavation by J. Hatzidakis.

FROM HERAKLION TO MALLIA

AMNISOS. The village is just over 4 miles east of Heraklion and has a fine beach. Two interesting archeological sites are situated close by: a Minoan villa ● *94*, at the base of the hill, and an Archaic sanctuary to the northwest of it. The villa site, facing the sea, is fenced off, but sufficiently compact to be surveyed from outside the perimeter. The

Archaic sanctuary consists of a large, circular, open-air altar, dating from the 6th century BC and dedicated to Zeus Thenatas. The enormous blocks used in the foundation wall were taken from a Late Bronze Age building.

THE EILEITHYIA CAVE. Also called *Neraidaspilios* (the "Nymph grotto"), the cave is situated on the other side of the highway. It is closed to the public but a key can be obtained from the guardian at the site of Nirou Khani, some 3 miles away. The sloping entrance leads to a stalagmite whose mounded shape could be thought to bear some resemblance to the belly of a pregnant woman. The votive objects unearthed (displayed in the Archeological Museum of Heraklion) indicate that the sanctuary was dedicated to Eileithyia, the goddess of childbirth, worshiped from 3000 BC until the early Christian era.

NIROU KHANI. The site is closed to the public but can nonetheless be viewed from the exterior. In 1918 the archeologist Xanthoudides unearthed a villa covering an area of 850 square yards, probably from Late Minoan I (1550 BC). The surviving ground floor includes some forty rooms. The main entrance was through the east court where "horns of consecration" were found. The south court seems to have formed a cloister at the heart of

Four days

the residential apartments. The room of the double axes to the west no doubt constituted the main sanctuary; several of these sacred weapons were found there. In the northwest room several steatite lamps were discovered. The banquet hall, to the north, was decorated with frescos. In the northeast room, containing three altars, symbolic sacrifices were offered to the gods.

SKOTINO. The name of the hamlet of Skotino, 2½ miles to the south of the main road, means "dark" and refers to the cave used as a religious sanctuary between Middle Minoan I and the Roman period. In it the archeologist Davaras found bone needles and three bronze votive statuettes from Late Minoan I, now in the Archeological Museum of Heraklion ▲ 156. At the entrance stands a 17th-century chapel alongside the ruins of an older one.

MALLIA. The Bay of Khersonisos offers a succession of fine sandy beaches as far as Mallia, where the village dates back to Venetian times when it was known as "Villa de Maglia". Its church, dedicated to the Panaghia, dates from the same period: two icons bear the date 1495.

Limin Khersonisou occupies a section of the ancient site of Khersonisos, the port for Lyttos during Minoan times. It remained important until the early Byzantine era. The remains of two moles of the Roman harbor are still visible.

▲ THE PALACE OF MALLIA

The site was occupied from Neolithic times. A first palace was built in around 1900 BC, roughly contemporary with those at Knossos and Phaistos. Like them, it was destroyed in around 1700 BC. A second palace was erected at the same site soon after; this stood until 1450 BC. It was based on a relatively straightforward plan and built with local materials (limestone and sandstone). The remains that can be seen today are predominantly those of the Neo-palatial structure. It is thought that a part of the site was reoccupied during Late Minoan III.

THE SOUTH WING
The tour of the palace begins in the west court (1), across which runs a raised, paved path that would have served as a processional way. To the right are a series of storerooms. In the corner are four enormous grain silos in two rows (2).

ROYAL APARTMENTS (4)
A long corridor (3) leads to a labyrinth of rooms. In the center stands the Megaron (5); this was accessible on three sides through *polythyra* (walls pierced with openings). To the left is a room with a central pillar (6) whose base is still visible. A staircase leads down to a lustral basin (7) ● 89 preceded by an antechamber (8). The Queen's Megaron connects with that of the King's, where the east wall gave onto a light-shaft (10).

occupies the east corner. Just before the north court (14) is an "oblique" structure (13), standing at an angle; this was perhaps a Mycenean sanctuary. The northeast court is surrounded by stores and workshops (15) to the west, north and east, where supplies of grain and olive oil were stored in giant *pithoi*. To the left of the keep court is a corridor running alongside a hypostyle hall (16) ● 88. Flanked

by an antechamber with a central column, this contains two asymmetrical rows of six pillars, of which only the bases survive. The function of this room is not precisely known; it was possibly the palace kitchen, with a banquet hall on the floor directly above it.

THE CENTRAL COURT
In front of this hall, at the north end of the central court (18), columns supported a portico (17).

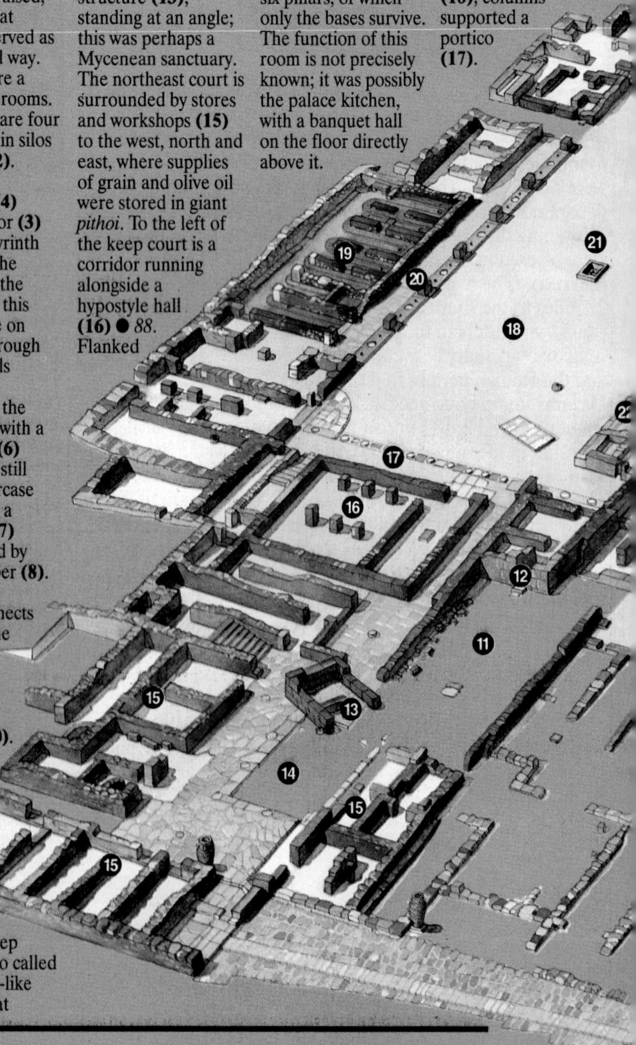

THE NORTH WING. The keep court (11) is so called after the keep-like tower (12) that

RECONSTRUCTION OF THE PALACE
The central courtyard, light-shafts, lustral basin, storerooms and so on form a series of asymmetrical blocks, cubes and rectangles.

THE EAST WING

This houses the storerooms; the six compartments (**19**) contain a system of channels designed to collect spilt liquid. The east side of the central court also had a portico, consisting of alternating columns and pillars (**20**); the portico and arcade no doubt supported an identical upper-story colonnade. The holes between the columns and pillars suggest that the court would have been fenced off to protect the crowd during contests. The court (**18**) measures 52 yards long by 25 yards wide. In its exact center is a mysterious altar-pit (**21**) where animals may have been sacrificed during religious rites.

THE LOGGIA

The raised platform flanked by two columns, known as the "loggia", appears to have been the throne room (**22**). Behind it a staircase leads down to the "Treasury" (**23**), a two-columned room where an ax in the shape of a leopard was discovered. Beyond the grand staircase that led to the upper story (**24**) is a paved crypt (**25**): in it, double axes and other sacred symbols are carved on two large pillars; coupled with the animal bones, the evidence appears to indicate that sacrificial rites took place here. A large room (**26**) is situated opposite the courtyard altar; it has a portico and light-shaft and was probably an important cult area. The steps of the monumental staircase (**27**), of which four remain, would have been used as tiered seats. Slightly above the level of the court is the celebrated *kernos* or cupped stone (**28**), a unique object. The large round stone measures 35½ inches in diameter, with a central hollow surrounded by thirty-four smaller ones; it was designed to receive *panspermia*, the harvested first fruits offered to the goddess of fertility. Further rooms on the west side of the court constitute the south sanctuary (**29**). Workshops (**30**) are situated to the east of the south entrance.

▲ THE PALACE OF MALLIA

Mythology links the site of Mallia with
Sarpedon who was king of the region,
son of Zeus and Europa, and younger
brother of Minos. In 1915 the archeologist
Joseph Hatzidakis began excavations; at
this time, traces of buildings were only
just noticeable as shallow outcrops
overlooking the plain. The French School
of Athens took over in 1922; since then it
has systematically explored the palace,
the surrounding town and the burial ground
known as Khrysolakkos.

ROYAL ACROBAT SWORD
The engraved gold-leafed
disk (above, right) of the
handle carries the image
of an acrobat bent
double, his
head arched
back to touch
his feet.
This sword
dates from
the end
of the
Proto-palatial
period. Today
it is displayed in
the Archeological
Museum of
Heraklion ▲ *154*.

THRESHOLD. This is a
characteristic feature of Minoan
architecture ● *90*.

THE WEST COURT
This paved esplanade **(1)** is crossed
by a "processional" way, also paved,
which is slightly raised and runs
almost parallel to the monumental
west or main façade of the two-story
palace. Entrance to the Palace of
Mallia is via this large, irregularly
shaped area.

**CORRIDOR OF
THE WEST STOREROOMS**
This long corridor **(3)**, open to the sky,
was originally split into two sections by a
dividing wall. It leads to a cluster of nine
storerooms, arranged in rows.

The meaning of these signs incised in stone has yet to be deciphered; they may be masons' marks, religious symbols or even some sort of early written script.

The excavations at Mallia unearthed a rich trove of objects. Notable among these is the well-known bee pendant ● *46*, the most remarkable of all Minoan jewels, and the triton shell ▲ *202*. Above, four earthenware cups dating from the Neo-palatial period.

ROYAL AXE IN THE SHAPE OF A LEOPARD
This schist object dates from 1650 BC. It is displayed in the Museum at Heraklion. Minoan art has left us numerous images of animals and birds. Its artists knew how to capture the effect of movement with their remarkable aptitude for "photographing" nature, particularly wild beasts and their habitat; bestiaries of exotic animals: lions, boars, bulls, deer, crocodiles and antelopes; as well as strange hybrids or fantastic creatures.

THE DRIROS TRIAD
This group of three statuettes, known as the Driros triad, dates from the 7th century BC and is thought to represent Leto and her two children, Apollo and Artemis. They constitute the oldest sculptures of hammered bronze to have been discovered in Greece (Archeological Museum of Heraklion ▲ 154).

THE MIRABELLO DISTRICT

Beyond Mallia the main road heads inland through the gorge of Vrakhasi. Leave the highway to join the old road to Haghios Nikolaos; this leads to Vrakhasion and the lush Mirabello valley. The villages of Latsida, Voulismeni and Neapolis follow. Latsida possesses two old chapels of the Venetian period: the Panaghia Keragonitissa and Haghia Paraskevi, both of which are decorated with 14th- and 15th-century frescos.

DRIROS. The site of ancient Driros is situated just under 2 miles to the northeast of the main road on the summit of St Anthony's hill, whose two crests mark the acropoli. The city developed on a site occupied from the Archaic period. It retained its influence until 220 BC when political conflict split its inhabitants and led to its destruction at the hands of enemies. The oldest and most significant monument to survive is the temple of the Delphinian Apollo, or Apollo Delphinios ● 97, dating from the 7th century BC. Still in place behind a central hearth inside the sanctuary, which measures some 8 yards long by 5 yards wide, are a table for offerings, a ledge for votive objects and a stone altar in the form of a box in which goats' horns have been found. The Delphinian Apollo was celebrated in the form of a dolphin (*delphin* in Greek), a guise adopted by the god to guide Greek sailors toward new colonies. The ruins of a second, Classical temple (490–323 BC) were incorporated by the Venetians into the Catholic church of St Anthony (Haghio Antonios). Driros lies just over 10 miles from Haghios Nikolaos.

FROM HERAKLION TO LASSITHI

ARKHANES JEWELRY
Burial grounds dating from 2500 to 1250 BC have been unearthed on the hill at Phourni. Many of these tombs contained grave-gifts of jewelry in gold, glass or semi-precious stones. Crete was not rich in gold and solid gold jewels are a rarity. The sheer elegance, delicacy and harmonious play of colors make these pieces masterworks of their kind. These examples are made of sard, a brown type of chalcedony.

ARKHANES ★. The road from Knossos leads to Arkhanes, some 9 miles south of Heraklion: the church of Haghia Triada retains its early 14th-century frescos, while the church of the Panaghia ● 101 possesses some Byzantine icons. A well-preserved Minoan palace dating from 1600 BC has been partially excavated on the site of the village; no doubt this was a summer palace for the kings of Phaistos. With the help of the guardian it is possible to see the floors of the two superb paved rooms to the northwest of the excavation area. On the hill at Phourni just over a mile away, remains of a Minoan necropolis have been discovered: *tholos* tombs dating from the Pre-palatial and Proto-palatial periods; funerary structures, one of them based on an absidal plan and containing nearly two hundred sepulchres; and, for the first time in Crete, a Mycenean grave-circle with six burial shafts.

MOUNT JUCHTAS. A dirt track between Arkhanes and Vathipetro leads to the top of Mount Juchtas, a distance of 2 miles. The accompaniment of a guide is advisable for any exploration of the caves; the view from the summit is quite superb. The site of Vathipetro is 2½ miles south of Arkhanes; here the archeologist Spyridon Marinatos exposed the ruins of a 6th-century BC Minoan villa ● *94*. At Anemospilia on the north slope of the hill, the Sakellaraki archeologists discovered the ruins of a three-roomed Minoan sanctuary ● *95*, whose contents hinted at bloodthirsty goings-on. On an altar was discovered the skeleton of a young man with a bronze sword planted in his chest. The same room contained two other skeletons. The finds may well indicate that the Minoans engaged in human sacrifice; such interpretations remain controversial.

MONI AGARATHOS. On the way to the monastery of Agarathos a byroad offers a detour via the village of Mirtia, where a museum is dedicated to Kazantzaki ▲ *146*. The oldest reference to Moni Agarathos is contained in a document of 1520, now in the Bodleian Library in Oxford. The monastery was an important seat of learning in the last century of Venetian domination. The village of Thrapsano ● *76*, 3 miles to the south, is renowned for its potters who still employ age-old techniques.

MONI GOUVERNIOTISSA ★. Two and a half miles to the east, beyond Kastelli and the River Langada, the old monastery of Gouverniotissa nestles among olive groves, cypresses and carob trees. It was founded in the reign of Nikephoros II Phokas (963–9) and retains its 14th-century frescos, some of which were damaged at the end of World War Two. The church once housed 16th- and 17th-century icons, now displayed in the Historical Museum in Heraklion ▲ *152*.

AVDOU. In the village of Avdou, 3 miles beyond, all four churches date from the 14th and 15th centuries and all are decorated with mural paintings. Those of Haghios Konstantinos were painted in 1445 by the brothers Manuel and Ioannis Phokas, who probably also executed the paintings in Haghios Georgios. Not far from Avdou are two caves, that of Haghia Photini and that of Phaneromeni, in which Marinatos discovered objects of Archaic origins.

MONI KERA KARDIOTISSA. Beyond the village of Gonies the road winds uphill toward the Lassithi plateau. Between the villages of Krasi and Kera stands the monastery of Kera Kardiotissa, at a height of 2,067 feet on the wooded slope of Mount Dikte and yielding splendid views. The exact date of its foundation is unknown although it certainly stood during the second Byzantine period (961–1204). It contains a copy of its famous icon of the Kardiotissa (now in Rome), executed during the 16th century. Restoration work begun in 1970 under the direction of Manolis Borboudakis has revealed important wall paintings from the Byzantine renaissance in the *katholikon* of the monastery.

The workshops in the village of Thrapsano display fine examples of Cretan pottery.

THE KAZANTZAKI MUSEUM, MIRTIA ★ The Museum (left) celebrates the life of Nikos Kazantzaki and contains original editions of his books, sets and costumes from his plays and many of his personal belongings.

ICON OF THE VIRGIN OF MONI KERA KARDIOTISSA This monastery is dedicated to the Nativity of the Virgin.

PANAGHIA ORPHANIS This icon, dated 1650, is one of the treasures of Moni Agarathos, which include the superb 17th- and 18th-century altar lamps adorning its church.

LIBATION VASE FROM MOUNT KARPHI
This unusual rhyton, shaped as a cart drawn by oxen represented only by their heads, dates from the 11th century BC. Its geometric style and cylindrical garments are characteristic of the end of the Sub-Minoan period.

Below, entrance to the Cave of Zeus.

THE WINDMILLS
There were at one time around 10,000 windmills ensuring the supply of water, but many have since been replaced by motorized pumps. Yet enough old examples with sails remain ● *110* to justify Lassithi's nickname, "Plain of the Windmills".

6th-century BC statuette representing Zeus.

MOUNT KARPHI. Beyond Kera the road continues to wind upward toward the Lassithi plateau. Past the village Mount Karphi looms into view in the east, where in 1934 John Pendlebury unearthed a Post-Minoan sanctuary and tomb. These discoveries revealed that after the collapse of the Minoan civilization the inhabitants of towns such as Knossos and Phaistos took refuge in the mountains of Karphi and Patela, near Haghia Varvara, where they were better able to defend themselves from the invaders of Crete. The road climbs up to the Ampelos pass from which, at an altitude of nearly 3,000 feet, rows of windmills can be seen scattered across the north slope. On a clear day the view is magnificent and stretches right along the coast from Heraklion to the bay of Mirabello and Haghios Nikolaos. Beyond the Ampelos pass the road opens out into the Lassithi plateau.

THE LASSITHI PLATEAU

This vast undulating plain is some 2,790 feet above sea level; it stretches approximately 7 miles from east to west and nearly 4 miles from north to south. The chain of mountains round it forms a natural barrier punctuated by just nine passes.
HISTORY. The earliest traces of occupation were found in the Trapeza Cave: it appears that the site was occupied up until

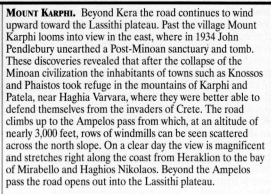

Middle Minoan I (1950–1850 BC), when the dwellings were transformed into tombs and the cave turned into a sanctuary. The plain itself seems to have been inhabited around 1760–1550 BC when troglodite dwellers left the caves to settle there.
FROM LAGOU TO PSYKHRO. The road winding around the high plain links sixteen villages: the Trapeza Cave is to the east of Tzermiado; at Marmaketo, a group of farm buildings has been converted into an ethnological museum; a short distance before Mesa Lassithi a road leads up to the Kroustalenia monastery, which stands on a superb site.
THE CAVE OF ZEUS. The village of Psykhro, situated to the southwest, is the departure point for excursions to the cave which, according to mythology, was the birthplace of Zeus ▲ *226*.
It was discovered by local people and later explored by the archeologists Hatzidakis and Halbherr, then by Arthur Evans, and between 1899 and 1900 by D. G. Hogarth, who discovered traces of human occupation from the Middle Minoan to the Archaic period. More recent excavations have established that it was reoccupied during the Greco-Roman era. Today it is thought that the cave was originally a sanctuary dedicated to the Minoan mother-goddess, and that the cult of Zeus Dikteon was introduced only after the arrival of the Myceneans toward the end of the Bronze Age. Leaving the plateau at the village of Mesa Lassithi, take the road toward Haghios Nikolaos.

HAGHIOS NIKOLAOS
AND SURROUNDINGS

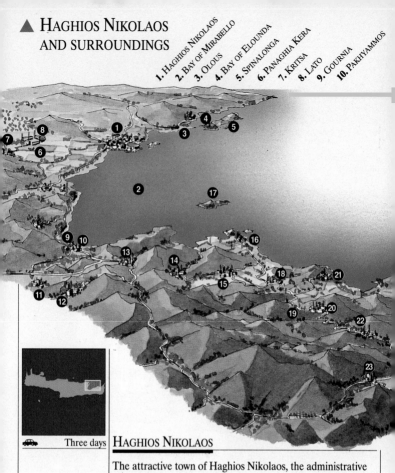

Three days

HAGHIOS NIKOLAOS

HAGHIOS NIKOLAOS
It was not until the 1960's that this peaceful little port began to attract foreign tourists in increasing numbers, transforming itself into a charming seaside resort; its numerous beaches extend along the west side of the bay of Mirabello. Today the town has one of the most efficiently developed tourist infrastructures. The picturesque heart of Haghios Nikolaos is centered around the quayside and tiny Voulismeni lake with its attractive canal and picturesque harbor.

The attractive town of Haghios Nikolaos, the administrative seat of the Lassithi province, is situated on the west side of the bay of Mirabello. Its origins go way back to a period when it was the port of ancient Lato Etera. Its present name dates from the Byzantine era and derives from a contemporary chapel dedicated to Saint Nicolas, erected to the north of the town on the road to Elounda. Under Venetian occupation the fishing village of Haghios Nikolaos really developed. This was when the name "Porto di San Nicolo" was adopted; the harbor, however, was known as "Mandragio", or "Mandraki" in Greek. Up on the hill, on the site of a Doric acropolis, the Venetians built a fort from which they dominated the entire bay and its "Mirabello", or "Lovely View".

THE FORTRESS OF MIRABELLO. The regional administrative offices today occupy the site of the Venetian fortress of Mirabello, from which both bay and region derive their name. The building suffered serious earthquake damage in 1303 only to be reduced to ruins by the Venetian–Turkish conflicts, then subsequently abandoned. Parts of the building were still intact at the end of the Turkish occupation, but not a trace of it remains today.

LAKE VOULISMENI. This lake is the main tourist feature of Haghios Nikolaos; around it is a string of cafés, restaurants and souvenir shops. The lake is linked to the harbor by a canal, dug in 1870, that is crossed by a small bridge. This sheltered stretch of water provides a mooring for small boats. Captain Spratt, visiting Haghios Nikolaos five years before the canal was cut through, described the lake in these terms: "To the east of the cove known as the 'Mandragio' of San Nicolo lies a round pond of briny water some 150 yards across and barely 20 yards from the sea. Yet this pond is 210 feet deep in its center, a depth only reached by the sea some 2 or 3 miles from port. Local tradition has it that the pond is fathomless and links up with the nether worlds of lost spirits. The sides of the basin must drop straight down, like a funnel, beneath the water. However, there is no indication that this is a volcano chimney or even the result of volcanic activity, as no igneous rock has been discovered in the surrounding area. Yet since a small stream appears to run from it toward the sea, I would rather imagine that this is the ancient mouth of a major spring or some underground river which, coming down from the mountains, would have found an outlet here."

THE ANCIENT HARBOR. The promontory enclosing the south end of the harbor was originally the port of the ancient city of Lato, situated 3 miles to the west of Haghios Nikolaos. Virtually nothing remains of it today, other than the odd crumbling ruin.

The village of Haghios Nikolaos is superbly positioned on one of the most beautiful bays of the island. Slopes planted with olive and almond trees surround the town, which is often described as the "St Tropez of Crete". But when the town's lively atmosphere seems too much, there is always the ready option of a trip to one of the natural or archeological sites close by.

THE FORTRESS OF MIRABELLO
This was built in 1206 by Enrico Pescatore, a Genoese adventurer and Count of Malta who reigned over Crete for six years before being overthrown by the Venetians in 1212.

201

Skull adorned with a wreath of golden olive leaves (1st century AD).

TRITON SHELL
Some thirty shells 12 inches long have so far been found, dating from between the 18th and 15th centuries BC. The Mallia triton (LM I), made of chlorite schist, is exceptionally beautiful with its delicate relief carvings.

THE ARCHEOLOGICAL MUSEUM ★. The museum was founded in 1970 and is second in Crete only to that of Heraklion. It stands on Konstantinou Paleologou street, which begins at the canal and is the main road out of town. Seven rooms contain recent finds from archeological sites in eastern Crete, dating from the Neolithic to the end of the Greco-Roman era. An eighth room contains exhibits that illustrate the folklore and traditional crafts of eastern Crete up to recent times.

ELOUNDA AND SPINALONGA

OLOUS. From the corniche road following the bay of Mirabello to the north, the island of Spinalonga comes into view. It was previously a peninsula but the Perou canal, cut through at the end of the last century, now parts it from the shore. The large island runs parallel to the coast for about 2 miles, creating a kind of narrow bay. The site of Olous, the ancient harbor of Driros, stands at the isthmus. In ancient times subsidence caused the flooding of a large part of the city; the neck of land sank and was reduced to its present size. In calm weather the remains of the harbor can still be seen in the shallows, while a few ruins are visible on the isthmus and surrounding area. The principal remains can be found at a site some 100 yards from the shore, where archeologists have unearthed a former Byzantine basilica with a mosaic floor depicting maritime scenes.

THE ISLAND OF SPINALONGA ★. In ancient times, a fortress erected on the islet of Kalidona-Spinalonga guarded the entrance to the harbor of Olous. This was still

The Bay of Elounda.

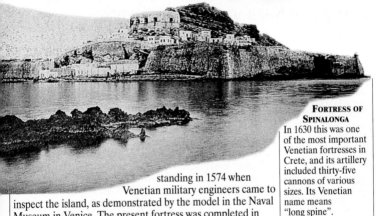

standing in 1574 when Venetian military engineers came to inspect the island, as demonstrated by the model in the Naval Museum in Venice. The present fortress was completed in 1579 under the governor-general, Jacopo Foscarini. The island was so well defended that it withstood all Turkish raids until 1715, despite the otherwise complete Turkish victory over Crete in 1669. A village existed in the shadow of the fortress until, in 1903, the Cretan authorities decided to found a leper colony on the islet. The ghostly remains of the village can be seen within the fort's ramparts.

ELOUNDA. One of the most famous beaches in Crete stretches out opposite the island at the fishing village of Elounda, now a hugely popular tourist base. Near the Minos Palace Hotel stands a Byzantine church dedicated to Saint Nicolas; keys to it can be obtained from the tourist office in Haghios Nikolaos, which takes its name from the saint. It is tentatively dated to the beginning of the Second Byzantine era, no doubt shortly after Nikephoros Phokas recaptured Crete from the Saracens in 961. Restoration work undertaken in 1968 uncovered frescos dating from the late 10th or early 11th century, along with 14th-century mural paintings that include a Pantocrator, or Christ in Glory, in the dome of the church.

THE PANAGHIA KERA ★

The lovely Church of the Panaghia Kera ● *100* is situated some 6 miles to the west of Haghios Nikolaos on the road to Kritsa. This domed church, dedicated to the Assumption of the Virgin, was founded in the 13th century and comprises three naves. Its plan is almost cruciform, with three semicircular apses forming the east end of the nave and side aisles. Originally the building consisted only of the larger, central nave surmounted by a cupola resting on four pillars and a high cylindrical drum, characteristic of late Byzantine churches. The south aisle, dedicated to Saint Anne, the mother of the Virgin, was added at the beginning of the 14th century; the north aisle, dedicated to Saint Anthony, was completed towards the middle of the same century. The mural paintings, no doubt the work of local artists, are contemporaneous with the three stages of the church's construction.

FORTRESS OF SPINALONGA
In 1630 this was one of the most important Venetian fortresses in Crete, and its artillery included thirty-five cannons of various sizes. Its Venetian name means "long spine".

PANAGHIA KERA
From the exterior the three apsidal windows constitute the most elaborate feature. They are very narrow and let in very little light.

THE FRESCOS OF THE PANAGHIA KERA
The decoration traces the art of fresco painting from the primitive type of the early nave to the "renascent" style of the north and south aisles. Elements of landscape and everyday objects increasingly feature, producing scenes of greater realism and visual depth.

203

WEAVING AT KRITSA
The village of Kritsa is renowned for its traditional woven textiles, which the villagers lay out for sale on their doorsteps.

KRITSA ★ AND SURROUNDINGS. To the southwest of the Panaghia Kera the charming village of Kritsa perches at an altitude of 984 feet on a slope of Mount Dikte (Oros Dikti), amid olive groves and carob trees. Four Byzantine churches with 14th-century frescos are situated in the vicinity; the frescos in the chapel of Haghios Ioannis are dated 1370 by a dedicatory inscription, while those in Haghios Konstantinos are dated 1354–5. Down the Kroustas road, at the head of the valley, stands the church of Haghios Ioannis Theologos, or St John the Evangelist; this was once part of the monastery of Toplou and was erected during the Second Byzantine period. The iconostases of the naves are particularly beautiful.

LATO ★

Just over one mile to the north of the Panaghia Kera, a dirt road leads off to the site of ancient Lato, a distance of 2½ miles. Lato's origins probably date back to the time of the Dorian invasions; it became the main town of the region during the Archaic period (7th century BC) and flourished in the Classical and Hellenistic periods. Its port, Lato Pros Kamara, lay at the southern point of present-day Haghios Nikolaos.

GOURNIA

The Minoan site of Gournia ● *92* is 12 miles from Haghios Nikolaos. The excavations carried out between 1901 and 1904 by Harriet Boyd-Hawes revealed that the site was inhabited from the beginning of the 2nd millennium BC. The town was prosperous, apparently due to its agriculture, stock and crafts, and survived until 1450 BC when it seems to have been destroyed by the same event that wiped out Knossos and other major centers. It is spread across the slopes of a hill; from the summit, paved roads radiated out from a long courtyard that flanked what may have been a small palace. Gournia may have been recolonized between the years 1300 and 1200 BC. This must have been a small settlement, whose inhabitants simply occupied the ruins of the Minoan city. Gournia did not survive the Bronze Age, and gradually faded into oblivion. It is not mentioned in any ancient text and its Minoan name is not known. The present name derives from the small stone drinking troughs known as *gournes* that have been discovered in front of most of its houses.

THE SITE OF LATO
The ruins are spread across the slopes of a hill, on top of which are two acropolis peaks that offer a splendid view. The most interesting part of the site centers around the agora, which was considered by R. E. Wycherley to be a prime example of an Archaic Greek city agora with strong Minoan influences. Arranged around this irregularly shaped area can be seen: a 3rd-century public building, or *prytaneion*, ● *97*; a colonnaded building, or stoa; a monumental niche, or exedra; a sanctuary; a round stone, possibly a threshing floor; and a broad flight of steps leading to a theater, where two stumps of columns are still standing.

EASTERN CRETE

1. HAGHIOS NIKOLAOS
2. PAKHYAMMOS
3. KAVOUSI
4. PSEIRA
5. MOKHLOS
6. TOURLOTI

Four days

PSEIRA AND MOKHLOS
Above, marine-style vase from Pseira (Archeological Museum of Haghios Nikolaos). Right, bull-shaped rhyton (Archeological Museum of Heraklion) ▲ 152 from the islet of Mokhlos (below).

SITIA
The brightly colored houses rise in tiers up the slopes of the hill of Kastro.

FROM PAKHYAMMOS TO SITIA

The road from Pakhyammos to Sitia passes close by a number of archeological sites. Close to Kavousi, on the Vronda ridge, a village dating from between 1200 and 875 BC has been excavated. On the islets of Pseira and Mokhlos in 1908, Richard Seager discovered the remains of villages that were occupied during all three Minoan periods. Just under 4 miles after Kavousi, a superb view of the Bay of Mirabello opens out; the road then climbs up through cypresses to Tourloti, a hamlet of Venetian origins. Three sites in the vicinity have been found: a Post-Minoan village on the Kastri hill; Late Minoan III tombs to the northeast of Mirsini; and burial chambers from the Post-palatial period on the Aspropilia hill. The objects found at these sites have joined the collections in the Archeological Museums at Haghios Nikolaos ▲ 202 and Sitia. Before long the main road reaches the villages of Mesa Mouliana and Exo Mouliana, nestling at the foot of a valley whose vineyards produce a highly regarded wine. Not far from Mesa Mouliana, in 1903, Xanthoudides discovered important funerary objects from the Mycenean and Geometric periods. The church of Haghia Triada at Mesa Mouliana and the chapel of Haghios Georgios at Exo Mouliana both contain fresco decoration from the Venetian period and are worth a detour.

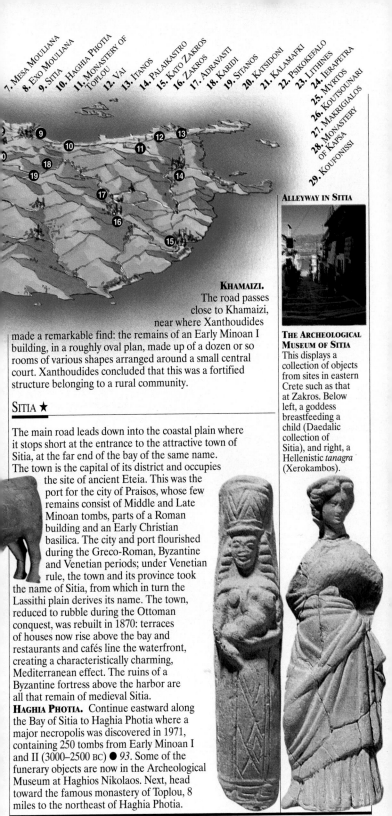

7. Mesa Mouliana
8. Exo Mouliana
9. Sitia
10. Haghia Photia
11. Monastery of Toplou
12. Vai
13. Itanos
14. Palaikastro
15. Kato Zakros
16. Zakros
17. Adravasti
18. Karidi
19. Sitanos
20. Katsidoni
21. Kalamafki
22. Psikokefalo
23. Lithines
24. Ierapetra
25. Myrtos
26. Koutsounari
27. Koutsigialos
28. Makrigialos
29. Monastery of Kapsa
30. Koufonissi

ALLEYWAY IN SITIA

THE ARCHEOLOGICAL MUSEUM OF SITIA
This displays a collection of objects from sites in eastern Crete such as that at Zakros. Below left, a goddess breastfeeding a child (Daedalic collection of Sitia), and right, a Hellenistic *tanagra* (Xerokambos).

KHAMAIZI.
The road passes close to Khamaizi, near where Xanthoudides made a remarkable find: the remains of an Early Minoan I building, in a roughly oval plan, made up of a dozen or so rooms of various shapes arranged around a small central court. Xanthoudides concluded that this was a fortified structure belonging to a rural community.

SITIA ★

The main road leads down into the coastal plain where it stops short at the entrance to the attractive town of Sitia, at the far end of the bay of the same name. The town is the capital of its district and occupies the site of ancient Eteia. This was the port for the city of Praisos, whose few remains consist of Middle and Late Minoan tombs, parts of a Roman building and an Early Christian basilica. The city and port flourished during the Greco-Roman, Byzantine and Venetian periods; under Venetian rule, the town and its province took the name of Sitia, from which in turn the Lassithi plain derives its name. The town, reduced to rubble during the Ottoman conquest, was rebuilt in 1870: terraces of houses now rise above the bay and restaurants and cafés line the waterfront, creating a characteristically charming, Mediterranean effect. The ruins of a Byzantine fortress above the harbor are all that remain of medieval Sitia.

HAGHIA PHOTIA. Continue eastward along the Bay of Sitia to Haghia Photia where a major necropolis was discovered in 1971, containing 250 tombs from Early Minoan I and II (3000–2500 BC) ● 93. Some of the funerary objects are now in the Archeological Museum at Haghios Nikolaos. Next, head toward the famous monastery of Toplou, 8 miles to the northeast of Haghia Photia.

207

The icon entitled "Megas ei Kyrie", "Lord Thou Art Great", is a major work by the Cretan painter I. Kornaros (1745–96) and dates from 1770. It measures some 52 by 33 inches, and includes several hundred figures in its sixty-one small scenes, each of which is labeled with a verse from the Epiphany prayer that the work illustrates. This post-Byzantine icon belongs to a tradition dating from the time of the Paleologi, yet is enriched by motifs of Renaissance origin. Recent restoration work has done full justice to the brilliance and subtle contrasts of the colors.

"CROSSING THE JORDAN WITH THE ARK OF THE COVENANT"

The Hebrews walk across the River Jordan, led by Joshua dressed as a Byzantine general. The priests carry the Ark of the Covenant containing the Tablets of the Law. Behind the mountain stands the city of Jericho.

"THE CREATION"

To the left is a figure representing one of the four elements of the Creation: that of light, symbolized by fire. In the center, God the Father pronounces the words of Genesis: "Let the waters under the heaven be gathered together unto one place".

"THE HOLY TRINITY IN MAJESTY"

A seated old man represents the Father, a younger man, the Son; the dove symbolizes the Holy Ghost and a globe, the Earth. The hierarchy of angels encircles them: archangels, angels, seraphim, cherubim and so on.

"JONAS SPEWED FROM THE WHALE'S BELLY"

Jonas, who refuses to obey the Word of God commanding him to go to Nineveh, falls into the water and is swallowed by a whale. Three days later he is spewed up onto the shore of Nineveh, represented here at the left.

"THE WORK OF IOANNIS KORNAROS, TWENTY-FIVE YEARS OF AGE, THANKS TO THE MOST REVEREND HIGOUMENE PARTHENIOS, MONK, KNOWN AS KAPHOUROS, IN THE FIFTH YEAR OF HIS OFFICE, 1770."

INSCRIPTION

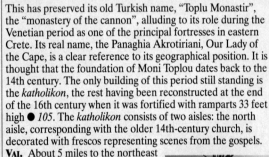

MONI TOPLOU
Three inscriptions are set into the façade of the church. One slab is part of the so-called Arbitration of Magnesia that relates how, in the 2nd century BC, Itanos fought with Ierapytna, modern Ierapetra, over control of the Temple of Diktean Zeus.

Above, coin of Itanos; below, the Bay of Itanos.

MONI TOPLOU ★

This has preserved its old Turkish name, "Toplu Monastir", the "monastery of the cannon", alluding to its role during the Venetian period as one of the principal fortresses in eastern Crete. Its real name, the Panaghia Akrotiriani, Our Lady of the Cape, is a clear reference to its geographical position. It is thought that the foundation of Moni Toplou dates back to the 14th century. The only building of this period still standing is the *katholikon*, the rest having been reconstructed at the end of the 16th century when it was fortified with ramparts 33 feet high ● *105*. The *katholikon* consists of two aisles: the north aisle, corresponding with the older 14th-century church, is decorated with frescos representing scenes from the gospels.

VAI. About 5 miles to the northeast of Moni Toplou is one of the finest stretches of beach in the whole of Crete; its powdery sand, tinged with pink, is fringed by a palm grove. The palm trees, *Phoenix Theophrastii*, are related to the date palm and were first described by the founder of botany, Theophrastus (370–288 BC), after whom they are named.

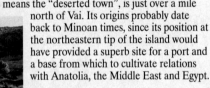

ITANOS. The site of ancient Itanos, whose Greek name of Erimoupolis means the "deserted town", is just over a mile north of Vai. Its origins probably date back to Minoan times, since its position at the northeastern tip of the island would have provided a superb site for a port and a base from which to cultivate relations with Anatolia, the Middle East and Egypt.

PALAIKASTRO

PALAIKASTRO
This superb site is right next to the sea.

Returning to Vai, continue directly toward Palaikastro, 5 miles to the southeast.

THE SITE OF PALAIKASTRO. The site is just a mile from the village of Palaikastro, on the Bay of Grandes. It was first investigated between 1902 and 1904 by R. C. Bosanquet of the British School, who unearthed a large Minoan village and the ruins of a sanctuary from the Hellenistic period, identified as the celebrated Temple of Diktean Zeus. The most important find was an inscription with a segment of a hymn to the god, possibly sung during the dance of the Kouretes ● *37*. The 3rd-century AD inscription is exhibited in

the Heraklion Museum and provides proof that the cult of Zeus was still practiced during the Early Christian era.

THE HILLS OF KASTRI AND PETSOPHAS. Further remains have been unearthed in the vicinity: on Kastri, the ruins of a fort built during Early Minoan I, then reconstructed at the end of Late Minoan III; on Petsophas, a peak sanctuary of Middle Minoan origins, containing numerous votive statuettes that are today displayed in the Museums of Sitia, Haghios Nikolaos and Heraklion ▲ *156*.

ZAKROS

The hamlet of Ano Zakros is 10 miles to the south of Palaikastro; just out of the village a road leads through plantations of olive and banana trees and along the shore to the coastal remains of the most important Minoan site in eastern Crete.

THE ARCHEOLOGICAL FINDS. The Minoan city bears the name of the neighboring village. The first archeological investigations were carried out at the end of the 19th century by Federico Halbherr and Luciano Mariani. In 1901 the English archeologist D. G. Hogarth unearthed ten houses from the Late Minoan period, and made important finds dating from the Mycenean era. In 1961 Nicolas Platon, for the the Greek Archeological Society, began

new excavations, which continue to the present day. His efforts were soon rewarded by the discovery of a palace whose size is only exceeded by those at Knossos ▲ *162*, Phaistos ▲ *178* and Mallia ▲ *192*. The center of a large city and a harbor were also excavated. It is thought that a palace was first built in the early 2nd millennium BC since remnants have been unearthed beneath the second palace, which dates from 1600 BC. It was seriously damaged in 1500 BC, perhaps due to an earthquake; it was immediately rebuilt only to be completely destroyed in 1450 BC.

▲ THE PALACE OF ZAKROS

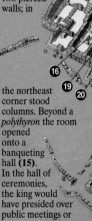

Zakros was truly a labyrinthine complex, as were the other Minoan palaces on Crete; covering over 7,100 square yards, it contained 250 to 300 rooms on two floors, possibly even three. It centers around a grand central courtyard and consists of royal apartments, cult places, storerooms and so on. The town area flanking the palace has been partially excavated. Most of the houses, whether attached to the palace or villas belonging to dignitaries, date from the Neo-palatial period.

The principal entrance **(2)** to the palace (orange slabs) is to the northeast of the complex, from the stretch of paved road **(1)** leading up from the harbor across the town. Beyond the entrance is the northeast court **(3)**, from which a corridor **(4)** leads to the northeast corner of the central courtyard **(5)**, measuring 33 yards long by 13 yards wide; this is not aligned on an exact north-south axis as are the esplanades of the other palaces. A stone altar stands in the northwest corner.

EAST WING. The royal apartments are situated to the east of the central courtyard with the King's Megaron **(6)** in the center and that of the Queen **(7)** to the north. The lustral basin (royal bathroom) **(8)** must have stood further back behind the northeast corner of the courtyard. A round cistern **(9)**, unique in Minoan architecture, is to the east of the King's Megaron; it measures 8 yards in diameter and must have collected water from a spring, possibly even serving as a ritual area. To the south of this is an underground square

fountain **(10)**, no doubt replicating the "fountain built with art" of the Odyssey; a similar well **(11)** stands at the southeast corner of the court. The southern area **(12)** was composed of workshops and possibly a living room reserved for the royal family.

WEST WING. The largest rooms are to the west of the court. In the northwest corner a vestibule **(13)** can be seen, with steps leading to an upper story. On the other side of a lateral corridor was the grand chamber known as the "hall of ceremonies" **(14)**, adjoined by a light-shaft; the southwest corner is flanked by two pierced walls; in

the northeast corner stood columns. Beyond a *polythyron* the room opened onto a banqueting hall **(15)**. In the hall of ceremonies, the king would have presided over public meetings or

religious rituals, these being followed by a feast in the banqueting hall. The area to the west of this large complex was filled with a cluster of small rooms: the sanctuary store **(16)** where various cult objects were placed; the archives

The different sections of the palace are arranged around the rectangle of the central courtyard with its stone altar (left). The finds constitute valuable evidence of the daily life of this wealthy city at the height of its power. They are today displayed in the Archeological Museums of Sitia and Heraklion ▲ 154.

(17) where Linear A tablets have been found; the sanctuary (18), a small room with a bench at the end wall; the treasury of the sanctuary (19), unique in the Minoan world in having escaped unplundered; the lustral basin (20), with a flight of steps leading down into it. The southern compartments contained stores and workshops (21). In the northernmost corner were further rooms, no doubt used as stores (22). A large room (23) whose ceiling was supported by six central wooden pillars must have been the palace kitchen, serving a banqueting hall directly above it. A fine paved portico with two wooden columns (24) opened into the north wing.

AN URBAN AREA. The ground plan consists of large "islands" of houses, surrounded by a complex network of paved roads and narrow streets (25). Near the "harbor road" (1) are the remains of what may have been either a bronze foundry or a potter's oven (26).

RITUAL OBJECTS The stone objects found at Zakros are fascinating. Take, for example, the superb rock crystal rhyton ● 44 from the treasury of the sanctuary; the butterfly (opposite page); and, above, the double axe together with the boldly shaped polychrome amphora (1450 BC), both originating from the lustral basin.

Reconstruction of the Palace of Zakros and the residential areas of the town.

LION FROM PRAISOS
During the
Post-Minoan period
Praisos was the
principal town of
the Eteocretans. It
occupied a strategic
position in the center
of the eastern
peninsula and had
two ports: Itia, to the
north on the bay of
Mirabello, and Stiles,
to the south on the
Libyan Sea. Ierapytna
was the

principal Dorian town
of eastern Crete and
the great rival of
Praisos during the
Greco-Roman period.
The rivalry resulted in
the destruction of
Praisos in 145 BC,
after which it was
neither rebuilt nor
reoccupied. Thus the
Eteocretans, the last
survivors of the
Minoan civilization,
disappeared forever.

FROM ZAKROS TO IERAPETRA

Back in the village of Ano Zakros, the road heads out
north as far as Adravasti, continues west via Karidi,
Sitanos, Katsidoni and Sandali, then turns south to
Kalamavka, after which it joins a main road. The village
of Nea Praisos is just over 4 miles to the northwest of
this intersection.

PRAISOS. From the village a dirt road leads down to the
site of ancient Praisos, where the first excavations were
carried out in 1884. Federico Halbherr discovered
numerous terracotta statuettes of idols along with
boustrophedon inscriptions ▲ *176* that have yet to be
deciphered: intriguingly, these use Greek characters
but the language is not Hellenistic. Some historians
believe it to be Eteocretan, a language spoken by
the peoples of Mycenean origin who retreated to
the mountains in the southeast of Crete and so
survived the centuries of Dorian invasions ● *46*.
Further excavations were undertaken in 1901 under
the direction of R. C. Bosanquet of the British
School. These studies revealed that the entire
region must have been inhabited during the
Neolithic period. The ruins at Praisos
indicate a city founded shortly after the
Bronze Age. This was spread over three
hills of which the highest, a natural stronghold,
must have been the city's heart; on one of the
other two, outside the city walls, was a peak
sanctuary. Archeologists also discovered
a necropolis, apparently in use from the
Mycenean period up to Hellenistic times.
In one of the tombs, exhumed in 1935,
the Greek archeologist Mavroidis found the bones of a
Praisos athlete, buried alongside his trophies; one such
is an amphora of 560–500 BC, quite possibly won in
Athens during the Panatheneian games.

LITHINES. The main road leading down toward the Libyan
Sea passes through Lithines, a village with origins in the
Byzantine period, although the first mention of it comes in a
Venetian census document of 1583. Its church of Haghia
Athanasios, dated by inscription to 1591, can still be seen,
along with a former sanctuary-cave dedicated to the Virgin,
which dates from the early years of the Venetian occupation.
A two-story defensive tower, or *pyrgos*, once stood in the
center of Lithines.

IERAPETRA ★

Some 7 miles south of Lithines the road joins the south coast along the Libyan Sea which it follows west for another 15 miles to Ierapetra. The modern town is spread around a promontory that constituted the site of ancient Ierapytna. It is thought that the name Ierapytna has Doric roots and that the town was established by the peoples of the Peloponnese during the Post-Minoan period. In its early history Ierapytna was eclipsed by Praisos, at that time the most powerful city in eastern Crete. Ierapytna, however, defeated and destroyed the city of Praisos, thus establishing control over the whole of the eastern peninsula and a large part of the south coast. This preeminent status

lasted until 67 BC, the year of the city's defeat at the hands of Quintus Metellus ● 47. The Romans rebuilt the town, which had been destroyed during the conflicts, and extended it. It flourished throughout the First Byzantine period but was once again destroyed in 824 by Saracen raids; it was possibly rebuilt during the Second Byzantine period. It regained a position of some importance under Venetian rule and became the capital of the region under the name of Ierapetra. Today it is the fourth town in Crete and the largest along the south coast; it is the capital of the district named after it. The town has a strong Mediterranean accent, with its pastel-colored or whitewashed houses, drenched in sunshine, clustering around the old Venetian fortress at the entrance to the harbor. Relics of Ierapetra's Turkish past consist of a minaret and an old *çesme*, or public fountain. The museum contains a small collection of archeological objects, some of which are from Ierapytna. Not a trace of the ancient city remains, although several Roman buildings are known to have survived until the 16th century, among them the harbor fortifications and a thermal bath.

THE FORTRESS OF IERAPETRA
This guards the entrance to the harbor and was built in 1626 by Francesco Morosini, who armed it with five large

cannons and 180 artillery pieces. In 1647, after a short siege, its commander Mouatsos yielded to the Turks. The conquerors rebuilt the town, which became the capital of eastern Crete and remained so until 1870. During Turkish rule Ierapetra's size did not increase, and the only event of note was the arrival of Napoleon in June 1798 en route for the Egyptian campaign. Left, the house where he supposedly spent the night.

215

PYRGOS
The site was explored by the Englishman G. Cadogan in 1970. On the summit of the hill the remains of a magnificent residence (1600 BC) that overlooked the sea have been unearthed.

MOTHER-GODDESS
A room near the southwest corner of the site of Phourno Koriphi may have been a sanctuary dedicated to the mother-goddess, as suggested by the discovery of an extraordinary clay figurine representing a female goddess (MA II). The sanctuary is the oldest domestic shrine known in Crete.

The main road west out of Ierapetra follows the contours of the coast. Just over 9 miles away, close to Myrtos, is the site of Phournou Koriphi, where English archeologists unearthed the remains of a village dating from early Minoan times (2500–2200 BC) ● 92. Its inhabitants clearly made a living from agriculture, pottery and textiles, as indicated by the pots and numerous objects excavated (weights for weaving looms, tools and so on) that are today shown in the museum at Haghios Nikolaos ▲ 201.

MYRTOS AND PYRGOS. Interesting archeological remains have been unearthed at Myrtos, perhaps most notably the Roman baths at the entrance to the village. The Greco-Roman city of Myrtos survived every period and lasted right up until 1943, when it was destroyed by the Germans. The villagers, believed to be members of the resistance, were executed. A further archeological site is found at Pyrgos, close to Myrtos, on a hill to the east of the River Kriopotamos. To date, the principal remains consist of a Minoan villa dating from 1600 BC, but the finds have established that the site was occupied as early as 2200 BC.

NEA ARVI. The main road climbs inland toward Pefkos; from here a minor road descends back to the coast and leads to Nea Arvi, a seaside village with a fine beach. Arvi is the site of the Greco-Roman city of Arvis, where numerous broken pots and archeological remains have been unearthed together with a remarkable marble sarcophagus. The village church dedicated to the Panaghia dates from the early Venetian period and is thought to have been erected on the site of a temple to Zeus Arbios. Some historians maintain that the temple was in fact on the site of Moni Arvis, a monastery built in 1880 on the slope overlooking the gorge behind the village.

ANO VIANNOS. Once back on the main highway, continue west to the village of Ano Viannos, perched high up in the mountains at 1,800 feet amid olive groves, vineyards and carob trees. Under Venetian rule Ano Viannos was the largest district in the region; two churches, Haghia Pelagia and Haghios Georgios, date from the early part of this period. Haghia Pelagia contains some remarkable frescos; an inscription states that these were executed during restoration of the church in 1360. Haghios Georgios also possesses frescos; a dedicatory inscription claims that these were executed in 1401 by the painter Ioannis Mousouros.

From Heraklion to Rethymnon

▲ From Heraklion to Rethymnon

1· Heraklion 2· Gazi 3· Rogdia 4· Palaikastro 5· Savathianon Monastery 6· Church of Haghia Pelagia 7· Phodele 8· Bali 9· Haghios Ioannis Monastery 10· Haghiou Pandeleimona Monastery 11· Panormos 12· Mount Stroumboi

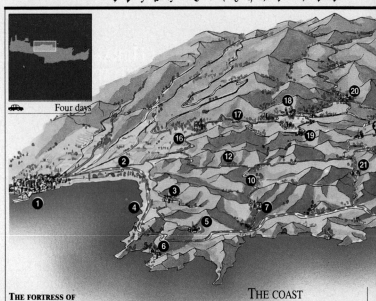

Four days

THE FORTRESS OF PALAIKASTRO

The Venetians restored this in the late 16th century when they were preparing to defend the island against the Turkish threat, but abandoned it in the final months of the Siege of Candia in 1669 ● 56. It was then occupied by the Turks, who in turn deserted it after it lost all strategic importance.

Haghio Grigorios O Dialogos, icon from Moni Savathianon.

THE COAST

ROGDIA AND PALAIKASTRO. Out of Heraklion, take the main highway toward the village of Gazi, where a sanctuary dating from Late Minoan III has been found. Shortly after, a minor road turns off toward Rogdia, an attractive village perched 985 feet up with a superb panoramic view over the gulf of Heraklion. It is thought that the village was founded during the Venetian period for although it is not mentioned in any census of the time its name is marked on the *Carta Basilicata* of 1618. The seaward view from the village takes in the ruined fort of PALAIKASTRO down below. Built in 1216, this was one of the fourteen forts erected by Enrico Pescatore, Count of Malta, to establish control over Crete ● 49.

THE MONASTERY OF SAVATHIANON ★. Out of Rogdia, take the road off to the left towards Moni Savathianon, a monastery dedicated to the Nativity. Its two-aisled *katholikon* is in turn dedicated to the "forty martyrs" and to Saint Savvas. Above the entrance a bas-relief decorated with acanthus leaves is inscribed with the date 1635; this seems to have been the year the new monastery was founded. A path crosses a bridge dated 1535 and leads to a chapel grotto dedicated to Haghios Antonios some 200 yards away; it was mentioned in a document of 1549 as having been part of the original monastery. This was converted into a nunnery at the end of the 1940's, when it was restored by ten or so nuns; today it is a flourishing institution.

HAGHIA PELAGIA. Returning to Rogdia, take the road north as far as Haghia Pelagia, a coastal village that in recent times has become a fashionable seaside resort. Recent exploration has revealed the existence of a Late Minoan I villa along with ruins dating from Classical and Hellenistic times, identified as those of the ancient city of Apollonia, destroyed by the Kydonians in 171 BC.

PHODELE ★. Some 4 miles along the highway a minor road branches off towards Phodele. The village dates back to Venetian times and is thought to have been built near a Byzantine settlement that was destroyed by the Saracens. The only Byzantine relic is the charming church of the Panaghia ● 100, at the end of a path bordered by orange trees. Phodele was traditionally believed to be the birthplace of Domenikos Theotokopoulos (1541–1614), known as El Greco ● 52, a theory that is not widely held today. The road leads to another monastery, Moni Haghiou Pandeleimona, just under 4 miles to the south.

BALI. Follow the highway for another 14 miles to reach the tiny seaside resort of Bali (Mpali). The village is set in a lovely bay on the site of Astali, the ancient port of Axos.

THE CHURCH AT PHODELE
This was built in the early 13th century over the nave of a previous 8th-century basilica that was probably destroyed by the Saracens at the same time as the rest of the village. The Phodele church contains fresco fragments, the oldest dating back to the early 13th century. There is also an inscription, dated 1323, making mention of a donor.

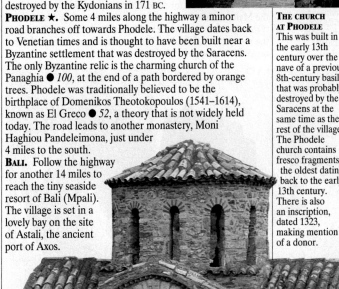

MONI HAGHIOU PANDELEIMONA
Right, icon from the monastery. Below, the Orthodox priest Neophytos Pediotis, who in 1866 fought with his monks alongside the Greek forces commanded by Captain Korakas, forcing the superior numbers of the Turkish army to surrender ● *64*.

THE MELIDONI CAVE
The chambers of the cave are adorned with magnificent stalagmites and stalactites whose columns create spectacular formations.

THE MONASTERY OF HAGHIOS IOANNIS. The turning for Moni Haghios Ioannis, also known as Moni Mpaliou, is just under a mile further along the main road. Dedicated to Saint John the Baptist, it was founded in the early 17th century; its basilica is decorated with frescos of the same period.

PANORMOS. The next village along this route is Panormos, occupying the site of the ancient port of the same name. During Venetian rule it was renamed "Roumeli Castelli", an allusion to a fort that no longer exists. The only trace of the old town of Panormos is an Early Christian basilica dedicated to Haghia Sophia, or Divine Wisdom, that was excavated by Kalokyris and Platon in 1948. They reconstructed a three-aisled edifice with a transept, nave and an atrium entrance. Panormos is 14 miles from Rethymnon along the main road.

THE MYLOPOTAMOS VALLEY

Leave Heraklion to the west in the direction of Gazi. Beyond the village, follow the route that skirts around Mount Stroumboulas then runs along the Mylopotamos River. The road passes the ruins of an old Turkish caravanserai, the KOUMBEDES, that during the Ottoman period served as a watering hole for travelers from Candia. The road carries on for a short distance west before reaching the Mylopotamos Valley, dominated to the left by Mount Ida (Oros Idi) and to the right by Mount Kouloukonas. Following the river, the road leads to Perama, the largest village of the region, 2½ miles from Melidoni.

> "BUT TALOS, THE MAN OF BRONZE, WITH ROCKS LOOSENED FROM A SOLID CLIFF, PREVENTED THEM FROM FASTENING THEIR ROPES TO THE LAND."
>
> APOLLONIOS OF RHODES, *THE ARGONAUTS*

THE MELIDONI CAVE. This cave is just under 2 miles west of the village of the same name. At the end of September 1823, when the region was laid waste by the Turkish army under the command of Hüseyin Pasha, 370 people took refuge here, mainly women, children and the old, while the majority of able-bodied men fought the occupier. The Pasha laid siege to the cave for several days; the besieged, for their part, refused to surrender and scored some victims in the enemy ranks. Eventually, on October 3, the cave entrance was blocked with brushwood and set alight by the besiegers; the rebels suffocated. The martyrs' bones are today preserved in an ossuary in a large chamber in the cave known as the "Heroes' room". A chapel dedicated to the Annunciation has also been erected outside the entrance; a ceremony to commemorate the martyrs is held there every year on the anniversary of the massacre.

Archeological research has revealed that the Melidoni cave was periodically occupied from the Neolithic era. During Classical times it was the site of the sanctuary of Hermes Tallaios, a regional cult in which the Greek god Hermes was associated with the mythical figure of Talos, the bronze giant.

THE MONASTERY OF ARKADI ★. From Perama, follow a series of by-roads that lead through Viranepiskopi, Loutra and Amnatos to Moni Arkadi, the most famous monastery in Crete. Below the monastery is a Turkish bridge of 1685. According to tradition the monastery of Arkadi was founded during the Second Byzantine period; however, no reference to it exists prior to the end of the 16th century. An inscription at the base of the bellcote refers to one of the first abbots, Klimis Khortatzis, and bears the date 1587. Moni Arkadi was one of the major Greek cultural centers of the Cretan Renaissance. Its monks had preserved a substantial collection of old manuscripts; the majority of these were subsequently stolen or destroyed. The monastery was sacked by the Turks on three separate occasions: in 1645, in 1823 and finally in 1866. During the siege of 1866 the besieged monks and refugees chose to explode their own powder magazines rather than surrender. Today the monastery is a national shrine and the heroic acts of its martyrs are celebrated every November 8.

TALOS THE GIANT
King Minos is supposed to have chosen Talos to guard Crete and his beloved Europa. He protected the island from invaders and prevented its inhabitants from leaving. The bronze giant strode round the island three times each day, hurling enormous boulders at any approaching vessels. But Talos had one vulnerable spot: his life depended on a plug of bronze in the artery of his leg. Medea drugged the giant and removed the plug; the *ichor*, or blood of the gods, ran out of the wound and Talos died, thereby allowing the Argonauts to land on Crete.

MONI ARKADI ● *102*
The church dates from the Cretan Renaissance and its magnificent portal dated 1587 is one of the finest examples of the style in Crete. The façade of the church displays a fine array of Corinthian colonnades, pilasters, classical bays and Baroque flourishes.

In autumn 1866 refugees, partisans and monks were besieged by the Ottoman army. The first attack was repulsed but a second assault brought down the entrance to the monastery. The besieged occupants chose death rather than surrender, blowing themselves up along with their last powder magazines. The shocking news of this self-sacrifice rang around the world and prompted many to rally to the cause of Cretan independence, among them European public and political figures of the century such as Guiseppe Garibaldi and the novelist Victor Hugo. Some ninety years later, Nikos Kazantzaki made the dramatic events of Moni Arkadi the subject of his novel *Freedom or Death*.

THE AIR FILLED WITH ROARS, THE CHRISTIANS ROARED, THE
TURKS ROARED.... IT WAS CRETE AND TURKEY, AND THEY FOUGHT.
FREEDOM! CRIED THE ONE. DEATH! REPLIED THE OTHER."

NIKOS KAZANTZAK

A Turkish army of 16,000 men under Mustapha Pasha Girilitis besieged the monastery; in it were 700 women and 287 men, among them twenty-five volunteers from mainland Greece and forty-five monks. The monastery was armed with only two cannons, two pieces of light artillery and a large supply of muskets. The Turks launched the assault on November 7.

On November 8 the Turks succeeded in destroying the main entrance to the monastery. Higoumene Gabriel gave the order to one of the partisans, Konstantin Giamboudhakis, to light the powder magazines. The explosion was such that only a handful of the besieged occupants escaped; 864 of them were killed and the others were taken prisoner. Turkish losses amounted to 3,000 dead and 1,500 wounded.

HIGOUMENE GABRIEL, ABBOT OF MONI ARKADI IN 1866.
The monastery museum also honors the bravery of this heroic priest, who has become one of the emblematic figures of the Cretan Resistance.

Above, fortified Venetian edifice in the little old town of Maroulas.

THE TYLISSOS SITE
The excavations undertaken between 1902 and 1903 under the direction of J. Hatzidhakis and more recently by Nicolas Platon have unearthed three Minoan villas dating from between 1600 and 1450 BC together with a number of objects now in the Archeological Museum of Heraklion. The three villas were erected on the site of earlier constructions of which only scant traces survive. The villas are laid out in similar fashion, each consisting of four rooms. The ground floor is made up of storerooms and workshops while the upper story would have contained living quarters. Villa A displays the typically irregular walls of Minoan architecture. Villa C has preserved fragments of its paving of red stucco.

Below, one of the charming doorways in the town of Tylissos.

One of the monastery buildings has been fitted out to accommodate the many visiting tourists. The forty or so monks offer hospitality for visitors who wish to spend the night. Entrance to the enclosure of the monastery is through the west façade, which was rebuilt after its destruction by Turkish artillery. At the far end of the courtyard stands the façade of the church with its double nave and two apses. There is a small museum devoted to the history of the monastery and the 1866 siege in a room to the southeast of the courtyard. The old refectory, where the bullet-holes are still visible, as well as the cell of Higoumene Gabriel, are open to the public. The roofless powder magazine is an impressive sight. From Moni Arkadi, the road down to the coast follows through Adele, then along to Rethymnon further west. The village of Maroulas south of Adele has a Venetian *pyrgos*: one of the grand seigniorial houses flanked by a tower from which the Venetian nobles surveyed their fiefs.

The north slope of Mount Ida

The third possible itinerary begins some 4 miles out of Heraklion, where a minor road turns off to climb up toward the villages situated on the north slope of Mount Ida.

TYLISSOS. Just under 4 miles after Gazi the road passes through Tylissos, a village whose pre-Hellenic name reveals its ancient origins. The village, which is mentioned in the registers of 1271, was in fact built over the ruins of the ancient Greek city of Tylissos, which was in turn founded on the site of a Minoan village of the Early Bronze Age.
SKLAVOKAMBOS. The road that runs west, winding around the northwestern foothills of Mount Ida, leads to a Minoan site known as Sklavokambos, or the "Valley of the Slavs", no doubt after the Slav village established here by Nikephoros Phokas ● *48*. The Minoan ruins were discovered during the construction of a road in 1930, and were excavated just before the outbreak of World War Two.

Anogia is once again a flourishing village, having been completely rebuilt following World War Two. It spreads in terraces across the slope of Mount Khameni at a height of 2,625 feet. The village possesses a strong sense of identity and is firmly attached to its heritage: an ancient dialect is still spoken there, and the inhabitants quite naturally don their traditional costumes during the song, dance and lyre contests that take place in the area from August 15. Anogia is also noted for its crafts, particularly its weaving in which the majority of the female population is still employed, producing bedspreads, wall hangings, napkins, cushions and bags embroidered in cotton or wool.

Marinatos exhumed the remains of a large villa dating from 1500 BC that must have formed the center of an important village destroyed by a fire during the Late Minoan period and never rebuilt.

KAMARIOTIS. The road leads to the mountain village of Gonies, built in an amphitheater formation, just over a mile from Sklavokambos, and from there to the village of Kamariotis. This was the birthplace of Evmenia Voria, a daughter of the village priest, who was taken by the Turks in 1645 when only three years old. She was taken to Istanbul, to the harem of the Topkapi Palace, where she was known as Rubia Gülnus, or "Spring rose". She became the favorite of the Sultan Mehmet IV (1648–87). Her two sons reigned as Mustapha II (1695–1703) and Ahmet II (1703–30).

ANOGIA ★. The large mountain village of Anogia is just 6 miles away, perched on the saddle of the hill. It seems that the village was founded in the early part of the 13th century by refugees from the neighboring town of Axos, which had been destroyed by the Venetians. In World War Two Anogia resisted the German occupation and was torched on August 15, 1944; the village was razed. All the men who had not fled to the mountains were executed. The only building to survive was the village church of Saint John the Baptist, which contains frescos of the early Venetian period.

Left, Minoan sarcophagus in the Archeological Museum of Heraklion ▲ 154.

225

BRONZE DRUM FROM THE CAVE AT MOUNT IDA
This relief shows Zeus flanked by two Kouretes ● *36*.

THE KOURETES DROWNING THE CRIES OF THE INFANT ZEUS
The "Ideon Antron" is considered by some to be the birthplace of Zeus, while others identify this with the "Dikteon Antron" ▲ *198*.

VIEW OF MOUNT IDA
The highest peak is Timios Stacros, or Psiloritis, at 8,056 feet. Psiloritis, which means the "High One", also refers to the whole range. It is snowcapped for half the year and often covered by clouds, and dominates the landscape from Heraklion to Rethymnon.

THE CAVE OF MOUNT IDA

At the south end of Anogia a road climbs up to the Nida plateau, 4,600 feet high and encircled by the peaks of Mount Ida. On the far side of the plain, to the south, a left fork leads to the tourist pavilion, the departure point for the twenty-minute walk to the famous "Ideon Antron", the Idean Cave. The entrance to the cave, which overlooks the west side of the plain from a height of 4,750 feet, was discovered by a shepherd in 1884 and investigated the following year by the Italian School. Further archeological exploration was undertaken in 1982 under the direction of Sakellarakis. The entrance is 29 feet high and 88 feet wide; above it is a Latin inscription that marks the cave as a sanctuary of Idean Zeus. On the south side an altar has been cut from the rock; below this are the foundations of a house, used by the guardian of the shrine during the Roman era. Inside the entrance a labyrinthine passage leads to the main chamber, which measures 115 by 131 feet, with a maximum height of 198 feet. The cathedral-like subterranean chamber must have formed the old sanctuary, while another room, recently discovered, seems to have been a secret shrine dedicated to the cult of

Idean Zeus. Excavations over the last few years have unearthed fragments dating back to the Late Neolithic era, along with more recent remains that suggest that the cave was used as a cult site from the Middle Minoan to the Roman period. Ivories from Syria and the Middle East, dating from the 8th century BC, have been discovered. The most impressive objects, however, display distinctly Oriental characteristics and consist of shields with relief patterns and a bronze drum. These objects, today on show in the Museum at Heraklion ▲ *156*, would no doubt have been used during ceremonies in which the dance of the Curetes was reenacted around a representation of Rhea giving birth to Zeus ● *37*.

Axos. The village of Axos is just over 6 miles northwest from Anogia. A ruined chapel dedicated to Saints Eleftherios and Modestos stands just outside the village. This dates from the Second Byzantine period but incorporates older architectural fragments. Another ruined Byzantine church stands in the middle of the village. Archeological exploration has

established that the site was occupied from the Late Minoan III period, around 1400 BC. A few remains on the summit of the hill date from a city that grew up between the Archaic and Hellenistic periods. The most important object to have been discovered at this site is a superb bronze helmet, today on display in the Archeological Museum at Heraklion ▲ *156*. The city seems to have survived up to the Venetian occupation, since the chapel that Pashley found below the acropolis is dedicated to Haghios Ioannis and dates from the late 14th or early 15th century. On one wall he noted a white marble plaque with an inscription in ancient Doric, which was originally on one of the walls of the ancient city.

MONI KHALEPAS AND MONI DISKOURI. Two old monasteries, Moni Khalepas and Moni Diskouri, are situated close to Axos along the road that turns off to the right at the crossroads next to the chapel. The Diskouri monastery is a sister house of Moni Khalepas, which seems to have been founded in the early part of the 16th century. Today only one monk, based at Moni Diskouri, is left to look after the two monasteries.

MARGARITES
This attractive village has long been renowned for its pottery.

Village of Prines.

ILLUMINATED MANUSCRIPT
Moni Arsani lists some old manuscripts among its treasures. The work of the monks, these were often illuminated, as in this example depicting Saint George.

The road rejoins the Mylopotamos River shortly after the village of Garazo; after 8 miles head toward Margarites then take the road to Prines; a minor road leads to Eleftherna, a village near the site of the same name.

ELEFTHERNA. The ancient city was discovered by Spratt in 1855 and occupies a long thin promontory between two rivers. The only approach to it is along a gully once guarded by a massive defensive tower. It was built in the 9th century BC and occupied until the Second Byzantine period. It was no doubt because of its naturally fortified site that the town was one of the most powerful Dorian city-states. It was nonetheless conquered by Quintus Metellus in 67 BC ● 47. Spratt discovered a number of ancient ruins in and around the site, among them the foundations of houses, two First Byzantine churches, a mutilated statue, a temple platform and two bridges. One of these, dating from the Hellenistic period, is still standing. More recently, the eroded bust of an Archaic *kouros* has been discovered; this stylized representation of a young man personifying Apollo, dating from 630 to 620 BC, is now on display in the Archeological Museum of Heraklion ▲ 154.

VIRANEPISKOPI. The road runs northwest through the villages of Erfi, Viranepiskopi and Arsani.

The church of Haghia Eirene at Viranepiskopi was erected on the ruins of an 11th-century basilica, in turn built over an ancient temple dedicated to Britomartis or Diktina, the Cretan goddess of fertility.

THE MONASTERY OF ARSANI. The Arsani monastery, probably founded shortly after 1600, is only a short distance from here. The *katholikon* dedicated to Haghios Georgios dates from only 1888, replacing an earlier church destroyed by the Ottomans. Each year Arsani celebrates the Feast of Saint George ● 80 on April 23.

RETHYMNON

Rethymnon preserves numerous relics of its past. Archeological finds have established that the site was inhabited from the end of the Minoan period. Its ancient origins are also evident in the number of documents referring to "Rethymnos" or "Rethimna", names whose suffixes are characteristic of pre-Hellenistic Greek place-names.

✕ Two days

Cretan revolutionary.

HISTORY

Rethymnon was not important during Roman times and Strabo makes no reference to it in his description of Crete. All that is known of its Byzantine history is that it was destroyed by the Saracens then rebuilt after Nikephoros Phokas recaptured Crete. Rethymnon expanded under Venetian rule to become the third largest town in Crete after Candia and Khania. Its inhabitants played a major part in the insurrections under Venetian and Turkish occupation. During the Cretan Renaissance the town, renowned for its intellectuals, writers and artists, was dubbed the "new Athens". One of its major figures was the poet Marinos Tzanes Bounialis, whose *Cretan War* describes the Turkish conquest of Crete between 1645 and 1669.

THE SIEGE OF RETHYMNON. After conquering Khania the Turkish forces turned their attention to Rethymnon, attacking by sea and by land and torching the surrounding villages ● 54. The Venetian troops, made up of Dalmatian and Slav mercenaries, tried in vain to withstand the attack but were forced to retreat inland to the fortress; here they joined the garrison and the town dwellers, who numbered approximately 8,500 people. The fortress surrendered at the end of November 1645 after a siege lasting twenty-three days.

A CHANGING POPULATION. After the capture of Rethymnon a large number of Turkish troops settled in the town, where they were later joined by Candiots fleeing the besieged capital. The ethnic combination of Cretans and Greek refugees cohabiting with Turks was not entirely peaceful:

the inhabitants of Rethymnon and the surrounding region frequently rose up against the occupier and such revolts were followed by brutal reprisals against the Christian population ● *61*. These massacres caused some to flee while others, in greater numbers, converted to Islam; before long Muslims outnumbered Christians. The situation was reversed following the end of occupation in 1897, subsequent union with Greece in 1913, and finally in 1923 the departure of the last Turks, exchanged for Greek refugees. After more than seven centuries of foreign occupation Rethymnon became a truly Greek town, as Pandelis Prevelakis in his *Tale of a City*, published in 1938, explained: "Rethymnon is a small town, sitting almost in the center of the north coast of Crete. It is more typically Greek than any other Greek town and has managed to preserve, as few old Greek towns have, the color and spirit of every epoch from its past… ."

THE CAPTURE OF RETHYMNON
While the Turkish fleet bombarded the fortress, the land forces tried to gain control of the promontory. Although weakened and suffering the loss of a number of officers, the besieged occupants managed to score thousands of victims among the enemy ranks. Following the outbreak of a cholera epidemic, however, the governor was forced to surrender and Pasha Hussein took control of the town and the harbor. The garrison and some 1,500 inhabitants fled by boat while the remainder of the population was imprisoned; the young women and children were sent to Istanbul to be sold in the slave markets.

231

▲ THE HOUSES OF OLD RETHYMNON

The architectural legacy of the Venetian and Turkish periods is particularly well preserved in Rethymnon. The monumental structures – Fortetza, ramparts, main gateway, Loggia, Rimondi fountain and *palazzo* – were built between the 15th and 17th centuries by local master masons who were influenced by their contacts with Italian architects, but also by reading the treatises of Sebastiano Serlio and Andrea Palladio. The Cretans adapted the new architectural vocabulary to suit the esthetic traditions of the island, thus creating a distinctly Cretan architectural style. Mosques and typical houses, with their propped wooden kiosk-balconies overlooking the street, are souvenirs of the Ottoman occupation, and of 19th-century rule in particular.

A FUSION OF STYLES
During the 15th and 17th centuries when the new Renaissance ideals were the order of the day, relations developed between Venetian high society and the Cretan nobility. Renaissance architecture, and above all its specifically Venetian form, made use of local building methods and materials. The *xostego*, the closed wooden balcony, derives from the Byzantine *iliakos* typical of Balkan architecture from the 18th century onward. Construction of them was encouraged and sometimes even imposed by the Turkish rulers. More often, such kiosks were incorporated into older, Venetian-style houses. A large number of these urban dwellings still survive, particularly along the old thoroughfares of Thessalonikis, Vernardou, Soulion, Tsouderon, Ethnikis Andistasis and Arkadiou streets.

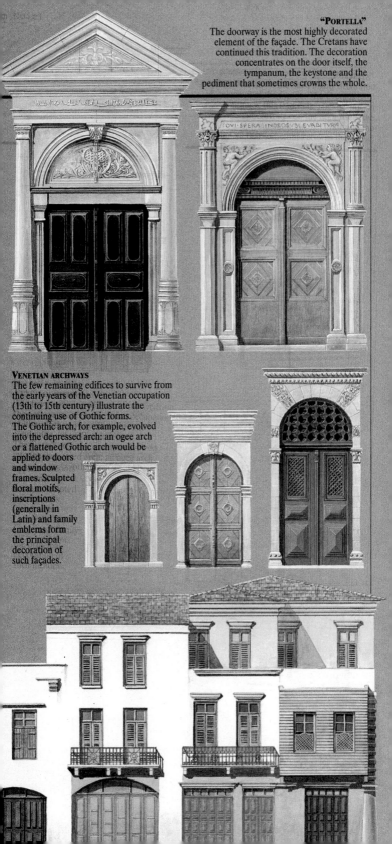

"PORTELLA"
The doorway is the most highly decorated element of the façade. The Cretans have continued this tradition. The decoration concentrates on the door itself, the tympanum, the keystone and the pediment that sometimes crowns the whole.

VENETIAN ARCHWAYS
The few remaining edifices to survive from the early years of the Venetian occupation (13th to 15th century) illustrate the continuing use of Gothic forms. The Gothic arch, for example, evolved into the depressed arch: an ogee arch or a flattened Gothic arch would be applied to doors and window frames. Sculpted floral motifs, inscriptions (generally in Latin) and family emblems form the principal decoration of such façades.

▲ THE PALACES OF RETHYMNON

The Cretan *palazzo* is more sober in appearance than its Venetian counterpart; its façade lacks the strong horizontal delineation between the stories that characterizes the palaces of Venice. Yet the biggest difference lies in one distinctly Cretan feature, adapted to the island's climatic conditions: the roof of the upper story is entirely flat, or very slightly inclined to allow rainwater to run off into a cistern, and is whitewashed.

THE ROOF TERRACE
This typically Mediterranean feature has survived on Crete from ancient times right up to the present day. In the absence of a piped system of running water it served as a private cistern to collect rainwater. Tiled roofs are, in fact, a relatively recent development. This rubblestone wall (left) built with limestone and mortar is coated with a mixture of red clay-like earth,

THE INTERIOR ARRANGEMENT OF THE PALACES
The *katoï*, or first floor, housed the stores, workshops and servants' quarters. The second story, or *mezzado*, was reserved for the public duties of the lord. The third and final story was composed of private apartments, or *anoï*: these included a *portego* (reception and dining room), the *kamares* or bedrooms, and the kitchens. A typical feature of these buildings was the inclusion of an interior courtyard, sometimes two, as was common long ago during Minoan times.

234

sand and whitewash.

The décor applied by a sculptor, or *intagliatoros*, adds a personal touch to each building. Such "signatures" are applied with particular care to entrance doorways to create a more imposing effect. The rich but muted principal colors of ocher, blue, red and pink serve to emphasize the architectural and decorative features, particularly on the neoclassical buildings. The door itself is surrounded by a frame of pillars and columns, with bases, shafts and capitals. An impost supports the fall of the arch or the tympanum across it. The quoins are also frequently decorated with carved foliage or sculpted figures. The keystone may be emphasized by a simple protuberance, or by a carved leaf decoration. The varied geometrical patterns of the wooden double doors are as tastefully finished as the surrounding décor.

THE FORTETZA ● 107

THE FORTETZA ● 107

The main building of old Rethymnon is the imposing Venetian fortress that stands at the far end of the promontory to the north of the town. An ancient Greek city once stood on this site, followed by a Byzantine citadel, the Palaikastro, whose remains lie buried under the foundations of the existing fort, erected in the 16th century. Two successive attacks by the Turkish fleet, led first by Barbarossa in 1538 then by Uluch Ali Pasha in 1562, exposed the weaknesses in the town's defenses and the Venetian council resolved to build a new fortress. The original plans drawn up by Sanmichele ● 54 were adapted and implemented by the Venetian military engineer Sforza Pallavicini. Work began on September 15, 1573; the walls were completed during the summer of 1577, with the exception of those along the shore which were completed the following year. It took six more years to complete the buildings inside the ramparts, among them the Venetian governor's residence, garrison quarters, administrative buildings, powder magazines, a hospital, lodgings for the town's inhabitants during times of siege and a Catholic chapel of Saint Spyridon.

THE FORT'S MOSQUE. The mosque built for the Turkish garrison at Rethymnon has recently been restored. The interior of its cupola is covered with mosaic decoration, rare in Ottoman art; the upper portion of its *mihrab* (niche indicating the direction of Mecca) is carved with stalactite-shaped motifs. The old prison at the entrance to the Fortetza houses the Archeological Museum.

THE ARCHEOLOGICAL MUSEUM ★

This fascinating collection displays excavated finds from Rethymnon and its district, together with Roman bronzes retrieved from a shipwreck off the coast of Haghia Galini ▲ 242. The most interesting exhibits were discovered in 1947 behind the secondary school to the southeast of the public gardens. They consist of eight different vase specimens, some intact, others fragmented, from a Middle Minoan III tomb (1350–1250 BC) dug from the rock. These objects are the

THE FORTETZA
The imposing fortress, measuring 1,400 yards in circumference, hugs the side of the hill. It provides a splendid view over the town, the harbor and the surrounding countryside. The ramparts are reinforced by four bastions. The impressive main gate is the only entrance from the town.

The dome of the fort's mosque

THE ARCHEOLOGICAL MUSEUM
The museum contains a variety of objects: jewels, tools and votive statuettes from the Neolithic era, Minoan ceramics, Roman and Byzantine architectural fragments and sarcophagi, as well as a small Egyptian collection.
Right, a bronze statuette of Isis, dating from the 18th dynasty (1700–1400 BC).

oldest to have been discovered in Rethymnon and are a
strong indication that the town was founded toward the
end of the Bronze Age.

AROUND THE VENETIAN HARBOR

THE LOGGIA. From the southwest of the Venetian
harbor Nearchou street leads to the junction of Paleologou
and Arkadiou streets and to the Venetian Loggia at the
intersection. Each of the four façades of this fine
Palladian-style building is pierced by three arched
embrasures, while a short flight of marble steps leads to a
central doorway. The Loggia dates in all probability from
the late 16th or early 17th century when it was used as a
meeting place for the Venetian nobility in Rethymnon.
Under Turkish occupation it was converted into a mosque:
the base of a minaret can still be seen to the rear of the
building, together with several tombstones with turban
motifs in the garden next to it. Arkadiou street, running
alongside the beach, cuts through the old part of Rethymnon
where the finest examples of Venetian doorways and
wooden-balconied Turkish houses can be seen.

THE RIMONDI FOUNTAIN ● 109. To the west of the Loggia,
at the junction of Paleologou and Thessalonikis streets,
stands the last monumental fountain erected by the
Venetians in Rethymnon. This is the Rimondi fountain, a
magnificent Renaissance structure with four Corinthian
columns framing three water-spouting lions' heads. The
monument dates from 1629 and bears the name of Alvise
Rimondi, the Venetian rector of the town at the time.
The fountain was originally
protected from the elements
by a domed structure, of which
three of the four pillars still
survive, along with a fragment
of the dome.

THE CENTER

**THE FORMER
NERANDZES MOSQUE.** South of
the Rimondi fountain and
Pertkhaki street is the former
Nerandzes mosque, whose most
impressive feature is its tall
minaret ● 112. This was
originally the Venetian church
of Santa Maria, mentioned from
1227, which was converted into
a mosque shortly after the Turks
captured Rethymnon. It was
renamed the Odeon and is today
used as a concert hall. Its most striking architectural
feature is its arched entrance, situated at the far side of
the building next to the minaret. It is flanked by two high
pedestals, each of which supports a pair of Corinthian
half-columns whose capitals are surmounted by an
architrave; each pair is separated by an impost with two
levels of rounded niches.

The area extending
west and southwest
from the Venetian
harbor is the oldest
part of the town.
The harbor, with its
pastel-colored
houses, is most
picturesque; note the
multicolored fishing
caiques and the old
lighthouse that stands
at the far end of the
jetty. The nearby
restaurants, serving
freshly caught fish,
are some of the best
in town.

RIMONDI FOUNTAIN
The arch next to it
shelters a shop.

**THE NERANDZES
MOSQUE**
A spiral staircase of
133 steps climbs up
to the top of the
minaret, from which
there is a magnificent
view over the town.

237

THE MARKET
The Porta Guora, also known as "Megali Porta", the Grand Gate, opens into the market, always lively and colorful, with displays of cheese, fruit and vegetables, fish and meat, superb round loaves, honey and so on. The numerous tiny stalls crowd together in this district, selling tourist goods and crafts: jewelry, embroidery, leather, pottery and woven textiles. There is even the odd antique stall. Sit in one of the many tavernas and cafés, sip a drink and watch the Cretans play cards or *tavli*, Cretan backgammon.

THE PINK MOSQUE OF KARA MUSTAPHA
This stands at the corner of Victor Hugo Street. Its fountain and minaret are virtually in ruins.

ODOS ETHNIKIS ANDISTASIS. South of Ethnikis Andistasis street another Turkish minaret stands at the entrance to the Square of the Four Martyrs. The square and its church are named after the four determined individuals who resisted Turkish rule and were hanged at this spot. The road passes under the arch of a fine neoclassical gateway; this is the Porta Guora, the only surviving portal of the old Venetian ramparts. Its name derives from Giacomo Guoro, the rector of Rethymnon in the second half of the 16th century.

TO THE SOUTH OF THE OLD TOWN

THE PUBLIC GARDENS. Apart from the Venetian harbor and the beach, one of the most pleasant spots in Rethymnon is the beautiful municipal park, whose entrance is at the intersection of Ethnikis Andistasis and Pavlou Koundouriotou streets. The park is laid out over the site of the former Turkish cemetery, of which hardly a trace survives. Every year at the end of July a wine festival ♦ *284* takes

place in the gardens, accompanied by much celebration, dancing and folk music. The flowers are also well worth seeing during March and April, and Rethymnon is renowned for its hot-house plants.

THE FORMER KARA MUSTAPHA MOSQUE. Another major monument, the former Kara Mustapha mosque, or Kara Moussa Pasha, is situated at the far end of Arkadiou street; it can also be reached via Gerakari street. It was originally a Franciscan building, erected at the beginning of the Venetian period. It was converted into a mosque immediately after the Turkish conquest of 1645, by Kara Mustapha Pasha, the Grand Vizir of Sultan Ibrahim and commander of the first troops to land on Crete. The building's Venetian origins are evident in the fine neoclassical entrance and the ribbed vaults inside. The building forms a cube surmounted by nine cupolas that were added, along with the minaret, during the Turkish period. Today the building is used by the Department of Byzantine Antiquities of Rethymnon and plans to turn it into a museum are under consideration.

SOUTH OF RETHYMNON

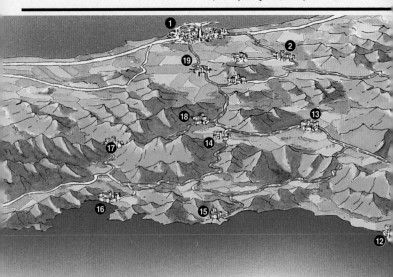

Three days

VILLAGE OF THRONOS-SYBRITA
This charming village stands on what was part of ancient Sybrita, once the most powerful city-state in this part of Crete, stretching across the southern slopes of the hill.

Right, monument at Apostoli, where the village commands a superb view over the Psiloritis (Ida) range.

AROUND MOUNT VRYSINAS

KHROMONASTIRI. From Rethymnon, take the road that leads south through the Sfakoriako valley. Khromonastiri is the first village to appear on the north slope of Mount Vrysinas, which rises to 2,800 feet. Its church dedicated to Haghios Eftikhios is thought to date from the Second Byzantine period, shortly after the Saracen conquest of Crete in 961 ● 48. It is still decorated with its original 11th-century frescos, among the earliest examples of this period in Crete.
PRASES. Continue further south toward the picturesque village of Prases, where several Venetian houses still stand. The cemetery chapel dedicated to the Panaghia contains remnants of 14th-century frescos. At the junction just over a mile outside the village, a right-hand turn takes you along the south slopes of Mount Vrysinas and leads up to the Phalanna site where, in the 1960's, Nicolas Platon unearthed two Archaic houses; the main road, to the left, leads to the Amari district.

THE AMARI DISTRICT ★

The number of Byzantine churches in the beautiful Amari valley is unequaled anywhere else in Crete. Much of the information relating to them comes from the inventory established by Giuseppe Gerola at the turn of the century in his *Monumenti Veneti nell'Isola di Creta*.
ANCIENT SYBRITA. The villages of Apostoli, Gena, Thronos and Kalogeros all lie

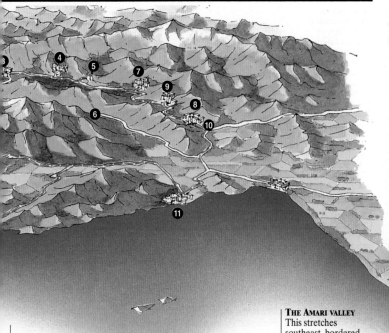

THE AMARI VALLEY
This stretches southeast, bordered to the northeast by the Psiloritis massif and to the southwest by Mount Kedros. One of Crete's most beautiful valleys, this fertile paradise nestles between the mountains where villages perch on slopes planted with olive groves.

in the northwest part of the Amari valley, and stand within the borders of the ancient state of Sybrita, whose city was to the north of Thronos: traces of the city walls survive, along with a monumental gateway. In each of the villages stands a frescoed 14th-century church: Haghios Nikolaos at Apostoli, Haghios Onouphrios at Gena, Haghios Ioannis Theologos at Kalogeros and, at Thronos, the church of the Panaghia.

THRONOS. Its church of the Panaghia, the Dormition of the Virgin, was erected over the foundations of an Early Christian basilica, whose mosaic floor is thought to date from the 4th century. Restoration work was undertaken in 1491 and in 1558, as the two inscriptions indicate. Its frescos are of two distinct stylistic periods: early 14th century and late 14th or early 15th century. Not far from the village of Kalogeros stands the Church of St John the Evangelist, whose 15th-century frescos are also worth a look.

AMARI. From the former monastery of Asomatom a road leads to Monastiraki, close to the site of Kharakas where archeologists have found an important Minoan settlement and palace. From here the road leads to the village of Amari, the "capital" of the district until the Venetian period, and the country retreat of the island's nobility. In the chapel of Haghia Anna, just outside the village, frescos dated at 1225 are among the earliest to have been found in Crete.

241

THE PORT OF HAGHIA GALINI
The village of Haghia Galini has recently been transformed into a seaside resort. Pleasure craft now outnumber the fishing boats in summer and hotels and pensions have multiplied along the steep roads that lead down to the Libyan Sea. Boat trips to the sea caves ♦ *310* are offered.

THE SPILI FOUNTAIN
This large village, today a bishop's see, is abundantly watered. Spili gives the impression of having been built around its springs. One of them flows from a handsome Venetian fountain with a row of nineteen lion-head waterspouts ● *109*.

VIZARI AND PHOURPHOURAS. Return to Moni Asomaton and continue south as far as Vizari where, to the west of the village, lie the remains of a Roman city and the ruins of a 7th-century Byzantine basilica. The Arab coins discovered in the debris suggest that the city was destroyed by the Saracens. Just over a mile away in the center of the village of PHOURPHOURAS, perched at 1,100 feet, the church of the Panaghia contains remnants of 14th- and 15th-century frescos.

PLATANIA. From Phourphouras, a minor road leads north to Platania. Three caves are situated close to the village in the foothills of Mount Timios Stacros: that of Diogenes at 2,700 feet; that of Kissospelios at 3,300 feet; and that of Pan at

nearly 6,000 feet, venerated as the god's lair during ancient times. The mountain shepherds still play on an instrument similar to Pan pipes. The road to the south of Phourphouras descends deep into the Amari valley, leading to the south coast via the village of APADOULOS, whose church of Haghios Georgios is decorated with frescos. Just before the entrance to the village Davaras discovered a *tholos* tomb of the Late Minoan period.

THE HAGHIOS VASSILIOS DISTRICT

Although discreetly placed, the Lion of St Mark, emblem of the Serenissima Republic, is unmistakable here.

HAGHIA GALINI. This picturesque fishing village is situated on the shores of the Libyan Sea and boasts a beautiful beach; however, it is overcrowded in summer due to the number of tourists. To find a more tranquil swimming spot it is worth exploring on foot the beaches that lie further west, since there is no access to the coast by road between Haghia Galini and the Preveli monastery. Apart from its fine beach Haghia Galini possesses an attractive church dedicated to the Panaghia, thought to date from the Venetian period.

SPILI. The main road climbs north, then west, flanked by Mount Kedros (5,800 feet) to the north and Mounts Vouvala (3,100 feet) and Siderotos (3,700 feet) to the south. The road leads to Spili, a large village where it is well worth pausing for a moment in one of the cafés that line the main street. Spili is refreshingly cool and shady, and its old houses and four

churches lend the village an unmistakable charm. Apart from the famous fountain, the other Venetian building in Spili is the Chapel of the Transfiguration.

THE GORGE OF KORTALIOTIKO. The road leads west to Koxare then turns south toward the monastery of Preveli. It passes through the impressive gorge of Kortaliotiko, where the Megapotamos River has its source next to the chapel of Haghios Nikolaos. Out of the gorge, the road turns west toward the village of Asomatos where, staying with the river, a left turn leads to the Preveli monastery.

MONI PREVELI ★. The river is crossed by a bridge dating

from Venetian times; on the other side of it, beyond an abandoned tower that formed part of the old buildings, the impressive monastery of Preveli suddenly comes into view. The buildings form two separate groups: the first, the Kato (lower) monastery, which is today deserted, looks over the Libyan Sea; the second, the Piso (upper) monastery, is situated at the foot of the Megapotamos valley, and is still occupied by two monks and a guardian. The date of the monastery's foundation has not been established, but research undertaken by Professor Tombakis of the University of Athens plausibly dates it to the Venetian period. It was destroyed by the Turks in 1646, then rebuilt and opened once more in the years prior to 1700. In 1797 George V, the Ecumenical Patriarch of Constantinople, published a bull granting Moni Preveli the status of *stavropigiako*, making it directly answerable to the Patriarchate and safeguarding it from the Turkish authorities. The monastery, which owned extensive lands, thereby became extremely prosperous. Under Turkish

ICON FROM MONI PREVELI
A small museum in the monastery displays precious objects together with 17th- and 18th-century icons. A miraculous gold and silver cross is preserved in the church.

THE ARMENI NECROPOLIS
Excavations have unearthed a Mycenean tomb along with several others from the Late Minoan period ● 95. The funerary objects (sarcophagi, jewelry, vases) discovered in the tombs are now displayed in the Archeological Museum at Khania ▲ 279. The cemetery at Armeni is one of the largest in Crete but, to date, no trace of the town attached to it has been found. This city, however, must have been of considerable size given the extent of the cemetery.

occupation the monks created several clandestine schools in the villages of the region in order to spread Orthodox Greek culture and ensure a future generation of monks and teachers. Moni Preveli became a vital center of resistance and was once again demolished and rebuilt for the last time shortly after the uprising of 1866 ● 59. The monastery also provided shelter for the soldiers of the Allied troops that took part in the Battle of Crete during World War Two ● 65. A road leads from Moni Preveli to the nearby chapel of Haghia Photini, decorated with frescos dating from the late 14th and early 15th centuries. Another road leads to the palm-fringed Damnoni beach, where a welcome taverna provides a refreshing break before the traveler returns to the road.

FROM PLAKIAS TO RETHYMNON

PLAKIAS ★. Just north of the monastery, at Lefkogia, a road leads west toward the bay of Plakias. The village of Plakias has become one of the main seaside resorts along the coast of the Libyan Sea. Numerous hotels, along with a holiday village, are dotted around its magnificent beach. The bay is sheltered at either end by the two promontories of Cape Kakomouri and Cape Stavros. Retrace the road leading to Myrthios through the Kotsifos gorge, beyond which the main road to Rethymnon can be joined.

ARMENI. The most interesting halt is situated halfway, at Armeni; this was one of the Armenian villages established by Nikephoros Phokas ● 48 shortly after his recapture of the island in 961. The move was part of a Byzantine program to re-establish the Christian culture following the Saracen occupation. Roughly a mile outside the village, a turning is signposted to an ancient site, the Minoan cemetery discovered in 1969 by the Greek archeologist Tzedakis.

FROM RETHYMNON TO KHANIA

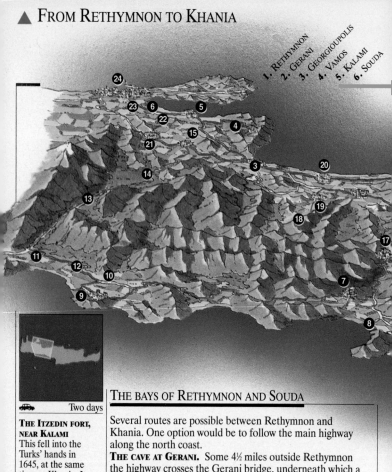

1. RETHYMNON
2. GERANI
3. GEORGIOUPOLIS
4. VAMOS
5. KALAMI
6. SOUDA

Two days

THE ITZEDIN FORT, NEAR KALAMI
This fell into the Turks' hands in 1645, at the same time as Khania. It has since retained its Turkish name.

THE BAY OF SOUDA
This is long and narrow and punctuated by several islets; on one of them, Souda, stands a Venetian fortress. An arsenal can also just be made out.

THE BAYS OF RETHYMNON AND SOUDA

Several routes are possible between Rethymnon and Khania. One option would be to follow the main highway along the north coast.

THE CAVE AT GERANI. Some 4½ miles outside Rethymnon the highway crosses the Gerani bridge, underneath which a sanctuary cave was discovered in 1967. The objects unearthed indicated that the cave was in use from the Late Neolithic era, probably as a cult site dedicated to the great mother-goddess. These cult objects, along with bone and obsidian tools dating from the same period, are now on show in the Archeological Museum in Heraklion ▲ 154.

THE BAY OF SOUDA. The highway follows the coast as far as Georgioupolis, then cuts across the base of the triangular Vamos peninsula to approach the bay of Souda near Kalami; from here there is a view over the whole bay, encompassing the cliffs of the big Akrotiri peninsula ▲ 264 on the far side. To the south the Malaxa massif is visible, forming part of the range of the White Mountains (Levka Ori) whose distant peaks dominate the horizon.

VENETIAN FORTRESSES ★. An old Venetian fortress, still known by its Turkish name of Itzedin, stands on the Kalami promontory. Another stands on the islet of Souda. Both were constructed by the Venetians toward the end of the 16th century with the purpose of protecting entry to the bay. The fortress on the islet resisted the Turks right up to 1715 and was one of the last three Venetian strongholds to fall, along with those at Spinalonga and Gramvousa, an islet situated off the northwest tip of Crete ▲ 202. The highway continues along the coast as far as the port of Souda, situated near the far end of the bay. It then crosses the base of the Akrotiri peninsula, before reaching the outskirts of Khania.

EASTERN SPHAKIA

A second option would be to travel from Rethymnon to Khania in a great loop that takes in the south coast via Selia, a village on the bay of Plakias. From here, the winding corniche road continues west between the mountains and the Libyan Sea, passing through a series of perching villages.

FORTRESS OF FRANGOKASTELLO ★.
The first by-road down to the coast leads to a fort ● 106 whose Venetian name, "Franco Castello", signifies the "Frankish fortress". Frangokastello, on its isolated promontory surrounded by sea, would have been one of the most impressive sites along the south coast of Crete. The fortress was built in 1371 by the Venetians and is now,

along with that of Ierapetra, the only fort to survive on the south coast ▲ 214. It is square-built and its walls, punctuated by four square towers at the corners, are extremely well preserved. Inside the walls are the remains of various buildings added during the Turkish occupation. The fortress looks down onto a beach of pinkish sand which is popular in summertime; the water here is shallow and protected by reefs. A number of small Byzantine churches are dotted along the coast.

KHADZIMICHALIS AND THE FORTRESS OF FRANGOKASTELLO
On May 18, 1828 this fortress was the site of a famous battle in which 1,000 besieged Greeks, led by General Khadzimichalis, were massacred by the 14,000 men of the army of Mustapha Pasha; it is claimed that Khadzimichalis was himself decapitated by the Turkish general. After they left, the rebels were buried by the villagers while a

nun collected the remains of Khadzimichalis and buried them in the crypt of the Haghios Kharalambos chapel.

▲ CAFÉS AND TAVERNAS

In Crete, the café is an institution and around it centers the social life of the male population. Whether a quiet retreat for the solitary-minded, a meeting place for a *parea* or "group of friends", a hang-out for a local professional group or party, the café occupies a special place in the daily lives of the Cretans, whether villagers or town-dwellers. *Stekia*, *ouzeries*, *rakadika*, *mezedadika* or *kapilia* are all versions of the traditional café, offering one specialty or another; the café, however, rarely has just one function and what it may offer depends on the customer, the time of day or simply pot luck. Bar, cigarette-kiosk, post-office, or even grocery, the *kafenio* is in its own way the very hub of the village.

CAFÉ SCENES
Seated at their tables in silence, often alone, the old men sip their coffee. A game of *tavli* may be started. Depending on the arrivals, conversations strike up. Some unfold their newspapers; others absentmindedly play with the amber beads of their *komboloï*. On occasion, the chairs are shifted to face the other way. Greetings are exchanged; a debate begins. After the offices shut, an informal "little parliament" session may begin: notables hold forth between *mezedes* and glasses of *raki* or *ouzo*.

THE TAVERNAS
These are the people's restaurants, where the tablecloths are more often than not paper ones. Space is tight but usually includes a small terrace under trellises. The menu is generally limited to the dish of the day, which usually arrives at the café ready-cooked from the baker's oven in large, round, shallow *tapsia* (pans).

"I HAVE DRUNK SWEET WINE AND DRY WINE. PURE AND INTACT LIKE A YOUNG CRETAN VIRGIN. AND WITH THE "RAKI" THAT I SWILLED ROUND MY MOUTH, I FELT MY WEAKENED FORCES REGAIN THEIR STRENGTH."

I. BRILLAKIS-KAVAKOPOULOS

From Frangokastello to Komitades the coast road is bordered with tiny villages perched in the foothills of Mount Agatha: right, the church of the Panaghia at Komitades, the last surviving trace of the Thymiani monastery where the Sphakians held their meetings prior to the War of Independence; below, the church of Nomikiana.

THE ASKYPHOU PLATEAU
This fertile region draws its main income from walnuts and potato crops; in springtime the fields are a carpet of yellow flowers.

THE CHURCH OF FRANGOKASTELLO. This is situated to the northeast of the fort; it is built on the site of an Early Christian basilica, of which parts of the mosaic floor survive.

KOMITADES. The coast road continues through the villages of Kapsodasos and Patsianos. The 13th-century Byzantine church of Haghios Georgios is close by, decorated with frescos by the Cretan painter Ioannis Pagomenos; signed and dated 1313, these are still in extremely good condition. Beyond Nomikiana, Vouvas and Vrakas lies the village of Komitades, with the beautiful church of the Panaghia nearby.

THE NIMBROS GORGE. A main road runs north through the spectacular Nimbros Gorge; this is some 4 miles long and only 6 to 10 feet wide in parts, while the two sides, forming steep walls, rise to a height of nearly 1,000 feet. The colored strata and the angles of the sides are evidence of the dramatic earthquake that split the rock in prehistoric times.

THE ASKYPHOU PLATEAU. On the far side of the gorge lies Imbros and then Petres, the southernmost village of the splendid Askyphou plateau which is bordered to the east by Mounts Agatha (5,000 feet) and Tripali (4,900 feet) and to the west by Mount Kastro (7,300 feet), part of the White Mountains massif. A minor road leads to Goni, where a ruined Turkish fort stands on a commanding height. The small town of Askyphou, at a height of 2,300 feet, is a pleasant place in which to stop and perhaps taste the local cheese pastry specialty, *mizithra*, in one of the cafés or tavernas. To the far north

THE CHURCH OF ASKYPHOU
The village of Askyphou is the main village on the plateau.

of the plain, the ravine of Lagos Katre was a major battle site during the Cretan revolts against the Turks in 1770, 1821 and 1866 ● 61. After crossing the ravine, the road dips down into the expanse of the Apokoronas plain to join Vryses and the main road for Khania.

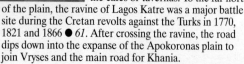

THE APOKORONAS DISTRICT

The third possible itinerary between Rethymnon and
Khania would be an exploration of the hinterland with its
villages and monasteries.

MONOPATI KASTELLOS. The village of Kastellos, 7½ miles
south of Rethymnon, is the first stop; here, crowning a rocky
slope, are the ruins of one of the fourteen forts erected by the
Genoese adventurer Enrico Pescatore in 1206.

THE MONASTERY OF HAGHIOS PROPHITIS ILIAS (ROUSTIKA).
The monastery of the Holy Prophet of Elias is 10½ miles
further west at the village of Roustika. Its fine library was
damaged by the Ottomans during raids in 1823 and 1866
● *61*: some of the original volumes are now housed in the
Bibliothèque Nationale in Paris.

MYRIOKEPHALA AND ITS MONASTERY. Some 12 miles to the
southwest lies Argyroupolis, built on the site of ancient Lappa
of which a few ruins remain. A Dorian city-state, destroyed in
67 BC, stood on the same site. The village of Myriokephala,
4 miles south, lies 1,650 feet up in the foothills of the White
Mountains. Its monastery dedicated to the Virgin Mary is one
of the oldest in Crete. Its foundation is attributed to Haghios
Ioannis O Xenos, the 10th-century Cretan evangelist monk
Saint John Xenos (the Stranger), who was canonized in 1632.
The church is the only monastery building not to have been
destroyed by the Ottomans in 1831. In the *katholikon* are
frescos dating from the 11th and 12th centuries, one of the
few examples of mural painting from this period to have
survived. The monastery's most precious object is a Byzantine
icon representing the Birth of the Virgin, supposedly painted
by the "beloved physician", Saint Luke.

**MONI HAGHIOS
PROPHITIS ILIAS**
This monastery
dates from the
Venetian period,
as indicated by the
dates of 1637 and
1641 carved on the
bell-tower and on a
lintel. Its church
contains a superb
carved wooden
iconostasis,
decorated with
icons from the
Second Byzantine
period. The
monastery which,
with its extensive
agricultural
property, was
once upon a time
prosperous, has
seen its large
community reduced
to a small handful
of monks today.
However, the annual
fair on July 20 has
remained a popular
feast day, drawing
many of the
inhabitants from the
surrounding area.

Above, the Vryses monument. Right, "Our Lady of the Fountain of Life" from the monastery of Khrysopighis.

THE SITE AT APTERA
The site has been under excavation since just after World War Two. Archeologists have unearthed the ruins of two Greek temples, a well, a small Roman theater and Byzantine remains. The objects uncovered are now in the Archeological Museum at Khania ▲ 179.

FROM EPISKOPI TO VRYSES. From here, take the road north as far as Episkopi, before continuing west along the byroads. In the Apokoronas district Pashley identified Dramia as being the site of ancient Hydrameion (Idramia); a few remains dating from Hellenistic times can still be seen. For a relaxing break, there is a choice of either Georgioupolis, an old fishing village that is now a seaside resort, or alternatively Lake Kournas, one of Crete's two lakes. From Georgioupolis, continue toward the White Mountains, following the river as far as the charming village of Vryses. Close to the village of Vaphes some 2 miles to the south is the cave of Kyronerida; one of the two old chapels it shelters is decorated with Byzantine frescos. To the west of Vryses a minor road passes through four attractive villages – Nipos, Fres, Kyriakosselia and Penomia – whose Byzantine churches

contain their original frescos; those at Fres are especially fine.
NEO-KHORIO AND STYLOS ★. A network of tiny roads leads to Neo-Khorio, a village situated among extensive olive groves encircled by orange and mandarin plantations. The beautiful old village of Stylos to the northwest is adorned with delightful fountains shaded by majestic plane trees. It possesses two Byzantine churches: Haghios Ioannis, with paintings from 1280, and Monastira. A tomb of the Late Minoan III was discovered not far from the village.

APTERA ★. Beyond a tributary of the Kiliaris the road leads to Aptera, one of the principal cities of the period between the 5th century BC and the Hellenistic era. At that time it was surrounded by 2½ miles of walls, the remains of which can be seen along a 650-yard stretch. Aptera's strategic position overlooking the bay of Souda gave it importance during the Roman and First Byzantine periods. It was partially abandoned after suffering damage in an earthquake in AD 700, then finally destroyed by the Saracens in 828.
MONI KHRYSOPIGHIS. The highway follows the bay of Souda, passing close by the monastery of Khrysopighis, the "monastery with the gold fountain"; it is dedicated to the Panaghia Zoodokhos Pigi, "Our Lady of the Fountain of Life". It was founded in the 16th century next to a sacred spring, from which it derives its name, and was abandoned at the turn of the 20th century; it later became a convent. It is reasonably well preserved today. A Minoan settlement and a Neo-palatial villa have been discovered to the south of it.

KHANIA

🎒 Three days

THE SIEGE OF KHANIA
In 1644 a vessel escorting a dignitary of the Ottoman Empire was intercepted by the Knights of Malta and the plunder brought back to Khania. Such an act of piracy, albeit fairly commonplace at the time, provided the Sultan with an excuse to blame the Venetians: since the fall of Cyprus, Crete had formed the last obstacle in the way of Ottoman expansion. The invasion of the island began in the summer of 1645 with an attack on Khania by a major fleet under the orders of Yusuf Pasha. The town was captured after a siege lasting fifty-seven days.

HISTORY

Khania occupies the site of ancient Kydonia, once the most powerful city in western Crete. Excavations undertaken in 1965 in the old Kastelli district confirm that the site was occupied during the Neolithic era and the Minoan period.
THE VENETIAN OCCUPATION. The Venetians arrived in 1252 and founded a new city, which they called La Canea. In 1266 the town fell to the Genoese, who controlled it until 1290. Once they had recaptured the town, the Venetians set about its reconstruction, building the basilica, the governor's palace and the houses that can still be seen in the Kastelli district.

THE OTTOMAN OCCUPATION. The town was captured by the Ottomans in 1645 and renamed Khania. In 1850 it became the capital of the island. Captain Spratt, visiting in 1855, described the population in terms of a fascinating mix of Greek Christians, Turkish Muslims and Sephardic Jews.

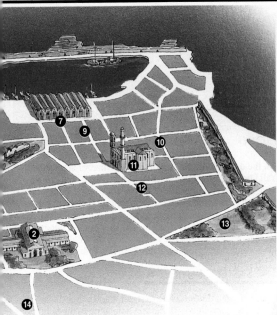

KASTELLI
Decorative features around the doors and windows characterize the Venetian-style houses. Below, the Mosque of the Janissaries, built in 1645, the oldest mosque in Crete.

INDEPENDENCE. When Khania regained its independence in 1898, it retained its position as capital of the island. Following union with Greece in 1913 it became the administrative capital, a role taken over by Heraklion in 1971.

THE VENETIAN HARBOR ★

PLATEIA ELEFTHERIOU VENIZELOU (VENIZELOS SQUARE). This picturesque square, better known as Plateia Santrivani, opens out from the southeast corner of the inner harbor. The seafront promenade, or *paralia*, is lined with cafés and restaurants. The harbor itself is sheltered by a long jetty, with, at its western tip, a Venetian lighthouse that was restored by the Egyptians between 1830 and 1840. On the opposite side of the harbor entrance stands an old tower, known as the Firka, which marks the start of the city walls.

THE PORT OF KHANIA IN THE 18TH CENTURY
The projecting balconies on the Venetian houses are Ottoman additions.

THE COVERED MARKET

This vast cruciform building, surmounted by a cupola, was built in 1911 along the same lines as the municipal market of Marseilles. It is divided into specialized areas, those of the butchers and fishmongers being the most lively. Between the stalls, merchants walk around selling their various wares. Tiny restaurants are dotted about, adding to the general clamor of this animated and colorful market.

THE HARBOR MOSQUE.
On the quayside to the east of the inner harbor stands the Yali Djami, literally the "mosque of the shore" but known by its more common name of the Mosque of the Janissaries ● *112*, a relic of the Ottoman occupation. The Hotel Plaza which stands opposite probably housed a Koranic school during the Ottoman occupation. The fountain set into its façade, below the staircase leading from the small hallway to the second story, probably dates from the Venetian period.

THE KASTELLI DISTRICT ★

In Venetian times Kanevaro street, known then as the "Corso", was lined with houses belonging to the nobility. It leads to the center of the Kastelli district. This little hill overlooking the harbor formed the ancient stronghold; its present form probably dates from 1252 when La Canea was founded by the Venetians. The new inhabitants erected a cathedral and a palace. Remains of the surrounding ramparts can still be seen in places; these were constructed in 1537 by Sanmicheli ● *56* at the request of the Venetians who feared a Turkish invasion. These fears were effectively realized, and the citadel fell.

MINOAN REMAINS. Halfway along Kanevaro street an important Minoan site has been unearthed by a team of Greek and Swedish archeologists; this may have been a palace complex, since Linear A tablets, clay seals, and a lustral bath decorated with frescos were found. The complex was destroyed at the same time as the palace at Knossos, in the Minoan III period, but seems to have been rebuilt during the last two centuries of the Bronze Age, when it may have developed into an important Minoan city. Kydonia continued to play a crucial role in the Roman and Byzantine eras.

IMPRESSION ON A CLAY SEAL OF THE SECOND HALF OF THE 15TH CENTURY BC

This reveals an astonishing representation of the town, with its god or prince of protection standing on the peak of the mountain. The seal was discovered on the acropolis of Kastelli at Khania.

ODOS LITHINON. Lithinon street is the most attractive in the Kastelli district; it is the first left turn off Kanevaro street from the direction of Santrivani Square. The street is lined with fine houses and climbs to a cul-de-sac at the top of a rise where the building housing the Venetian Archives stands; according to the inscription this dates from 1632.

THE FORMER RECTOR'S PALACE. A stroll through the maze of tiny streets to the northeast of Kastelli leads inevitably to the ruins of an elegant palace; this building, the Arcade of San Marco, was the residence of the Venetian Rector of Khania and also the administrative seat of western Crete.

THE VENETIAN ARSENALS. A flight of steps runs down to the cobbled quayside; to the east, this leads to the 15th-century Venetian arsenals where large galley ships were repaired. Moored along the quayside of the inner harbor are rows of fishing boats and pleasure craft, together with old caiques that were once used for maritime trade. Not far from here is the Venetian Loggia, now in ruins. Further east toward the shore of the outer bay the seaward bastion that marks the end of the city walls can be seen, with the winged Lion of St Mark set in its walls.

KHIONES AND SPLANZIA

The area behind the arsenals is known as the Khiones district, while further south is that of Splanzia. During the Venetian period both were inhabited by a working population which was predominantly Greek. Today these are still popular districts where women and children fill the streets by day, while in the evening the menfolk reappear at the usual time to sit at their doorsteps or on café terraces. The best way to explore these districts is by strolling casually through the narrow streets.

PLATEIA 1821. The name of this square commemorates the year that the War of Independence began. The plane tree in the square is sadly infamous as the hanging tree used by the Turks for defiant Cretans. On the other side of the square stands the church of Haghios Nikolaos Splanzias.

THE VENETIAN ARSENALS
On a map published by Coronelli in 1689, thirteen or fourteen of these arsenals can be counted; originally there seem to have been twenty-three. Of these vast vaults, nine have survived, most of them in good repair and still in use.

THE CHURCH OF HAGHIOS NIKOLAOS
It is flanked on one side by a campanile and on the other by a minaret, added by the Ottomans.

"LA CANEA",
ENGRAVED BY
IOANNES PEETERS,
18TH CENTURY
Note that the Venetian lighthouse and the great basilica of St Francis have been crowned by crescents, the emblem of the Ottoman rulers.

This old Turkish hammam near the cathedral is today used as a bronze foundry.

EX-VOTO
This clearly shows the feelings of the Cretans during the German occupation. It is today on show in the Historical Museum on Sphakianakis Street, which traces the Cretan resistance movement under the various occupations.

POSEIDON AND AMYMONE, DETAIL FROM A ROMAN MOSAIC OF THE 3RD CENTURY AD
Roman Kydonia was a prosperous settlement and its villas were decorated with sumptuous mosaic floors: the works displayed in the Archeological Museum date primarily from the 2nd and 3rd centuries AD. They illustrate, for the most part, scenes from mythology. One of these villas, richly decorated with scenes from episodes of the Dionysiac cycle, has been named the "House of Dionysus" after them.

A 16th-century chapel, the Haghii Anargyri, stands behind the church and is dedicated to Saints Cosmas and Damian. The chapel of San Rocco, founded in 1630, stands to the northwest of the square. The public gardens at the far end of Tzanakakis street are the legacy of a Turkish pasha. They contain a small zoo, where *kri-kri* (native goats) can be seen ■ *32*.

THE EVRAIKI DISTRICT

This was the Jewish quarter from the Venetian period until World War Two. Of the rare survivors among the Jews deported by the Germans, only a handful returned to settle in Khania. To the west of the market, Halidon street cuts through the city walls erected by the Venetians in the mid-16th century. South of this thoroughfare, the imposing Shiavo bastion overlooks the square dominated by the Greek Orthodox cathedral of Khania, the Trimartyri or "Three Martyrs", dedicated to the Annunciation and erected in 1865. The rather more modest Catholic cathedral, dedicated to the Assumption, is close by. At the north end of Halidon street stands the imposing 14th-century Venetian church of St Francis. This is the best preserved of the Latin churches; it has been well restored and today houses the Archeological Museum.

St Francis is the largest of
the twenty-three churches
built by the Venetians.
It was originally graced with a
campanile but that has long since
disappeared. It was converted into
a mosque by Yusuf Pasha who
added a minaret; the base of this
survives in the adjoining
garden. The museum was
founded in 1963 and fills
the central nave of the church,
which was restored between 1977
and 1981. The collection displays
artefacts found in the Khania district.

THE MINOAN EXHIBITS. The excavations
carried out by I. Tzedakis in 1965 unearthed
a number of objects from the Minoan period that
are now on show in the museum; these consist primarily
of vases, figurines and painted sarcophagi. Other Minoan
sites have been discovered in the surrounding area: in the
hills, the Late Neolithic cave of Platyvola; close to Perivolia
the cave of Mameloukou; and on the coastal plain, the site
of Nerokourou. The most remarkable piece, since it is the
only one of its kind, is undoubtedly the clay seal of Late
Minoan II origin bearing the impression of a villa. The
majority of artefacts in the collection date from the Late
Minoan III (1400–1100 BC) when Kydonia was an important
craft center, exporting its products to mainland Greece.
The collection of inscribed tablets in Linear B dates from
this period.

THE IRON AGE. The Geometric period
is illustrated by a number of funerary
objects. More of these date from the
Classical and Hellenistic periods (4th to
2nd century BC), indicating an increase
in prosperity: the finest sculptures of this
period are from the temple of Asklepios
at Lissos, near Syia on the south coast.
The Roman period is represented by the
superb mosaics that once decorated the
villas of Kydonia along with colored glassware from a local
workshop at Tarra ▲ 272.

THE GARDEN. In it are displayed architectural remains
from the Greco-Roman, Venetian and Ottoman periods.
The *sadirvan*, from which Santrivani Square derives its
name, is in the far corner. One of the funerary stones in the
courtyard is crowned by a sculpted turban, now supported
by a Corinthian capital. Towards the back of the courtyard
is a monumental Venetian portal,
surmounted by a shield representing a
male bust in an armored helmet, possibly
a rector of Khania. The portal opens
onto what was once the *medrese* of the
Yusuf Pasha Mosque.

TANAGRA, LATE 4TH CENTURY BC
The gentle grace
and elegance of this
terracotta figurine
reveals the influence
of the celebrated
sculptor Praxiteles
(mid-4th century BC)
who reinvented
Greek classical art:
a subtle play of curves
brings the attractive
female figure
to life.

A ten-sided Turkish
fountain, embellished
with fine columns
and a calligraphic
inscription, stands
in the garden of
the Archeological
Museum.

CLAY CHILD'S TOY
This dates from
the late 8th century
BC and was found
in a tomb at
Gavalopmouri, near
Kisamos Kastelli.

THE MARITIME MUSEUM

At the far end of Angelou street stands the Firka tower which houses the Maritime Museum; in it are displayed a number of documents that related to the modern history

of Khania.

A photograph of Prince George, High Commissioner of the island, dates from his arrival in 1898. In another photograph, taken on the harbor in 1913 at the time of union with Greece, the inhabitants can be seen celebrating the end of seven centuries of foreign occupation. The collection also contains some fine model boats, coats of arms and so on. In summer, shows, plays, concerts and folk dancing all take place at the foot of the Firka tower.

THE HOUSES OF KHANIA

The Venetian and Ottoman occupants have clearly left their mark. In the house on the left, the wooden upper story is characteristic of Ottoman architecture; in that to the right, the stone dressings around the door and window indicate the Venetian style.

TOPONA ★

To the west of Santrivani Square follow Zambeliou street, lined with old Venetian houses, as it leads through the Evraiki district to the Topona district. To the left, Kondailaki street leads to a fine Venetian palace; recently restored, this now houses an expensive restaurant. This street, like the next ones, leads up to the Shiavo bastion. At the opposite end of Skoufon street is a fine Venetian gateway. This is the Porta Retimiota (Rethymnon gate) erected by the Venetians and renamed Kale Kapi (Gate of the Fort) by the Ottomans. It was once surmounted by a bas-relief showing the Lion of Saint Mark, now in the Archeological Museum.

THE WALLS. The Topona district begins more or less at the intersection of Skoufon and Zambeliou streets. Not far from here is Theotokopoulou street, a picturesque alleyway that runs the length of the Venetian fortifications; it is linked by several stairways to the *paralia*. Topona was the Muslim quarter of Khania, deriving its name from the *tophane*, the cannon foundry that once stood against the walls. The street leads to the far end of the promontory and to the quayside, where the Firka tower stands. Nearby is the best preserved section of Sanmicheli's ramparts. The 3-mile wall is flanked on the exterior by a ditch some 55 yards wide and 11 yards deep. The Venetians called the formidable redoubt San Demetrio (1546–9). The walls that extend from it to the Shiavo bastion are virtually intact, along with the ditch, where the locals cultivate their vegetable gardens.

THE FIRKA TOWER. Retrace your steps and turn down Angelou street, on the right. This is one of the most attractive streets in Khania; the houses generally date from the Venetian period. The most interesting building is the large tower that was part of the first Venetian edifices. It was destroyed during World War Two but has since been magnificently restored. The tower's history is linked with the Liberation of Crete: in 1913, for the first time, the Greek flag was raised by King Constantine, in the presence of Elephtherios Venizelos ● *64*.

AROUND KHANIA

1. KHANIA 2. THERISO 3. ZOURVA 4. MESKLA 5. PHOURNES 6. ALIKIANOS

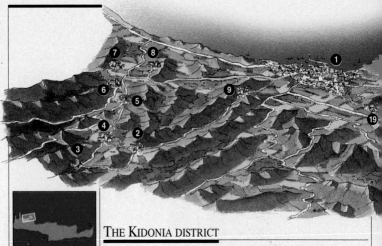

Two days

THERISO ★
Eleftherios Venizelos ● 62 lived here for a long period; his mother was born here also. His house has been turned into a museum. In it, in 1905, the first assembly of Cretan nationalists was held, thus marking the first step on the road toward *enosis* (union with Greece), which came about eight years later. Theriso is also a good starting point from which to climb the peaks of the White Mountains.

THE KIDONIA DISTRICT

The majestic peaks of the White Mountains (Levka Ori) dominate the landscape of western Crete. To the west of the Malaxa massif overlooking the Bay of Souda, the great coastal plain of Khania stretches out between the White Mountains and the sea. With its vineyards, olive and orange groves and numerous farms, this is one of the most fertile regions of Crete. Leaving Khania to the north, take the road signposted to Theriso, a distance of some 9 miles. This route crosses the coastal plain and one of the most attractive gorges in Crete, the Theriso Pharagi gorge, to lead to the foot of the northern slopes of the White Mountains. The cave of Sarakini was discovered near Theriso, its pottery contents indicating occupation from the Neolithic era. It served on several occasions, as did numerous other caves, as a refuge for local inhabitants during periods of war or occupation.

THE WHITE MOUNTAINS. To the south of Theriso loom the twenty-odd peaks of the Levka Ori, of which Mount Pakhnes at 8,042 feet is the highest. Like those of the Ida range to the east, the peaks of the White Mountains are snowcapped for over half the year. The top of Mount Pakhnes remains snow-covered until the end of June; from Khania the first rays of dawn can be seen gilding its white crest.

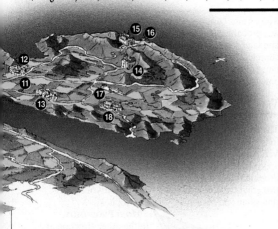

MESKLA
At the entrance to the village a tiny road climbs up toward the Metamorphosis Sotirou, dedicated to the Transfiguration of Christ, which was built in the early part of the 14th century. The narthex was added later. Well preserved frescos in its nave are dated 1302. An inscription mentions the painter Theodoros Daniel and his nephew Mikhail Veneris. The paintings in the narthex are dated 1403.

MESKLA. Beyond Theriso the road loops round through the village of Zourva, the highest hamlet on the north flanks of the White Mountains, to reach the heart of the Riza and Meskla region. Meskla has two churches. Alongside a huge modern church stands the Koimis tis Panaghia, dedicated to the Assumption of the Virgin and dating from the Second Byzantine period. It was built over the foundations of a 5th- or 6th-century basilica, from which fragments of a mosaic floor survive.

THE PORTOKALOKHORIA. For a scenic return trip to Khania, a circuitous route beyond Meskla leads northwest through Phournes and Alikianos. Together with Skines, these villages are known as the Portokalokhoria, or "orange villages". Their extensive orange groves are dubbed the "Garden of Eden".

ALIKIANOS. The village of Alikianos was the scene of a Cretan insurrection led by the Sphakiot chieftain Georgios Kandanoleou in the early part of the 16th century. Kandanoleou formed an independent government in the regions of Sphakia ● 59 and Riza, with Meskla as its base. He and his family were massacred by Francesco Molini, the Venetian governor and local aristocrat. In the village, the charming 13th-century Byzantine church of Haghios

Georgios contains frescos dating from 1430 by Pavlos Provatas. On the way to Kouphos a narrow path leads to the church of Haghios Ioannis, notable for its fine architecture and Greek-cross plan.

HAGHIA. The road toward Khania continues through the village of Haghia. A left turn at the first crossroads leads to the ruined church of the Panaghia. This was the episcopal church of the Greek Orthodox bishop of Kydonia during the Second Byzantine period and throughout Venetian rule. The earlier church,

PHOURNES
Above, the church at Phournes; left, picking oranges. Phournes alone possesses 120,000 orange trees, while Skines has 90,000; a big Orange Festival takes place every year in the Portokalokhoria during Easter Week ● 82. The main agricultural output in the plain consists of the production of oranges and mandarins.

MONASTERY OF HAGHIA TRIADA
At the foot of Tzobomylos, the monastery nestles in a sea of green made up of olive trees, vines and cypresses.

CRETAN RESISTANCE FIGHTERS BRANDISH THE GREEK FLAG ON THE AKROTIRI, 1897
Above the beach at the hamlet of Stavros, near Cape Tripiti, is the cave of Lera; it is named after the head of the Cretan insurrection who used it as a clandestine base during the War of Independence.

whose ruins have not yet been excavated, was probably erected during the First Byzantine period and later destroyed during the Saracen invasions. The present church dates from the 10th or 11th century and incorporates numerous elements from the previous building. Haghia is only 5 or so miles from Khania on the main road.

THE AKROTIRI PENINSULA

The Akrotiri peninsula begins at the city gates of Khania; follow the signs east out of the town. Signs for the "Tafi Venizelon", the tomb of Eleftherios Venizelos, appear approximately 4 miles further on; it is sited on the hill of Prophitis Ilias. On a terrace overlooking the sea two great crosses mark the tombs of both the statesman and his son Sophokles.

MONI PRODOMON. In the other direction, the road leads toward Korakies, where a pause in one of the tavernas allows you to take in the magnificent view over the entire Bay of Souda. Close by is the convent of HAGHIOS IOANNIS PRODOMOS, whose foundation is thought to date back to the Venetian occupation; the embroidery of the nuns is highly regarded.

THE BAY OF KALATHAS. A side road leads north, via Kounoupidiana, to the west coast and the superb beach of the bay of Kalathas.

THE MONASTERY OF HAGHIA TRIADA ★. Returning to Kounoupidiana, take the minor roads leading northeast to reach Moni Haghia Triada, the monastery of the Holy Trinity ● *105*, also known as Moni Zangarolo after its founders. The oldest description of Haghia Triada is by a man called Savary who visited the monastery in 1670 and whose depiction evokes a

MONI GOUVERNETO
The monastery stands on a charming site on the north side of the Akrotiri peninsula. In the center of the monastic buildings, a fortress with corner towers, is the church of the Panaghia Theotokos, Our Lady the Mother of God, barrel-vaulted and embellished with elegant Renaissance motifs ● *102*.

MONI HAGHIA TRIADA
The monastery was founded in 1630 by Lavrentios and Ieremias Zangaroli, two brothers from a Venetian noble family who converted to the Greek Orthodox faith. In the 19th century it housed a college of theology. Its church is a fine cruciform building with two chapels, Zoodokhos Pigi and St John the Theologian. The bell tower dates from 1864.

monastic existence much as it is lived today in Crete: "The monastery possesses all the accoutrements of a farm, with oil and wine presses and all the tools needed to work the land. The priests devote their time to prayer and recitation of the liturgy while the brothers tend to the fields. The monastery resembles a small republic blessed with a wealthy government, whose citizens apply themselves to their work and lead a life of devotion, serenity and joy." Haghia Triada is the most important monastery of the Akrotiri. In it, a Renaissance chapel dated to 1632 still survives, whose portal and campanile display distinctly Venetian characteristics.

THE MONASTERY OF GOUVERNETO ★. A short distance beyond here lies Moni Gouverneto, the monastery of Our Lady of Angels. From the exterior this 16th-century edifice appears to be quite a stronghold, and clearly reflects Venetian influences. It possesses two churches, one dedicated to the Panaghia Theotokos and the other to Haghios Ioannis Xenos, Saint John the Stranger, also known as "Ermitis", the hermit. This saint, who is still much venerated, spent a large part of his life in western Crete. He retired to the cave of Katholiko where he died at the end of the 11th century. Several icons dating

from the 15th century are dedicated to him in the small chapel of the monastery. A path, whose steps are cut from the rock in places, leads to the Moni Katholiko and to several cave sanctuaries at the far end of the peninsula. A walk of ten minutes or so will take you to a sanctuary known from ancient times as the "Bear Cave". A chapel at its entrance is dedicated to the Panaghia Arkoudiotissa, Our Lady of the Bear. Inside is a stalagmite that in ancient times was sacred to the cult of Artemis. The goddess, who was venerated as the protector of animals, is always represented with a bear at her side.

265

STERNES
To the right on entering the village the ghostly outline of a ruined Venetian villa comes into view, its staircase silhouetted against the sky.

MONI KATHOLIKO ★. The path continues toward a stream and after about twenty minutes the roof of the 12th-century Moni Katholiko comes into view. A flight of 130 rock-cut steps leads down to a first cave, then a second and larger cave in which Haghios Ioannis Xenos is said to have lived the last years of his life, before his burial by the monks of his order. Inside, a tiny chapel has been cut from the rock and dedicated to the saint, whose feast day is October 7. Although deserted in the 17th century, the monastery retains a quite extraordinary atmosphere.

THE CAVES. Those at the northern extremity of the Akrotiri peninsula were probably refuges during the Neolithic era. The German archeologist Jantzen discovered human skulls in the cave of Koumarospilia, dating from at least 3400 BC. Dorothea M.A. Bates, who lived in Khania before World War Two, discovered ancient objects and human bones in each of the caves.

THE SOUTH OF THE PENINSULA. To return to Haghia Triada, take the route south; this leads first to Paxinos, with its

Monastery of Paxinos.

MONI KATHOLIKO
The ruins of the monastery can still be seen here and there in a ravine spanned by an old stone bridge, probably built at the same time as Moni Katholiko.

15th-century Venetian monastery. Sternes is some distance away, close to the airport. The village has two churches; the first is dedicated to Haghii Pantes, "All Saints", the second to the Annunciation. Near the second a Minoan villa has recently been unearthed, along with houses and catacombs that appear to date from the Early Christian era. Beyond Sternes the road leads to a beach opposite a Venetian fortress on the islet of Souda. The return road to Khania follows the west side of the bay, as far as the port of Souda ▲ 246. Here, on a superb site in the crook of the bay, is the Commonwealth War Cemetery.

THE GORGE OF SAMARIA

▲ THE GORGE OF SAMARIA

🥾   One day

THE PLAIN OF KHANIA
In this fertile plain
are olive groves,
vineyards and
market gardens
along with
glasshouses
producing tomatoes,
cucumbers,
watermelons and
more recently,
bananas. The orange
groves and lemon
plantations are
concentrated around
the Portokalokhoria
▲ 263.

FROM KHANIA TO THE OMALOS PLATEAU

Between 6 am and 1pm a bus service provides a link
between Khania and Omalos, some 23 miles to the
south at the head of the national park of the gorge
of Samaria. It is well worth leaving as early as
possible to allow enough time for the hike
down this famous gorge.
THE PLAIN OF KHANIA. The bus follows
the main highway across the plain
of Khania, heading southwest.
After the turning for
Alikianos ▲ 263 it
bears southeast
towards Phournes
▲ 263, then
directly
south as
far as
Lakki, climbing the first foothills of the White
Mountains (Levka Ori). With the increase in altitude
chestnut and plane trees begin to appear, along with
terraces of olive trees.
LAKKI. Some 15 miles from Khania, the road passes through
the peaceful and majestic village of Lakki. Perched 1,640 feet
up, this is the final village before the Omalos plateau. It was

founded during the Venetian period by
Sphakiot resistance fighters and has
played a major role in the Cretan
insurrections. Its magnificent church
rises above the tiled roofs of the houses.
The twisting road continues upward,
threading its way between the rocks
as far as Omalos.

THE SAMARIA NATIONAL PARK

In ancient times the
trees of Samaria
were felled to make
columns for palaces
and masts for sailing
ships; they were
exported as far
as Egypt.

This was created in 1962 and consists of the Omalos plateau
and the gorge of Samaria which, running for 11 miles, is the
longest gorge in Europe and takes between five and seven
hours to descend. Nearly 450 plant species grow here ■ 32;
higher up the slopes a rarely seen wild goat known as the
kri-kri may be spotted, along with badgers, weasels and
stone-martens, while birds of prey soar above.

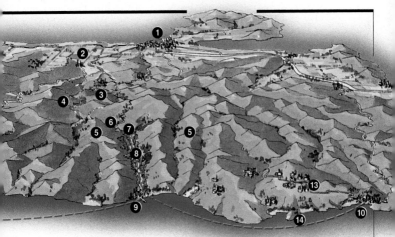

1. KHANIA 2. ALIKIANOS 3. LAKKI 4. OMALOS 5. WHITE MOUNTAINS 6. HAGHIOS NIKOLAOS 7. SAMARIA 8. GORGE OF SAMARIA 9. HAGHIA ROUMELI 10. KHORA SPHAKION 11. PALAIOKHORA 12. SOUYIA 13. ANOPOLIS 14. LOUTRO

THE OMALOS PLATEAU. Over the last pass the Omalos plain comes suddenly into view; at an altitude of 3,445 feet, it stretches across nearly 15 square miles. It is enclosed by brown hills and mountains rising to a height of nearly 8,000 feet. In winter the plateau is covered with snow, which melts in the spring thaw to form a shallow seasonal lake. The streams pouring from it run into a huge cavern, the *katavothron*, visible from the top of the pass. There is an enormous variety of wild plants in the plain, which form carpets of flowers in the spring; flocks of grazing sheep are dotted here and there.

OMALOS. The road leads to the hamlet of Omalos, the only village on the plateau; a tourist office can be found here, along with a restaurant and a few rooms for those wishing to spend the night (camping is forbidden in the national park).

XYLOSKALO. The route down into the gorge of Samaria begins at the village of Xyloskalo (4,025 feet), accessible on foot from Omalos. The view from here is superb: the White Mountains stretch toward the east, while the barren peak of Mount Gigilos (6,580 feet) rises up in the south, its flanks sloping down into narrow wooded valleys of pines and plane trees. Unmarked paths parallel to the official route, which is often crowded, can be taken. These quieter paths have the additional benefit of being closer to the wild fauna. Xyloskalo means "Wooden Staircase", and the first path leading down into the gorge was in effect built from logs by the local mountain folk. The date of its construction is unknown, but the name was already in use in 1834 when Pashley rode up the gorge from Haghia Roumeli as far as the village of Samaria. The Xyloskalo path is well laid out, with wide steps and a ramp along the side of the precipice at the steepest point; on the way down there are springs to quench the thirst. As the path descends deeper into the valley it gradually narrows to the width of a narrow mule trail.

DITTANY
This fragrant plant ■ *32* grows wild only on the steepest mountain slopes. It is loved for its rich scent and is used in infusions; today it is cultivated close to Heraklion.

Beyond Lakki the typical scenery of the Phrygana ■ *32* dominates the terrain: this arid scrub is carpeted with thyme in some parts, with pastel-colored beehives here and there.

269

THE GORGE OF SAMARIA

Over the first mile the path is shaded with pine trees: this is the steepest and most vertiginous section, as over this short distance it descends some 3,200 feet. The descent leads to the upper gorge and to the Neroutsiko, followed by the Riza Sykias springs, providing a thirst-quenching halt.

HAGHIOS NIKOLAOS. In a clearing further along stands a small, white, slate-roofed church dedicated to Saint Nicholas. The clearing is fringed with pines and magnificent cypresses, said to be the tallest in Crete and possibly even the descendants of those used as the pillars for the great palace at Knossos.

THE RIVER. Beyond the church of Haghios Nikolaos the path is gentler, although the walls steadily narrow as it reaches the bottom of the gorge. The noise of running water can soon be heard and flat stones just beneath the water carry the path across the rapids. The water spills from pool to pool, bordered with oleanders, its green and turquoise reflections mirroring the rocks and the greenery.

SAMARIA. The path passes through a more arid landscape where the vegetation huddles in small sun-scorched clumps, to reach a wooden bridge and the village of Samaria, marking the halfway point. The village is now deserted; its inhabitants were rehoused when the national park was created. Two churches still stand: the CHRISTOS CHAPEL, to the west of the gorge, and the chapel of OSSIA (BLESSED) MARIA to the east, the older and more interesting of the two. It was built in 1379 and contains original frescos dating from the Byzantine Renaissance. The chapel, known as Santa Maria by the Venetians, gave its name to the village and gorge. It once possessed a fine

THE GORGE
The path disappears completely in places, forcing hikers to hop from stone to stone to cross the river, when it can only just be traced again on the opposite side. The gorge gradually narrows to the *sideroportes* or "iron gates" where the corridor is just 10 feet wide, while its walls rise up to 1640 feet.

icon, painted in 1740 by a Sphakian artist; since 1962 this has been preserved in a monastery on Mount Athos.

THE "SIDEROPORTES", OR "IRON GATES". Beyond the village of Samaria the path follows a narrow trail winding between massive cliffs some 1,000 to 1,300 feet high. The path penetrates deeper into the gorge, crossing and recrossing the flowing river and its green oases.

A small sanctuary built by Sphakian mountain folk during the Ottoman period can be seen to the left of the path. The entrance to the *sideroportes* now looms into view. Its walls of split and jagged rock, glistening with rusty reds and shades of brown, are striped with lines of anthracite gray that have no doubt been traced by rivulets of water. Each of these three "gates" is narrower and higher than the preceding one; the last one is just over 10 feet wide at river-bed level while its walls, rising to a height of over 1,640 feet, lean together at the top to form a near-complete arch. From the path, a long way down at this point, only a tiny strip of blue sky is visible, while rays like the sunset are reflected on the walls of the ravine. Beyond the *sideroportes* the gorge opens out into a peaceful valley shaded by an olive grove which is surrounded by cypresses, pines, oaks and a few plane trees. After hours of hiking along a rocky path and crossing seemingly endless fords, the walk down through the valley to the coast is pleasantly gentle.

THE END OF THE GORGE

THE SPHAKIOT WARRIORS
The province of Sphakia was relatively independent throughout the various periods of Venetian and Ottoman occupation, because of its virtually inaccessible geographical position. But its ability to maintain a core of resistance was equally due to the courage of its inhabitants, who organized themselves into powerfully armed clans. Even today an abduction or a theft of livestock can trigger a vendetta.

THE OLD VILLAGE OF HAGHIA ROUMELI. The Samaria National Park ends at the level of the original village of Haghia Roumeli, whose inhabitants left in 1962 and were resettled a mile and a half further down on the coast. The village church of Haghios Georgios dates from the Venetian period. The ruins of an Ottoman fort can be seen further along, together with the remains of another Venetian church, dedicated to the Madonna of Haghia Roumeli. Although this dates from the 16th century, fragments of a mosaic floor indicate that it was constructed over a Roman temple. Spratt was the first to mention this building, suggesting that the church had been built on the site of a temple of Apollo linked with the ancient city of Tarra.

LOUTRO
The walk from Haghia Roumeli to Loutro is extremely pleasant and takes about five hours. The journey can also be made by boat. The village of Loutro occupies the site of ancient Finix, the port of the prosperous city of Anapolis whose wealth was based on maritime trade. Barely a trace remains of this glorious past. The fine chapel of Sotiros Christou possesses frescos of the 14th and 15th centuries. A walk to the west of the village leads to a few straggling Roman, Byzantine and Venetian ruins.

KHORA SPHAKION
The sheer cliffs down to the sea are at their most spectacular between Khora Sphakion and Loutro.

Archeological exploration has since revealed that Tarra was founded towards the end of the 5th century BC and survived until the 5th century after Christ. In the early Hellenistic period, beginning around 300 BC, Tarra was one of half a dozen cities along Crete's south coast that made up the Oreioi league, joined later by Gortyn and Cyrenaica. At this time Tarra was already known for its temple of Artemis, to which the Cretan goddess of hunting, Britomartis, had been assimilated. The temple seems to have been one of the most significant cult sites of the Kydonians, the ancestors of the Sphakians.

THE NEW VILLAGE OF HAGHIA ROUMELI. The new village is fringed by a beach of white pebbles, where the swimming is good. It also offers a number of tavernas in which to have a meal while waiting for the boat for Khora Sphakion (6 nautical miles) or Palaikhora (8 nautical miles), from where a bus can be caught back to Khania.

KHORA SPHAKION AND ANAPOLIS. From the small picturesque port of Khora Sphakion, whose fine church is dedicated to the Transfiguration, a road leads to Anapolis, the main town of the Sphakion region, perched high up in the mountains; it can also be reached along a dirt track from Loutro. Nearby, the ruins of the ancient Minoan city of Anapolis are still visible. The village was a center of resistance and was torched by the Venetians in 1365, and again by the Ottomans in 1867.

THE ISLAND OF GAVDOS. A small caique, usually twice a week, links the island with Palaikhora (18 nautical miles) ▲ *280* and Khora Sphakion (12 nautical miles). The island, wooded with pines and cedar trees, offers mooring at Karabe where two tavernas sit side by side next to a small jetty.

ISLAND OF GAVDOS
This island to the southwest of Crete was the ancient Clauda of antiquity, where in legend the nymph Calypso seduced Ulysses. The crystal-clear water of its bays could hardly be more enticing to the bather.

Among its natural features are some magnificent beaches plus the cape at Tripiti, to the south, which is overlooked by three natural arch formations. Gavdos was for a long time a pirates' haunt. During the Byzantine period, its inhabitants numbered over eight thousand. Today its forty-odd inhabitants grow olives and breed goats, whose flesh is prized as a delicacy.

The old village of Haghia Roumeli.

WESTERN CRETE

1 • HAGHIA MARINA
2 • HAGHII THEODORI
3 • PLATANIAS
4 • MALEME
5 • KOLYMBARI
6 • GONIAS MONASTERY
7 • RODOPOS

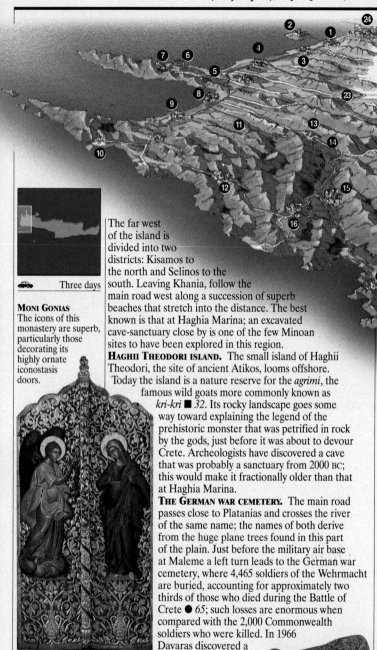

Three days

MONI GONIAS
The icons of this monastery are superb, particularly those decorating its highly ornate iconostasis doors.

Right, Minoan seal depicting a sheep (Archeological Museum of Heraklion).

The far west of the island is divided into two districts: Kisamos to the north and Selinos to the south. Leaving Khania, follow the main road west along a succession of superb beaches that stretch into the distance. The best known is that at Haghia Marina; an excavated cave-sanctuary close by is one of the few Minoan sites to have been explored in this region.

HAGHII THEODORI ISLAND. The small island of Haghii Theodori, the site of ancient Atikos, looms offshore. Today the island is a nature reserve for the *agrimi*, the famous wild goats more commonly known as *kri-kri* ■ *32*. Its rocky landscape goes some way toward explaining the legend of the prehistoric monster that was petrified in rock by the gods, just before it was about to devour Crete. Archeologists have discovered a cave that was probably a sanctuary from 2000 BC; this would make it fractionally older than that at Haghia Marina.

THE GERMAN WAR CEMETERY. The main road passes close to Platanias and crosses the river of the same name; the names of both derive from the huge plane trees found in this part of the plain. Just before the military air base at Maleme a left turn leads to the German war cemetery, where 4,465 soldiers of the Wehrmacht are buried, accounting for approximately two thirds of those who died during the Battle of Crete ● *65*; such losses are enormous when compared with the 2,000 Commonwealth soldiers who were killed. In 1966 Davaras discovered a large Minoan tomb near the cemetery; this was a square chamber whose funerary objects included an agate seal engraved with an *agrimi*. Just over 3 miles away the road leads into

Kolymbari and the base of the Rodopos peninsula, where German archeologists have unearthed the ruins of a sanctuary dedicated to Diktynna, dating from the 2nd century AD.

THE MONASTERY OF GONIAS

In the corner of the peninsula stands Moni Gonias, the "Monastery of the Corner", founded in 1618. The original church was destroyed by the Turks. The present buildings date from 1662 but were restored in 1798 and later modified between 1878 and 1884. There are several fine mural paintings along with some superb icons dating from the 17th and 18th centuries. The most striking among these is an *Annunciation* dating from 1618 on the iconostasis door leading to the sanctuary (opposite, below), together with two icons by the famous Cretan painter Konstantinos Palaiokapas: a *Crucifixion* (1630) and a *Saint Nicholas* (1637). Both these works are housed in the tiny museum, which also contains a display of ecclesiastical vestments and historical documents. Outside the west gate is a fountain with the inscription: "O gentle flowing Spring, let me drink from your water, for water is pure and essential to Life. Erected at the expense of the former Metropolitan of Crete, Kyrios Kallinikos, August 10, 1708". A path from the fountain leads west to a hill and the old church. This dates from the 13th century and preserves a few remains of its original frescos.

BUST OF HADRIAN
Boats leaving from Kolymbari offer excursions to the Rodopos peninsula. In the bay of Menies lies the ruined temple of Diktynna, a pre-Hellenic goddess later identified with Artemis. Several Greco-Roman statues that once adorned it are displayed in the Archeological Museum of Khania.

MONI GONIAS
Despite being fortified the monastery was unable to withstand the assault of 50,000 Ottomans on June 13, 1645, which constituted the first wave of the invasion of Crete. Several of the monks who fled returned in 1651 to set about the restoration of the monastery. This was again attacked by the Ottomans in 1841 and bombarded by a warship in 1867: a cannonball can still be seen in the seaward ramparts.

275

The Villa Trevisani near Kastelli Kisamos.

Bas-relief bacchanal discovered on the site of ancient Polyrrhenia.

KASTELLI–KISAMOS. Returning to the Kolymbari turn-off, continue west along the main road. Beyond a pass, the plain of Kastelli and the bay of Kisamos (Kolpos Kisamou) stretch out below; the bay is bordered to the east by the Rodopos peninsula and to the west by that of Gramvousa. At the end of the road, to the southeast, are the Hellenistic ruins of the ancient town of Falassarna. Just over 4 miles before Kastelli is a sign for Travasiana, so-called after the Villa Trevisani, built during the Venetian period. Kastelli Kisamos occupies the site of ancient Kisamos, which was the port for the city of Polyrrhenia. A certain number of ruins discovered by John Pendlebury point to its being inhabited from 800 BC right up to the Greco-Roman period. Kisamos became an independent city-state during the 3rd century AD and was the seat of a bishop during the First Byzantine period. Following its destruction by the Saracens, the town was rebuilt by the Venetians, who fortified it during the 16th century. The name Kastelli derives from this fort. Recent excavation has uncovered several relics of the ancient city, including sections of a theater, Roman baths, a 3rd-century villa decorated with fine mosaic floors and an aqueduct.

POLYRRHENIA

A fortified acropolis once stood on the hill, occupied first by the Byzantines and then by the Venetians. The buildings were carved from the rock; they spread in terraces across the slopes of the hill. From the shards discovered on the site it seems that ancient Polyrrhenia, the name of which means "many herds", was founded during the Archaic period. The city lasted throughout the Greco-Roman period. Destroyed by the Saracens, it was rebuilt shortly after the reconquest of the island by Nikephoros Phokas ● 48 and later became an important Venetian stronghold.

POLYRRHENIA. The village of Polyrrhenia is just over 4 miles south of Kisamos. Here on a shoulder of the hill stands the church of the Ninety-nine Martyrs, erected over the foundations of a Hellenistic building that was possibly a 4th-century BC temple. Stone slabs with ancient inscriptions have been reused and set in the walls. The principal remains of ancient Polyrrhenia consist of the city fortifications punctuated by semicircular towers. These were no doubt contemporary with the Hellenistic temple; they were repaired in Roman times and rebuilt by the Byzantines, then by the Venetians after them.

THE ENNEAKHORIA

Continuing south toward Topolia the road slowly climbs the slopes of Mount Koutroulis, which rises to 3,514 feet. Several of the mountain villages have Byzantine churches decorated with

The handsome front of the Villa Rotonda (left) in the village of Kalathenes, between Polyrrhenia and Topolia.

frescos: that of Haghios Pandeleimon at Aikirgianis; that of Haghios Georgios, which dates from 1330, at Tsourouniani; while further east around Voulgaro are the churches of Haghios Nikolaos at Mouri, Haghios Georgios at Makronas and Haghia Varvara at Latziana. The church of Haghia Paraskevi in the picturesque village of TOPOLIA possesses frescos dating from the early Venetian period. The road then enters an impressive gorge some 5,000 feet long, which opens out at Koutsomatados. It then passes through an attractive group of villages known as the Enneakhoria, "nine villages". This designation actually includes fifteen hamlets, all of them beautifully situated. The Enneakhoria is thought to occupy the site of the ancient city-state of Inakhorium, whose name, somewhat corrupted, has survived. Elos, perched 1,837 feet up in the heart of a forest of chestnut trees, is one of the most picturesque of these villages. It has two frescoed Byzantine churches. The villages following are Perivolia, Kephali and Vathi, whose church of Haghios Georgios, on the village square, is decorated with frescos dated 1284. South of here a path leads left to a church dedicated to Saint Michael the Archangel ● *101*, containing 14th-century frescos. The Enneakhoria continues further west with Pappadiana, Amigdalokephali, and its church dedicated to the Transfiguration of Christ and decorated with frescos from 1320, and lastly Keramoti, whose red-tiled roofs can be picked out at the bottom of a valley.

The cave of Saint Sophia near the gorge of Koutsomatados was inhabited from the Neolithic period.

The church of the village of Vlatos, between Koutsomatados and the Enneakhoria.

THE MONASTERY OF KHRYSSOSKALITISSA

From Vathi a dirt track leads to the bay of Stomio; nearby looms Moni Khrysoskalitissa, the monastery of Our Lady of the Gold Steps. Legend has it that the staircase leading to it included one gold step and that only the untainted were able to recognize it, thanks to the intercession of the Virgin. The origins of Moni Khrysoskalitissa are far from clear. The recent discovery of fragments dating from the final Minoan periods point to the existence of a settlement during the Bronze Age. It is also quite possible that the promontory attracted hermits during the Byzantine period; the monks of Moni Gonias may have erected an earlier monastery here at the beginning of the Venetian period. This would have served as a refuge to all those attempting to escape the oppression of the Venetians or Ottomans.

MONI KHRYSOSKALITISSA
This monastery forms an isolated citadel on a rocky promontory that drops abruptly to the sea, above which it rises to a height of 115 feet. From time immemorial it has been a haven for shipwrecked victims washed up on the Elaphonisi point to the south of the promontory.
A few monks still inhabit it.

Vines cover nearly 2,223,000 acres of Cretan soil: a third of the vineyards produce red and white wines, while two thirds produce table grapes or raisins, known as Smyrne sultanas. The cultivation of vines in Crete dates back to the Minoan period, when it was still unheard of in mainland Greece and Europe. It was mainly concentrated in the region around Knossos, where a wine press over 4,000 years old has been discovered. Crete would thus appear to be the cradle of wine, whose precious nectar was so favored by the gods of legend.

The Cretan vineyards spread across the hilly slopes, flanked by groves of olive trees.

The grape harvest begins around August 16 following the Feast of the Panaghia.

WINES. In the 16th century wine constituted the main comestible exported by Venetian Crete: at that time the most coveted wines were the perfumed Muscat and the famous Malmsey, which was rich but sweet. Today the vineyards produce several grape varieties. The four major red wines of the island are from Arkhanes, Peza, Daphnes and Sitia.

> "THERE, AS IN COUNTLESS OTHER MEDITERRANEAN COUNTRIES, A GENIE OF THE VINE EXISTED, TO BE CAST OUT OR ELSE APPEASED."
>
> PAUL FAURE

In some cantons the wine is mixed with juniper berries or aniseed. Retsina wine, white or rosé, is flavored with pine resin.

DIONYSOS
The Greek god of wine and inebriation, Dionysos was the son of Zeus and the nymph Semele. Wine and sultana festivals are important events at Epano, Kastelli Kisamos and Perama ♦ 284.

SULTANAS
The yellow sultana grapes, seedless and extremely sweet, are mainly grown in central and eastern Crete. They are harvested in mid-August when their sugar content is over 25 percent. The grapes are first immersed in a bath of potassium carbonate which splits the skin of the fruit to let the juices escape. They are then hung on racks exposed to the sun and wind. At the end of the cycle they will be packed in the KSOS factory in the capital, where they will be graded, packaged and sold throughout the European Community.

279

Above, the beaches
of Elaphonisi.

PALAIOKHORA
The new village
of Palaiokhora
has become an
extremely pleasant
holiday spot
thanks to its
long, beautiful
beaches.

ELAPHONISI BAY. A dirt track from the monastery leads
south and after some 3 miles arrives in the crook of the bay
of Elaphonisi. This is the site of one of the finest beaches
in the island, a great curve of pinkish sand bordered with
tamarisks, with a lagoon enclosed by coral reefs.

PALAIOKHORA. Returning to Vlatos, take the road to
Palaiokhora. Old Palaiokhora is situated on a promontory
overlooked by the ruins of a Venetian fortress, while the
new village has grown up along the eastern shore of the
isthmus. A huge beach shaded with tamarisks stretches west

along the tiny bay of Selinou Kastelli,
whose name derives from the fortress
erected by the Venetian governor
Marino Gradenigo in 1282 in order
to guard the two bays. The building
has recently been restored and is open
to the public.

KANDANOS. The district of Selino is
renowned for its numerous churches
dating from the Byzantine and early
Venetian periods. These are particularly
numerous between Palaiokhora and
Kandanos, the capital of the Selino
district, and often contain original
frescos, some of which are by the great
Cretan painter Ioannis Pagomenos.
Kandanos is 10½ miles north of
Palaiokhora. During the Byzantine
period it was the see of the Greek

VOUKOLIES
Above, the tiny
church of Haghios
Konstantinos at
Voukolies. The
village is the market
center of this fertile
region where olive
groves and vineyards
abound. The region
produces cereals,
wine and chestnuts.
A market is held
every Saturday.

Below, the bus
for Palaiokhora.

Orthodox church, while under the Venetians it was that of
the Roman Catholic church; both have left the region rich in
art and architecture. To cite but a few of the most interesting
churches in the area, from south to north: that of the Nativity
at Kadros; Haghios Issidoros near Kakodiki; and Haghios
Georgios at Plemeniana. The village of ANISARAKI, to the
east of Kandanos, has no less than four churches of the 14th
and 15th centuries, all of them frescoed: Haghia Anna,
Haghios Georgios, the Panaghia and Haghia Paraskevi.
From Anisaraki the road leads south to SOUYIA, a tiny village
on the site of ancient Syia, of which a few Roman ruins are
left. The modern church was built over the foundations of
an Early Christian basilica whose mosaic floor, with its
deer and peacock designs, is quite
remarkable. To the west of
Souyia, straggling in the
undergrowth, lie the
remains of the temple
of Asklepios and a
building of Roman
origin from ancient
Lissos. From
Kandanos the
main road
leads to
Voukolies
and from
there
toward
Khania.

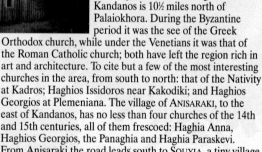

PRACTICAL INFORMATION

Greece has been a member of the European Community since 1981: nationals of most countries will encounter no particular entry restrictions. Crete's beaches and historical sites make it a very popular destination in the high season, therefore it is advisable to book your flights and hotel accommodation in advance.

FORMALITIES

An identity card or valid passport is sufficient for a short stay. A visa is needed for a stay of longer than three months.

CUSTOMS

Greece's customs regulations are the same as elsewhere in the European Community. You may export items to a maximum value of £300/$480 per person. This sum is not divisible, however: items of higher value cannot be shared among several people.

CURRENCY

There is no limit on the amount of foreign currencies which may be brought into Crete, but you may not import more than Dr 100,000, nor export more than Dr 25,000, per person.

HEALTH

You will need an official prescription to bring certain medicines onto Greek territory. You can obtain from your Social Security office a form guaranteeing the reimbursement of healthcare costs incurred abroad.

ANIMALS

You may bring your pets to Crete with you, provided they have a recent certificate of health (six months for cats, one year for dogs) stating that they have been vaccinated against rabies. However, if you are staying in a hotel you should find out if pets are allowed there. Remember that animals returning to the UK must undergo six months' quarantine.

VEHICLES

If you are traveling in your own car, bring vehicle registration documents and your insurance card, as well as your driving license (national or European). You will also need a driving license to hire a car in Crete.

PURE CRETE
79 George Street
Croydon
Surrey CR0 1LD
Tel. 0181 760 0879

KOSMAR VILLA HOLIDAYS
358 Bowes Road
London N11 1AN
Tel. 0181 368 6833

For details of other travel companies offering holidays in Crete, contact the Greek Tourist Agency.

UK AND US EMBASSIES IN CRETE

AMERICAN EMBASSY
91 Vassilisis Sophias Avenue
10160 Athens
Tel. (1) 721 29 51

BRITISH EMBASSY
1 Ploutarkhou Street
Kolonaki,
Athens
Tel. (1) 723 62 11

INFORMATION

IN THE UK
GREEK TOURIST AGENCY
4 Conduit Street,
London W1R 0DJ
Tel. 0171 287 1369

IN THE US
GREEK TOURIST OFFICE IN NEW YORK
Olympia Towers,
645 Fifth Avenue
5th floor
New York,
N.Y. 10022
Tel. (212) 421 5777

GREEK TOURIST OFFICE IN CHICAGO
168 North Michigan Avenue,
Suite 600,
Chicago,
IL 60601
Tel. (312) 782 1084

GREEK TOURIST OFFICE IN LOS ANGELES
611 West 6th Street,
Suite 2198
Los Angeles,
CA 90017
Tel. (213) 626 6696

MAJOR AIRLINES THAT FLY TO GREECE

IN THE US
AMERICAN AIRLINES
For flight information
Tel. (800) 228 8356

TWA
For flight information
Tel. (800) 221 2000

UNITED AIRLINES
For flight information
Tel. (800) 241 6522

IN THE UK
BRITISH AIRWAYS
For flight information
Tel. 0181 759 2525

OLYMPIC AIRWAYS
11 Conduit Street
London N1R
Tel. 0171 409 2400
or 0171 409 3717

SOME SPECIALIST TRAVEL COMPANIES IN THE UK

SIMPLY TRAVEL
Chiswick Gate
598–608 Chiswick High Road
London W4 5RT
Tel. 0181 994 4462

GREEK ISLAND WANDERING
51A London Road
Hurst Green
East Sussex
TN19 7QP
Tel. 01580 860733

OLYMPIC HOLIDAYS LTD
Olympic House
30/32 Cross Street
London N1 2BG
Tel. 0171 359 3030

SIMPLY SIMON HOLIDAYS
1–45 Nevern Square
Earls Court
London SW5
Tel. 0171 373 1933

TYPICAL COST OF A ONE-WEEK STAY (SEVEN NIGHTS)

◆ For a couple taking a charter flight, and staying in mid-range accommodation:
Flight £400
+ Hotel £370
+ Restaurants £230
= £1000
◆ A couple with two children, traveling with a tour operator:
Fixed price including flight, hotel and full board = £1860
◆ For a couple taking a scheduled flight, and staying in top-of-the-range accommodation:
Flight £900
+ Hotel £890
+ Restaurants £510
= £2300

◆ WHEN TO GO

CALENDAR OF THE SEASONS		
SPRING		**March to May**

Easter is still the most important festival in the Orthodox calendar: celebrations are lavish in Crete, as elsewhere in Greece.

FIRST MONDAY OF MARCH	**LENT,** PUBLIC HOLIDAY
MARCH 25 INDEPENDENCE DAY	**NATIONAL FESTIVAL** PUBLIC HOLIDAY
EASTER MONDAY	PUBLIC HOLIDAY
GOOD FRIDAY, EASTER SATURDAY PUBLIC HOLIDAYS	**PROCESSIONS** of the Epitaphion, a chance to hear the most beautiful Byzantine hymns
APRIL 23 ST GEORGE'S DAY	In Asi Gonia, gathering of all the shepherds and distribution of sheep's milk
MAY 1	**LABOR DAY,** PUBLIC HOLIDAY

★ Churches lit by candlelight, Easter Saturday at midnight

MARCH	48°–64°
APRIL	52°–72°
MAY	59°–79°

SUMMER		**June to August**

Summer is the festival season at Heraklion and Rethymnon. But in Crete religious traditions are strongest of all: there are many events celebrating the different saints' days.

JULY TO AUGUST	**HERAKLION FESTIVAL** Concerts, theater, opera
JULY TO AUGUST	**RETHYMNON FESTIVAL** In twenty-seven towns and villages
END OF JULY	**FESTIVAL OF DIONYSOS WINE FESTIVAL** In the municipal park
JULY 26	**FESTIVAL OF SAINT PARASKEVI** Candlelit procession to the cave of Skotino, folk music and dancing
AUGUST 15 PUBLIC HOLIDAY	**FEAST OF THE ASSUMPTION OF THE VIRGIN** Dancing and fireworks

★ Visit the cave of Skotino

JUNE	66°–86°
JULY	70°–90°
AUGUST	70°–90°

AUTUMN		**September to November**

From now on, out of the tourist season, the festivals held in out-of-the-way villages retain their traditional character. It is customary to offer hospitality to visitors who come to take part in the festivities.

SEPTEMBER TO OCTOBER	**DISTILLATION OF *RAKI*** Celebrations in the squares of many villages, especially around Sitia.
OCTOBER 7	**FESTIVAL OF JOHN THE EVANGELIST** In the Gouverneto monastery at Akrotiri
NOVEMBER 7–9	**COMMEMORATION** At Arkadi monastery
NOVEMBER 11	**FESTIVAL OF HAGHIO MINAS** At Heraklion

★ Hear a *lyra* being played in a village square

SEPTEMBER	66°–82°
OCTOBER	61°–75°
NOVEMBER	55°–68°

WINTER		**December to February**

Religious festivals take place practically all winter in Greece.

DECEMBER 25 PUBLIC HOLIDAY	**CHRISTMAS**
JANUARY 1 PUBLIC HOLIDAY	**NEW YEAR'S DAY**
JANUARY 5 PUBLIC HOLIDAY	**EPIPHANY**
A FORTNIGHT BEFORE LENT	**HERAKLION** and **RETHYMNON** Carnival with processions and festivities
LAST MONDAY BEFORE LENT	Kite-flying

★ Carnival at Rethymnon

DECEMBER	50°–64°
JANUARY	46°–59°
FEBRUARY	46°–59°

☀ sunny and hot	☁ changeable to cloudy	☁ rainy	☁ cold, snow possible

The minimum and maximum temperatures for each month are given in degrees Fahrenheit

PUBLIC HOLIDAYS

January 1:
New Year's Day
January 6:
Epiphany
March 25:
Annunciation,
national holiday
in memory of the
uprising against
the Turks in 1821
Good Friday:
Some shops
and offices
are closed
Easter Saturday:
offices are closed

**Easter Sunday
and Monday:**
Orthodox Easter
May 1:
Labor Day
August 15:
Assumption of
the Virgin
October 28:
Ochi ("No") day, in
memory of Greece's
refusal of Mussolini's
ultimatum in 1940
December 25 and 26:
Christmas Day,
St Stephen's Day

WEATHER FROM MAY TO OCTOBER

	MAY	JUNE	JULY	AUG	SEPT	OCT
DAY TEMPERATURE						
	68°	75°	79°	79°	73°	68°
NIGHT TEMPERATURE						
	61°	68°	73°	73°	68°	46°
HOURS OF SUNSHINE DAILY						
	10	12	12	11	10	7
NUMBER OF RAINY DAYS						
	4	2	0	1	2	7
TEMPERATURE OF THE SEA (DAYTIME)						
	66°	73°	75°	77°	75°	73°
TEMPERATURE OF THE SEA (NIGHT-TIME)						
	54°	61°	63°	64°	59°	55°

SPECIAL TIP
THE BEST TIME TO VISIT CRETE

The island has the advantage of a
slight breeze which makes the heat
more bearable than in mainland Greece.
Spring and autumn are still the best times
to visit the archeological sites, however,
and to avoid the summer crowds. The sea
is still warm enough for swimming and
the plant life is at its best: verdant
and brightly colored.

MAPS

Road signposting in Crete is
patchy, especially in out-of-the-way
areas. It is best to buy a good map.
These are sold in the kiosks or *peripteros*,
and in bookshops: the best ones are
Hannibal (1/275,000), Efstathiadis
(1/200,000), Nelles (1/200,000) and
Harms (1/80,000).

CLOTHING

In summer, bring
light clothes, a hat
and sunglasses.
Do not forget to
bring a cardigan or
jacket, however, as
the evenings can
be cool. In spring
and autumn bring
a wind-cheater or
anorak and a pullover
for the evening and
for days of *meltemi*
(Etesian wind from
the north). Formal
clothes are not
necessary. If you
are invited to a
Cretan home,
casual clothes are
sufficient. Bring
flat, comfortable
shoes for visiting
archeological sites.
When visiting
churches, women
should not have
bare arms: always
carry a shirt, a
cardigan or a shawl
so as not to be
caught unprepared.

WHAT TO BRING

The light wind can
disguise the strength
of the sun's rays:
a sun-cream is vital,
especially for your
first days in Crete.
You should also
be aware that the
change of water
and naturally
occurring bacteria
can sometimes
cause stomach
upsets, as can
olive oil. However,
pharmacists on
the island are quite
used to dealing
with these and
other difficulties
and can solve them
easily. Proprietary
medicines are
cheap, so you will
not need to bring
extensive supplies.
Films and
flashlights can be
bought in large
towns, as in
Greece, but prices
are high: it is a
good idea to bring
these with you.

WHAT TO READ

Ill Met by Moonlight
(1948) by W.S. Moss,
a moving account of
Cretan resistance in
World War Two.
Zorba (1946), *Letter
to El Greco* (1961),
both by Nikos
Kazantzaki, the
leading Cretan writer.
The Cretan (1957)
by Pandelis
Prevelakis, a quest
for freedom.
The Greek Islands
by Lawrence Durrell.
*The Colossus of
Maroussi* (1941)
by Henry Miller, an
account of his
journey with
Lawrence Durrell.

DISTANCES BETWEEN ATHENS AND OTHER EUROPEAN CITIES

London   1,906 miles
Paris   1,820 miles
Berlin   1,827 miles
Rome   777 miles
Madrid   2,362 miles

From Athens to Crete is around 250 miles: allow twelve hours for the boat crossing.

BY AIR

Charter flights are usually cheaper than the airline scheduled flights, and many fly direct to Crete in season, from Easter to around October 15. Otherwise there are no direct flights between the UK and Crete and it is necessary to fly to Athens and then continue to Crete via a domestic flight or ferry crossing.

CHARTER FLIGHTS

These are booked through travel agents and tour operators and fly from several airports in the UK, such as Manchester, Newcastle, Bristol, Birmingham and Glasgow as well as from Gatwick and Heathrow. There are well over a hundred tour operators or travel agents in the UK offering flights to Crete: for further details, see page 283 or contact the Greek Tourist Agency in London.

CHEAP FARES

◆ British Airways operate a system of cheap fares from Monday to Thursday. Offers change every fortnight, however, so contact the airline for up-to-the-minute details on flights to Athens.
◆ Olympic Airways in London also offer seasonal flight bargains which compare favourably with charter flight fares.

BRITISH AIRWAYS

Daily flights to Athens depart from London Gatwick North Terminal at 9.10am, and from Heathrow Terminal 4 at 1.40am and 11pm. Full fare around £490 return in high season, £350–£382 in September and around £300–£332 through the low season. Airport tax of £21.70 covers both London and Greece.

OLYMPIC AIRWAYS

Daily flights to Athens from Heathrow Terminal 2 depart at 12.30pm. There is also a high season flight at 4.40pm and, daily except Wednesdays, a 10.30pm flight. These arrive at Athens Olympic (West) Terminal, from which you can catch domestic flights to Crete.

BY TRAIN

Regular departures from London's Victoria station, via Paris. Tel. 0171 834 2345

BY CAR AND FERRY

You should allow at least five days on the road, traveling via France, Germany, Austria and Hungary, to reach Athens. Once there, the regular ferry service provides a connection between Piraeus, the port of Athens, and the main towns on Crete's north coast. The crossing is free of charge for children of under four years and half-fare for children of four to ten years. Standard foot passenger fare £12–£16. Vehicle charge £30–£45.
PIRAEUS–HERAKLION Departs each day at around 7pm.
PIRAEUS–RETHYMNON Departs each day at around 7pm.
PIRAEUS–KHANIA Departs each day at around 8pm.

PARIS
LYONS
MARSEILLES

NAPLES

FROM THE UK

MEDI

COST OF THE TRIP, INCLUDING RETURN

From the U.K.	Duration	Rough price
Scheduled flight (change at Athens)	4 h	£375
Charter flight (direct to Crete)	4 h	£250
By train to Athens (including ferry crossing)	62 h	£330
By car and ferry (typical cost for two people)	120 h	£450

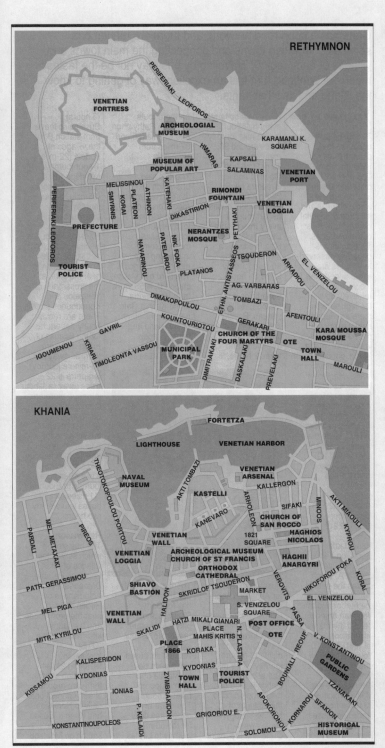

RETHYMNON

PERIFERIAKI LEOFOROS

VENETIAN
FORTRESS

ARCHEOLIGIAL
MUSEUM

KARAMANLI K.
SQUARE

HMARAS

KAPSALI

SALAMINAS

VENETIAN
PORT

MUSEUM OF
POPULAR ART

MELISSINOU

KATEHAKI

RIMONDI
FOUNTAIN

SMYRNIS
KORAI
PLATEON
ATHINON

VENETIAN
LOGGIA

DIKASTIRION

PREFECTURE

NAVARINOU
PATELAROU
NIK. FOKA

NERANTZES
MOSQUE

PETYHAKI

TSOUDERON

ARKADIOU

EL. VENIZELOU

PLATANOS

TOURIST
POLICE

AG. VARBARAS

ETHN. ANTISTASSEOS

DIMAKOPOULOU

TOMBAZI

AFENTOULI

GERAKARI

KARA MOUSSA
MOSQUE

GAVRIL

KOUNTOURIOTOU

CHURCH OF THE
FOUR MARTYRS

OTE

IGOUMENOU

KRIARI

TIMOLEONTA VASSOU

MUNICIPAL
PARK

DIMITRAKAKI

DASKALAKI

PREVELAKI

TOWN
HALL

MAROULI

KHANIA

FORTETZA

LIGHTHOUSE

VENETIAN HARBOR

THEOTOKOPOULOU PORTOU

NAVAL
MUSEUM

VENETIAN
ARSENAL

AKTI TOMBAZI

KALLERGON

AKTI MIAOULI

KASTELLI

ARHOLEON

SIFAKI

MINOOS

KANEVARO

CHURCH OF
SAN ROCCO

KYPROU

MEL. METAXAKI

PIRECS

VENETIAN
WALL

1821
SQUARE

HAGHIOS
NICOLAOS

PARDALI

VENETIAN
LOGGIA

ARCHEOLOGICAL MUSEUM
CHURCH OF ST FRANCIS

HAGHII
ANARGYRI

KORAI

PATR. GERASSIMOU

ORTHODOX
CATHEDRAL

VEROVITS

NIKOFOROU FOKA

MEL. PIGA

SHIAVO
BASTION

HALIDON

SKRIDLOF TSOUDERON

MARKET

EL. VENIZELOU

MITR. KYRILOU

VENETIAN
WALL

SKALIDI

HATZI MIKALI GIANARI
PLACE
MAHIS KRITIS

S. VENIZELOU
SQUARE

PASSA

REOUF

BOUNIALI

V. KONSTANTINOU

KALISPERIDON

N. PLASTIRA

POST OFFICE

OTE

PUBLIC
GARDENS

KISSAMOU

KYDONIAS

PLACE
1866

KORAKA

KYDONIAS

TZANAKAKI

IONIAS

ZYMBRAKIDION

TOWN
HALL

TOURIST
POLICE

KORNAROU

SFAKION

KONSTANTINOUPOLEOS

P. KELADI

GRIGORIOU E.

APOKORONOU

SOLOMOU

HISTORICAL
MUSEUM

Crete has a good road network, and there are regular bus services both within towns and connecting the main towns and villages of each region. Traveling by bus may not be the fastest means of transport, but it is an excellent way of getting to know the island and its inhabitants.

TRAVELING BY BUS

Taking the bus is of course the cheapest way of getting around. The network is quite well organized and covers the whole of the island, linking the regional capitals with most outlying villages. Timetables are generally observed, the drivers are experienced, and the vehicles are relatively new. In the high season there are departures nearly every hour on the main routes in the north of the island, connecting Khania, Rethymnon, Mallia, Haghios Nikolaos and Sitia. For more details you can obtain a leaflet from the local bus services (KTEL) in the main towns. Telephone numbers of KTEL:
Haghios Nikolaos: (0841) 22 234
Heraklion: (081) 283 925
Khania: (0821) 23 024
Rethymnon: (0831) 22 212

HERAKLION

Heraklion has three bus stations. Station A, which serves the east of the island, is near the harbor and the Venetian arsenals, behind the marina.
Information:
tel. (081) 24 50 20
You should allow one hour's journey time to get to Khersonisos and Mallia, which are 23 miles from Heraklion. Buses depart half-hourly. Buses to Haghios Nikolaos also leave every half-hour; the 43-mile journey takes around 90 minutes.
To get to Istron, Gournia and Ierapetra takes 2½ hours (a journey of 65 miles); buses depart roughly every three hours. Buses leave for Sitia five times a day at least; the 90-mile journey takes 3½ hours. There are two departures daily for the Lassithi plateau, Psykro and the Dikte cave; the journey is 43 miles long and takes 2 hours.

Buses also leave for Akharnes nearly every hour (30-minute journey, of 11 miles); for Haghia Pelagia they leave four times daily (30-minute journey, of 19 miles). The second bus station is also near the harbor, next to the Institute of Marine Biology; it serves western Crete and the major northern route between Rethymnon and Khania (55 and 87 miles from Heraklion, respectively).
There is also a bus which takes the old Rethymnon road. This is of course a longer journey but the route passes through some interesting little mountain villages. The third bus station, station B, is 55 yards from Hanioporta, at the Khania Gate. It serves the south of the island and some villages.
Information:
tel. (081) 25 59 65

There are several departures each day for Gortys, Phaistos and the plain of Messara (a 40-mile, 2-hour journey).
At least six buses leave each day for Matala (the 47-mile journey takes 2 hours).
There are two departures daily for the 50-mile journey to Lentas (3 hours).
Buses also leave from station B for the villages of Fodele (22-mile, 1-hour journey, two departures daily), and Anogia (25-mile, 1-hour journey, four departures daily).

HAGHIOS NIKOLAOS

Information: tel. (0841) 22 234 and 28 284
The bus station is near the lake, at the crossroads of Venizelou and Koundourioti streets. There are regular, hourly departures for the villages of Kritsa and Kera (6 miles away, 15-minute journey). Ierapetra is 22 miles away (a 1-hour journey); there are ten departures each day.
At least seven buses leave for Sitia each day (the 47-mile journey takes 1½ hours). It is a 40-minute journey to Elounda (11 miles away); buses leave every two hours.

RETHYMNON

The bus station which serves the villages of Viran Episkopi, Perama, Dafnedes and Apladiana is on Hiroon Square, near the promenade and the tourist information office (OTE).
Information:
tel. (0831) 29 644
In the high season there are around fifteen connections daily to Heraklion and Khania. Buses leave from the station on Moatsou

ΠΛΑΤΕΙΑ
ΑΓ. ΑΙΚΑΤΕΡΙΝΗΣ
ΙΣΤΟΡΙΚΗ ΜΟΝΗ ΤΟΥ ΣΙΝΑ

ΛΕΩΦΟΡΟΣ
ΝΙΚ. ΠΛΑΣΤΗΡΑ
ΗΡΩΙΚΟΣ ΣΤΡΑΤΗΓΟΣ κ ΠΟΛΙΤΙΚΟΣ

and Dimokratias streets.
Buses also leave here for the villages of Armeni, Spili, Haghia Galini, Plakias, Rodakino and Gonia.
The urban bus network also serves the suburbs of Atsipopoulo, Perivolia and Adele, as well the major hotels. All buses pass through Koundourioti Avenue.

Khania

The KTEL bus station is at 7, Kydonias Street. Information: tel. (0821) 23 052 and 23 306
In addition to connections with other towns of the northeast (already mentioned), the bus network serves the villages of Kalathas-Stavros (three times daily), Kastelli–Kisamos (every hour), and Kastelli–Kisamos–Falassarna (twice daily).
There are two departures daily for Chora Sfakion and two departures, early in the morning, for the gorge of Samaria.

Traveling by taxi

The taxis waiting outside airports generally cover long-distance journeys. Official fares are posted inside every airport. Even so, it is generally best to agree the fare for the journey with the driver before setting out. The general style of driving is quite aggressive: even if you are running short of time it is probably not necessary to say so. The main taxi ranks in the town center of Heraklion are opposite the Loggia, in front of the Astoria Hotel and on Kornarou Square.

Car hire

Here the only problem is choosing. In Heraklion, car hire agencies can be found on August 25 Street, between the harbor and Lion Square. In Khania they are near the Venetian Harbor. The major agencies also have branches at airports. You may prefer the big names to less well-known companies – although in the latter it is possible to negotiate

competitive rates. It is a good idea to check two-wheeled vehicles thoroughly before hiring, especially at seaside resorts. A B license is required for motorbikes over 50 cc; an A licence for those over 250 cc. It is always wise to take extra care when driving in town: rights of way are rarely observed, drivers often go through red lights, and emergency stops are generally the order of the day. In Heraklion there are a number of "blue zones" in the centre of the town, Liberty Square and Plastiras Avenue, where you have to have a parking ticket, which can be purchased at the nearest kiosk. In theory, speed limits are 50 km/h (30 mph) in built-up areas, 80 km/h (50 mph) outside built-up areas, and 100 km/h (62 mph) on the island's main roads. In an emergency you can contact the ELPA (Automobile Club of Greece) at:
Heraklion
junction of Knossou Avenue and Papandreou Street, Tel. (081) 28 94 40
Khania
junction of Apokoronou and Skoula Streets, Tel. (0821) 260 59

Social relations in Crete are not subject to a rigid or fussy code of behavior, so the number of serious blunders a foreigner can make is limited. Nevertheless, language obviously poses a number of difficulties and traps. Even if you can speak Greek fluently, you should not attempt to pass yourself off as a native Cretan – nothing could teach this, and the islanders will instinctively find you out.

HOW TO BEHAVE IN CRETE

To get to know Cretan hospitality you only need to strike up a conversation. But do take special care to check how words are stressed in your dictionary: altering the main cursing gesture which is widespread throughout the Mediterranean. By the same token, do not be shocked or misled if a villager spits lightly on the ground when greeting you: he has no doubt complimented your health or the beauty social status of your hosts, and whether they are accustomed to foreigners. In general, follow your instincts. Crete's main towns may be by the sea, but this does not make them seaside resorts: when visiting, you should obviously avoid

For Cretans it is a point of honor to eat well and treat their guests with hospitality, so do not be afraid to show a hearty appetite. Excuses like "being on a diet" will not go down well. After all, a local proverb says that "fat is beautiful". Cretans are generous, hospitable, with the gift of *philotimo* – an untranslatable expression, suggesting their sense of what is due to you and to themselves; they will happily open their houses, their wine cellars, and their hearts to you. If you are planning to pay a visit to a church or a monastery, avoid wearing shorts. Trousers are also inadvisable for women. Have a long skirt or tunic with you, just in case. A detail: the orthodox sign of the cross is made from right to left. If you are thinking of hitch-hiking, be sure to dress discreetly and, whenever possible, travel with a companion. Even though tourism has become well-established in Crete over the last twenty years or so, foreign women can still be the subject of fantasies which can be sparked off even by trivial things. If you are

An informal gathering at the local village café.

stress can change a word's meaning completely. You might say "awful", thinking you are talking about carpets; or you may get sent to the nearest glazier when you ask the way to the mosque. However, in the main tourist areas English is generally spoken very proficiently. Some gestures should be deliberately avoided: holding the arms away from the body, with palms raised and fingers spread out, is the *moutza*, a of your children, but considers it wise to ward off ill fortune, or avoid committing *hubris*, (the sin of pride) to be on the safe side. Avoid offending national sensibilities by ordering a "Turkish" coffee: ask for a *hellinikoss* instead. In souvenir shops in large towns you do not have to haggle. If absolutely necessary, act as if you are going off to another shop. If you are invited into a Cretan home, everything depends on the age and shorts and sandals. Relations may be very casual, but in matters of dress a certain decorum is required, particularly for women. Cretans' idea of time is not Anglo-Saxon: "Come in the afternoon" means after 6pm. You can call people on the telephone up to 10pm, but it is best to avoid calling during the siesta, between 3pm and 5pm, especially in the summer. Meals are generally eaten quite late: lunch around 2pm, dinner at 9pm.

traveling alone, do not forget that some hotels – even the larger ones – encourage their staff to make themselves very available to guests: over-friendliness on your part, however innocent in intent, could be interpreted as encouragement. *Kamaki* – semi-professional harpooning or taking for a ride – is virtually a sport, or business, throughout Greece: it could end up costing you dearly!

A picturesque Cretan grocery store.

WHERE TO STAY

Average prices for each class of hotel are fixed by the government. However, the overall quality of accommodation can vary enormously even within a single class. And do remember that it is best to reserve hotel rooms during the high season.

LUXURY HOTELS
Spacious rooms or suites, with air conditioning and en-suite bathrooms. Additional facilities might include a swimming pool, private beach, saunas, tennis, bar, restaurant, taverna.

CLASS A HOTELS
Very comfortable rooms, with air conditioning and bathrooms. They generally have a swimming pool, restaurant, bar, maybe even a private beach and a discotheque.

CLASS B HOTELS
Rooms may have air conditioning; they will have bathrooms or washrooms with shower. Many often have their own taverna or restaurant.

CLASS C HOTELS
Rooms of a medium or simple standard, with washroom and private WC.

CAMPING
Crete has fourteen officially registered campsites. You can obtain their addresses from the Greek Tourist Office. Camping elsewhere is forbidden.

PRIVATE LODGINGS
This is extremely common in small towns and villages, both by the sea and in the mountains. You can obtain information on these from local tourist offices.

OTHER
It is also possible to rent flats or bungalows, or apartments in holiday villages. Again, contact a local tourist office.

FOOD

meat: *kreass*
meatballs: *keftedhakia*
lamb chop: *paidhakia*
pork chop: *yhirini britzola*
veal cutlet: *mia moskharissia*
fillet: *ena bonn fileh*
fish: *psari*
squid: *kalamaria*
octopus: *khtapodi*
mullet: *barbouni*
French fries: *tighanitess patatess*
rice: *pilafi*
bread: *psomi*
cheese: *tyri*
green salad: *marouli*
mixed salad: *khoriatiki salata*
beer: *bira*
coffee: *kafess*
Turkish coffee: *hellinikoss*
instant coffee: *enass ness*
with sugar: *glykoss*
without sugar: *sketoss*
medium: *metrioss*
with milk: *meh ghala*
well-done: *kala psimenoss*
water: *nero*
mineral water: *emmfyalomeno*
wine: *krassi*
white: *asspro*
red: *kokkino*

SPECIALTIES
barbounia: red mullet, served whole
moussakas: aubergines, mince, potatoes and béchamel sauce
pastitsio: macaroni, mince and bechamel sauce
souvlaki: meat kebabs with spices and tomatoes; these may be served in pitta bread
keftedhes: spicy meatballs
taramosalata: puree of fish roe mixed with olive oil and spices
tzatziki: salad of cucumber, yogurt and garlic
manouri: sheep's milk cheese
madares: meat stew with cheese and potatoes
spanakopites: spinach-filled pastry parcels
tyropites: cheese-filled pastry parcels

Taverna Vassilis in Heraklion.

THE PRICE OF A TELEPHONE CALL (IN DRACHMA PER MINUTE)

HERAKLION	Cost of the first 3 minutes	Cost per additional minute	
	455 Dr	152 Dr	UK
	358 Dr	119 Dr	SWITZERLAND
	1066 Dr	355 Dr	US/CANADA

THE COST OF SENDING A TELEGRAM (IN DRACHMA)

Basic rate	Cost per additional word	
1211 Dr	48 Dr	UK/EUROPE
1211 Dr	91 Dr	US/CANADA

TOURIST INFORMATION

LOCAL TOURIST OFFICES

Haghios Nikolaos:
20, Akti I. Koundourou
tel. (0841) 223 57
Khania:
6, Akti Tombazi
tel. (0821) 433 00
Heraklion:
1, Xanthoudidou Street
tel. (081) 22 82 03
Rethymnon:
El. Venizelou Avenue
tel. (0831) 291 48 or
241 43
Sitia:
Iroon Polytekhniou
Square
tel. (0843) 249 55

CURRENCY

Currency and
traveler's checks
can be changed in
banks and post
offices, and in the
many travel agents,
which have the
advantage of
being open over
the weekend, but
they do charge a
higher rate of
commission.
The pound sterling
is equivalent to
approximately
350 Drachma,
the dollar to about
585. Banks give
the best rates of
exchange, although
only the Kredit
Bank is equipped
with automatic
cashpoints that
will accept Visa
cards, in the major
tourist locations.

BANKS

Cretan banks are
only open from
8am to 2pm,
Monday to Thursday,
and from 8am to
1.30pm on Fridays.
In the high season,
and in all the
provincial capitals,
a bank is open for
changing currency
between 5pm
and 7pm, and
on Saturdays.

MONEY

The Greek unit of
currency is the
Drachma; it was
once divided into
100 lepta, but this
unit is no longer
used. There are
5 Dr, 10 Dr, and
20 Dr coins: coins
of the same
denomination may
be different sizes,
however, which often
causes mistakes.
Notes in circulation
are: 50 Dr, 100 Dr,
500 Dr, 1,000 Dr
and 5,000 Dr.

SOME USEFUL TELEPHONE NUMBERS

EMERGENCY
Emergency
number:100
Ambulance: 166
Fire service: 199

PRACTICAL INFORMATION
Tourist police: 171
Road emergencies
or assistance: 104
Buses: 142

TIME

CRETAN TIME

GMT + 2 hours, in
other words two
hours ahead of the
UK, seven hours
ahead of United
States Eastern
Standard time.

SHOP OPENING TIMES

Shops are open
from 8am until
1.30pm; and then
from 5pm to 8pm
on working days.
Many kiosks and
shops are open
continuously
between 8am and
10pm, seven days
a week.

SIESTA

In common with
other Mediterranean
countries, many
shops are closed
during the hottest
hours of the day,
between 3pm
and 5pm.

CREDIT CARDS

Payments by
visa card are
accepted in most
of the more
expensive hotels
and restaurants in
the tourist resorts,
and also in some
souvenir shops.
Credit cards can
also be used to
withdraw money
over the counter
at branches of the
Commercial Bank
of Greece or the
Ionian Bank.

POST OFFICES

Post offices are open from Monday to Friday between 8am and 7pm, or in some places between 8am and 2pm. The letter boxes are yellow and generally rather difficult to locate. Stamps can be purchased in shops selling postcards, in post offices or the yellow post-office caravans situated in main squares and parks. Mail can be collected at the *poste restante* in the central post office of any town. Eurocheques can be changed in post offices.

TELEPHONE AND TELEGRAMS (O.T.E.)

To send a telegram or make a telephone call you will need to go through the O.T.E., which has offices in most large towns. They are generally open between 8.30am and 11pm. For some bizarre reason it is often easier to telephone abroad

from some kiosks and tavernas, at rates which are little higher than those of the O.T.E.

TELEPHONE DIALLING CODES

Khersonisos/Mallia: 0897
Haghia Galini: 0832
Haghios Nikolaos: 0841
Heraklion: 081
Khania: 0821
Mires/Messara: 0892
Palaiokhora: 0823
Pyrgos: 0893
Rethymnon: 0831
Sitia: 0843
To telephone from the UK, dial 00 30 followed by the town code without the first 0. To telephone the UK, dial 00 44, followed by the area code without the first 0.

NEWSPAPERS

The main English-language newspapers and magazines are easy to obtain, the day after publication, in large towns and tourist centres; prices are high, however.

WHAT THINGS COST

COFFEE OR TEA: 80 TO 200 DR

ONE BREAKFAST: 600 TO 1000 DR

ONE LITER OF PETROL: 200 TO 240 DR

A MEAL IN A TAVERNA: 2500 TO 5000 DR

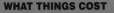

ONE GLASS OF WINE OR BEER: 200 TO 400 DR

ONE POSTCARD WITH STAMP: 90 DR

A MUSEUM ENTRANCE TICKET: 400 DR

A DOUBLE ROOM: 8000 TO 12,000 DR

Rhyton in the shape of a bull, Archeological Museum, Heraklion

Mallia

Gortyn

Verisi-Idomeneo fountain, Heraklion

North entrance to the palace of Knossos

Zakros

Morosini fountain,
Heraklion

Haghia Triada monastery

Fresco
at Toplou
monastery

Hellenic
statue,
Archeological
Museum,
Haghios
Nikolaos

297

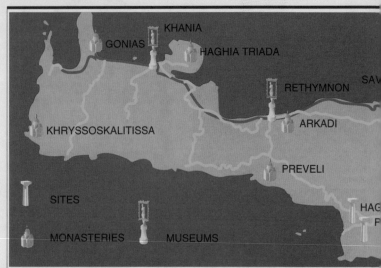

• ARKADI monastery	east of Rethymnon	Open 8am–1pm and 5pm–7pm daily. Sundays and public holidays 10am–5pm
• KHANIA Archeological Museum	21, Halidon Street Tel. (0821) 24 418	Open 8am–7pm. Sundays and public holidays 8am–6pm closed Tuesdays
Historical Museum	20, Sphakianaki Street Tel. (0821) 226 06	Open 8am–1pm. Closed Sat, Sun and public holidays
Maritime Museum	Akti Koundouriotou Tel. (0821) 264 37	Open 10am–7pm, Saturdays 7pm–9pm. Closed Mondays
• KHRYSSOSKALITISSA monastery	47 miles from Khania	Open 9am–1pm and 4–7pm daily
• GONIA monastery	Rhodopos peninsula	Open 9am–1pm and 4–7pm daily
• GORTYN site	29 miles from Heraklion	Open 8.45am–3pm daily
• GOURNIA site	12 miles from Haghios Nikolaos	Open 8.45am–3pm, closed Sundays and public holidays
• HAGHIA TRIADA site	2 miles from Phaistos	Open 8.45am–3pm daily. Sundays and pub. holidays 9.30am–2.30pm
monastery	Akrotiri peninsula	Open 9am–2pm and 5–7pm daily
• HAGHIOS NIKOLAOS Archeological Museum	74, K. Paleologou Street Tel. (0841) 224 62	Open 8.45am–3pm. Sun. and public holidays 9.30am–2.30pm closed Tuesdays
• HERAKLION Archeological Museum	2, Xanthoudidou Street Tel. (081) 22 60 92	Open 8am–7pm. Sundays and public holidays 8am–6pm closed Mondays
Historical and Ethnographic Museum	Kalokerinou Street Tel. (081) 28 32 19	Open 9.30am–1pm, 3–5pm closed Sun. and public holidays
Nikos Kazantzaki Museum	at Mirtia 12 miles from Heraklion	Open Mar. 1 to Oct. 31, Mon., Tues., Sat., Sun. 4–6pm Wed., Fri. 9am–1pm, closed Thurs Sun., pub. hols 9.30am–2.30pm
Venetian Fortress	in the harbor	Open daily 8.45am–3pm
• IERAPETRA Kostoula Archeological Museum	Adrianou Street	Open 8.45am–3pm. Sundays and public holidays 9.30am–2.30pm Closed Tuesdays

• KATO ZAKROS site	eastern tip of the island	Open 9am–7pm daily. Sundays and public holidays 10am–5pm
• KNOSSOS site	near Heraklion	Open 8am–7pm daily. Sundays and public holidays 8am–7pm
MALLIA site	21 miles from Heraklion	Open 8.45am–3pm daily. Sundays and public holidays 9am–2.30pm
• PANAGHIA KERA	near Kritsa	Open 8.45am–3pm daily. Sundays and public holidays 9am–2pm
• PHAISTOS site	23 miles from Heraklion	Open 8am–7pm daily. Sun. and public holidays 8.30am–6pm
• PREVELI monastery	23 miles from Rethymnon	Open 8am–1pm and 5–7pm daily
• RETHYMNON Archeological Museum	220, Arkadiou Street Tel. (0831) 240 68	Open 8am–3pm. Sundays and public holidays 8am–noon closed Mondays
Museum of History and Folk Art	28, Messolonghiou Street	Open 9am–1pm & 7–9pm Closed Sundays and Mondays
Venetian Fortress		Open out of season 9am–5pm, in season 8am–8pm
L. Kanakakis Gallery	Himaras Street Tel. (0831) 218 47	Open 10am–2pm and 5–8pm. Closed Mondays
• SAVATHIANA monastery	near Rodgia	Open 8am–noon and 4–7pm daily
• SITIA Archeological Museum	E. Venizelos Street Tel. (0843) 239 17	Open 9am–3pm. Sundays and public holidays 9.30am–2.30pm closed Tuesdays
Folklore Museum	Arkadiou Street Tel. (297) 323 98	Open 9.30am–3.30pm closed Sundays
• TOPLOU monastery	17 miles from Sitia	Open 8am–4pm and 4.30–7.30pm daily
• TYLISSOS site	9 miles from Heraklion	Open 9am–3pm daily. Sundays and public holidays 9am–2pm
• VATHIPETRO and PHOURNI site	12 miles from Heraklion	Open Mondays, Fridays and Saturdays, 9am until evening

The Tria-Tetarta bar at Heraklion

Cretans of all ages are very convivial and love to go out at night, whether to a taverna, a bar or discotheque, or for an impromptu *venghera* with friends. There is certainly no lack of choice. However it must be said that there is a rapid turnover among bars and nightclubs in the large towns: many of them last no longer than one summer.

The choice is wide: the traditional Cretan *kendro*, an orchestra with *lyra*, *lauto* and sometimes violin, especially popular in the villages; café-bars and discotheques playing jazz, continental Greek and modern Anglo-American music, catering for every mood... and a number of night-clubs where small groups, generally of young people, play an authentic repertory of *rembetika*, popular songs of the harbors and refugees of Asia Minor, of marginals and outcasts (the earliest compositions date from 1800).

HERAKLION

BARS AND DISCOTHEQUES
Behind Lion Square, in the narrow alleys going down to the harbor, there are many small, pleasant bars and discos, often in old buildings which have been restored.

GUERNICA
2, Andreou Kritis Street
Tel. (081) 28 29 88
CAFÉ JASMIN
6, Haghiostefaniton St
Tel. (081) 28 16 14
AVGO
15, Koraï Street
Tel. (081) 22 35 80
In the center of town, near the Astoria Hotel.
IDAION ANDRON
In Koraï Street
Tel. (081) 24 20 41
NOTOS
Sarandaporou Square
Tel. (081) 22 67 87

DISCOTHEQUES
VENETO
9, Epimenidou Street
Tel. (081) 22 09 18
FLOU AND DIESSI
Daskaloyannis Square
Tel. (081) 34 18 55
NAOS
9, Haghiostefaniton St
RAFFINARIA
Tel. (081) 22 17 70
In a Venetian gallery, on the corner of Ikarou Avenue, at the foot of the city walls.

PIANO-BARS AND RESTAURANTS
TRIA-TETARTA
Theotokopoulou Street
Piano-bar on the harbor, in a neoclassical building.
DORÉ
Liberty Square
Tel. (081) 22 52 12

Piano-restaurant with terrace.

CABARET
TROMBONI
Makariou Boulevard

TAVERNAS WHERE "REMBETIKA" ARE PLAYED
PALAZZO YTTAR
Epimenidou Street
Tel. (081) 22 60 61
TA PERIX
At Carteros, beyond the airport.
Tel. (081) 24 56 19

TAVERNAS WHERE CRETAN MUSIC IS PLAYED
ARIADNI
92, Knossou Avenue, on the road to Knossos
Tel. (081) 23 19 94
AVYSSINOS
At Spilia, past Knossos
Tel. (081) 23 33 55
AROLITHOS
On the road to Anogia
Tel. (081) 82 10 50

KHANIA

CAFÉ-BARS AND DISCOTHEQUES
ANAYENISSI
By the old harbor
Tel. (0821) 72 768
At the foot of the Venetian wall.
ANEKDOTO
On the corner of Skoufon and Zambeliou
CAFÉ KRITI
22, rue Kallergon

Near the Venetian arsenals, with traditional music.
FAGOTTO
16, Anghelou Street, behind the Maritime Museum.
Tel. (0821) 57 487
Classical music to 9pm, then jazz and blues.
PRAXIS
3, Skoufon Street
Closed Sundays.
1920's-style bar with a charming little courtyard.
STREET
Venetian harbor
Rock music.
TA 2 LUX
8, rue Sarpidon
Near the Venetian harbor.
UTOPIA
At Platanias
Bar with garden

OUZO BARS
VASSILIKO
Akti Enosseos

"Trompe-l'œil" Bistro at Khania

Sign of the Skala discotheque at Khania

SKALA
16, Sarpidonos Street
Street runs parallel to
Akti Enosseos.
HAMMAM
By the Venetian harbor,
near Firkos
Eastern music.

RETHYMNON

**BARS AND
DISCOTHEQUES**
1600
16, Radamanthou Street
In the old town, in
what used to be an
oil press. Dance
music: European
earlier in the evening.
Greek later on.
FIGARO
21, rue Vernardou
Tel. (0831) 29 431
In the old town,
behind the Nerantzes
mosque. 20's-style
decor; Greek music.
ODOD ONIRON
8, Photaki Street
Tel. (0831) 50 448
In the old town, not
far from the Loggia.

European and
Greek music.
Attractive décor,
mainly young people
and students.
AFTER EIGHT
83, Venizelou Street
Tel. (0831) 21 227
Greek music,
student crowd.
TAXIMI
27, Nearkhou Street
Rembetika after
11pm.
CARIBBEAN
In the Platanos
suburb
Open noon to 4am.
Music: jazz,
Latin-American.
Frequented by
locals and students.

The small bars
do not always
have telephone
numbers. This is
rarely a problem,
however, as they
are usually all in
the same district
of the town.

SUMMER FESTIVALS

Many cultural
events – concerts
and various
performances –
are held during
the tourist season.
The authorities of
the major towns
make it a point of
honor to organize
their own festival
each summer.

HERAKLION

Every year the
town council
organizes concerts,
theatrical
performances,
choirs, ballet,
Greek or Cretan
evenings, music,
traditional dance
and song, recitals
etc. Major national
and international
artists take part.
The various events
take place outside,
in the open-air
Kipotheatro
Kazantzaki theater
near the New
Gate and the Oasis
gardens. Details
of the programs
can be obtained
from the public
relations office at
the town hall.
Tel. (081) 22 71 02,
22 12 37, 22 72 02

and 24 29 77.
Tickets can be
purchased in the
kiosks on Lion
Square, Kornarou
Square and at the
Kipotheatro
Kazantzaki itself.

KHANIA

There is an
annual festival
organized by the
town council.
Concerts of
classical and
contemporary
music, theater etc.
The events take
place in the
arsenals of the old
Venetian port, in
the East Moat
theater and in the
theater of the
Peace Park.

RETHYMNON

Every summer at
the Fortetza, the
town of Rethymnon
organizes a series
of concerts and a
festival devoted to
medieval and
Renaissance
theater. Every July
the town puts on
a wine festival; this
is held in the
public gardens.

SUMMER CINEMA

The summer cinemas have long been
almost an institution in Crete – an oasis
of coolness, the air perfumed with jasmine
and frangipani, nostalgically evoked by
singer-composer Yannis Kelaïdonis. Their
numbers have fallen over recent years –
enjoy them while they last. All films are
shown in their original language.

HERAKLION
(from May to October):
- Galaxy, 96, Akadimia street
- Pallas, 4, Arkhimidous street
- Romantika, 26, Leftheraiou street
KHANIA
In the gardens of the municipal park
RETHYMNON
Asteria, Melissinou street

You can get to know the Cretan landscape in a number of different ways: strolling through it on foot, on a boat trip, or on horseback. Above all Crete offers you the opportunity to try a range of nautical sports, from windsurfing to the pedalos which can be hired on beaches and in hotels.

There are several tour operators in the UK offering special activity holidays in Crete: these include golfing, mountain-biking, rural retreats, scuba diving, sports, walking, plus tuitional sailing, windsurfing and other watersports. Less strenuous holiday specialties on offer include history, holistics, mythology, natural history, naturism, painting, amateur photography and traditional settlements.

For further information, contact:
The National Tourist Organization of Greece
4 Conduit Street
London W1R 0DJ
Tel. 0171 734 5997
Fax 0171 287 1369

GREEK MOUNTAIN CLUB (O.S.E)
HERAKLION
74, Dikaiossynis Avenue
Tel. (081) 227 609
KHANIA
3, Mikhelidaki Street
Tel. (0821) 24 647
RETHYMNON
143, Arkadias Street
Tel. (0831) 22 411

WALKING AND TREKKING

Mountaineering clubs at both Heraklion and Khania organize regular excursions which vary in length and difficulty. At Heraklion, Wild Nature organizes a range of tours that combine trekking, jeep and bicycle in quite magnificent yet little-known parts of the island, with an English-speaking guide and a cook (minimum of eight participants).
Information:
George Tsalikakis
20–22 Malikouti Street
Tel. (081) 71 202, 22 52 52 and 24 19 19

WALKS IN CRETE

ARMENI
If you are a good walker, you can go from Heraklion to Armeni on foot: this takes about four hours both ways. Leave from Koundouriatou Avenue, the large road which crosses the town, in front of the municipal

SKIING

You can go skiing in the Cretan mountains, on deserted pistes served by only two ski-lifts. For more information, contact the Greek Mountain Club (O.S.E.)

gardens. Head in the direction of Khania. As you leave the town, turn left toward Gallou. The asphalt road goes uphill, by the side of a verdant ravine. After reaching the village (some 45 minutes' walk), take a right turning to the monastery of Saints Peter and Paul. From here there is a beautiful view over the sea. The road becomes a dirt track at this point. After thirty minutes you will reach the village of Somatas, and fifteen minutes later the necropolis of Armeni. Continue along the track to the foot of Mount Vrisinas, where there is a magnificent view over Rethymnon. Carry on downhill toward the hamlet of Risvani-Metokhi (ten minutes), reaching the ruins

of Irfan Bey's house a little further along. Fifteen minutes later you will see a church made of porous stone, built by one of the last Cretan stonemasons. After this, orchards and vines stretch ahead of you, with Evliyias hill in the middle, covered with pine trees. There is a play area for children, as well as wooden tables and chairs for picnics. Pause, finally, by the church of St John to enjoy a beautiful view over Rethymnon, which you can reach in less than twenty minutes.

THE PRASSANO GORGES
The walk from Rethymnon to the gorges takes from five to six hours; it can only be done in summer, from June to October. It is

Small port at Gramvousa

Snowcapped summits at Alikampo

advisable to take drinking water with you. Cross the town, heading eastward toward Heraklion. In the suburb of Perivolia, turn right toward Amari. After the village of Prassies ▲ *240* and the junction for Mirthios, Selli, etc., stop at the first turning on the road. If the walk seems too long, you can take the Amari bus and continue on foot from there. Take the dirt track down toward the Platanias Valley and follow one of the paths leading to the river bed. After walking some 300 yards under the shade of the plane trees, you will arrive at the junction of this stream with the main river. In less than thirty minutes you will come to the first entrance to the gorges, still walking along the river bed. The gorges are 500 feet high in places, with abundant plant life: planes, laurels, carob trees, roses, olive trees, and chestnut trees. After the third gorge the walls are not so high. You can follow the track on the left of the river, coming to a three-arched bridge. Continue along the track. After coming to the old road

between Rethymnon and Heraklion, you can take the bus back into town, or walk back along the beach (3 miles) after a well-earned dip in the sea.

BOAT EXCURSIONS

ON THE NORTH COAST
From Heraklion you can reach the neighboring island of Dia, a wildlife reserve with chamois deer. Departure from

the marina, every morning at 10am, return at 4pm. From Elounda you can hire a boat to visit the fortified island of Spinalonga ▲ *202*.

ON THE SOUTH COAST
From Makry-Yalos you can go on an interesting excursion to Koufonissi, formerly Lefki. From Ierapetra there are daily departures for Gaïdouronissi, with its magnificent beaches and little cedar groves in the dunes.
HERAKLION:
Magic Day in Dia, Idomeneos Street.

DEEP-SEA DIVING

Diving with equipment is strictly forbidden and

punishable with hefty fines. The Cretans, seeking to protect the archeological heritage of their coasts, have even outlawed the photography of submerged objects which may have archeological interest.

TENNIS

Most large hotels have tennis courts. You can also play and have lessons at tennis clubs in the main towns.

KHANIA
Dimokratias Street
Tel. (0821) 240 10 or 21 293
HERAKLION
Doukos Beaufort Street
Tel. (081) 226 152 (after 2pm)

HORSE RIDING

The riding club on the beach of Amnisos-Karteros offers you the chance to explore the Cretan countryside or to take riding lessons.

CLUB KARTEROS
tel. (081) 282 005

Cretan grocery at Heraklion

Cobbler at Rethymnon

Leather goods shop near the Rimondi fountain at Rethymnon

Traditional Cretan products – jewelry, leather, pottery and weaving – as well as specialty foods can be found in both small villages and shops in large towns.

FOOD

Oil, raisins, honey, aromatic and medicinal plants: since antiquity Crete has been a paradise for botanists and herbalists.

HERAKLION
The market on 1866 Street has all the atmosphere of an oriental bazaar. There is an excellent shop selling local produce at 17 Kosmon Street, at right angles to 1866 Street.

KHANIA
Taste a *bougatsa* – a cheese pastry parcel – at **IORDANIS**, 18 Plastiras Street, opposite the town market or at 4 Sifaka Street by the Venetian harbor. Also look for some *loukoumadhes* in Potier Street: a delicious local specialty filled with honey.

RETHYMNON
Local products can be found in Ethn. Andistassis Street and Petykhaki Square. You can purchase medicinal plants at 58 Souliou Street in a charming shop the Cretans call a "polyclinic".

JEWELRY

Metalwork is a Cretan tradition

going back thousands of years. They produce beautiful jewelry in gold and silver, sometimes decorated with semi-precious stones.

HERAKLION
One of the most highly rated shops is Fanourakis, on the corner of 25 Avgoustou Street and Kalokairinou Avenue. But the town has many specialist jewelers, mainly located in 1821 Street, Kalokairinou Avenue and Dikaiosynis Avenue. These include:
- **TO FIDI:** 71, 1821 Street
- **Io:** 5, Daidalou Street
- **TZEDAKIS:** 18, Kalokairinou Avenue
- **ARIANE,** 21 Dikaiossynis Avenue

You can also find antique jewelry at 11 Daidalou Street.

KHANIA
Most of the jewelry shops are in Khalion Street and in the Venetian quarter.

RETHYMNON
Beautiful, mainly traditional jewelry at **PAPADOURAKIS**, 70 Akti Koundourioti, and in the shops on Souliou Street.

LEATHER GOODS

This traditional craft of Asia Minor has become established

in Crete. Shoes and belts are excellent value here as elsewhere in Greece. You can even buy *stivania* in specialist shops, the superb leather boots which used to be an indispensable part of the national Cretan costume.

HERAKLION
Shops in Korai, Daidalou and Argyraki Streets and on Kalokairinou Avenue.

RETHYMNON
You can order Cretan boots made to measure at 63 Souliou Street. The main leather goods shops are at 198 Arkadiou Street, on Petykhaki square, and at 1 and 17 Souliou Street.

KHANIA
Skrydlof and Khalidon Streets are the best places to go for top-quality leather goods.

CERAMICS, POTTERY

If you are not able to visit the villages of Thrapsano
▲ *197* or Margarites
▲ *288*, where the pot-making tradition goes back over 5,000 years, you can find some of their products in the shops in larger towns.

HERAKLION
BARCO
7 Koraïs Street
Lovely ceramics and other high-quality craft products.
VOLTONE
25 Idomeneos Street, near the Archeological Museum.

WEAVING, EMBROIDERY

These crafts have a centuries-old tradition in Crete.

HERAKLION
ELENI KASTRINOYANNI
Xanthoudidou, opposite the Archeological Museum
A long-established shop with a good reputation.
BOURAS
2 Marogheorghi Street, near St Minas
Beautiful woven cloth from northern Greece, sold by the meter.
EVA GRIMM
25 Avgoustou Street
Wonderful antique fabrics.
RETHYMNON
30 Souliou Street – also shops on Arkadiou and Ethnikis Andistassis Streets.

SPECIAL INTEREST TRIPS

The Koules fortress at Heraklion

The Loggia at Rethymnon

The remains of the Venetian occupation, dating from the 13th to the 17th centuries, are concentrated mainly in three towns in Crete: Heraklion, Khania and Rethymnon. Less important monuments – ruins and fortresses, watch towers, villas or small aristocratic houses – survive throughout the island, in a few remote villages. However, visitors interested in Venetian architecture should not rely on the list of Venetian monuments drawn up by Giuseppe Gerola between 1905 and 1932: sadly, urbanization, indifference and ignorance have destroyed in a few years what three centuries of turbulent history had left untouched.

HERAKLION (1)

Although the Venetian quarters of the old city of Candia vanished long ago, the town still has some of the most beautiful monuments on the island: the city wall with its seven strongholds, designed by the engineer Micheli Sanmicheli; the Koules Rocca al Mare fortress protecting the port, built in the 12th century, destroyed by earthquakes, and rebuilt between 1523 and 1540; the church of St Titus, seat of the Latin bishop, which was rebuilt several times; the Palladian Loggia (1626–8), in 25 Avgoustou Street, which was recently restored – formerly a meeting place for Venetian aristocrats, it now houses the town hall; the Sagredo fountain; the small church of St Mark with its two naves, dating from the 13th century, today an exhibition hall decorated with reproductions of frescos from the 13th and 14th centuries; the Morosini fountain, built in 1626, on Lion Square, its basin supported by lions from a 14th-century monument; the Bembo fountain of 1588 on Kornarou Square at the far end of the picturesque Market Street (the headless classical statue which adorns it came from Ierapetra); the Greek monastery of Madonna Akriotirina behind the market, in the Haghia Triada quarter; St Catherine of Sinai, a small pink church next to St-Minas cathedral (which has been converted into a museum and now houses a remarkable collection of Cretan School icons).

AROUND HERAKLION

At Kanli Kastelli, 12 miles southwest of Heraklion, are the remains of the La Rocca citadel (2), built over the ruins of the fortress constructed by Nikephoros Phokas in the 10th century, after the conquest of the Arabs. At Rogdia ▲ 218, 9 miles east of Heraklion, the Modino tower (3) offers a splendid view over the bay.

HEADING EASTWARD

The citadel (4) on the island of Spinalonga ▲ 202 was built in 1579, on the order of Proveditore Jacopo Foscarini, to protect the bay of Elounda from attacks by Turks or pirates. It eluded Ottoman control until 1715. Admiral Spratt, who visited it in the 19th century, described it as a miniature Gibraltar. From 1903 until the 1950's it was used to house

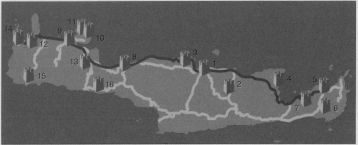

The arsenals of Khania

Frangokastello to the south of Khania

lepers. The beautiful fortress of Casarma **(5)** at Sitia ▲ *207* was built by Errico Pescatore at the beginning of the 13th century and then enlarged by the Venetians. Today it houses a summer theater where the annual Kornaria festival is held. It is worth making a detour to see the abandoned village of Etia **(6)**, a fomer estate of the Di Mezzo family, on the road linking Sitia and Ierapetra. From here you can reach the medieval village of Voila, half a mile from Handras. After Makry-Yalos on the southern coast, a walk inland leads to the ruins of the Monforte fortress **(7)**, built in the 13th and 14th centuries, not far from the villages of Stavrokhori and Krya. It has a fine view over wild hilly scenery.

RETHYMNON (8)

This is without doubt the most interesting town for lovers of Venetian architecture. The old town, which was carefully restored twenty years ago, has a large number of charming small palazzi within a small area – notably in Arkadiou, Vernadou,

N. Phokas, Arabatzoglou and Klidi streets. Monuments to see include the Venetian ramparts and Fortetza citadel ▲ *236*, built in 1574, on the Palaiokastro hill to the northwest of the town; the Rimondi fountain, built in 1629 on Petykhaki Square; the churches of San Francesco and Our Lady of the Angels, and finally the Loggia, a Palladian-style monument in Arkadiou Street.

KHANIA (9)

This small Venetian port, dominated by its lighthouse, was originally able to accommodate up to forty galleys. There are many traces of the Venetian occupation, scattered across the town, from the arsenals to the superb aristocratic residences of the Topanas and Ovraiki quarters, with Latin inscriptions on the porches, coats of arms on the pediments and paved internal courtyards. Behind the small port is a maze of winding alleys, sometimes connected by arches: Zambeliou, Skoufon, Theotokopoulou and Gamba are among the most interesting of these. Splendid

arched passageways can be seen in Moskhon and Veneri Streets. The fortifications and the remains of the city wall date from the beginning of the 12th century. The Loggia, at 43 Khalidon Street, formerly a meeting place for Venetian noblemen, has a façade decorated with coats of arms and a Latin inscription. The San Francesco basilica,

which houses the Archeological Museum, was formerly the monastery of Minori Osservanti. Remains of the old Venetian archives are found on the Kastelli hill, Lithinon Street; the church of San Marco in Haghiou Marcou Street has beautiful Romanesque arches. The small church of San Rocco, in 1821 Square in the Splanzia quarter, was built in the 17th century.

AROUND KHANIA

On the north side of the Akrotiri peninsula, it is a twenty-minute walk to the monasteries of Giancaroli de Gouverneto **(10)**

and Katholiko **(11)** ▲ *266*, heading downhill toward the sea. The walk is delightful, and you can visit the caves of Karkoudospilia and Katholiko on the way, as well as seeing very old hermitages carved into the rock on the hillside. Villa Clussia and Villa Trevisan **(12)**, dating from 1500, can be seen at Drapanias in the province of Kisamos. Brosnero **(13)**, 23 miles from Khania in the province of Apokoronou, has the remains of the Alikadi tower. On the island of Gramvousa, which can be reached by boat from Kastelli Kisamos, you can see the impressive Venetian fortress **(14)** of 1579.

SOUTH OF KHANIA

In the village of Palaiokhora Selinou, which overlooks the Mediterranean Sea 47 miles to the south of Khania, are the remains of the Marino Gradonico citadel **(15)**, which was built in 1279, destroyed by the pirate Barbarossa in 1539, and then rebuilt by B. Dolfin in 1595. Frangokastello **(16)**, around 6 miles from Khora Sphakion ▲ *272*, was built in 1373 and became a focus for Cretan revolutionary struggles against foreign occupation.

Church of St Catherine at Heraklion

Monastery of Gouverneto

Crete has many archeological remains: Minoan, Archaic, Greek and Roman. Sometimes this overshadows the fact that the island as a whole also has an impressive number of monasteries, churches and chapels of considerable beauty, set in magnificent scenery.

HERAKLION AND ITS SURROUNDINGS

The church of St Catherine **(1)** ▲ *148* is now a museum, housing magnificent icons by Damaskinos, the

establishments. As the Ottoman threat grew the monasteries moved away to the foot of Mount Ida.

PALIANIS CONVENT
Records of this convent at Venerato **(2)** go back to AD 668. It was probably built on the remains of an early Christian basilica. A rather unusual form of religion survives here even today: worshipers venerate a tree, the "holy Myrtle". In the neighboring village of Avgheniki, there is a holy cypress tree within the walls of the Stavromenos monastery **(3)**.

since antiquity, on the site of a temple dedicated to Zeus the Savior. It was visited in 1415 by the Florentine traveler Buondelmonti. Evidence shows that this sacred mountain near the palaces of Knossos and Archanes was used as a place of worship from the Minoan period onward. As well as the shrine of Psili Korfi and the holy caves, the Minoan "human sacrifice" temple at Anemospilia ▲ *197* is not far away, offering a splendid view over the bay of Heraklion.

ST TITUS BASILICA (7)
This triple-naved basilica, which was built at Gortyn ▲ *177* in the 5th century, is one of the most important Christian monuments in Crete. To the south, the Asteroussia mountains, which overlook the Messara plain and the Mediterranean Sea, harbored a large number of monasteries, hermitages, and chapels decorated with frescos, some of them cut into the rock-face. This wild region, far from towns and villages, was a sacred area

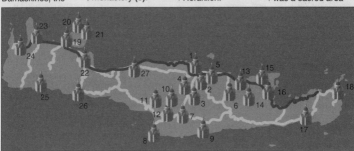

leading figure of the Cretan School. There are many important monasteries near Heraklion. Many date from the Venetian occupation, when Candia was the island's administrative, religious and intellectual center. Most were probably built on the sites of much older

KYRIA ELEOUSSA MONASTERY (4)
This monastery at Kroussonas-Kitharida is now in ruins; it is one of the oldest in Crete, dating from the 11th century.

CHURCH OF CHRIST THE SAVIOR (5)
The four-naved church was built on Mount Juchtas, a place of worship

AGARATHOU MONASTERY (6)
The historic monastery was a brilliant intellectual center, a breeding ground for patriarchs and humanists whose portraits hang in the entrance hall. It is a typical example of the Cretan fortified monastery, built on a hillside.

even in Minoan times; it became one of the focal points of Cretan Christianity. The monasteries of Odigitrias **(8)** ▲ *188* and Koudouma Haghiofarango **(9)** are evidence of this. The monasteries of Vrontissou **(10)** and Valsamonero **(11)**, on the foothills of Mount Ida, were founded before the

Monastery of Odighitria   *Toplou chapel*   *Arkadi monastery*

Venetians came to Crete. They were flourishing religious and intellectual centers, with famous copyists' workshops, and played an important role in the Cretan Renaissance. Several icons by the Cretan master Mikhail Damaskinos were kept at Vrontissou until 1800: they are now exhibited at the church of St Catherine in Heraklion. The superb chapel of St Fanourios **(12)**, at Voriza, has a beautiful iconostasis and frescos. On August 27, the saint's day, there is a procession with the blessing of bread, and the church is decorated with branches.

LASSITHI

The church of Haghios Andonios in the village of Avdou **(13)** ▲ *197*, 25 miles from Heraklion on the road to the Lassithi plateau, is decorated with 14th-century frescos. The churches of Haghios Georgios and Haghios Konstandinos were built in the 15th century. The Kera Kardiotissa monastery (14) ▲ *197*, ouside the village of Krasi a few miles from the Lassithi plateau, has a beautiful chapel decorated with an exquisite iconostasis. Combine a visit to the church of St Antony **(15)** at Fourni with an excursion to the austere Driros hill, which has ruins of a sizable Archaic town. On the road into the village of Kritsa ▲ *204* is the triple-naved church of the Virgin of Kera **(16)**, with its fine 14th-century frescos. The monastery of Kapsa **(17)** is magnificent, standing against a cliff by the sea, a few miles from Makry-Yalos – it is only a pity that there are shops in it now. The fortified monastery of Toplou **(18)** ▲ *207* stands in austere terrain beyond Sitia, on the road leading to Vai; this used to be one of the most powerful monasteries in Crete.

KHANIA (19) AND ITS SURROUNDINGS

In the town itself, the small church of Haghi Anarghyri is decorated with lovely Byzantine frescos. The church of St Madeleine in the Halepa quarter is built in the Russian Byzantine style.

GOUVERNETO (20) This rich fortified monastery ▲ *265* on the Akrotiri peninsula was built at the beginning of the Venetian occupation, on the site of an earlier building dedicated to Our Lady of the Angels. Celebrations are held on October 7 and November 21. Also on the Akrotiri peninsula, the impressive "monastery of cypresses", Haghia Triada ▲ *264*, is well worth a visit.

ST JOHN THE STRANGER (21) Not far to the north, in a ravine, with its church carved into the rock face. This is supposed to be the site of the first Orthodox monastery founded in Crete, in the 6th or 7th century. An impressive cave near the monastery was a place of worship. The church of the prophet Elias **(22)** is at Armeni-Kalyves; a large festival is held there on July 20.

GONIAS ODIGHITRIA (22) This monastery ▲ *275* in the province of Kisamos was built at the beginning of the 17th century, on the magnificent bay of Kolymbari 16 miles from Khania. There is a collection of icons by the Cretan School. At Episkopi, 19 miles from Khania to the south of Kolymbari, is the church of St Michael the Archangel **(24)**, built in a circular shape, with interesting mosaic floors and beautiful frescos by Byzantine artists in the 12th century.

CHURCH OF ST GEORGE (25) This church, at Komitades in the Sfakia province, has frescos by Pagomenos. Panaghia I Thymiani **(26)** is also worth seeing: it was a focus of the 1821 revolution. The modern church at Souyia **(27)** ▲ *280* houses magnificent mosaics from an early Christian basilica by the sea.

RETHYMNON REGION

The monastery of Arkadi **(28)** ▲ *275* is a symbol of Crete's struggle for independence. When it was besieged by the Turkish army in 1866, monks and revolutionaries set fire to the monastery's stores of gunpowder rather than surrender.

Loutro

Koufonissi

With over 160 miles of coastline and a large number of islands, Crete has many beaches, with white or gray sand, shingle, red or white rocks, and warm, crystal-clear water. Many large hotels have their own private stretch of waterfront, but there are also public beaches where you can enjoy watersports such as canoeing, windsurfing and waterskiing. Some of the smaller islands are ideal for fishing.

CRETE'S MOST BEAUTIFUL BEACHES

The Cretan sea has quite strong currents, especially in summer, and can be dangerous – particularly near Rethymnon, and between Stalida and Mallia. It is therefore not advisable to swim too far from the shore: emergency provisions are basic, at best. In summer the *meltemi* wind can rise suddenly: some beaches on the south coast are wonderful but very exposed; Plakia ▲ 244, Frangokastello ▲ 247 and Xerokampos are unsuitable in these conditions. However, there are plenty of sheltered creeks throughout the island.

NORTH COAST

There are some beautiful beaches near the large towns, but these tend to be packed on Wednesday afternoons and at the weekend. Close to Heraklion, there are sheltered beaches at Lygaria or Haghia Pelagia ▲ 219, 12 miles east, or at Limenas Khernisou, 19 miles west. Close to Rethymnon, you can choose between the small inlet at Petres, 6 miles to the west, and the superb Bali bay ▲ 219, to the east. Near Khania, there are charming inlets to be found on the

Akrotiri peninsula ▲ 265.

EAST COAST

There is a superb, peaceful bay with a series of sheltered inlets at Itanos, just over a mile to the north of Vai ▲ 210. Itanos, owned by Moni Toplou, is not crowded with tourists. The inlet closest to Vai has the advantage of offering some shade from the sun. The water is not very deep here, but it is sometimes cluttered with seaweed. The road leads directly to the second beach, where the rocks can be rather slippery. The most beautiful beach is to the north, heading toward the headland of Sideros. Here you will need a sunshade. At the foot of the Kastri hill, right by the Palaiokastro ruins ▲ 218, is the beautiful, sandy Iona beach: the water is blue-green and shallow. There are some excellent fish tavernas near the landing stage.

SOUTH COAST

Near Phaistos ▲ 178 you will enjoy the long, sheltered beach of Komos with its white sands. Here too there are plenty of tavernas, including the excellent Mystical View which overlooks the bay. On the other side of the Asteroussia mountains, near Lendas, is the splendid inlet of the Haghios Savas caves. To the west of Haghia Galini, an asphalt road across the hills leads to the pleasant Haghios Georgios beach. Further on, a dirt track leads to the peaceful Haghios Pavlos inlet. Here there are fish tavernas and rooms to let facing the island of Paximadia. A path from Preveli monastery ▲ 243 leads to another idyllic creek. If you have been walking through the Samarian gorge ▲ 267, you can stop off to enjoy the cool waters of peaceful Loutro bay on your way back to Khora Sphakion.

CRETE'S ISLANDS

If you want to get off the beaten track, we can recommend

Gramvousa

Haghiofarango

Gavdos

some of the islands to the south of Crete. Here you can enjoy the beaches, fishing, diving and quiet archeological rambles.

KOUFONISSI

The island facing the Goudoura Koufonissi headland, formerly Lefki, has a daily connection with Makrigialos on the mainland. The landscape is almost African, with sparse wild grass on which a few herds of goats used to feed. Tamarisk trees have just been planted here. There are

splendid beaches of white sand, at the foot of chalky cliffs, and the waters teem with fish.

GAVDOS

This island is about three hours from Paleochora ▲ 280: it is the southernmost point of the European continent. There are still a few dwellings scattered on the island. Few trees grow here: figs, carobs, and some cedars. Some claim to have identified this island as Homer's Ogygia, the island

of the nymph Calypso: islanders will be happy to point out her cave. The island was a pirates' lair in the Middle Ages, and then a place of exile; today it is a fishermen's paradise.

GAIDOURONISSI

A one-hour boat trip from Ierapetra ▲ 215, Gaidouronissi is known as "Donkey Island", or, more poetically, Khryssi, the "Golden Island". It is like the ideal desert island, with its sand dunes and small groves of

cedars. The water is clear and shallow, and the coarse white sand has a surprising number of tiny shells in it. It is best to bring a picnic basket with you, some bottles of water and a flask: the only taverna here is generally stormed by holidaymakers. However, you can consult the invaluable map in the taverna, which points out all the things to see on this charming hideaway: archeological remains, cave, and creeks.

◆ WORDS AND PHRASES

◆ BASICS ◆

Yes: *nai*
No: *okhi*
With: *me*
Without: *khoriss*
What: *ti*
Why: *yati*
Where: *pou*
When: *pote*
How: *poss*

◆ POLITESSE ◆

Please: *parakalo*
Thank you: *efkharisto*
Thank you very much: *efkharisto poly*
Excuse me: *sig-nomi*, *me singkhorite*
Don't mention it: *tipota*
Goodbye: *khairete*, *adio*
Hello: *kalimera*
How are you? *ti kanete?*
Very well: *poli kala*
OK: *enn daxi*
Good evening: *kalispera*
Good night: *kali nykhta*
Hi! *y asou*

◆ TIME, DATES ◆

Now: *tora*
Later: *meta*
What time is it? *ti ora ine?*
Morning: *proi*
Midday: *messimeri*
Afternoon: *apoyema*
Evening: *vradhi*
Night: *nykhta*
Today: *simera*
Tomorrow: *avrio*
Yesterday: *khtess*
Day: *(i)mera*
Week: *vdhomada*
Monday: *dheftera*
Tuesday: *triti*
Wednesday: *tetarti*
Thursday: *pemmti*
Friday: *paraskevi*
Saturday: *savato*
Sunday: *kyriaki*
Month: *minass*
January: *ianouarios*
February: *fevrouarios*
March: *martios*
April: *aprilios*
May: *mayos*
June: *younios*
July: *youlios*
August: *avgoustos*
September: *septemmbrios*
October: *octovrios*
November: *noemvrios*
December: *dhekemmvrios*
Year: *khronos*

◆ NUMBERS ◆

One: *ena*
Two: *dhio*
Three: *tria*
Four: *tessera*
Five: *pennde*
Six: *exi*
Seven: *efta*
Eight: *okhto*
Nine: *ennia*
Ten: *dheka*
Twenty: *ikossi*
Thirty: *triannda*
Forty: *sarannda*
Fifty: *peninnda*
Sixty: *exinnda*
Seventy: *evdhominnda*
Eighty: *oghdonnda*
Ninety: *eneninnda*
(One) hundred: *ekato*
(One) thousand: *khilia*

◆ TRAVELING ◆

Airport: *aerodhromio*
Airplane: *aeroplano*
Boat: *karavi*
Harbor: *limani*
Bus station: *stathmos leoforion*
Luggage: *aposkeves*, *bagazia*
Porter: *akhthoforos*
Automobile: *aftokinito*
Driving licence: *adhia odhighissis*
How much does it cost per day? *posso kostizi tinn imera?*
Taxi: *taxi*

◆ ON THE ROAD ◆

Road: *dhromos*
Garage: *garaz*
The car has broken down: *to aftokinito ekhi vlavi*
Fill it up, please: *to yemizete me vennzini, parakalo*
Gasoline: *vennzini*
Normal, super, unleaded: *apli, souper, amolivdhi*
Could you check...? *parakalo, elennxte...*
Oil: *to ladhi*
Tires: *ta lastikha*

◆ GETTING AROUND ◆

Are we on the right road for...? *imaste sto sossto dhromo ya...?*
Sea: *thalassa*
Mountain: *vouno*
Village: *khorio*
Beach: *paralia*
North: *voria*
South: *notia*
East: *anatolika*
West: *dhitika*

◆ IN TOWN ◆

Bus: *leoforio*
Where is the bus for...? *pou inai to leoforio ya...?*
Bus-stop: *stasi*
Where is...? *pou inai...?*
How far? *posso makria inai?*
Near: *konnda*
Far: *makria*
Right: *dhexia*
Left: *aristera*
Center: *kenndro*

Street: *dhromos, odos*
Avenue: *leoforos*
Square: *platia*

◆ MONEY ◆

Bank: *trapeza*
Money: *khrimata, lefta*
I would like to change some...: *thelo nallaxo merika...*
Do you take credit cards? *pernete pistotiki karta?*
Travelers' checks: *travelers' checks*

◆ VISITS ◆

Open: *anikhto*
Closed: *klisto*
Ticket: *isitirio*
Church: *ekklissia*
Castle: *kastro*
Palace: *palati*
Ruins: *arkhaia*
Museum: *moussio*
Temple: *naos*
Theater: *theatro*
May I take a photograph? *boro na paro mia fotografia?*
Entrance: *issodhos*
Exit: *exodhos*

FINDING ◆ A ROOM ◆

I would like a room: *tha ithela ena dhomatio*
A single room, a double: *ena mono, ena diplo*
With two beds: *me dhio krevatia*
With bath: *me banio*
With shower: *me douss*
What does it cost for a night? *pia inai i timi ya mia nykhta?*
Breakfast: *to proino*

◆ EATING OUT ◆

Restaurant: *estiatorio*
Taverna: *taverna*
Lunch: *messimeriano fayito*
Dinner: *vradhino fayito*
Menu: *kataloghos*
May we have a table, please? *boroume na ekhoume ena trapezi?*
Coffee: *enan kafe*
Coffee with milk: *enan kafe me ghala*
Tea: *ena tsai*
Dessert: *ena glyko*
Hot: *zesto*
Cold: *kryo*
A glass: *ena potiri*
Plate, dish: *piato*
Water: *nero*
Mineral water: *emmfayalomeno*
Wine: *krassi*
Bottle: *boukali*
Beer: *bira*
Meat: *kreass*

Fish: *psari*
Vegetables: *khortarika, lakhanika*
Potatoes: *patates*
Bread: *psomi*
Sugar: *zakhari*
Rice: *rizi*
Salad: *salata*
Soup: *soupa*
Cheese: *tyri*
Fruit: *frouta*
Bill: *loghariasmos*

◆ POST OFFICE ◆

Post office: *to takhydhromio*
Where is the nearest post office? *pou inai to takhydhromio?*
Stamp: *ghramatossimo*
Letter: *ghrama*
Postcard: *karta*
Telegram: *tileghrafima*
Could you get me the following number...? *borite na mou parete aftonn tonn arithmo...?*

◆ EMERGENCIES ◆

Pharmacy: *farmakio*
I need a doctor: *khriazomai ena yatro*
Dentist: *odhontoyatro*
Ambulance: *asthenoforo*
Hospital: *nossokomio*
Police officer: *astynomikos*
Police station: *astynomia*

◆ SHOPPING ◆

Kiosk: *periptero*
Shop: *maghazi, katastima*
Cheap: *ftino*
Expensive: *akrivo*
Market: *agora*
Baker's: *fournos*

HANDY ◆ PHRASES ◆

I do not understand: *dhenn katalavaino*
I would like...: *thelo...*
Where can I make a phone call? *pou iparkhi tilefono?*
How much does it cost? *posso kani?, posso kostizi...?*
It is too expensive: *inai poly akrivo*
What is it? *ti inai afto?*
When does it open...? *ti ora anighi?*
When does it close...? *ti ora klini?*
A packet of cigarettes, please: *ena paketo tsighara, parakalo*
Can you help me? *borite na me voithissete?*

USEFUL ADDRESSES

☀ VIEW
C CENTRAL LOCATION
⊡·· ISOLATED
⊕ LUXURY RESTAURANT
◑ TYPICAL RESTAURANT
○ BUDGET RESTAURANT
🏛 LUXURY HOTEL
🏠 TYPICAL HOTEL
⌂ BUDGET HOTEL
🅿 CAR PARK
🚗 SUPERVISED CAR PARK
☐ TELEVISION
⌂ QUIET
🛏 SWIMMING POOL
▭ CREDIT CARDS ACCEPTED
⚘ REDUCTIONS FOR CHILDREN
✗ PETS NOT ALLOWED
♫ MUSIC
🎺 LIVE MUSIC
☎ ROOM WITH TELEPHONE

◆ Choosing a Hotel

314

♦ < 5,250–12,250 Dr (£15–£35)
♦♦ 12,250–21,000 Dr (£35–£60)
♦♦♦ < 21,000 Dr (£60)

	PAGE	PRICE	VIEW	QUIET	GARDEN, TERRACE	BAR	CAR PARK	RESTAURANT	SWIMMING POOL
AMNISOS									
Lakis	318	♦			●	●	●		●
Minoa Palace	318	♦♦	●	●		●	●	●	●
BALI									
Bali Beach	318	♦	●		●	●		●	●
KHANIA									
Amphora	318	♦♦	●	●				●	
Casa Delphino	319	♦♦	●	●					
Doma	319	♦♦	●	●					
Kastelli	319	♦		●					
Pandora	319	♦♦	●						
Porto Del Colombo	319	♦	●	●					
Porto Veneziano	319	♦♦	●	●			●	●	
Tina	319	♦							
KHERSONISOS									
Khersonisos Maris	319	♦♦				●		●	●
Creta Maris	319	♦♦♦			●	●			●
Nana Beach	319	♦♦	●		●	●		●	●
Silva Maris	319	♦♦						●	●
Zorba Village	319	♦♦♦				●		●	●
ELOUNDA									
Astir Palace	320	♦♦♦			●	●			●
Elounda Mare	320	♦♦♦	●	●	●	●		●	●
Elounda Marmin	320	♦♦♦				●	●	●	●
Elounda Palm	320	♦♦	●		●		●		●
PHODELE									
Domingo	320	♦		●					
HAGHIOS NIKOLAOS									
Apollon	321	♦		●					
Crystal	321	♦		●					●
Domenico	321	♦	●	●					●
El Greco	321	♦				●	●	●	
Minos Beach	321	♦♦♦	●		●	●		●	●
Pangalos	321	♦	●				●		
Saint Nicolas Bay	321	♦♦♦	●		●	●		●	●
HAGHIA PELAGIA									
Capsis Beach	320	♦♦♦	●		●	●		●	●
HERAKLION									
Agapi Beach	323	♦♦			●	●		●	●
Akti Zeus	323	♦♦♦				●		●	
Astoria Capsis	323	♦♦				●	●		●
Atlantis	323	♦♦	●	●		●	●		●
Atrion	323	♦♦		●	●	●			
Daidalos	323	♦				●			
El Greco	323	♦							
Esperia	323	♦		●		●	●		
Galaxy	323	♦♦				●		●	●
Irini	323	♦♦	●	●	●				
Lato	323	♦♦	●	●	●	●	●		
Lena Hotel	323	♦		●					
Marin	323	♦	●	●					
Mediterranean	323	♦♦	●		●				
Petra	323	♦♦		●	●				
Xenia	323	♦♦	●	●		●		●	

	PAGE	PRICE	VIEW	QUIET	GARDEN, TERRACE	BAR	CAR PARK	RESTAURANT	SWIMMING POOL
IERAPETRA									
KAMIROS	323	♦							
PETRA MARE	324	♦♦	●			●		●	●
KALI LIMENES									
KARAVOVRISSI BEACH	324	♦							
KASTELLI–KISAMOS									
KISAMOS	324	♦	●						
KATO ZAKROS									
POPY	324	♦	●						
POSEIDON	324	♦							
KOLYMBARI									
ARION	324	♦♦						●	●
KRITSA									
ARGYRO	324	♦							
LENDAS									
BUNGALOWS LENDAS	324	♦	●	●					
ROOMS FOR RENT	324	♦	●	●			●		
MALLIA									
ALEXANDER BEACH	325	♦♦			●	●		●	●
GRECOTEL MALLIA PARK	325	♦♦				●		●	●
IKAROS VILLAGE	325	♦♦	●		●			●	●
KERNOS BEACH	325	♦♦♦	●		●	●		●	●
SIRINES BEACH	325	♦♦♦	●			●		●	●
MATALA									
ZARIFIA	325	♦	●			●			
MOKHLOS									
ALDIANA CLUB	325	♦♦				●		●	●
ARETOUSA	325	♦	●	●			●	●	
ERMIS	325	♦	●	●					
MELTEMI	325	♦	●	●			●		
MYRTOS									
ESPERIDES	325	♦			●	●			●
MERTIZA STUDIOS	326	♦		●					
VILLA MARE	326	♦	●	●			●		
PALAIOKHORA									
MALI	326	♦	●	●					
PALAIOKASTRO									
MARINA VILLAGE	326	♦♦	●	●	●			●	●
PHAISTOS									
YANNIS	326	♦	●	●			●		
RETHYMNON									
ADELE MARE	327	♦♦♦				●		●	●
CRETA STAR A	327	♦♦				●		●	●
CRETA ROYAL LUXE	327	♦♦				●		●	●
EL GRECO	327	♦♦			●	●		●	●
LEO	327	♦							
PALAZZO RIMONDI	327	♦♦		●	●				
RETHYMNO HOUSE	327	♦		●					
RITHIMNA	327	♦♦				●		●	●
SITIA									
ELYSÉE	327	♦	●						
HELIO-CLUB SITIA BEACH	327	♦♦	●			●		●	●
MARESOL	327	♦♦				●		●	●
VAI	327	♦					●		

◆ CHOOSING A RESTAURANT

♦ < 5,250 Dr (£15)
♦♦ 5,250–7,000 Dr (£15–£20)
♦♦♦ < 7,000 Dr (£20)

	PAGE	PRICE	VIEW	EATING OUTSIDE	SETTING	CRETAN SPECIALTIES	FISH SPECIALTIES	LIVE MUSIC	TYPICAL
AMNISOS									
AMNISOS TAVERN	318	♦	●	●	●		●		
ANOGIA									
MITATO	318	♦			●				
ARKHANES									
RODAKINIES	318	♦				●			●
AXOS									
SOFIA	318	♦							●
KHANIA									
AERIKO	319	♦	●	●			●		
AKROYALI, CHEZ MYLONAKIS	319	♦♦							●
THE PANORAMA	319	♦♦	●			●			
TO PLATANI	319	♦							
THE RETRO	319	♦♦	●	●	●				
TOURKIKO	319	♦	●	●					
KHERSONISOS									
DRAPIERIS	319	♦				●			
ELOUNDA									
KALYPSO	319	♦♦	●	●					
POULIS NICOLAS	319	♦♦	●				●		
VRITOMARTIS	319	♦♦	●				●		
PHODELE									
EL GRECO	320	♦	●	●	●				
PIRAIKO	320	♦	●						
HAGHIA PELAGIA									
VOTSALO	320	♦♦					●		
HAGHIOS NIKOLAOS									
AKRATOS	321	♦♦	●				●		
THE BOUILLABAISSE	321	♦♦♦	●				●		
MYRTO	321	♦	●	●		●			
LAKE RESTAURANT	321	♦♦♦	●				●		
VASSILI	321	♦♦	●	●					
HERAKLION									
ANTIGONI (TAVERNA)	322	♦		●					●
EMVOLO	321	♦					●		
ERGANOS	321	♦		●		●			
GALERA (TAVERNA)	322	♦					●		
GIOVANNI	321	♦							●
GORGONA (TAVERNA)	322	♦		●			●		
HILOTAS	322	♦		●	●				
HIPPOKAMBOS (TAVERNA)	323	♦					●		
ITAR	322	♦	●					●	
KONAKI	322	♦						●	

	PAGE	PRICE	VIEW	EATING OUTSIDE	SETTING	CRETAN SPECIALTIES	FISH SPECIALTIES	LIVE MUSIC	TYPICAL
KYRIAKOS	322	♦		●					
LUCULLO	322	♦	●	●					
TERZAKIS (TAVERNA)	323	♦				●			
TO STEKI (TAVERNA)	323	♦		●	●	●			
VANGHELIS	322	♦							
VIA VENETO	322	♦	●						●
YAKOUMIS (TAVERNA)	323	♦							
IERAPETRA									
ACROPOLIS	323	♦	●	●		●			
EL GRECO	323	♦	●				●		
GORGONA	323	♦	●				●		
KALI LIMENES									
KARAVOVRISSI BEACH	324	♦							
TAVERNA	324	♦	●						
KATO ZAKROS									
ANESIS	324	♦				●			
KNOSSOS									
KHRIAZOMENOS	324	♦				●			
KRITSA									
CASTELLO	324	♦				●			●
MALLIA									
CORALI	325	♦	●	●					
MATALA									
TA KYMATA	325	♦	●				●		
ZAFIRIA	325	♦	●				●		
ZEUS BEACH	325	♦	●				●		
MOKHLOS									
THE SEA SHELL	325	♦	●	●	●		●		
PALAIOKASTRO									
ANESIS	326	♦							
PANORMOS									
CAVOS	326	♦	●	●			●		
MOURAGIO	326	♦	●	●			●		
PHAISTOS									
YANNIS	326	♦		●	●				
RETHYMNON									
ALANA	327	♦	●		●		●		
AVLI	327	♦♦♦	●	●	●		●		
CHEZ VASSILIS	327	♦♦					●		
PETRINO	327	♦			●		●		
PARADISOS (TAVERNA)	327	♦							
SITIA									
ELYSÉE	327	♦	●	●			●		

1. AMPHORA 2. CASA DELPHINO 3. DOMA 4. KASTELLI 5. PANDORA 6. PORTO DEL COLOMBO 7. PORTO VENEZIANO 8. TINA

KHANIA

(map labels) FORTETZA · LIGHTHOUSE · VENETIAN HARBOR · THEOTOKOPOULOU · AKTI TOMBAZI · KASTELLI · KALLERGON · AKTI MIAOULI · KYPROU · PORTOU · PREOS · MEL. BETAKAKI · PAIDARI · KANEVARO · ARHOLEON · SIFAKI · MINOOS · 1821 SQUARE · SHIAVO BASTION · SKRIDLOF TSOUDERON · MARKET · NIKIFOROU FOKA · MEL. PIGA · S. VENIZELOU SQUARE · EL. VENIZELOU · ANCIENT VENETIAN WALL · HATZI MIKALI GIANARI · MAHIS KRITIS SQUARE · PLASTIRA · V. KONSTANTINOU · MITR. KYRILOU · SKALIDI · 1866 SQUARE · KORAKA · YASSA · PUBLIC GARDENS · KALISPERIDON · KYDONIAS · ZYMBERAKIDON · BONIALI REDUF · TZANAKAKI · KISSAMOU · IONIAS · P. KELAIDI · APOKORONOU · KORNAROU SFAKION · HISTORICAL MUSEUM · KONSTANTINOUPOLEOS · GRIGORIOU E. · SOLOMOU

AMNISOS

Area code tel 081

RESTAURANT

AMNISOS TAVERN
By the beach.
Tel. (081) 22 22 82
Open 9am–10pm.
Closed out of season.
Taverna with a lovely terrace.
Specialty: red mullet.
2,000–5,000 Dr
🍴 🅿

ACCOMMODATION

LAKIS
Tel. (081) 24 33 17
Closed Nov.–Mar.
A stone's throw from the sea, twenty white rooms, decorated with excellent taste. Swimming pool and bar with terrace. Good service.
8,750–12,250 Dr
⌂ 📶 ≋ 🚗 ▭

MINOA PALACE
Amnisos beach
Tel. (081) 22 78 02/24
Open Apr.–Oct.
124 air-conditioned rooms with attractive marble bathrooms. Bar, restaurants, discotheque, swimming pool, tennis court, etc. Faultless reception and service.
12,250–21,000 Dr
⌂ ⌂ 🍴 ≋ 🚗 ▭ ♫

ANOGIA

Area code tel. 081

RESTAURANTS

MITATO
At the bottom of the village
Tel. (081) 312 77
Open 11am–11pm.
Closed out of season.
Wooden taverna, well maintained. Local cuisine.
Specialty: meat dishes.
1,400–3,500 Dr
◑

ARKHANES

Area code tel. 081

CULTURE

ARCHEOLOGICAL MUSEUM
Open daily
8.30am–2.30pm,
closed Tues.

SITES

Necropolis of Phourni, less than 1 mile away. Temple of Anemospilia, about 2 miles away. Minoan villa of Vathypetro, about 2 miles away.

RESTAURANT

RODAKINIES
Village square
Tel. (081) 75 13 88
Open 11am–11pm.
A taverna where the villagers gather to eat, drink coffee and chat. Young, friendly proprietor.
1,750–3,500 Dr
◑ 🅿 ◯

AXOS

Area code tel. 0834

RESTAURANT

SOFIA
Main road
Tel. (0834) 610 23

Open 9am–10pm.
Closed out of season.
A typical taverna, with friendly service.
Specialty: meat dishes.
1,750–3,500 Dr
◐ ◯

BALI

Area code tel. 0834

ACCOMMODATION

BALI BEACH HOTEL
By the beach
Tel. (0834) 942 10/11
Vast rooms with balcony and bathroom, looking out over the Bali gulf. Private beach. Restaurant, bar.
8,750–12,250 Dr
≋ ≋ ☎

KHANIA

Area code tel. 0821

PRACTICAL INFORMATION

TOURIST OFFICE
40, Kriari Street (4th floor.)
Tel. (0821) 264 26

CULTURE

ARCHEOLOGICAL MUSEUM
Halidon Street
Tel. (0821) 244 18
Open Mon. 12.30–7pm,
Tue.–Fri. 8am–7pm,
Sat. Sun. 8.30am–3.30pm.

HISTORICAL MUSEUM
20, Sfakianaki Street
Open Mon.–Fri.
9am–1pm, 3–5.30pm.

NAVAL MUSEUM
Akti Koundourioutou
Open Tue.–Fri.
10am–7pm, Sat. 7–9pm.
Closed Mon.

CRETAN HOUSE
46, Khalido Street
Closed Sat.

ACCOMMODATION

AMPHORA
2, Parodos Street
Theotokopoulou
Tel. (0821) 932 26
Building dating from the 18th century, with Ottoman and Venetian influences. Parquet floors in rooms. The restraint and elegance of the décor make for a very pleasant stay in this superb hotel.
14,000–21,000 Dr
🏛 🅲 ⌂ 🍴 ▭

CASA DELPHINO
9, Theophanous Street
Tel. (0821) 930 98
*There are twelve exquisite
suites in this 17th-century
Venetian dwelling. Warm
and friendly service.*
19,250–22,750 Dr
🏠 🇨 ⌂ 🌙 ▭

DOMA
124, E. Venizelou Street
Tel. (0821) 217 72.
Open Mar.–Oct.
*Patrician household run
with impeccable taste.
Quiet; view of the sea.
About 14,000 Dr*
🌙 ⌂

KASTELLI
39, Kanevaro Street
Tel. (0821) 570 57
Closed Nov.–Mar.
*Charming hotel, with
ornate and pleasant style.
Very welcoming reception.
7,700–8,750 Dr*
🏠 🇨 ⌂ ▭

PANDORA
29, Lithinon Street
Tel. (0821) 435 88
*Rooms with cooking
facilities and view of the
harbor, in a building in the
neoclassical style.
17,500–21,000 Dr*
🌙 🏠 ⌂

PORTO DEL COLOMBO
Corner of Theophanous
and Moskhon Streets
Tel. (0821) 509 75
*Lovely hotel. Paneling
and parquet floors in the
rooms. Ideal location.
8,750–12,250 Dr*
🏠 🇨 ⌂ 🌙 ▭

PORTO VENEZIANO
Akti Enesseos Limenos
Tel. (0821) 293 11
Open all year.
*Quiet, air-conditioned
hotel, with restaurant.
Good views.
15,750–17,500 Dr*
🌙 🅿 ⌂

TINA
3, Bouniali Street
Tel. (0821) 425 27
*Plain but comfortable.
4,200–8,750 Dr*
⌂

RESTAURANTS

AERIKO
Koum Kapi district
*By the sea. Attentive
service. Specialties: fish
and meat dishes.
2,800–5,000 Dr*
🌙

AKROYALI, CHEZ MYLONAKIS
Nea Khora. Akti Papanikoli
Tel. (0821) 581 37
*Best of all the tavernas
in this district.
4,200–5,000 Dr*
◑

THE PANORAMA
Malaxa
*On a hillside
overlooking the bay.
Cretan specialties:
herb or cheese
turnovers, with raki.
4,200–6,300 Dr*
🌙

TO PLATANI
Rethymnon road, just over
a mile outside Souda
Tel. (0821) 894 94
*Friendly family-run
taverna.
Specialties: meat dishes.
2,000–4,200 Dr*
○

THE RETRO
Halepa, 1, Mavroghenidon
Tel. (0821) 583 86
*Garden and pleasant
setting. Cosmopolitan.
4,200–6,300 Dr*
🌙

TOURKIKO
Galatas village
*The only Turkish taverna
on the island. Generous
helpings, fine view, large
courtyard.
1,400–2,800 Dr*
🌙 ○

SHOPPING

CARMELA
Angelou Street
*Modern ceramics in
every style.*

COVERED MARKET
Halidon Street
*A large number of
craftsmen's stalls
offering a wide variety
of wares.*

TOP HANAS
Angelou Street
*Antique embroidery and
carpets.*

KHERSONISOS

Area code tel. 0897

RESTAURANT

DRAPIERIS
Lassithi road,
Pano-Hersonissos
Tel. (0897) 21 15 84
*Family-run taverna.
Generous helpings.
Specialties: stuffed
courgettes.
1,400–2,800 Dr*
◑ ○

ACCOMMODATION

KHERSONISOS MARIS
By the beach
Tel. (0897) 236 01.
*Bar, restaurant,
snacks, swimming pool.
15,750–17,500 Dr*
⌐

CRETA MARIS
Limenas Hersonissou
Tel. (0897) 221 15
*Hotel and bungalows;
architecture in the
Aegean style. Fitted out
in luxurious style, with
private beach, swimming
pool, watersports, tennis,
open-air cinema.
31,500–36,750 Dr*
🏠 ⌐

NANA BEACH
By the beach
Tel. (0897) 227 06
Open Apr.–Oct.
*Hotel and bungalows,
bar, two restaurants,
snack bar, open and
covered swimming
pools, sauna, tennis.
16,800–19,250 Dr*
🌙 ⌐

SILVA MARIS
Limenas Hersonissou
Tel. (0897) 228 50
*Hotel and bungalows.
Architecture in the
style of a traditional
Cretan village.
Lovely swimming pool,
restaurant, shops.
13,300–21,000 Dr*
🏠 ⌐

ELOUNDA

Area code tel. 0841

RESTAURANTS

KALYPSO
In the square
Tel. (0841) 414 24
Open 9am–4pm, 7–11pm.
Closed out of season.
*An attractive dining
room with a terrace
looking over the port;
friendly, obliging and
faultless service.
Chic location.
Specialties: seafood.
4,200–7,000 Dr*
◍ ▭ 🌙

POULIS NICOLAS
Schisma Eloundas
Tel. (0841) 414 51
Open 11am–3pm, 6–11pm.
Closed out of season.

*You can try out all
the seafood specialties
with your feet dangling
in the water! A little
expensive.
Specialties: lobster,
crayfish.
3,500–8,750 Dr*
◍ ▭ 🌙

VRITOMARTIS
In the harbor
Tel. (0841) 413 25
Open 10am–11pm.
Closed out of season.
*Among the boats in
the harbor. Fish dishes
predominate on the
varied menu. Specialties:
depend upon the catch.
3,500–5,000 Dr*
◑ 🌙 🅿

ZORBA VILLAGE
Anissara beach
Tel. (0897) 226 04
Open Mar.–Oct.
*113 bungalows and
36 apartments,
restaurant, bar, beach,
swimming pools, tennis,
watersports.
28,000–31,500 Dr*
🌙 ⌐

1. APOLLON   2. DOMENICO   3. EL GRECO   4. PANGALOS

ACCOMMODATION

ASTIR PALACE
By the beach
Tel. (0841) 415 80
Open Mar.–Oct.
A hotel fitted out to a high level of luxury, albeit not entirely successfully.
26,250–54,250 Dr

ELOUNDA MARE
Haghios Nikolaos road
Tel. (0841) 411 02
Open Mar.–Oct.
This establishment is situated on the gulf of Mirambello. Cheerful flower borders surround the startlingly white bungalows, many of which have access to a swimming pool. The Yacht Club serves a wide range of grilled fish. In the evening, the Old Windmill taverna offers a selection of Greek specialties.
33,250–56,000 Dr

ELOUNDA MARMIN
Schisma Eloundas
Tel. (0841) 415 13
Open Apr.–Oct.
Small luxury complex. Bungalows with swimming pool, bar, etc. Fairly average service, but you get what you pay for.
15,750–42,000 Dr

ELOUNDA PALM
Elounda
Tel. (0841) 418 25
Open Apr.–Oct.
All the rooms are spacious and look out over the sea. The hotel also has access to a freshwater swimming pool, a children's playground and a car park.
15,750–17,500 Dr

HAGHIOS NIKOLAOS

(map with streets: PRINGIPOS, KORISSIS, MILETOU, KOUNDOUROU, ETHNIKIS ANTISTASEOS, PALEOLOGOU, THEOTOKOPOULOU, PERIKLEOUS, GEORGIOU, THERMOPILON, NIKOLAOU, PLASTIRA, KAZANTZAKIS, SOLOMOU, TITOU, DIMOKRATIAS, PLASTIRA, LOUKAREOS, KONDYLAKI, LAKE VOULISMENI, OMIROU, 28 OKTOVRIOU, KOUNDOUROU, MARTIOU, SFAKIANAKI K., LASTHENI, PASSERAS, SAROLIDI, AKTI THEMISTOKLI, MILOU, ARIADNIS, EVAN., VENIZELOU SQUARE, OTE, MONDATSOU, TSELEPI, AKTI PANGALOU, VRILOU, KONTOGIANI, MINOS, EL.VENIZELOU, TAVIA, KOZIRI I., KASTEL MIRAMBELOU, SFAKIANAKI N., AXGHLOPOULOS)

PHODELE
Area code tel. 0815

RESTAURANTS

EL GRECO
Tel. (0815) 212 03
Open 11am–3pm, 6–10pm.
Closed out of season.
Sheltered, close by to a small stream. The taverna menu is ideal for a light meal.
1,750–3,500 Dr

PIRAIKO
Tel. (0815) 213 73
Open 11am–4pm, 6–10pm.
Closed out of season.
A very short walk from the preceding restaurant, it offers the same quality of cuisine: limited in variety but well prepared. Specialties: meat dishes.
1,750–3,500 Dr

ACCOMMODATION

DOMINGO
Tel. (0815) 112 08
Open all year
The only hotel in Phodele to be found in the village itself.
5,000–8,750 Dr

GORTYN
Area code tel. 0892

CULTURE

ARCHEOLOGICAL SITE
Open Mon.–Fri. 8am–7pm,
Sat. Sun. 8.30am–3pm
(5pm in winter).

GOURNIA
Area code tel. 0842

CULTURE

MINOAN SITE
Open 9am–3pm.

HAGHIA PELAGIA
Area code tel. 081

RESTAURANTS

VOTSALO
By the beach
Tel. (081) 81 10 22
You can sit out on the terrace just a couple of steps from the water and sample freshly caught fish and shellfish.
3,500–7,000 Dr

ACCOMMODATION

CAPSIS BEACH
Haghia Pelagia
Tel. (081) 81 11 12
A large hotel complex built on the Haghia Pelagia peninsula. Attractive location. This hotel offers all the facilities one would find in a much larger hotel.
43,750–56,000 Dr

HAGHIA TRIADA
Area code tel. 0892

CULTURE

MINOAN SITE
Open Mon.–Sat. 9am–3pm, Sun. and public holidays 9.30am–2.30pm.

HAGHIOS NIKOLAOS

Area code tel. 0841

PRACTICAL INFORMATION

TOURIST OFFICE
In the harbor,
20, Akti Koundourou
Tel. (0841) 223 57

POST OFFICE
9, October 28 Street

CULTURE

ARCHEOLOGICAL MUSEUM
68, Paleologou Street
Tel. (0841) 22 462
Open Tue.–Sat. 9am–3pm,
Sun. 9.30am–2.30pm.
Closed Mon.

MUSEUM OF POPULAR ART
Next to the tourist office.
Open 9.30am–1pm,
5–8.30pm

RESTAURANTS

AKRATOS
15, Omirou Street
Tel. (0841) 227 24
Open 11am–11pm.
Closed out of season.

Overlooking the small lake by the harbor, offering a very wide menu. A little expensive but the quality is excellent. Specialties: fresh fish.
3,000–7,700 Dr

THE BOUILLABAISSE
Amoudi beach
Tel. (0841) 223 45
Fish restaurant on the Minos Beach. Good for the view and the shellfish.
About 8,750 Dr

MYRTO
7, Kitroplatia Street
Tel. (0841) 241 48
Open 9am–11pm.
Closed out of season.
On a rather isolated beach, therefore quiet. The service is prompt and the proprietors obliging. Good food. Specialties: souvlaki, moussaka.
2,450–5,000 Dr

LAKE RESTAURANT
17, Omirou Street
Tel. (0841) 224 14
Open 11am–11pm.
Closed out of season.
Fish restaurant with impeccable service but high prices. Specialties: shrimps, fish soup.
4,200–8,750 Dr

VASSILI
16, I. Koundourou Street
Tel. (0841) 282 01.
A traditional taverna on the waterfront in Crete's "Saint-Tropez".
About 5,000 Dr

ACCOMMODATION

APOLLON
9, Minos Street
Tel. (0841) 230 23
Closed Oct.–Mar.
In the center of town, 72 well-furnished, very traditional rooms; close to the beach.
5,000–7,000 Dr

CRYSTAL
Some distance from the town, bordering on a small beach.
Tel. (0841) 244 07
Closed Oct.–Mar.
Charming hotel with swimming pool. Geared toward tourists but quiet.
7,700–12,250 Dr

DOMENICO
3, Argyropoulou Street
Tel. (0841) 228 45
Closed Nov.–Mar.
South of the town, next to the bus station. Pleasant reception and traditional décor. View of the sea.
8,750–12,250 Dr

EL GRECO
Akti Kitroplatia
Tel. (0841) 288 94
Open Mar.–Dec.
45 double rooms, bar, restaurant car park.
8,750–12,250 Dr

MINOS BEACH
Amoudi beach
Tel. (0841) 223 45/9
Open Apr.–Oct.
Spectacular bungalows built on the rocks, by the sea. Lovely garden. Swimming pool and private beach. Good food.
22,750–52,500 Dr

PANGALOS
17, Tselepi Street
Tel. (0841) 221 46
Closed Oct.–Mar.
A few yards from the beach; small but friendly family-run hotel. Rooms with balconies.
6,300–8,750 Dr

SAINT NICOLAS BAY
By the beach
Tel. (0841) 250 41/43
Open Mar.–Nov.
130 air-conditioned bungalows, with mini-bars and radios. Private beach and two salt-water swimming pools. Two restaurants and a taverna.
17,500–59,500 Dr

HERAKLION

Area code tel. 081

PRACTICAL INFORMATION

POST OFFICE
Daskaloyanni Square,
near Eleftherias Square.

TOURIST OFFICE
Xanthoudidou Street,
opposite Archeological Museum.

CULTURE

HAGHIA EKATERINI, CHURCH AND ICON MUSEUM
Haghia Ekaterini Square
Open Mon. Wed. Sat.
9.30am–1pm, Tue. Thur.
Fri. 5–7pm. Closed Sun.
and public holidays.
Entry about 350 Dr.

VENETIAN FORT
Tel. (081) 28 62 28
Open Mon.–Sat.
8.45am–3pm, Sun. and
pub. hols 9.30am–2.30pm.
Entry 350 Dr.

KHRONAKIS HOUSE
Paleologou Street
Open Mon.–Fri.
10am–1pm.
Ancient pasha's residence, recently restored.

ARCHEOLOGICAL MUSEUM
Eleftherias Square
Tel. (081) 22 60 92
Open Tue. Fri. 8am–7pm,
Sat. Sun. 8.30am–3pm,
Mon. 11am–5pm.
Entry: about 525 Dr.

HISTORICAL AND ETHNOGRAPHIC MUSEUM
Kalokairinou Street, west of the fort
Tel. (081) 28 32 19
Open Mon. Sat. 9am–1pm
and 3–5.30pm. Closed
Sun. and public holidays.
Entry: about 350 Dr.

ART GALLERY
In the old St Mark's Church, Lions Square
Open Mon.–Sat.
9am–2pm. Closed Sun.

RESTAURANTS

EMVOLO
Miliara cul-de-sac,
off Evans Street
Tel. (081) 28 42 44
Cretan specialties.
1,400–2,800 Dr

ERGANOS
G. Ghiorgiadou Avenue
Tel. (081) 28 56 29
Small terrace. Cretan specialties.
1,750–2,800 Dr

GIOVANNI
12, Korais Street
Tel. (081) 24.63.38
Open noon.
Greek cuisine. Friendly ambience. Small bar.
2,800–3,500 Dr

HERAKLION

CRETAN SEA

KOULES FORTRESS

VENETIAN HARBOR

HARBOR MASTER'S OFFICE

MAKARIOU

KOUNDOURIOTON SQUARE

VIRONOS

EPIMENIDOU

EL GRECO PARK

E. VENIZELOS SQUARE

DOUKOS

MERAMBELOU

HATZIDAKI

MOROSINI FOUNTAIN

DEDALOU

BEAUFORT

SAINT CATHERINE'S CHURCH

DIKEOSSYNIS

ELEFTHERIAS SQUARE

IKAROU

M. GIANARI

DASKALOYANNIS SQUARE

BEMBO FOUNTAIN KORNAROU SQUARE

AVEROF OTHONOS

TRIS KAMARES

TRIESTOU ANOPOLEOS

HILOTAS
Panaghitsa Square,
Mastabas district
Tel. (081) 25 72 53
Open in the evening.
Closed Wed.
*Pleasant setting,
high-class cuisine,
attentive service,
attractive terrace.*
1,400–3,500 Dr
◐

ITAR
16, Epimenidou Street
Tel. (081) 22 60 61
Open in the evening.
*On the first floor of
an ancient Venetian
palace. Live band
playing Greek music.*
2,450–4,200 Dr
◐ ♫

KONAKI
At Kokkini Hani, in the
suburbs of Heraklion
Tel. (081) 761 229
Open Tue.–Sun.
Closed Mon.
*International cuisine plus
Greek specialties. Music
on Thur. Fri. Sat. Sun.*
3,500–5,000 Dr
♫

KYRIAKOS
53, Dimokratias Avenue
Tel. (081) 22 46 49
Open noon.
Closed Wed.
*Traditional, well-prepared
Greek cuisine in plain
surroundings. Pleasant
terrace on one of the
main roads in the town.*
2,800–3,500 Dr
◗ ▣

LUCULLO
5, Korais Street
Tel. (081) 22 44 35
Open 12.30–4.30pm and
8pm–1am.
*Pleasant setting and a
pretty courtyard. Italian
specialties.*
2,800–5,000 Dr
☩

VANGHELIS
Karteros
Tel. (081) 24 56 26
*One of the best menus in
the Heraklion district.
Strongly recommended.*
3,150–4,550 Dr
◐

VIA VENETO
Epimenidou Street
Tel. (081) 28 54 30
Open in the evening.
*Fine view of the harbor
and the Venetian fortress.
Piano-restaurant.
Night club.*
4,200–5,000 Dr
☩ ♫

TAVERNAS

ANTIGONI
Knossou Avenue
Tel. (081) 23 02 70

Open noon, closed Sun.
*Generous Greek
cuisine. Warm-hearted
welcome. The terrace
is a bit small.*
2,000–3,500 Dr
◐ ○

GALERA
185, Leoforos Knossou
Tel. (081) 21 10 32
*Restaurant specializing
in fish.*
2,000–4,200 Dr

GORGONA
13, Viglas Street
Tel. (081) 28 95 16
Open Sat. only.
*Greek specialties,
pikilia, charming
central garden.*
1,750–2,800 Dr
◐ ○

HIPPOKAMBOS
Sophias Venizelou
Street
Tel. (081) 28 02 40
Open noon.
*Unpretentious, friendly
atmosphere, prompt
service. Tourists
welcomed.
Specialties: seafood
and fish.
1,750–3,500 Dr*
○

TERZAKIS
Haghiou Dimitriou
Square
Tel. (081) 22 14 44
Open noon.
*Various mezedes.
2,450–3,500 Dr*
❶

TO STEKI
Rue Viglas
Tel. (081) 22 54 00
Open in the evening.
*Terrace under a vine
trellis, range of Greek
specialties: pikilia.
1,750–2,800 Dr*
❶ ○

YAKOUMIS
8, Theodoraki Street
Tel. (081) 28 02 77
*In a narrow street
perpendicular to
the market street;
succulent lamb chops.
2,000–3,500 Dr*
❶ ○

ACCOMMODATION

AGAPI BEACH
Amoudara
Tel. 81 25 05 02
Open April to Oct.
*180 rooms,
100 bungalows,
12 suites. Bar, two
swimming pools,
snack bar, restaurant,
café, taverna,
discotheque, shops,
three tennis courts,
watersports.
Half-board only.
22,750–36,750 Dr*
⇱ ♫

AKTI ZEUS
Linoperamata
Tel. 81 82 15 03
Open Apr.–Oct.
*380 rooms, 9 fully
equipped suites, roof
garden, air-conditioning,
bars, restaurants,
discotheque, cafeteria,
watersports, tennis,
miniature golf.
Half-board only.
31,500–35,000 Dr*
⇱ ♫

ASTORIA CAPSIS
5, Eleftherias Square
Tel. (081) 22 90 12
*Central, a stone's throw
from the Archeological
Museum and bordering
a pedestrian precinct.
Roof garden with
swimming pool, bar, tea
room. Very pleasant.
17,500–22,750 Dr*
🏨 🅒 ⅏ 🚗 ▭

ATLANTIS
2, Igias Street
Tel. (081) 22 91 03
*One of Heraklion's most
luxurious hotels, with
swimming pool, tennis,
billiards, etc., near the
Archeological Museum.
Good restaurant,
terrace, shopping
arcade, panoramic
view of the harbor.
17,500–22,750 Dr*
🏨 🅒 ⅏ ⇲ 🚗 ▭

ATRION
9, K. Paleologou Street
Tel. (081) 24 28 30
Open all year.
*Modern, peaceful,
snack bar, in-room TV,
patio and garden.
14,000–15,750 Dr*
⌂

DAIDALOS
15, Dedalou Street
Tel. (081) 24 48 12
*Central, comfortable,
bar, TV in room. Not
far from the Morosini
fountain and the shops.
8,750–10,500 Dr*
⌂ 🅒 ▭

EL GRECO
4, 1821 Street
Tel. (081) 28 10 71
*Very central, near the bus
station for Knossos.
7,000–8,750 Dr*
⌂ 🅒 ▭

ESPERIA
22, Idomeneos Street
Tel. (081) 22 85 56
*Very close to the
Archeological Museum, in
a small quiet back street.
Bar, roof garden, rooms
with en-suite bathrooms.
7,700–9,800 Dr*
🏨 🅒 ⌂ 🚗 ▭

GALAXY
67, Dimokratias Avenue
Tel. (081) 23 88 12
Open all year.
*Modern. Bar, restaurant,
café, sauna, swimming
pool, attractive rooms.
22,750–26,250 Dr*
⇲

IRINI
4, Idomeneos Street
Tel. (081) 22 97 03
*Air-conditioned rooms,
terrace with a view over
the harbor. Quiet.
13,300–16,800 Dr*
⅏ ⌂

LATO
15, Epimenidou Street
Tel. (081) 22 81 03
*Excellent view over
the Venetian Harbor.
Terraced garden
where one can sit
and have a drink.
TV and bar in rooms.
11,200–13,300 Dr*
🏨 🅒 ⌂ ⅏ 🚗 ▭

LENA HOTEL
10, Lahana
Tel. (081) 22 32 80
*Small, clean and quiet
family-run hotel.
Generous breakfast.
About 5,000 Dr*
🏨 ⌂

MARIN
12, Doukos Beaufort
Tel. (081) 22 47 36
*Right next to the harbor,
view of the sea.
Rooms with shower or
bathroom, elevator.
Traditional furniture.
10,500–12,250 Dr*
⌂ 🅒 ⌂ ⅏ ▭

MEDITERRANEAN
Dikeossynis Square
Tel. (081) 28 93 31
*Central location, with
terraced garden.
Some very pretty and
well-decorated rooms,
but average service.
12,250–15,750 Dr*
🏨 🅒 ⌂ ⅏ ▭

PETRA
55, Dikeossynis Street
Tel. (081) 22 99 12
*Near Eleftherias Square.
Plenty of charm, and a
secluded courtyard
where one can take
breakfast. Spacious
rooms.
12,250–14,000 Dr*
🏨 🅒 ⌂ ▭

XENIA
2, Venizelou Street
Tel. 81 28 40 00
*Has the advantages of
being opposite the
museum and close to
the sea. Large restaurant
room, bar, good service
and irreproachable
management.
15,750–21,000 Dr*
🏨 ⌂ 🚗 ▭

IERAPETRA

Area code tel. 0842

RESTAURANTS

ACROPOLIS
Opposite the harbor
Tel. (0842) 236 59
Open 9am–4pm, 6–11pm.
Closed out of season.
*A lot of tourists, but
an attractive terrace.
Specialties: squid,
souvlaki.
2,000–5,000 Dr*
○ ▭ ⅏

EL GRECO
By the sea
Tel. (0842) 287 91
Open 6–10pm.
*Hotel restaurant. Stylish
service, fine cuisine.
Specialties: fish.
2,000–5,000 Dr*
❶ ▭ ⅏

GORGONA
By the sea
Open 9am–11pm.
Closed out of season.
*Situated in the midst of
many other waterfront
restaurants, this one
has preserved its
authenticity.
Specialties: kalamari,
swordfish.
2,000–5,000 Dr*
❶ ▭ ⅏

ACCOMMODATION

KAMIROS
15, M. Kothri Street
Tel. (0842) 287 04
*In an old city dwelling
which boasts some
handsome features,
including marble
staircases. The rooms
are a little stark,
although reception is
cordial. A good hotel
for business travelers.
7,000–8,750 Dr*
🏨 🅒 ▭

323

PETRA MARE

By the beach
Tel. (0842) 233 419
Open Apr.–Oct.
Tennis, swimming pool, restaurant, discotheque, shops.
17,500–21,000 Dr

NIGHTLIFE

CHEZ VICTOR
By the sea
Tel. (0842) 255 16
Open 8–3am.
Good music, young crowd, cocktail bar.

XANADU
Coast road
Tel. (0842) 262 80
Open 10pm–4am.
Closed out of season.
Large, traditional discotheque.

KALI LIMENES

Area code tel. 0892

RESTAURANT

KARAVOVRISSI BEACH
Lentas road
Tel. (0892) 422 02.
Open 8am–9pm.
Closed out of season.
Simple fare: salads, filled rolls.
1,750–3,500 Dr
○

TAVERNA
Lendas road
Tel. (0892) 422 04.
Open 11am–10pm.
Closed out of season.

Superb view over the bay.
Specialties: rib of lamb.
1,400–2,800 Dr
○

ACCOMMODATION

KARAVOVRISSI BEACH
At the village limits
Tel. (0892) 422 02
Open Apr.–Oct.
Small rooms painted blue.
Shared showers.
3,500–5,000 Dr

KASTELLI-KISAMOS

Area code tel. 0822

SITE

Polyrrhinia, roughly 4 miles to the southwest

ACCOMMODATION

KISAMOS
Town center
Tel. (0822) 220 86
A small, fairly new hotel. Sea views.
5,600–7,000 Dr

KATO ZAKROS

Area code tel. 0843

CULTURE

MINOAN PALACE
Open Mon.–Sat.
9am–5pm,
Sun. and public holidays
10am–5pm.
At the eastern tip of Crete, at the end of a bumpy road but in a superb location, the last of the great Minoan palaces is a must for sightseers.

RESTAURANT

ANESIS
Tel. (0843) 933 74
Open 9am–11pm.
Closed out of season.
Friendly. Specialties: cheese turnovers, red mullet, swordfish.
1,750–4,200 Dr
○

ACCOMMODATION

POPY
By the beach
Tel. (0843) 933 77
Open Apr.–Oct.
Rooms to rent, ornate, with or without showers. Unbeatable views.
5,000–7,000 Dr

POSEIDON
By the beach
15 rooms with or without showers.
5,000–7,000 Dr

KNOSSOS

Area code tel. 081

CULTURE

MINOAN PALACE
Tel. 81 23 19 40
Open Mon.–Sat 8am–7pm,
Sun. 8am–6pm,
out of season 8am–5pm.

RESTAURANT

KHRIAZOMENOS
Before the aqueduct on the Haghia Irini road.
Tel. (081) 23 19 15
Well-prepared traditional Cretan cuisine.
1,400–2,800 Dr
○ ◐

KOLYMBARI

Area code tel. 0824

ACCOMMODATION

ARION
By the beach
Tel. (0824) 229 42
Small, comfortable hotel. Half-board only.
12,250–14,000 Dr

KRITSA

Area code tel. 0841

CULTURE

PANAGHIA KERA
A mile or so from Kritsa

Open Mon.–Sat
8.30am–3pm,
Sun. 8.30am–2pm.

SHOPPING

A small village renowned for the high quality of its weaving.

RESTAURANT

CASTELLO
The main square
Tel. (0841) 512 54
Open 11am–4pm, 7–9pm.
Closed out of season.
In the midst of all the souvenir stalls, this restaurant comes as a welcome break.
Specialties: Greek salad, souvlaki.
2,000–3,500 Dr
○

ACCOMMODATION

ARGYRO
Entrance to the village
Tel. (0841) 516 13.
Closed out of season.
6 good, clean rooms.
2,000–5,000 Dr

LENDAS

Area code tel. 0892

ACCOMMODATION

LENDAS BUNGALOWS
Tel. (0892) 222 72
Closed Nov.–Mar.
20 bungalows, fairly close to the sea but some distance from the center, prettily decorated, with showers and washrooms.
5,000–8,750 Dr

ROOMS FOR RENT
Kali Limenes road
Tel. (0892) 422 04
Closed Nov.–Mar.
Along a bone-shaking road, an unusual spot to stop and enjoy complete peace.
Eight bungalows with outside showers. Superb view of the sea.
3,500–5,000 Dr

MALLIA

Area code tel. 0897

CULTURE

MINOAN PALACE
Tel. (0897) 244 62
Open Mon.–Sat. 9am–3pm,
Sun. and public holidays
9.30am–2.30pm.

RESTAURANT

CORALI
By the sea
Open 9am–11pm.
Closed out of season.
*One of several
restaurants on this
very lively beach.
Well-prepared food.
Greek specialties.*
2,000–5,000 Dr
⌂ ▭ ⚊

ACCOMMODATION

ALEXANDER BEACH
By the beach
Tel. (0897) 321 24
Open Mar.–Oct.
*200 rooms, restaurant,
taverna, bars, swimming
pool, sauna, tennis
courts, watersports.*
12,250–17,500 Dr
⌇

**GRECOTEL MALLIA
PARK**
By the beach
Tel. (0897) 314 60
Open Mar.–Nov.
*180 rooms, bar,
restaurant, swimming
pool, watersports, tennis.*
15,750–28,000 Dr
⌇

IKAROS VILLAGE
By the beach
Tel. (0897) 312 67/9.
Open Mar.–Oct.
*Bungalows. Pretty
gardens. Sauna, taverna,
restaurant, tennis.*
14,000–21,000 Dr
⚊

KERNOS BEACH
By the beach
Tel. (0897) 314 21/5
Open Apr.–Oct.
*280 rooms, three bars,
restaurant, taverna,*

*miniature golf, tennis,
swimming pools, nursery,
shops. Half-board only,
rooms with sea view.*
22,750–33,250 Dr
⚊ ⌇

SIRINES BEACH
By the beach
Tel. (0897) 313 21
Open Apr.–Nov.
*Bar, tennis, swimming
pools, restaurant, night
club.*
33,250–38,500 Dr
⌇ ♫

MATALA

Area code tel. 0892

RESTAURANT

TA KYMATA
Tel. (0892) 423 61
Open 11am–11pm.
Closed out of season.
*By the beach, very good
cuisine, fresh fish, friendly
ambience. Good service.
Specialties: red mullet,
octopus, squid.*
2,800–5,000 Dr
◑

ZAFIRIA
Tel. (0892) 427 47
Open 11am–11pm.
Closed out of season.
*Beside the sea, taverna
at the hotel Zafiria.
Warm reception, plenty
of tourists. Specialties:
red mullet, sole.*
2,000–4,200 Dr
◑ ▭ ⚊ P

ZEUS BEACH
Tel. (0892) 427 30
Open 9am–10pm.
Closed out of season.
*Friendly proprietors.
Nearest to the caves.
Specialties: red mullet,
sole, swordfish.*
1,750–3,500 Dr
○ ⚊

ACCOMMODATION

ZAFIRIA
Tel. (0892) 421 12
Closed Nov.–Mar.
*This large hotel has a
taverna on the beach, a*

*bar and a breakfast
room. Considerate
service and sparkling
clean rooms.*
5,000–8,750 Dr
⌂ ◙ ⚊ ▭

MOKHLOS

Area code tel. 0843

CULTURE

*The islet blocking the
creek is an archeological
site; swimming is
permissible, although it
is important to watch out
for the powerful currents
in the channel.*

ACCOMMODATION

ALDIANA CLUB
Outside the village
Tel. (0843) 942 11
Open Apr.–Oct.
*Restaurant, swimming
pool, bar, discotheque,
watersports, tennis.
35 rooms and 100
bungalows.
Full board only.*
14,000–17,500 Dr
▭•• ⌇ ♫

ARETOUSA
In the harbor
Tel. (0843) 944 26
Closed Oct.–Mar.
*Extremely friendly,
English-speaking
proprietor. Lodgings
with a small taverna
where you can sample
authentic Greek
family cooking.*
4,200–5,000 Dr
⌂ ◙ ⌂ ⚊ 🚗

ERMIS
In the harbor
Tel. (0843) 940 74
Closed Oct.–Mar.
*Small establishment
with eight rooms kept
by an old fisherman.
Very good value;
outdoor showers.
Peace guaranteed!*
3,500–5,000 Dr
⌂ ◙ ⌂ ⚊

MELTEMI
Entrance to the village
Tel. (0843) 944 32
Closed Nov.–Apr.
*New and generally
very comfortable
apartments overlooking
the village and the
harbor. Very ornate.
Ask at the Sea Shell
taverna.*
6,300–8,000 Dr
⌂ ⌂ ▭•• ⚊ 🚗 ▭

RESTAURANTS

THE SEA SHELL
Tel. (0843) 944 32
Open 9am–10pm.
Closed out of season.
*A very pretty terrace
under an arbor, with
a view over the little
harbor and the fishing
boats. Friendly and
accommodating service.
Specialties: fish.*
1,750–4,200 Dr
◑ ⚊

MONI ARKADI

CULTURE

**MONASTERY
AND MUSEUM**
Open 8am–1pm, 2–7pm
(in summer).

MONI PREVELI

CULTURE

MONASTERY
Open 8am–1pm, 5–8pm.

MONT IDA

CULTURE

CAVE OF ZEUS
Open 10am–5pm.

MYRTOS

Area code tel. 0842

ACCOMMODATION

ESPERIDES
On the main road
outside the village.
Tel. (0842) 512 98
Closed Nov.–Mar.
*A tourists' hotel by the
side of the road, with
swimming pool, bar
and terrace.*
7,000–8,750 Dr
⌂ ▭•• ⚊ ⌇ 🚗 ▭

1. LEO **2. PALAZZO RIMONDI** **3. RETHYMNON HOUSE**

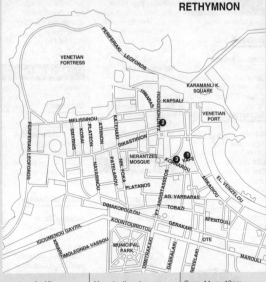

RETHYMNON

MERTIZA STUDIOS
Entrance to the village
Tel. (0842) 512 08
Closed Nov.–Mar.
*A delightful complex
of new and very well
equipped bungalows.
Charming proprietor.
Excellent value for
money.*
5,000–7,000 Dr
⌂ ⌂ ⌷•• ⌂

VILLA MARE
Tel. (0842) 512 74
Closed Nov.–Mar.
*A very pretty white
building with attractive
flowerbeds. Well kept;
sea views.*
5,000–8,750 Dr
⌂ C ⌂ ⛏ 🚗

PALAIOKHORA (SELINO)

Area code tel. 0823

ACCOMMODATION

MALI
Near the sea
Tel. (0823) 411 44
Closed Nov.–Mar.
*Very comfortable with
pleasant service;
views of the sea.*
7,000–8,750 Dr
⛏ ⌂

PALAIOKASTRO

Area code tel. 0843

CULTURE

*A fascinating
archeological site
about 12 miles from
Sitia. Near the sea, at
Roussolakkos, in the
midst of olive groves.
Digging continues to this
day. Further off are the*

*remains of a Minoan
kiln. There is a sanctuary
on the crest of the hill at
Petsofas.*

ACCOMMODATION

MARINA VILLAGE
Coast road
Tel. (0843) 612 84
Closed Nov.–Mar.
*An old, ornate country
house which has been
renovated. Children's
swimming pool, big
garden. Clean rooms.*
8,750–14,000 Dr
⌂ ⛏ 🛏 ⌂ ⌷ 🚗
⌷••

RESTAURANT

ANESIS
Coast road
Tel. (0843) 614 79
Open 11am–4pm, 6–10pm.
Closed out of season.
*Family cooking for a
modest sum in this
restaurant lying at some
distance from the town.
Simple, but good food.*
1,700–3,500 Dr
◑ P

PANORMOS

Area code tel. 0834

RESTAURANTS

CAVOS
In the harbor
Tel. (0834) 610 54
Open 11am–11pm.
Closed out of season.

*Unpretentious taverna
with a terrace.
Specialties: fish.*
1,750–3,500 Dr
○ ⛏

MOURAGIO
In the harbor
Tel. (0834) 512 97
Open 11am–11pm.
Closed out of season.
*Taverna with terrace.
Specialties: fresh fish.*
1,750–3,500 Dr
○ ⛏

PHAISTOS

Area code tel. 0892

CULTURE

MINOAN PALACE
Tel 89 29 13 15
Open Mon.–Sat
8am–7pm,
Sun. 8am–6pm.

ACCOMMODATION

YANNIS
Matala road
Tel. (0892) 914 94
*Charming reception.
Isolated rooms in the
garden. View over the site
of Phaistos. Outdoor
showers.*
4,200–5,000 Dr
⛏ ⌂ ⌷•• ⛏ 🚗

RESTAURANTS

YANNIS
Matala road
Tel (0892) 315 60

Open 11am–10pm.
*Family cooking, terrace
opening out onto the
garden. Fresh vegetables,
charming proprietors.
Quiet. Specialty: rabbit.*
2,000–4,200 Dr
◑ P

RETHYMNON

Area code tel. 0831

PRACTICAL INFORMATION

POST OFFICE
19, Moatsou Street
Taxis: main ranks near the
pier and in the square at
the municipal gardens.

TOURIST OFFICE
By the beach, Eleftherios
Venizelou Street
Tel. (0831) 291 48

CULTURE

VENETIAN FORTRESS
Open 9am–4.30pm.

ARCHEOLOGICAL MUSEUM
Old prison opposite the
fortress.Open Mon.–Sat.
8.45am–3pm,
Sun. 9.30am–2.30pm.
Closed Tue. and public
holidays.

HISTORICAL MUSEUM
28, Messolonghiou Street
Open Tues.–Sun.
9am–1pm, 7–9pm.
Closed Mon.

ACCOMMODATION

ADELE MARE
Old road from
Heraklion
Tel. (0831) 718 03
Open Mar.–Nov.
*60 bungalows and 50
rooms, bars, restaurant,
swimming pool, tennis,
day nursery.*
17,500–28,000 Dr

CRETA STAR A
AND CRETA ROYAL
LUXE
Old road from
Heraklion
Tel. (0831) 718 12
Open Apr.–Oct.
*320 rooms, bars,
taverna, discotheque,
indoor swimming pool,
sauna, gymnasium,
cinema, day nursery.*
15,750–22,750 Dr

EL GRECO
Old road from
Heraklion
Tel. (0831) 712 01
Open Apr.–Oct.
*320 rooms, bars,
self-catering, restaurant,
café, swimming pool,
watersports, three
tennis courts, miniature
golf, day nursery.*
12,250–28,000 Dr

LEO
2, Vafe Street
Near the museum
Tel. (0831) 261 97
*This richly decorated
little hotel is situated
in a tiny street in the
old town. Staff is
young and friendly,
but there are few
rooms.*
6,300–7,000 Dr

PALAZZO RIMONDI
21, Xanthoudidou Street
Tel. (0831) 512 89
*Luxury hotel at an
affordable price.
Superb décor,
enclosed courtyard
with fountain, lovely
bar. Exquisite suites.
Not to be missed.*
8,750–17,500 Dr

RETHYMNO HOUSE
1, Kornarou Street
Tel. (0831) 239 23
*These English-style
lodgings in a little alley
in the old town are run
by a charming and
considerate landlady.
A little old-fashioned.*
About 5,000 Dr

RITHMNA
Old road from
Heraklion
Tel. (0831) 294 91
Open Mar.–Nov.
*Bungalows and rooms,
four bars, self-catering,
restaurant, café, big
swimming pool, five
indoor tennis courts,
watersports, fitness
room, day nursery.*
13,300–26,250 Dr

RESTAURANTS

ALANA
11, Salaminos Street
Tel. (0831) 277 37
Open 11am–4pm,
6–11pm.
Closed public holidays.
*A traditional and
friendly taverna in the
old town. Pleasant
setting and high-class
menu. Specialty: fish.*
2,000–4,550 Dr

AVLI
22, Xanthoudidou Street
Radamanthyos
Tel. (0831) 292 57
Open 11am–3pm,
7–11pm.
*Without doubt the
town's most attractive
restaurant. Charming
enclosed courtyard with
pretty flowerbeds,
excellent décor.
Impeccable service;
good cooking with a
varied menu; the last
word in luxury.
Specialties: lobster,
crayfish.*
6,300–11,200 Dr

CHEZ VASSILIS
In the Venetian Harbor
Tel. (0831) 229 67
Open all year.
*Specialties: fish and
seafood.*
5,000–7,000 Dr

PETRINO
Salaminos Street
Tel. (0831) 264 10
Open 11am–3pm, 6–11pm.
*An attractively decorated
restaurant behind the
Rimondi fountain. Soft
lighting, perfect cuisine.
Specialties: seafood.*
2,000–5,000 Dr

"PARADISOS" TAVERNA
(CHEZ GAVALAS)
Platanias
*Family taverna with a
flamboyant proprietor.
Excellent meat croquettes.*
2,000–5,000 Dr

SITIA

Area code tel. 0843

CULTURE

ARCHEOLOGICAL
MUSEUM
Ierapetra road
Open Mon.–Fri. 8am–3pm,
Sat. Sun. 9am–2.30pm.

ACCOMMODATION

ELYSÉE
By the beach
14, K. Karamanli Street
Tel. (0843) 234 27
*Spacious and
comfortable rooms,
elegant bathrooms.*
7,700–10,500 Dr

HELIO-CLUB SITIA
BEACH
By the beach
Tel. (0843) 288 21
Open Apr.–Oct.
*150 rooms, bars, two
swimming pools,
discotheque, theater,
restaurant.*
13,300–22,750 Dr

MARESOL
Haghia-Photia
Tel. (0843) 289 50
*26 bungalows, bar,
restaurant, taverna,
swimming pool, tennis,
volleyball, waterskiing,
sailing club.*
13,300–22,750 Dr

VAI
September 4 Street
Tel. (0843) 222 88
*Fairly new building in
the town center.
44 spacious rooms
with bathrooms.*
6,300–8,750 Dr

RESTAURANT

ELYSÉE
14, K. Karamanli Street
Tel. (0843) 223 12
Open 11am–4pm,
6–10pm.
*Restaurant with a
large terrace. Fine
cooking, pleasant
atmosphere.
Specialties: squid,
red mullet.*
1,750–3,500 Dr

VARVARI
(MYRTIA)

Area code tel. 081

CULTURE

N. KAZANTZAKI
MUSEUM
Tel. (081) 74 24 51
Open Mon. Wed. Sat.
Sun. 9am–1pm, 4–8pm,
Tue. Fri. 9am–1pm,
Closed Thurs.
Closed Oct.–Mar.

VORI

Area code tel. 0892

CULTURE

ETHNOLOGICAL
MUSEUM
Open 10am–6pm
(during the season).

327

Appendices

ESSENTIAL
◆ READING ◆

◆ BREWSTER (R.):
*The Island of Zeus:
Wanderings in Crete*,
Duckworth, London,
1939.
◆ CADOGAN (G.):
*Palaces of Minoan
Crete*, Barrie & Jenkins,
London, 1976.
◆ GRAVES (R.):
Greek Myths, Cassell &
Co. Ltd., London, 1968.
◆ PALMER (L.R.):
*Mycenaeans and
Minoans*, 2nd edn,
Faber and Faber,
London, 1965.

GENERAL
◆ INTEREST ◆

◆ ALLBAUGH (L.):
*Crete: A Case Study of
an Underdeveloped
Area*, Princeton
University Press,
Princeton, 1953.
◆ BOWMAN (J.): *Crete*,
Jonathan Cape,
London, 1978.
◆ BRYANS (R.): *Crete*,
Faber & Faber, London,
1969.
◆ EDEY (M.): *Lost World
of the Aegean*,
Time-Life, New York,
1975.
◆ ELLIADI (M.N.): *Crete,
Past and Present*,
Heath, Cranton,
London, 1933.
◆ FIELDING (X.):
The Stronghold,
Secker and Warburg,
London, 1953.
◆ HAWKES (J.):
The World of the Past,
Alfred A. Knopf,
New York, 1963.
◆ HAWKES (J.): *Dawn of
the Gods*, Random
House, New York, 1968.
◆ HAWKES (J.):
The Atlas of Early Man,
St. Martin's Press, New
York, 1976.
◆ LEAR (E.): *The Cretan
Journal*, Denise Harvey
& Co., Athens, 1984.
◆ PLATON (N.):
Crete, Nagel,
Paris/Geneva/New York,
1968.
◆ POWELL (D.):
The Villa Ariadne,
Hodder & Stoughton,
London, 1973.
◆ SANDARS (N.K.):
The Sea Peoples,
Thames and Hudson,
London, 1978.
◆ SMITH (M.L.): *The
Great Island, A Study of*

Crete, Longmans,
London, 1965.
◆ VAUGHAN (A.C.):
*The House of the
Double Axe: the
Palace at Knossos*,
Weidenfeld and
Nicolson, London, 1960.
◆ WUNDERLICH (H.):
The Secret of Crete,
Souvenir Press,
London, 1975.

◆ NATURE ◆

◆ BATTYE (A.B.R.T.):
*Camping in Crete. With
notes upon the animals
and plant life of the
island*, Wilhertz and
Co., London, 1913.
◆ CAUGHEY (B.) AND
CAUGHEY (N.):
*Crete off the beaten
track*, Cicerone,
Milnthorpe, 1989.
◆ GODFREY (J.) AND
KERSLAKE (E.):
*Landscapes of
eastern Crete, a
countryside guide*,
Sunflower, London,
1986.
◆ GODFREY (J.) AND
KERSLAKE (E.):
*Landscapes of western
Crete, a countryside
guide*, Sunflower,
London, 1987.
◆ TURLAND (N.J.),
CHILTON (L.) AND PRESS
(J.R.): *Flora of the
Cretan area, annotated
checklist and atlas*,
HMSO, London, 1993.

◆ PREHISTORY ◆

◆ ALEXIOU (S.):
Minoan Civilisation,
Spyros Alexiou Sons,
Herakleion, 1973.
◆ ALSOP (J.): *From
the Silent Earth*,
Harper & Row, New
York, 1964/Secker &
Warburg Ltd, London,
1965.
◆ BRANIGAN (K.):
*Dancing with death,
Life and death in
southern Crete,
3000–2000 B.C.*,
Hakkert, Amsterdam,
1993.
◆ BURN (A.R.) AND BURN
(M.): *The Living Past of
Greece*, Penguin Books,
Harmondsworth, 1980.
◆ DANIEL (G.):
The Idea of Prehistory,
C.A. Watts, London,
1962/Penguin,
Baltimore, 1964.
◆ FAURE (P.): *La Vie*

*Quotidienne en Crète
au temps de Minos
(1500 BC)*, Librairie
Hachette, Paris, 1973.
◆ HOOD (S.): *The Home
of the Heroes, the
Aegean before the
Greeks*, Thames and
Hudson, London, 1967.
◆ HUTCHINSON (R.W.):
Prehistoric Crete,
Pelican, London, 1962.
◆ LUCE (J.V.): *The End
of Atlantis*, Thames and
Hudson, London, 1969.
◆ MARINATOS (S.):
Crete and Mycenae,
Thames and Hudson,
London, 1960.
◆ MATTON (R.): *La Crète
au Cours des Siècles*,
Collection de l'Institut
Français d'Athènes,
Athens, 1957.
◆ MELLERSH (H.E.L.):
Minoan Crete, G.P.
Putnam, New York,
1968/Evans Brothers
Ltd., London, 1967.
◆ RENFREW (C.):
*The Emergence of
Civilisation: The
Cyclades and the
Aegean in the Third
Millenium BC*, Methuen,
London, 1972.
◆ RENFREW (C.):
*Before Civilisation: the
Radiocarbon Revolution
and Prehistoric Europe*,
Jonathan Cape,
London, 1973.
◆ STYLIANUS (A.):
Minoan Civilisation,
Spyros Alexiou Sons,
Herakleion, 1973.
◆ TRUMP (D.):
*The Prehistory of the
Mediterranean*, Penguin
Books, Harmondsworth,
1981.
◆ WARREN (P.): *The
Aegean Civilisations*,
Elsevier-Phaidon,
London, 1975.
◆ WILLETTS (R.F.):
*Everyday Life in
Ancient Crete*, Batsford,
London, 1969.

RECENT
◆ HISTORY ◆

◆ BUCKLEY (C.):
Greece and Crete,
H.M.S.O., London,
1952.
◆ CLARK (A.):
The Fall of Crete, Blond,
London, 1962.
◆ FIELDING (X.): *Hide
and Seek*, Secker and
Warburg, London, 1954.
◆ HEYDTE, BARON VON
DER, TRANS. MOSS (W.S.):
Daedalus Returned,

Crete 1941, Hutchinson,
London, 1958.
◆ MILLER (W.):
*The Ottoman Empire
and its Successors*,
Cambridge Historical
Series, Cambridge,
1927.
◆ MOSS (W.S.):
Ill Met by Moonlight,
Harrap, London, 1948.
◆ PSYCHOUNDAKIS (G.):
The Cretan Runner,
John Murray, London,
1955.
◆ RENDEL (A.M.):
Appointment in Crete,
Wingate, London, 1953.
◆ STEWART (I.McD.G.):
*The Struggle for Crete,
20 May–1 June 1941, A
Story of Lost
Opportunity*,
Oxford University
Press, London, 1966.
◆ WAUGH (E.):
Evelyn Waugh Diaries,
Weidenfeld and
Nicolson, London, 1976.
◆ WOODHOUSE (C.M.):
Apple of Discord,
Hutchinson, London,
1948.
◆ ZACHARIADOU (E.A.):
*Trade and Crusade,
Venetian Crete and the
Emirates. . . 1300–1415*,
Hellenic Institute of
Byzantine Studies,
Venice, 1983.

RELIGION
◆ AND SOCIETY ◆

◆ GUTHRIE (W.K.):
*The Religion and
Mythology of the
Greeks*, Cambridge
Ancient History, Vol. 2,
Cambridge Univ. Press,
Cambridge, 1961.
◆ GOODRICH (N.):
The Ancient Myths,
New American Library,
New York, 1960.
◆ HOOKER (J.T.):
'Minoan religion in
the Late Palace Period',
in Krzyszkowska (O.)
and Nixon (L.) Eds.,
*Minoan Society:
Proceedings of the
Cambridge Colloquium,
1981*, Bristol Classical
Press, Bristol, 1983.
◆ KERENYI (K.):
*The Gods of the
Greeks*, Grove Press,
New York, 1960.
◆ LEVY (G.R.):
The Gate of Horn,
Faber and Faber,
London, 1948.
◆ MALINOWSKI (B.):
*Magic, Science and
Religion*, Doubleday,

New York, 1954.
◆ MARINATOS (N.): *Art and Religion in Thera: Reconstructing a Bronze Age Society*, D. and I. Mathioulakis, 1984.
◆ NILSSON (M.): *The Minoan-Mycenean Religion*, G.W.K. Gleerup, Lund, 1950.
◆ RUTKOWSKI (B.): *The Cult Places of the Aegean*, Yale University Press, New Haven, Conn., 1986.
◆ WILLETTS (R.F.): *Cretan Cults and Festivals*, Routledge and Kegan Paul, London/Barnes and Noble, New York, 1962

◆ ART AND ARCHEOLOGY ◆

◆ COTTRELL (L.): *The Bull of Minos*, Evans, London, 1953.
◆ EVANS (A.): *The Palace of Minos*, Macmillan & Co. Ltd., London, 1921-36.
◆ FALKENER (E.): *A Description of Some Important Theatres and Other Remains in Crete*, Turner, London, 1854.
◆ GEROLA (G.): *Monumenti Veneti nell'Isola di Creta*, Istituto Veneto di Scienze, Lettere ed Arti, Venice, 1905-32.
◆ GRAHAM (J.W.): *The Palaces of Crete*, Princeton University Press, Princeton, 1962.
◆ HALL (H.R.): *Aegean Archeology*, Philip Lee Warner, London, 1915.
◆ HALLAGER (E.): *The Mycenean Palace at Knossos*, Medelhavsmuseet, Memoir 1, Stockholm, 1977.
◆ HIGGINS (R.A.): *Minoan and Mycenaean Art*, Oxford University Press, New York, 1967/Thames & Hudson, London, 1967.
◆ HOOD (S.): *The Arts in Prehistoric Greece*, Penguin Books, Harmondsworth, 1978.
◆ KALOKYRIS (C.): *La Peinture Murale Byzantine de l'Ile de Crète, 1954, Cretica Chronica*, Heraklion.
◆ MOSSO (A.): *The Palaces of Crete and their Builders*, Fisher Unwin, London, 1907.
◆ PALMER (L.R.): *The Penultimate Palace of Knossos*, Edizioni dell'Ateneo, Rome, 1969.
◆ PENDLEBURY (J.D.S.): *The Archeology of Crete*, Methuen, London and New York, 1939.
◆ PLATON (N.): *Zakros: the Discovery of a Lost Palace of Ancient Crete*, Scribners, London, 1971.
◆ WILSON (D.): *The New Archeology*, Alfred A. Knopf, New York, 1974.

◆ LITERATURE ◆

◆ HOMER: *The Iliad*, trans. Rieu (E.V.) Penguin, London, 1950.
◆ HOMER: *The Odyssey*, trans. Rieu (E.V.) Penguin, London, 1946.
◆ KAZANTZAKI (N.): *The Odyssey: a Modern Sequel*, Trans. Friar (K.), Secker & Warburg, London, 1958.
◆ KAZANTZAKI (N.): *Freedom or Death*, Bruno Cassirer, Oxford, 1956.
◆ KAZANTZAKI (N.): *Zorba*, Bruno Cassirer, Oxford, 1959.
◆ MARSHALL (F.H.) AND MAVROGORDATO (J.) TRANS: *Three Cretan Plays*, Oxford, 1929.
◆ MILLER (H.): *The Colossus of Maroussi*, Heinemann, London, 1960.
◆ MORGAN (G.) KALOKKAIRINOS ED.: *Cretan Poetry: Sources and Inspiration*, Iraklion, 1960 (offprint from Cretika Chronica, Vol. XIV).
◆ NOTOPOULOS (J.A.): 'Homer and Cretan Homeric Poetry', American Journal of Philology, Vol. LXXIII, 3.
◆ PREVELAKIS (P.): *Chronique d'une Cité*, Gallimard, Paris, 1960.
◆ PREVELAKIS (P.): *Le Crétois*, Gallimard, Paris, 1962.
◆ PREVELAKIS (P.): *The Sun of Death*, Trans. Sherrard (P.), John Murray, London, 1965.
◆ RENAULT (M.): *The King Must Die*, Pantheon Books, New York, 1958.
◆ RENAULT (M.): *The Bull from the Sea*, Pantheon Books, New York, 1962.
◆ WEBSTER (T.B.L.): *From Mycenae to Homer*, Methuen & Co., London, 1958.

◆ FOLKLORE AND MUSIC ◆

◆ BAUD-BOVY (S.): *La Chanson Populaire Grecque du Dodecanèse*, Institut Néo-Hellenique de l'Université de Paris, Paris, 1936.
◆ DAWKINS (R.M.): *Folk Memory in Crete*, Folklore, 1930.
◆ DAWKINS (R.M.): *Soul and Body in Greek Folk Lore*, Folklore, 1942.
◆ LAWSON (J.C.): *Modern Greek Folklore and Ancient Greek Religion*, Cambridge, 1910.

◆ TRAVEL WRITINGS ◆

◆ BELON (P.): *Les Observations de Plusieurs Singularitez et Choses Memorables Trouvées en Grèce*, Paris, 1554.
◆ DAPPER (D.O.): *Description Exacte des Iles de L'Archipel, trans. from the Flemish*, Amsterdam, 1703.
◆ PASHLEY (R.): *Travels in Crete, 2 vols*, John Murray, London, 1837.
◆ POCOCKE (R.): *A Description of the East and Some Other Countries, 1738*, J. and R. Knapton, London, 1743–45.
◆ SPRATT (CAPT. T.A.B.): *Travels and Researches in Crete, 2 vols*, Van Woorst, London, 1967.
◆ TOURNEFORT (J.P.): *A Voyage in the Levant*, Trans. Ozell (J.), London, 1718.

◆ GUIDES ◆

◆ MICHAILIDOU (A.): *Knossos: a Complete Guide to the Palace of Minos*, Ekdotike Athenon, Athens, 1987.
◆ PALMER (L.R.): *A New Guide to the Palace of Knossos*, Faber & Faber, London, 1969.
◆ PENDLEBURY (J.D.S.): *A Handbook to the Palace of Minos at Knossos and its dependencies*, Macmillan & Co. Ltd., London, 1935.
◆ SAKELLARAKIS (J.A.): *Herakleion Museum: Illustrated Guide to the Museum*, Ekdotike Athenon, 1987.
◆ SPANAKES (S.): *Crete, A Guide*, Sfakianakis, Iraklion.
◆ STYLIANOS (A.): *A Guide to the Archeological Museum of Heraklion*, General Direction of Antiquities and Restoration, Athens, 1972.

◆ Glossary

◆ A ◆

◆ **Acropolis:** A fortified site, high up on a hill or rock, on which stood the major public buildings of a Greek city.

◆ **Acroterion** (plural Acroteria): Pedestal supporting an ornamental piece of statuary, on top of a pediment.

◆ **Adorer:** Baked-earth, ivory or bronze statuette, representing a male or female figure in a reverential pose.

◆ **Agora:** Public marketplace where citizens gathered.

◆ **Aisle:** Lateral division running alongside the central nave.

◆ **Ambulatory:** The aisle, or walk, around the choir.

◆ **Amphiprostyle temple:** Temple with colonnaded porticos at the front and rear, but not the sides.

◆ **Amphitheater:** Round or oval building with tiered seating where gladiatorial contests or animal fighting took place.

◆ **Amphora:** Generic name given to the handled vases used for storing and transporting liquids.

◆ **Apse:** Polygonal or semicircular space opening into an aisle, generally at the east end of a church.

◆ **Arch:** Curve of a ceiling vault or opening, either semicircular (Roman) or pointed (Gothic).

◆ **Architrave:** The lowest section of an entablature, resting on the column.

◆ **Archivolt:** The molding along the curve of an arch or portal.

◆ **Atlas** (plural, Atlantes): Male statue used in place of a column to support an architectural element.

◆ **Atrium:** Entrance courtyard to an ancient building or paleo-Christian church.

◆ B ◆

◆ **Barrel vault:** Vault whose arched section is semicircular.

◆ **Basilica:** The architectural source for early Christian churches, with either one or several naves.

◆ **Bond:** The cut and shape of the constituent parts of a wall. From the 11th and 12th centuries onwards, the bond of Greek churches consisted of alternating courses of bricks and masonry.

◆ **Bowl:** Shallow basin used in Roman baths; by extension, the somewhat larger basin of a fountain.

◆ C ◆

◆ **Capital:** Uppermost part of a column, which sits on top of the shaft.

◆ **Cavea:** Tiered area for spectators in an ancient theater.

◆ **Choir:** Screened section of a church reserved for the officiating clergy; generally includes the altar.

◆ **Church ornamentation:** Usually statuary or, more rarely, recessed reliefs. From the 14th century onwards, arcading, festoons and niches in the walls begin to appear.

◆ **Church plans:**
1) **Basilical plan:** Analogous with the paleo-Christian basilicas, the plan is oblong and consists of several aisles. The central aisle is illuminated by high windows.
2) **Inscribed Greek cross plan, with cupola:** A development of the cruciform paleo-Christian plan. From the 11th century onwards, the pillars supporting the dome were replaced by columns.
3) **Octagonal plan:** Octagon inscribed in a square and crowned with a cupola resting on eight columns, with linking arches.
4) **Triconch plan:** In Greece this is often combined with the inscribed-cross plan.

◆ **Circus:** Building with tiered seats used for chariot races. It was rectangular in shape and closed off by curved sections at either end, at which stood the oppidums.

◆ **Corbelling:** Overhanging course of an edifice.

◆ **Corinthian order:** The base of the column is composed of a plinth, a torus, two scotias between fillets separated by twin baguettes, and another torus. The shaft is fluted. The capital consists of a bell covered in leaves (usually acanthus); an abacus with concave sides; and between the stems that end in volutes (scrolls), a stalk bearing a flower sits in the center of the abacus.

◆ **Council:** Assembly of bishops that formulates the texts and decrees governing doctrinal questions and ecclesiastical discipline. The council is referred to as "ecumenical" when all the bishops attend.

◆ **Crossing:** Formed by the intersection of the nave and transept.

◆ **Cupola:** Dome that crowns a square space, supported by either pendentives or corner squinches that rest on pillars or columns.

◆ D ◆

◆ **Despot:** Governor of a province in the Byzantine Empire.

◆ **Diazoma:** Promenade half-way up, or at the top of the tiered seating of an ancient theater.

◆ **Dodecaorton:** Cycles of icons linked with dances and major feast days in the Byzantine liturgical calendar.

◆ **Dog-tooth cordons:** A repeating serrated molding, often found decorating the window surrounds in Byzantine churches.

◆ **Doric order:** The column is without a base. The shaft is fluted and separated from the capital by one or more annulets. The capital is composed of a neck, an echinus and an abacus. Between one and three fillets (or annulets) separate the neck from the echinus (the convex molding, or ovolo).

◆ E ◆

◆ **Drum:** The cylindrical lower section of a dome, generally octagonal from the exterior.

◆ **Entablature:** Section between the column and the pediment, made up of the architrave and the frieze.

◆ **Exedra:** A semicircular recess, usually with seats.

◆ **Extrados:** The outer curve of an arch or dome.

◆ F ◆

◆ **Foliate:** Stylized ornamental motif of interlaced leaves and branches.

◆ **Fresco:** A wall-painting technique where mineral pigments suspended in water are applied to wet plaster composed of sand and lime.

◆ **Frieze:** The horizontal band between the pediment and the architrave of the entablature, decorated with alternating metopes and triglyphs.

◆ H ◆

◆ **Hermeneutics:** A guide, or iconographic manual, used by painters of icons and churches in the Eastern Christian church.

◆ **Higoumenos:** Superior of a Greek Orthodox monastery.

◆ **Hypostyle chamber:** Room where the roof is supported by columns.

◆ I ◆

◆ **Icon:** A holy image in Orthodox religions. It can be painted on wood, ivory, metal etc.

◆ **Iconostasis:** Screen that separates the nave from the sanctuary, usually decorated with mural paintings and/or icons.

◆ **Ionic order:** The base of the column consists of a plinth, two scotias separated by two fillets, and a torus. The shaft is fluted. The capital is composed of an echinus, two volutes and an abacus. The echinus is generally decorated with ovolos and the space between the volutes may be embellished with festoons; in this case, the abacus often has a flower in the center.

◆ K ◆

◆ KARST: Limestone plateau that is heavily eroded.
◆ KATHOLIKON: The principal church of a monastery or parish.
◆ KOINE: Any dialect, spoken or written, which has become the common language of a larger area.

◆ L ◆

◆ LIBATION: A symbolic liquid (wine, milk or oil) offered up to a god, and often poured from a rhyton.
◆ LUSTRAL CHAMBER: Small, half-sunken rectangular room. Most likely used for bathing, purifications or other obscure rituals.

◆ M ◆

◆ MAGAZINE: Rows of rooms, perpendicular to the main palace complex, used for storing perishable foodstuffs.
◆ MEGARON: The principal chamber in a Mycenaean palace. Rectangular in shape, it consists of a porch (supported by two columns), a vestibule and a square room in whose center is a hearth surrounded by four columns.
◆ METOPE: The square space in a Doric frieze, often plain but sometimes decorated with a motif.
◆ METROPOLITAN: Presiding bishop.
◆ MINOAN ALTAR: Rectangular sacred table of modest size, with concave sides.
◆ MOSAICS: A more costly form of decoration than mural paintings. Mosaics were generally the preserve of Imperial institutions between the 10th and 13th centuries.
◆ MURAL PAINTINGS (ICONOGRAPHICAL SCHEME): Christ the

Pantocrator (the Almighty) is depicted in the cupola; a cycle of important feast days, numbering between seven and twelve, generally decorates the lunettes and vaults; apostles, patriarchs and prophets are represented on the upper portion of the walls and pillars. This basic scheme was enriched with numerous additions from the 10th and 11th centuries onwards.

◆ N ◆

◆ NARTHEX: The vestibule of a church (frequently crowned by a tribune) over which the roof of the nave extends.
◆ NECROPOLIS: Large burial city.
◆ NAVE: The main body of a church (the central aisle).
◆ NOME: Greek administrative district (rather like the Parisian "départments" or London boroughs).

◆ O ◆

◆ ODEON: Semicircular or semi-oval roofed theater with tiered seating, used for concerts.
◆ ORCHESTRA: Below the cavea in an ancient theater. This was the circular area, between the first rows of spectators and the pulpitum, on which the actors performed.
◆ ORDER: Architectural term referring to a column (base, shaft and capital) and its entablature (architrave, frieze and cornice); see under Doric order, Ionic order, Corinthian order.
◆ OROPHILE: Term given to a plant that grows in the mountains.

◆ P ◆

◆ PALACE: Monumental assembly of edifices, built around a rectangular central court planned on a north-south axis. The palace is situated in a town.
◆ PALATIAL: Chronology based on the Cretan palace system. The

divisions are: Prepalatial (3000–2100 BC); Protopalatial (the first palaces, 2100–1600 BC); Neopalatial (the second phase of palace building, 1650–1300 BC)
◆ PANTOCRATOR: Representation of Christ as the Almighty, the Ruler of the Universe.
◆ PARASCENIA: The supporting walls, at right angles to the backdrop, on either side of the stage in an antique theater.
◆ PEAK SANCTUARY: A cult site, perched high on a hill or mountain.
◆ PEDIMENT: Triangular gable composed of a tympanum framed by a cornice.
◆ PENDENTIVES: Spandrels, characterized by the triangular and concave shape of their intrados, effecting the transition between the square area formed by the walls and the cupola.
◆ PITHOS (PLURAL PITHOI): Large jar used for storing liquids or perishable foodstuffs, such as olive oil. Some of them, such as those at Knossos, stand head-high to a grown man.
◆ POLYTHYRON: A day-room or receiving chamber, composed of walls pierced through with a number of bays.
◆ POPE: Greek Orthodox priest.
◆ PORTICO: Open gallery formed by colonnades. Also refers to a colonnade projecting from the entrance to a building.
◆ PROPYLAEA: Monumental entrance, generally consisting of a columned portico.

◆ R ◆

◆ REDANS: System of movable wall panels, flush with the façade, which let in extra light. These also created interesting features.
◆ RHYTON: The most typical form of the Minoan sacred vessel. The rhyton is a libation vase with a pierced base, often conical in shape, and frequently

in the form of an animal's head.

◆ S ◆

◆ SANCTUARY: Room or structure which by its position and furnishings seems to have been used for cult purposes; found in palaces, houses, or set alone in villages or in the countryside.
◆ SQUINCHES: Small arches used as devices to support the drum of a dome, built across the corners of a square or polygon. Sometimes used instead of pendentives.
◆ STUCCO: A mixture of plaster and marble dust used to decorate surfaces. Also describes the decorative motif itself.

◆ T ◆

◆ TAUROKATHAPSIE: Bull-leaping: a public spectacle, characterized by sporting exploits involving bulls.
◆ TRANSEPT: Transverse arm of a church, at right angles to the central nave.
◆ TRIBUNES: High open galleries above the central nave. A feature of Greek churches and the early basilicas of Constantinople.
◆ TYMPANUM: The space between the lintel and the archivolt of a portal in church architecture.

◆ V ◆

◆ VILLA: Identifiable by its size, position and the quality of building materials. May be either rural or suburban.
◆ VOLUTES: Ornamental motif resembling a spiral, or scroll.
◆ VOUSSOIR: Curve or section of the curve of a vault.

◆ W ◆

◆ WALL, OR PIERCED CHAMBER: A Cretan invention, involving replacing a solid wall with a series of pillars that serve as entrances.

◆ Z ◆

◆ ZOODOCHOS PIGHI: Icon representing the Virgin and Child.

◆ LIST OF ILLUSTRATIONS

INDEX